# EXIT POLLS

# EXIT POLLS

## SURVEYING THE AMERICAN ELECTORATE, 1972–2010

SAMUEL J. BEST, *UNIVERSITY OF CONNECTICUT*
BRIAN S. KRUEGER, *UNIVERSITY OF RHODE ISLAND*

Ⓢ**SAGE** | **CQPRESS**

Los Angeles | London | New Delhi
Singapore | Washington DC

Los Angeles | London | New Delhi
Singapore | Washington DC

FOR INFORMATION:

CQ Press
An Imprint of SAGE Publications, Inc.
2455 Teller Road
Thousand Oaks, California 91320
E-mail: order@sagepub.com

SAGE Publications Ltd.
1 Oliver's Yard
55 City Road
London, EC1Y 1SP
United Kingdom

SAGE Publications India Pvt. Ltd.
B 1/I 1 Mohan Cooperative Industrial Area
Mathura Road, New Delhi 110 044
India

SAGE Publications Asia-Pacific Pte. Ltd.
33 Pekin Street #02-01
Far East Square
Singapore 048763

Acquisitions Editor:   Doug Goldenberg-Hart
Development Editor:   John Martino
Production Editor:   Gwenda Larsen
Marketing Manager:   Ben Krasney
Typesetter:   C&M Digitals (P) Ltd.
Cover Designer:   Michael Dubowe

Printed in the United States of America

*Library of Congress Cataloging-in-Publication Data*

Best, Samuel J.
Exit polls: surveying the American electorate, 1972–2010 / Samuel J. Best, Brian S. Krueger.

p. cm.
Includes bibliographical references and index.

ISBN 978-1-60871-741-5 (hardcover: alk. paper)

1. Exit polling (Elections)—United States. 2. Election forecasting—United States. I. Krueger, Brian S. II. Title.

JK2007. B47 2012
324.973′092—dc23          2011044553

This book is printed on acid-free paper.

12 13 14 15 16 10 9 8 7 6 5 4 3 2 1

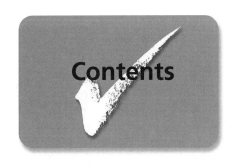

# Contents

Tables and Figures

## Chapter 4    Presidential Voting Preferences of Exit Poll Respondents

## Chapter 5    Congressional Voting Preferences of Exit Poll Respondents

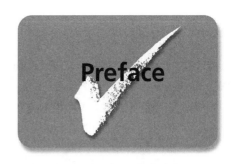

# Preface

The genesis of this project was election night 2008, when Barack Obama defeated John McCain to become our nation's first African American president. We were poring over the exit poll results, trying to put the numbers in some sort of historical context. We knew Obama had done exceedingly well with a wide range of groups, but just how well was open to question. Did African Americans make up a disproportionate number of voters, or did Hispanics exert a far greater impact than they had in the past? Did Obama attract as much support from Catholics as Ronald Reagan did, or as many female voters as Bill Clinton did? Did he reverse Democratic fortunes among white men, rural residents, or devout Christians?

As we tried to find answers to these questions and many more, we realized quickly that there simply was no easily accessible resource that allowed us to put national exit poll results in historical perspective. Previous polls had been catalogued in archives around the country, but each was stored in a unique format that was not conducive to easy compilation or manipulation. Consequently, the results of the exit polls could not be retrieved and compared to those of others undertaken at different points in time.

Considering the sheer number of national exit polls that had been conducted through the years, we realized that this was not an unfortunate oversight, but a glaring omission in the information age. Exit polls had been administered to voters departing the polling booth in every national election conducted since 1972. Data on these polls could be used to see how voters compared not only to those from an election or two earlier but also to those from generations before. Compiling and analyzing these trends seemed likely to yield unique and important insights on electoral politics.

During the past two years, we have undertaken the painstaking process of developing a single data set to identify trends and relationships in the exit polls. We developed an original coding scheme, applied it to each data file, and merged the results together into a user-friendly spreadsheet. We then used this unique data set to explore the composition and electoral choices of American voters.

This is the product of those efforts. In this volume, we present and discuss the electoral behavior of a wide range of groups in the active electorate. We reveal a number of interesting patterns, some of which will be familiar to readers and some of which have remained hidden until now. Together, they provide a compelling portrait of American voters over the past four decades.

# Acknowledgments

We take full responsibility for the numbers and interpretations that follow. Nonetheless, one does not complete a project of this size and scope without the help of a great many others.

Professor Monika McDermott sparked our intellectual interest in voter feedback years earlier. She introduced us to the ins and outs of exit polling, making us aware of endless research possibilities.

The polling group at CBS News provided a venue through which we could dive into the exit poll data. Director of Surveys Kathy Frankovic offered us the opportunity to analyze exit polls for the network, ultimately planting the seed for this volume. During its preparation, she also read and critiqued portions of the manuscript, correcting misunderstandings and identifying oversights. Her colleagues at CBS News—Sarah Dutton and Kevin Hechtkopf—provided valuable feedback on pieces we wrote for the network, prompting new questions that were pursued along the way. Fellow exit poll analysts Professor David Jones and Doug Schwartz, the director of the Quinnipiac University Poll, played the foil to many analyses and interpretations during the past several elections.

Several prominent survey methodologists imparted their knowledge about the intricacies of exit polling to us. Professor Stanley Feldman passed along valuable insights about the polling process through the years. Susan Pinkus, director of the *Los Angeles Times* poll, and Murray Edelman, former editorial director of the Voter News Surveys, provided background about the origin and evolution of the exit polls.

Our respective universities provided us with exceptional academic homes to foment and refine our ideas. At the University of Connecticut, Professors Lyle Scruggs and Jeffrey Ladewig were great sounding boards, offering critiques and insights that only improved the manuscript. Professors Oksan Bayulgen, Kristin Kelly, Peter Kingstone, Matthew Singer, and Heather Turcotte provided alternative perspectives, bringing to bear fields outside of electoral politics and encouraging us to consider less obvious interpretations. At the University of Rhode Island, Marc Hutchison provided valuable insights from the perspective of a comparative behavioralist. Shanna Pearson-Merkowitz pushed us to consider the geographic and state-level implications of our decisions. Kristin Johnson fortunately provided us elegant solutions to seemingly unsolvable, large data set problems. And Gerry Tyler was a strong supporter of the original idea, offering sage comments on the prospectus.

We are indebted to our editorial team at CQ Press. Doug Goldenberg-Hart extolled the virtues of the project before we were even fully aware of them. January Layman-Wood shepherded the project to completion, making sure we met our deadlines and remained true to our original vision. John Martino painstakingly edited draft after draft, dramatically improving its readability in the process. Amy Marks was an outstanding and patient copy editor.

We owe considerable gratitude to our family and friends who provided unconditional support during the two years it took us to put this book together. Robert Chisholm, Everett Finklestein, Scott Herlihy, Gus Monteiro, Neath Pal, and Geoffrey Schnirman provided a layman's perspective each week at the poker table. Sean Krueger served as unknowing timekeeper, sowing and reaping gargantuan gourds in his pumpkin patch to a cycle by which we monitored our progress. Our children, Alexander Best, Madeleine Best, and Melody Krueger, kept our priorities in perspective and recharged our batteries time and time again. Finally, our lovely spouses, Niki Best and Jennifer Krueger, to whom this book is dedicated, shouldered disproportionate burdens, eased our frustrations, and provided encouragement without which this book would never have been completed.

**About the Authors**

**Samuel J. Best** is associate professor of political science at the University of Connecticut. He has written numerous articles on public opinion and electoral behavior appearing in journals such as the *Journal of Politics*, *American Journal of Political Science*, *Public Opinion Quarterly*, *American Politics Research*, and *Political Behavior*. He has coauthored several books, including *Internet Data Collection* with Brian S. Krueger (2004), and coedited *Polling America: An Encyclopedia of Public Opinion* (2006). He has served as an exit poll analyst for CBS News since 2004 and administered and analyzed numerous surveys as the former director of the Center for Survey Research and Analysis at the University of Connecticut.

**Brian S. Krueger** is associate professor of political science at the University of Rhode Island. He has coauthored two books on polling and elections: *The Politics of Cultural Differences* (2002) and *Internet Data Collection* (2004). He has also written scholarly articles for journals such as *American Politics Research*, *Political Behavior*, *Public Opinion Quarterly*, and the *Harvard International Journal of Press/Politics*. He served as an exit poll analyst for CBS News during the 2008 election season.

# The Exit Poll Phenomenon

On election day in the United States, exit polls are the talk of the nation. Even before balloting has concluded, the media uses voters' responses about their electoral choices to project final results for a public eager for immediate information. Once votes have been tallied, media commentators from across the political landscape rely almost exclusively on exit polls to explain election outcomes. The exit polls show what issues were the most important in the minds of the voters. They identify how different groups in the electorate cast their ballots. They expose which character traits helped or hurt particular candidates. They even reveal voters' expectations of the government moving forward.

In the weeks and months that follow, exit polls are used time and again to give meaning to the election results. Newly elected officials rely on them to substantiate policy mandates they claim to have received from voters. Partisan pundits scrutinize them for successful and failed campaign strategies. Even political strategists use them to pinpoint key groups and issues that need to be won over to succeed in future elections.

Unfortunately, these same exit poll results are not easily accessible to members of the public interested in dissecting them. After appearing in the next day's newspapers or on a politically oriented website, they disappear quickly from sight as the election fades in prominence. Eventually, the exit polls are archived at universities where only subscribers are capable of retrieving the data. But nowhere is a complete set of biennial exit poll results available in an easy-to-use format for curious parties.

This book is intended to address this shortcoming. It is a resource for academics, journalists, and political observers alike who wish to explore the exit polls in order to understand the composition and vote choices of the active electorate during the past four decades. Inside, readers will find voters' responses to nearly three dozen questions asked repeatedly in the exit polls over time, including items tapping voters' demographic backgrounds, lifestyle choices, economic considerations, and political orientations. In addition, the book features the presidential and congressional preferences of voters possessing these characteristics, enabling readers to see the primary sources of Democratic and Republican support in these critical races.

The results of the exit polls are presented in three different ways to facilitate readers' understanding of them. Tables report the proportion of respondents selecting each response option available to them. Graphs permit visual inspection of trends in each question over time. Written interpretations guide readers through the intricacies of the tables and graphs.

Beyond reporting the longitudinal results of the exit poll questions, the book details a wealth of information about each question for every year it was asked, including the following:

The exact wording of both the question and the response options

The marginal distributions for each response option

The presidential and congressional vote choices for each response option

The number of respondents answering each question

The margin of sampling error for population projections

The book also provides the technical details explaining how all the numbers were computed. It describes how questions were selected and response options were merged over time. It documents how missing responses were handled. And, it explains how to properly read each table and graph to avoid common misperceptions. In the process, it aims to make the information accessible to even the most numerically challenged reader.

We begin by providing an overview of media-sponsored exit polling in the remainder of this chapter. We outline the history of the exit polls, describing their development, growth, and controversies over the years. Next, we explain how exit polls are conducted, detailing each phase of their implementation from questionnaire design to sampling methods to interviewing protocols to analytic procedures. Finally, we discuss the advantages and disadvantages of exit polls for understanding the composition and political preferences of the active electorate.

## A History of Exit Polls

Exit polling developed in the 1960s out of a desire by journalists to explain voting results to their audiences. Over time, it transformed from a modest effort at CBS News to estimate the outcome of the 1967 Kentucky gubernatorial election into a multimillion-dollar operation sponsored by a consortium of television networks and designed to project race winners and explain the preferences of numerous voting groups. Along the way, it overcame technical malfunctions, internal squabbles, and erroneous calls to become the centerpiece of media coverage of the elections.

### Prior Approaches to Explaining Voters' Choices

Historically, media outlets relied on preelection polls and precinct analysis to make sense of election outcomes. They offered insights into the voting behaviors of particular subgroups in the electorate. Unfortunately, both techniques had serious underlying methodological problems, capable of producing misleading conclusions about the composition and preferences of voters.

Preelection surveys typically sampled 1,000 to 1,500 adults nationwide about their backgrounds, issue positions, and candidate preferences in the last few weeks before an election. Although such surveys were administered close to election day, it often proved difficult for pollsters to differentiate respondents who indicated an intention to vote from those who would turn out to the polls. Worse, the ever-changing nature of the campaign made voting preferences susceptible to change until the moment ballots were cast. Compounding these challenges was the fact that the number of interviews completed, although seemingly large, was usually too small to enable analysis of many voter subgroups, particularly those that comprised less than a quarter of the active electorate, such as African American, Hispanic, or Jewish voters.

Another common approach used to understand election outcomes was precinct analysis. This involved identifying key precincts that were largely homogenous on a particular social or political characteristic and inferring the voting patterns of the group nationwide from their behavior in these jurisdictions. For example, analysts would identify precincts that were heavily African American and project the voting patterns of African Americans across the country. The problem was that the voting patterns of groups often varied across districts, at times, by considerable margins. For example, an analysis of African American precincts in the 1972 presidential election suggested that 13 percent of African Americans supported Republican nominee Richard Nixon, failing to capture the wide disparity in support of African Americans, ranging from 6 percent within inner-city precincts to 34 percent in wealthy suburban precincts.[1]

## The Beginnings of National Exit Polling

The elections unit at CBS News under the direction of Warren Mitofsky developed a method for forecasting elections and explaining outcomes that ameliorated the problems undermining preelection polling and precinct analysis. They randomly selected precincts from across a jurisdiction and interviewed select voters as they left polling stations. Although they were not the first pollsters to survey exiting voters—evidence indicates that this had been done as far back as the 1940s[2]— they were the first to use probabilistic sampling techniques so that their results could be inferred to the active electorate with a certain degree of confidence.[3]

The inspiration behind CBS's exit polling efforts surfaced in 1967.[4] The elections unit wanted a method for projecting election results before the full returns came in, either because of delays in acquiring information on sample precincts or varied poll closing times. George Fine, head of the market research company that assisted CBS in hiring field staff, suggested interviewing voters as they left the polling booth, citing the valuable feedback that exiting moviegoers had provided a film company with which he worked. Warren Mitofsky was drawn to the idea and, together with his CBS colleague Murray Edelman and statistician Joe Waksberg of the U.S. Census Bureau, developed a probabilistic method for selecting a sample of precincts across a jurisdiction and intercepting a subset of voters after they left the polls. They applied the approach to the 1967 Kentucky gubernatorial election with great success, making the first on-air prediction using information derived, in part, from an exit poll. The exit poll had proven far more consistent with the outcome of the election than a same-day telephone poll or an analysis of key precincts.

Building on their success, CBS expanded its efforts to twenty states in 1968. Again, though, the exit polls (which were limited to vote choice, gender, and race) were used only to facilitate projections in presidential, senatorial, and gubernatorial races. Although the thought of scrutinizing exit poll responses to understand the outcome of the election had arisen, there simply were not the technological means to immediately transmit individual responses collected in remote precincts to a centralized computer for analysis.

These logistical problems were worked out by the 1970 election, enabling CBS to administer a lengthier series of demographic questions to voters in a number of states and provide on-air analysis of them on election night. The network could now describe the voting patterns of key groups in these states, providing valuable insights to its viewers. Two years later, CBS cast an even wider net and conducted its first national exit poll of voters in select precincts across the contiguous United States.

By the 1984 presidential election, all three major networks and the *Los Angeles Times* were conducting independent, nationwide exit polls. They each crafted their own questionnaires, designed their own sampling methodology to select precincts and voters, and developed their own weighting procedures to ensure the representativeness of their findings.[5] Nonetheless, they were producing results similar to both each other and the actual outcome.

Table 1.1 shows the proportions of voters in several different demographic groups who chose Ronald Reagan for president in 1984 across each of the media-sponsored, national exit polls. Despite varying methodological approaches, the network exit polls produced comparable findings. In most subgroups, the difference in Republican vote choice across the polls did not exceed the margin of error.[6]

Initially, exit poll results were used simply to analyze election outcomes, providing context for actual vote counts. The networks soon realized, though, that exit polls could be used to project election results in advance of the returns and give them a leg up on the competition during election day. In 1980, NBC projected Reagan the winner of the presidential election at 8:15 p.m. This early call set off a storm of criticism because it occurred before the polls had closed in many western states, and with little more than 5 percent of the actual ballots tabulated.[7] Congressional hearings were held in Washington to look into the impact of early calls on turnout in late-closing precincts, and legislation was proposed, though never passed, to adopt uniform poll closing times.[8]

Despite the indignation, the other television networks followed suit quickly. All three networks used national exit poll results to project congressional races in the 1982 midterm elections. In 1984, all the networks called the winner of the presidential election between 8:00 and 8:30 p.m.

By the end of the 1980s, exit polling had become very expensive and yielded little competitive advantage. The networks spent millions of dollars each election cycle to hire thousands of temporary workers to gather the questionnaires and then compile and analyze the results.[9] They were competing for an on-air advantage that had shrunk from hours to a matter of minutes. As a result, the networks commenced talks after the 1988 presidential election to find ways to pool their efforts and fund a single exit poll.

**Table 1.1**  Ronald Reagan's Share of the 1984 Presidential Vote across Exit Polls

| Demographic | CBS-*New York Times* | ABC | *Los Angeles Times* |
|---|---|---|---|
| Male | 61% | 62% | 63% |
| Female | 57% | 54% | 56% |
| | | | |
| 18–29 | 58% | 57% | 60% |
| 30–59 | 59% | 58% | 59% |
| 60+ | 63% | 57% | 60% |
| | | | |
| White | 66% | 63% | 67% |
| Black | 9% | 11% | 9% |
| Hispanic/Latino | 33% | 44% | 47% |
| | | | |
| Catholic | 55% | 56% | 59% |
| Jewish | 32% | 31% | 32% |
| | | | |
| Democrat | 26% | 24% | 16% |
| Independent | 63% | 61% | 67% |
| Republican | 92% | 94% | 97% |
| | | | |
| Liberal | 29% | 25% | 32% |
| Moderate | 54% | 50% | 59% |
| Conservative | 81% | 81% | 82% |

*Source:* "Exit Polls Agree on Who Voted for Whom," *National Journal* 16 (1984): 2271.

The idea to share identical exit poll information sparked considerable debate. Critics raised concerns about projections and analysis deriving from a single source.[10] In the past, the polls had served as a check on each other and offered some assurances that the results were accurate. Worse, if a single entity ran into problems, the networks might have to wait hours or even days for actual votes to be tabulated before they could speak about the results.

Cost savings won out, though, leading CNN and the three major networks to form a consortium in 1990—Voter Research and Surveys (VRS)—to oversee a cooperative exit poll unit, similar to the National Election Service, a joint network venture that had been created in 1964 to compile precinct vote counts for the networks.[11] Warren Mitofsky was named to oversee the unit, which eventually hired 6,000 employees to administer exit polls across the nation. VRS was charged with projecting winners, whereas the networks were left to interpret the causes of the outcome. Network competition had shifted from forecasting to analysis.

## Problems with Projections and Partisan Skew

Unfortunately, the consortium confronted various challenges from the outset. In the 1990 midterm election, the computer program designed to process and weight the results malfunctioned, leaving numerous media outlets scrambling to explain the results. VRS attempted to correct the problem quickly by crafting a simpler weighting scheme, but it did not fully account for all the sampling considerations.[12] This method resulted in several questionable anomalies, such as a high Republican share of the black vote, which were not easily explained by political observers.[13] It was not until much later, when the election was well in the past, that programming errors were fixed and the results fell more in line with expectations.

In 1992, two problems came to the forefront that would burden exit-polling efforts for much of the next two decades. First, in accordance with their contract, VRS provided subscribers with early survey results by 1 p.m. to help media outlets develop storylines and organize their presentations. Mitofsky emphasized repeatedly that these results were preliminary and susceptible to change over the course of the day, warning that "looking at an exit poll halfway through the day is like announcing the final score of a football game at halftime."[14] Nonetheless, commentators characterized the races based on these early indicators, hinting at the outcomes in ways that appeared more definitive than they actually were. Worse, reporters leaked this supposedly embargoed information to friends, colleagues, and even the campaigns themselves, setting off both premature celebrations and handwringing across the political spectrum.

Second, and far more troublesome for the reputation of the exit polls, the preliminary exit poll results showed a partisan skew. They overstated Bill Clinton's share of the vote by 2.5 points in the 1992 presidential race and understated George H. W. Bush's share by 2.5 points, giving the impression that Clinton won by a far greater margin than the officially tabulated votes indicated.[15] The raw exit poll data had never been deemed "accurate" in the past prior to being weighted to the actual results, but with the release of early results, observable, but correctable, sampling errors gave the impression that the numbers were "off."[16]

VRS claimed the Democratic overstatement in the raw exit poll data was due to partisan differences in the willingness of voters to complete the exit poll, not to a poor selection of precincts or differential response rates by age, race, or gender. Republicans simply refused to participate at the same rates as Democrats, resulting in there being fewer Republicans in the raw exit poll results than there should have been. Mitofsky speculated that the disparity was due to different intensities of support for the candidates—Democratic voters were just more excited about voting for Clinton than Republican voters were about voting for Bush and, as a result, were more motivated to communicate this message by filling out the exit poll questionnaire; others thought it was due to Republicans in general having less confidence in the mass media.[17]

Despite the source of the partisan bias in the raw results, the exit polls were able to characterize accurately the voting patterns of demographic subgroups and partisan constituencies once they were weighted to match the official returns. The problem was that the data could not be corrected until the official results began coming in. As a result, the exit polls were susceptible to inaccurate vote projections on election night, especially early in the evening right after poll closings. Nonetheless, the cautious analysts at VRS still called all the races correctly in the 1992 election.

In 1993, VRS merged with the other related media consortium, the National Election Service, to save money.[18] The expanded unit was named the Voter News Service (VNS) and partnered the Associated Press (AP) with CBS, ABC, NBC, and CNN to oversee the provision of exit polls and vote counts (Fox News would join in 1996). Mitofsky, however, was unhappy with the new management structure. He left to form a new exit poll company, Mitofsky International, to compete directly with VNS.[19] Mitofsky International quickly peeled away several high-profile subscribers—including the *New York Times* and the *Washington Post*—that sought to have greater input in the design of questionnaires than they had at VNS. Murray Edelman, Mitofsky's second in command at CBS News and VRS, stepped in as editorial director at VNS.

This change in structure coincided with the reemergence of competitive race calling among the networks. In the prior two election cycles, the networks had deferred to VRS, waiting for them to project a winner before calling the race on the air. In the 1994 congressional elections, ABC News decided to form its own decision desk, comprised of polling experts and statisticians, to expedite the analysis and interpretations of the VNS projection models.[20] On election night, ABC accurately called a number of prominent races well ahead of their competitors. This success prompted the other networks to assemble their own decision desks. By 1996, all the networks were again calling winners in each state, at times well ahead of the VNS projections, which relied on far more conservative statistical models.

## The 2000 Election Debacle

Network competition to call winners culminated in the disastrous 2000 presidential election, when these systems of race projections broke down, and the networks wound up retracting their calls for the winner in Florida and presumptively the election, not once, but twice on election night. The trouble began early in the evening, when VNS alerted the networks around 7:50 p.m. that their statistical models predicted Al Gore the winner in Florida and that the networks should consider calling the state for Gore.[21] This prediction took place even though only 4 percent of the actual vote had been counted and numerous precincts in the Florida panhandle, which happened to be in the central time zone, remained open until 8 p.m.[22] Less than ten minutes later, the decision desks at all the networks and the AP agreed with VNS and announced Gore the winner in Florida.

Over the next hour-and-a-half, VNS discovered that vote-count data from Duval County had been entered incorrectly, making Gore appear as if he had many more votes than he actually did. After fixing this error, the statistical models used by VNS and decision desks at all the networks showed the race could no longer be projected safely for either candidate. By 10:18 p.m., all the networks announced they were moving the state back to the undecided category, prompting Jeff Greenfield of CNN to quip, "Oh waiter, one order of crow."[23]

The networks continued to track the actual vote tallies in Florida over the next several hours. They showed a consistent Bush lead but not one large enough to give any of the decision desks enough confidence to project him as the winner. With 97 percent of the precincts reporting, Bush's 50,000 vote lead finally appeared insurmountable to the networks.[24] At 2:15 a.m., Fox News called Florida and the presidency for Bush. Within five minutes, NBC, CNN, CBS, and ABC followed suit, announcing that Bush would be the forty-third president of the United States. Meanwhile, VNS and the AP chose not to call the race in Florida a second time, wary of the volatility in the data with the contest that close.[25]

During the next couple hours, new errors were discovered. VNS had underestimated the number of votes remaining to be counted. Two counties—Volusia and Brevard—had mistakenly entered their vote totals in favor of Bush. Once these mistakes were corrected, the race narrowed considerably, so much so that Bush's lead was inside the margin of error.[26] Around 4 a.m., one by one the networks began retracting their calls in Florida for Bush, announcing that a recount would be necessary to resolve the winner in the state as well as the race for the presidency. For many newspapers, though, it was too late and numerous morning editions featured headlines announcing Bush as the next president.[27] An embarrassment early in the evening had turned to a humiliation by the end, leading NBC News anchor Tom Brokaw to remark, "We don't just have egg on our face; we have an omelet."[28] Despite the resulting indignation, the exit polls were not responsible for the erroneous second call. In fact, the exit polls were at that point no longer part of the estimation models, having been replaced by actual vote counts—incorrect as they were in some cases—over the course of the evening.[29]

## New Crises and Controversies

After the election, VNS commissioned the Research Triangle Institute (RTI) to conduct an independent analysis of their data collection techniques and estimation models.[30] RTI found that VNS's sampling methods were sound and well designed for estimating the vote. However, they questioned VNS's projected winner formula and standard error calculations, arguing that VNS should make greater use of prior data. Of particular concern was that VNS had used only a single race to gauge past precinct turnout and vote preference in their projected winner formula. RTI also contended that the VNS models did not sufficiently account for early/absentee votes, pointing out that these votes accounted for 12 percent of the actual total vote in 2000 compared to the 7 percent assumed by the VNS models.[31] Finally, RTI thought that VNS could do more to verify incoming information and check for errors in the data.

As a result of this investigation, VNS overhauled their entire system for making projections, redesigning many aspects of the operation from scratch.[32] They modernized their computer hardware and updated their software. They redesigned their projected winner models, making greater use of past votes, revising weighting schemes, and developing new sampling error computations. They expanded the number of states in which they conducted preelection surveys of early/absentee voters and updated models estimating the share of the early/absentee vote received by each candidate. They also installed new quality control procedures, such as error correction notifications, to alert decision desks of significant corrections in turnout counts or vote tallies. Nearly all of these innovations, though, pertained to the procedures for determining a winner of a state on election night and not to the quality of the exit poll data.

Unfortunately, VNS did not have adequate time to fully test the new system. On election night 2002, the new computer system failed to properly integrate and analyze information imported from precincts around the country. Vote counts were processed so slowly that some of the networks stopped using them and turned to other sources, such as the AP, which was running a backup operation. Worse, VNS was unable to supply exit poll data to any of their clients that evening, leaving media outlets scrambling for explanations for the outcome. VNS claimed that fewer exit poll interviews were reported than expected at various planned intervals, making the results too unreliable for them to be confident in their accuracy.[33]

This was the final straw for the media partners in the consortium. In January 2003, VNS was disbanded, leaving the networks once again looking for an efficient and effective way to conduct exit polls.[34] Considering the complexity of the task, though, few options were available. Later that month, the major networks agreed to join forces again, creating the National Election Pool (NEP) to oversee the administration of a single, joint exit poll. NEP hired Edison Research, which had served as the backup system for CNN in the 2002 election, and Mitofsky International, to conduct the exit polls. Edison/Mitofsky would make projections, but each network would be responsible for the calls they made on the air.[35]

Despite the elimination of VNS and the changes made under NEP, the exit polls ran into major headaches again in 2004. Edison/Mitofsky did not make any incorrect projections on election day. However, the partisan skew in the measure of aggregate vote choice was higher than in previous elections. The preliminary data overstated the difference in the George W. Bush-John Kerry vote on election night by 5.5 percentage points, predicting a 51- to 48-percent advantage for Kerry rather than a 50.5- to 48-percent win for Bush.[36] This was the highest error in the preliminary results since the 1992 election and double the error found in the previous two presidential elections.

The discrepancy between the preliminary exit poll findings and the final election results was even greater in the competitive states. The exit polls predicted a Kerry victory in four states—Ohio, Iowa, New Mexico, and Nevada—in which Bush won, and overstated Kerry's support by 11 percentage points in Ohio, 9 points in Pennsylvania, and 8 points in Florida.[37] Considering the closeness of the election, the exit polls seemed to suggest that Kerry was capable of winning the 2004 election.

Political observers used these differences between the preliminary exit polls and the final results to support allegations of vote rigging and fraud in precincts deploying electronic voting machines, particularly in Ohio, where the state's twenty-seven electoral votes, enough to change the winner of the Electoral College from Bush to Kerry, was decided by 118,775 ballots.[38] Steven Freeman of the University of Pennsylvania calculated the odds of the exit polls in Ohio, Pennsylvania, and Florida being as far off the final outcome as they were as 662,000 to 1.[39] The National Election Data Archive, a nonpartisan group of mathematicians and statisticians promoting election reform, found that twenty-two of the forty-nine precincts in Ohio polled by Edison/Mitofsky had reported Kerry vote share results that had less than a 5 percent chance of occurring, based on the state's exit polls.[40] Rep. John Conyers, D-Mich., even used the exit polls as the basis for holding congressional hearings on vote irregularities in Ohio.[41]

Edison/Mitofsky disputed these charges in a follow-up report, contending that precincts with electronic voting had virtually the same rates of error as those using punch card systems.[42] They again attributed the bias to within-precinct error—error due to a systematic bias in the selection of voters within a precinct—and not to bias in the selection of precincts themselves. Bush voters were more likely to refuse to participate in the exit polls than Kerry voters. They hypothesized that the result was a function of the disproportionate numbers of interviewers under age thirty-five who administered the exit poll. Young people had more problems securing participation from voters than older respondents, perhaps because they were correctly perceived to have been more likely to have voted for Kerry.

Edison/Mitofsky also found that voting patterns within electoral groups were accurate once they were weighted to the official results. They found no evidence that the distribution of presidential vote choices within various demographic groups was biased, despite the vote choice of exit poll respondents overall overstating Democratic support.[43] Table 1.2 shows how the presidential

**Table 1.2** Comparison of Composition and Presidential Vote Choice in the 2004 National Exit Polls

| Demographic | NEP National Exit Poll | | *Los Angeles Times* National Exit Poll | | Difference between Polls (NEP–*Los Angeles Times*) | |
|---|---|---|---|---|---|---|
| | % of Respondents | % Voting for Bush | % of Respondents | % Voting for Bush | % of Respondents | % Voting for Bush |
| Male | 46% | 55% | 49% | 53% | –3% | 2% |
| Female | 54% | 48% | 51% | 49% | 3% | –1% |
| | | | | | | |
| Married Men | 30% | 60% | 31% | 59% | –1% | 1% |
| Single Men | 16% | 45% | 16% | 40% | 0% | 5% |
| Married Women | 32% | 55% | 30% | 57% | 2% | –2% |
| Single Women | 22% | 37% | 19% | 35% | 3% | 2% |
| | | | | | | |
| 18–29 | 17% | 45% | 20% | 43% | –3% | 2% |
| 30–44 | 29% | 53% | 32% | 52% | –3% | 1% |
| 45–64 | 38% | 52% | 36% | 54% | 2% | –2% |
| 65 or Older | 16% | 52% | 12% | 55% | 4% | –3% |
| | | | | | | |
| White | 77% | 58% | 79% | 57% | –2% | 1% |
| Black | 11% | 11% | 10% | 14% | 1% | –3% |
| Hispanic/Latino | 8% | 44% | 5% | 45% | 3% | –1% |
| Asian | 2% | 44% | 3% | 34% | –1% | 10% |
| | | | | | | |
| Protestant | 54% | 59% | 51% | 61% | 3% | –2% |
| Catholic | 27% | 52% | 25% | 55% | 2% | –3% |
| Jewish | 3% | 25% | 4% | 26% | –1% | –1% |
| | | | | | | |
| Weekly Religious Attender | 41% | 61% | 42% | 65% | –1% | –4% |
| Less Than Weekly Attender | 54% | 44% | 58% | 42% | –4% | 2% |
| | | | | | | |
| Own Guns | 41% | 63% | 36% | 65% | 5% | –2% |
| Do Not Own Guns | 59% | 43% | 64% | 43% | –5% | 0% |
| | | | | | | |
| First-Time Voter | 11% | 46% | 11% | 42% | 0% | 4% |
| Voted Before | 89% | 51% | 89% | 53% | 0% | –2% |
| | | | | | | |
| Union Households | 24% | 40% | 27% | 43% | –3% | –3% |
| Not Union Households | 76% | 55% | 73% | 54% | 3% | 1% |
| | | | | | | |
| Heterosexual | 96% | 53% | 96% | 53% | 0% | 0% |
| Gay/Lesbian/ Bisexual | 4% | 23% | 4% | 17% | 0% | 6% |

*Source:* Edison Media Research and Mitofsky International, "Evaluation of Edison/Mitofsky Election System 2004," 2005, pp. 63–64, www.ap.org/media/pdf/evaluationedisonmitofsky.pdf.

preferences of various demographic groups in the 2004 NEP national exit poll compared to the national exit poll conducted by the *Los Angeles Times*. For almost every group, there is virtually no difference in their size or presidential vote choice.

In the aftermath of the 2004 election, Edison/Mitofsky announced they would make several changes to address these issues. They committed to hiring interviewers from a broader age range and to training them more intensely in an effort to diminish the apparent differences in response rates among supporters of different candidates. Moreover, they would not release any results from the exit polls prior to 6 p.m. eastern time.[44]

Since 2004, less controversy has surrounded the exit polls. No serious technical problems have surfaced during the last three elections, enabling the media to prepare analyses of the outcome in a timely manner. Leaks of early wave findings have been contained. The preliminary exit polls have continued to overstate support for Democratic candidates; however, the final vote counts have had such large winning margins that the projected outcomes were no different.

## How Exit Polls Work

Conducting national exit polls in the United States is an enormous undertaking, requiring as long as two years to implement. The goal of the process is to collect information on a subset of voters that can be projected to the entire active electorate with a high degree of confidence. Numerous obstacles, though, stand in the way, threatening to undermine the effort and bias the results.

Exit polls, like most surveys, unfold in four distinct but often overlapping stages.[45] Researchers usually begin by developing procedures for drawing a probabilistic sample of voters whose responses can be inferred to the active electorate with a high degree of confidence. They develop a questionnaire, capable of both describing the types of voters participating in an election as well as offering insights into the reasoning behind their choices. Interviewers are trained and eventually employed to disseminate the questionnaires to and collect them from sampled voters on election day. The process concludes with the integration of voters' responses into a data set for analysis. The specific procedures used for each stage vary by polling organization; therefore, we focus our discussion on those procedures developed by Warren Mitofsky, Murray Edelman, and their colleagues at CBS and used by the polling units employed by the network consortium to conduct the last four national exit polls.

### Sampling

The first stage of the exit polling process centers on selecting a subset of voters to whom the questionnaire will be administered. To make valid inferences to the active electorate, a sample needs to be drawn that ensures every voter has some chance of being selected. Systematically excluding certain voters can bias the data collected and distort generalization to the active electorate.[46] At the same time, though, a representative sample of the active electorate requires a demographic mix of voters from across the states as well as across regions within a state, a challenging feat for pollsters relying solely on simple random sampling methods, whereby each voter has the same probability of being selected.

To reduce the threat of coverage error and to ensure that obvious subgroups in the population (for example, geographic regions) are represented, exit pollsters undertake a two-stage sampling process. The first stage involves choosing a subset of precincts from around the country. The second stage centers on interviewing a group of voters in each of the selected precincts. If sampling is done correctly, all voters nationwide will have a chance of being selected, and the responses of those interviewed can be used to make probabilistic inferences about the active electorate.

*Selection of Precincts.* National exit pollsters choose precincts by taking stratified probability samples in each of the states before drawing a national subsample from the state samples. This process involves sorting the precincts in each state into different categories or strata to guarantee that particular groups are represented adequately. To begin, precincts in each state are initially grouped into two strata according to their size to ensure the selection of smaller precincts.[47] Within each of these size strata, precincts are categorized by geographic region, usually between three to five regions in each state. For each state geographic region, precincts are ordered by their percentage vote for one of the major political parties in a previous election. Precincts are sampled from these strata with probabilities proportionate to the total votes cast in them in a prior election, so that every precinct has as many chances of being picked by pollsters as it has voters. The samples drawn in each state are then combined, and a national sample of precincts is selected from them using a previous presidential race to determine the relative number of precincts chosen from each state.

Typically, the total number of precincts selected in the national exit poll is between 250 and 300. Ultimately, the number of precincts chosen represents a tradeoff between sampling error and financial constraints. Research by Edison/Mitofsky has shown that the number of precincts selected has not been responsible for the Democratic overstatements that have continually appeared in the exit polls.[48] For example, they found that for the 2004 election the actual distribution of the presidential vote in the precincts used in the exit poll samples did not differ significantly from the actual vote distribution nationwide. In fact, these precincts overstated support for the Republican candidate, George W. Bush, but only by 0.4 points, on average, across the states.

*Selection of Individual Voters.* Within each precinct, interviewers are instructed to count all the voters exiting a sampled precinct and interview every $n$th voter.[49] The interviewing rate usually varies between every voter and one out of every ten voters depending on the size and expected turnout in each precinct. It is typically structured to ensure that interviewers collect responses from approximately a hundred voters over the course of the day.

Despite the apparent simplicity of the process, it is fraught with challenges. It can be difficult for interviewers to get close enough to polling places to intercept voters effectively. A number of states have imposed laws prohibiting pollsters from getting within a certain distance of polling places. Typically, these distance requirements have been between 50 and 300 feet, although, in the most extreme case, Hawaii forbade interviewers from getting within 1,000 feet. The news media have repeatedly brought lawsuits to overturn these efforts. To date, the courts have always sided on behalf of the media, ruling that such laws violate the First Amendment rights of the media to access newsworthy information.[50] Nonetheless, some restrictions remain. In the 2004 election, roughly 12 percent of interviewers reported having to stand more than 50 feet away from a polling location and 3 percent said they had to stand more than 100 feet away.[51]

Even when interviewers can get sufficiently close to a polling place, voters can still elude exit pollsters. Sometimes polling places contain multiple entry points, making it difficult to maintain an accurate count of voters. Other times, it can be challenging to intercept voters who are moving too quickly or exiting as part of a crowd. All told, about one in ten voters chosen for the sample are nonetheless missed by interviewers and therefore contribute no information.[52]

Finally, intercepted voters can refuse to complete the questionnaire. Voters refuse for a variety of reasons, including lack of interest or time, weather, concerns about privacy or media objectivity, or the demographic characteristics of the interviewer (for example, voters are less likely to respond to younger interviewers). The proportion of refusals varies by precinct, but typically it occurs in roughly a third of voters in the sample.[53]

Refusal rates, or for that matter miss rates, are not necessarily problematic, as long as the propensity of different groups to participate does not vary. However, if one group is more or less likely than other groups to complete exit surveys, their responses will be over- or underrepresented, thereby biasing estimates for the overall electorate. For example, the partisan overstatement repeatedly found in the national exit polls over the past several decades appears to be due to the greater willingness of Democratic voters to complete the exit polls, compared with their Republican counterparts. However, once this discrepancy has been corrected by weighting the exit polls to correspond with the actual vote, there has been no evidence that the vote estimates within groups are biased.

Nonetheless, the network exit polling organizations have undertaken a number of measures to reduce the threat posed by nonresponse. They have recruited interviewers with characteristics that correlate with higher response rates, such as prior survey interviewing experience and older age. They have emphasized training to better educate interviewers on how to handle evasive voters. Most important, they have imposed strict protocols for cases in which the voters intended to participate are either missed or refuse to complete the questionnaire. Interviewers are first instructed to record the *n*th voter's sex, race, and approximate age. This information allows the data to be adjusted for differential nonresponse on these three observable characteristics. Interviewers then commence the count again, selecting the *n*th voter. They are instructed not to substitute the *n*th voter with a more easily accessible alternative. If this procedure is performed correctly, the probability structure underlying voter selection will be maintained.

*Accounting for Early/Absentee Voters.* Some voters do not go to the polls in person on election day, casting ballots in advance by mail or at designated locations. Historically, citizens living overseas, deployed by the military, or away at school were permitted to mail an absentee ballot to the precinct containing their permanent residence. In recent years, a growing number of states have permitted all registrants to vote prior to election day, regardless of their rationale, in an effort to stimulate participation. Some states, such as Oregon, permit voters to mail their early/

absentee ballots, whereas others require voters to submit early/absentee ballots at designated on-site locations. By the 2010 election, as many as a third of the ballots cast by voters were done by means other than going to an election day polling station.[54]

National exit pollsters account for early/absentee voting by conducting telephone surveys in states where the rates of early voting are highest. VNS first incorporated early/absentee voting in 1996, surveying voters in California, Oregon, Texas, and Washington. By 2008, NEP was conducting telephone surveys in eighteen states, including Oregon, Washington, and Colorado, where the proportions of early voting were so high that no in-person exit polls were conducted on election day.

The telephone surveys are contracted out to different survey centers that administer them during the last week before the election. Respondents are chosen through random digit dialing. Because of the increased use of cell phones over the past few years, the exit polls now include cell and landline phone numbers in their samples. Respondents who indicate that they have already voted or intend to do so before election day are interviewed. They are administered essentially the same questionnaires as those given to exiting voters on election day. After a designated number of interviews have been conducted (usually based on the expected ratio of early/absentee to election day on-site voting), the data are weighted to reflect the probabilities of selection as well as key demographic characteristics in the state (such as race, age, and education).

On election day, the results from the absentee/early voter telephone surveys are combined with the on-site exit polls. Each group is then weighted in proportion to its contribution to the overall vote. When projecting the vote during election night, these weights are based on an estimate of their relative influence. After the election, the exit polls and absentee/early voter telephone surveys are forced to the proportions of the actual vote totals that they comprised in their respective states.

## Questionnaire Design

The exit questionnaires are designed by representatives from each of the networks in the consortium. They typically contain twenty-five to forty questions, many of which are carried over from past election years. To allow a greater number of questions, multiple versions of the surveys are usually administered, typically four in presidential election years and two in midterm election years (see Table 1.3). Each version contains both a unique and a common set of questions. The versions are interleaved on pads that can be removed sequentially by interviewers. After the surveys are returned, the versions are combined into a single data set for analysis.

The content of the questions covers a range of topics, including respondents' vote choices, physical traits, religious characteristics, lifestyle choices, political orientations, economic considerations, issue positions, and candidate evaluations. All the questions are close-ended, save those on vote choice, which provide space for respondents to write in candidates whom they selected but who were not amongst the options provided. Most questions contain two to four response options, including well-known scales such as ideological identification and presidential approval, which are truncated to three or four choices. Efforts are made to retain similar, if not identical, wording for questions on topics asked repeatedly over time.

**Table 1.3**   Number of Respondents in Each Version of the CBS/VRS/VNS/NEP Exit Poll, 1972–2010

| Year | Version 1 | Version 2 | Version 3 | Version 4 | Total |
|------|-----------|-----------|-----------|-----------|-------|
| 1972 | 17,595 | | | | 17,595 |
| 1976 | 15,300 | | | | 15,300 |
| 1978 | 8,808 | | | | 8,808 |
| 1980 | 15,201 | | | | 15,201 |
| 1982 | 7,855 | | | | 7,855 |
| 1984 | 9,174 | | | | 9,174 |
| 1986 | 8,994 | | | | 8,994 |
| 1988 | 11,645 | | | | 11,645 |
| 1990 | 10,565 | 9,323 | | | 19,888 |
| 1992 | 4,416 | 4,137 | 3,920 | 3,017 | 15,490 |
| 1994 | 5,742 | 5,566 | | | 11,308 |
| 1996 | 4,185 | 4,203 | 4,146 | 4,103 | 16,637 |
| 1998 | 5,747 | 5,640 | | | 11,387 |
| 2000 | 3,323 | 3,321 | 3,328 | 3,253 | 13,225 |
| 2002 | 9,095 | 8,777 | | | 17,872 |
| 2004 | 3,666 | 3,324 | 3,300 | 3,429 | 13,719 |
| 2006 | 7,008 | 6,858 | | | 13,866 |
| 2008 | 4,508 | 4,525 | 4,609 | 4,376 | 18,018 |
| 2010 | 4,623 | 4,725 | 4,635 | 4,149 | 18,132 |

*Source:* National exit polls. See the section in Chapter 2 entitled "Creating a Cumulative National Data Set: Selecting Exit Polls" (pp. 28–29).

Some exit poll questionnaires are translated into Spanish. Voters in precincts where Hispanics comprise at least 20 percent of the population are given the option of completing the exit poll in English or Spanish. In the 2010 election, eight states contained precincts offering a Spanish version of the questionnaire.

Despite the apparent straightforwardness of constructing exit poll questionnaires, the process presents a number of challenges to pollsters as they attempt to design an instrument in which every solicited voter will complete every question on the survey. For example, researchers have long debated questionnaire length. Longer questionnaires can yield more data about individuals, but fewer people want to complete them. Today, exit pollsters balance this tradeoff by limiting questionnaires to the front and back of a single sheet of paper.

Pollsters also weigh how to handle respondents who fail to complete any of the questions on the back side of the questionnaire. Typically, 3 to 5 percent of respondents leave the entire back side blank, despite reminders by interviewers to complete both sides. A number of questions placed at the end tend to be of great importance, covering key demographic variables such as household income, education, religious affiliation, and party identification. Exit pollsters use the information provided on the front side even if respondents do not answer any of the questions on the back side.

Finally, exit pollsters debate how to interpret individual questions skipped by respondents. An unanswered question could mean a respondent missed it inadvertently, was unsure how to answer it, could not find an acceptable response from among the options provided, or intentionally chose to skip it. This problem was exacerbated during the 1980s and early 1990s when exit pollsters included lists of characteristics at the end of the questionnaire and instructed respondents to check all that applied. National exit polls treat unanswered demographic questions as missing data and do not include them in the marginals and cross-tabulations provided to the network consortium on election night. Unanswered attitudinal questions, though, are interpreted as "don't know" responses for the purposes of election day analyses, unless they occur on a back side that is completely unanswered, in which case they are treated as missing data, as well.

## Interviewing

Exit questionnaires are disseminated by contracted interviewers at precincts across the country on election day. One interviewer is typically assigned to each precinct, although sometimes more than one interviewer is deployed in precincts deemed unsafe or anticipating high turnout. They are tasked with distributing and collecting exit poll surveys as well as collecting information on voter turnout and nonresponse.

Interviewers are recruited from across the country, primarily through job postings at various career centers and websites and through the recommendations of former exit poll interviewers. Their training unfolds in three phases. During the hiring call, interviewers are given an overview of the exit poll process as well as their particular responsibilities. Interviewers are then mailed instructions and a training video describing the procedures for intercepting voters, administering the questionnaire, and tallying misses, refusals, and overall turnout. Finally, interviewers participate in telephone rehearsals to ensure that they understand all aspects of the job.[55]

On election day, interviewers arrive at their assigned precincts when the polls open. After checking in with their supervisor, they make voting officials aware of their presence and where they intend to station themselves to conduct interviews. Interviewers attempt to stand as close to the precinct exits as possible. If voting officials attempt to prevent them from performing their task or distance them too far from the exits to be effective, they contact supervisors to attempt to resolve the situation.[56]

Interviewers approach the voters defined by their designated interviewing rates, introducing themselves and describing what is necessary to complete the exit poll. Their pitch typically includes assurances that the questionnaire can be completed quickly and confidentially. A badge identifying themselves as members of the consortium conducting the exit polls is worn to legitimize their request.

Once voters agree to participate, interviewers give them a pencil and a paper questionnaire affixed to a clipboard. Respondents self-administer the questions and complete the survey privately, typically standing a short distance from the interviewer. When they are finished, they fold the questionnaires and slip them through an opening in a closed box to ensure that their identities and answers remain confidential.

Interviewers take a short break every hour to tabulate responses. At three times during the day—late morning, midafternoon, and just before the polls shut down—interviewers call in to a centralized computing system the results of the exit poll as well as information on voters who were missed or failed to respond. During these breaks throughout the day, and after the precinct closes, interviewers attempt to secure actual turnout numbers and vote returns from precinct officials.

## Analysis of the Results

A centralized computing system receives exit poll results, completion rates, and turnout information from interviewers during election day. It tabulates the survey responses to each question across all precincts in a given electoral jurisdiction and weights the results to account for various sampling considerations. The findings are then integrated with cumulative precinct tallies of turnout and vote returns into various projection models to estimate vote totals for each candidate. This information is sent to the decision desks of the consortium members, who use them to "call" winners in various races and offer explanations of the outcomes.

The weights applied to the exit polls adjust for three different sampling considerations.[57] Initially, respondents are weighted for their probability of selection within a given precinct. This probability hinges on how many people voted overall in the precinct and the composition of voters who failed to respond. Both must be projected, at least initially, with the best available information. During the course of the day, interviewers provide turnout numbers based on their own counts or those provided by precinct election officials. Later in the process, as the actual final turnout figures become more available, they replace any remaining interviewers' estimates, often altering the weight in the process.

Respondents' probabilities of selection also hinge on the composition of voters. For example, the likelihood of selecting a female voter depends in part on the proportion of female voters who participated. Estimation of this ratio requires information on all voters in the sample, not just those who completed the survey. Interviewers are instructed to track the sex, race, and age of voters who were missed or chose not to participate. The frequency distribution of nonresponders is then compared to responders to determine if a discrepancy exists. If so, the data are adjusted to account for any of these discrepancies. However, nonresponse bias stemming from other nonobservable characteristics is not and cannot be corrected because interviewers have no way of identifying the attribute from afar. For example, because pollsters do not know the party identification of those who refuse to participate in the exit poll, the weight cannot account for nonresponse bias based on partisanship.

Also, exit poll results are weighted by the probability of precinct selection. Precincts within a state are adjusted to match their relative size in the state's active electorate. The exit poll results are then weighted to modify each state's contribution so that it matches the state's relative contribution to the election.

Finally, exit poll results are forced to the official turnout and the vote share given to the respective candidates in each precinct. This final adjustment is designed to correct for obvious sampling error in the exit polls that was not remedied when the probability of respondent and precinct selection was taken into account. This generates a data set that offers the greatest likelihood of understanding the electorate's voting patterns. The assumption underlying this weighting is that the officially reported vote counts are a valid representation of the ballots cast in an election. In recent years, this correction has been controversial, as some observers have argued that it obscures evidence of vote fraud. Such accusations, of course, presume that the exit polls are precise estimates of the actual vote and not the other way around. The nature of opinion polls, whereby survey error is ever present, and the history of the exit polls themselves, in which they have yielded a persistent Democratic overstatement in presidential vote choice, make this unlikely.[58]

## Advantages and Disadvantages of Exit Polls

National exit polls possess numerous advantages over their chief counterparts—preelection and postelection telephone surveys—for understanding the composition and vote choices of the active electorate.[59] Certainly, trends about *likely voters'* opinions drawn from standard public opinion surveys exist in our poll-saturated contemporary environment. Yet, compared to exit polls, standard public opinion surveys are less well suited to examine *voters'* attitudes and behaviors.

First and foremost, the exit polls are distinct in that they contact actual voters immediately after they depart polling locations across the nation. Because standard public opinion polls, such as the American National Election Study or Gallup Poll, do not capture respondents as they depart the voting booth, these standard surveys often fail to correctly identify voters from nonvoters.[60] These surveys are not even conducted on election day, but rather in the weeks and months preceding or following the election. As a result, individuals may project erroneously whether they will vote in the upcoming election or recall inaccurately whether they voted in the past election.[61] Political scientists have long known that many nonvoters misreport that they voted to come across as "good citizens" to the interviewers.[62] Accordingly, standard surveys routinely present voter turnout rates 15 to 20 percentage points higher than turnout rates reported by official election returns.[63] Worse, we know little about the recent patterns of overreporting given that the American National Election Study stopped conducting voter validation studies in 1990.

Given this challenge of overreporting, polling firms resort to correcting their survey data by using a variety of complex and often controversial predictive algorithms to reclassify many self-described voters as nonvoters.[64] This scheme is vulnerable to classifying nonvoters as voters, as well as voters as nonvoters, because the algorithms used to classify individuals rely on responses to questions about preregistration, turnout history, and campaign enthusiasm, rather than observable voting behavior. By contrast, exit polls overcome many of these problems with the benefit of immediate hindsight. Exit polls describe what voters thought and did at the polls only minutes earlier. There is simply no better way to capture actual voters in a sample than to station interviewers at hundreds of precincts nationwide on election day.

Exit polls also have the advantage of letting respondents self-administer the questionnaire and record their own responses, rather than requiring interviewers to read them the questions and document their answers, as in telephone surveys. This confidential self-reporting alleviates the pressures that respondents may feel to indicate that they cast a ballot or voted for a particular candidate when they did not, in an attempt to be judged favorably by an interviewer. By enabling voters to complete the questionnaires on their own, the exit polls greatly reduce the threat of social desirability bias that can plague telephone surveys, particularly on sensitive issues such as voters' electoral choices.

Finally, the national exit polls collect completed questionnaires from far greater numbers of respondents than telephone surveys. Preelection and postelection surveys conducted by media outlets typically number between 500 and 1,500 cases. Even the two most prominent academic surveys with a multidecade time series—the American National Election Study and the General Social Survey—rarely administer their surveys to more than 3,000 respondents (see Table 1.4). By comparison, the national exit polls have always involved at least 7,500 respondents and routinely top 15,000 cases, including in 2008, when the exit polls were administered to 18,018 voters, and in 2010, when they were administered to 17,504 voters. Not only do these larger sample sizes permit great confidence in the overall results, but they also permit analysis of a far greater number of subgroups that comprise a small proportion of the overall electorate. Take, for example, Jewish voters, who comprise only 3 percent of the electorate. In a large standard survey of 2,000 people, Jews will only make up roughly sixty cases, resulting in a margin of error in excess of 12 points.

Despite their unique strengths, exit polls are not without their shortcomings. They are a type of sample survey, and as such are vulnerable to the four types of survey error: sampling error, coverage error, nonresponse error, and measurement error.[65] These errors can manifest themselves in two forms: (1) bias in the population estimates, and (2) decreases in the precision of population

**Table 1.4** Number of Respondents in Postelection Polls, 1972–2010

| Year | CBS/VRS/VNS/NEP National Exit Poll | American National Election Study | General Social Survey |
|------|------|------|------|
| 1972 | 17,595 | 2,285 | 1,613 |
| 1974 | Not administered | 1,575 | 1,484 |
| 1976 | 15,300 | 1,909 | 1,499 |
| 1978 | 8,808 | 2,304 | 1,532 |
| 1980 | 15,201 | 1,408 | 1,468 |
| 1982 | 7,855 | 1,418 | 1,506 |
| 1984 | 9,174 | 1,989 | 1,473 |
| 1986 | 8,994 | 2,176 | 1,470 |
| 1988 | 11,645 | 1,775 | 1,481 |
| 1990 | 19,888 | 1,980 | 1,372 |
| 1992 | 15,490 | 2,255 | 1,606 |
| 1994 | 11,308 | 1,795 | 2,992 |
| 1996 | 16,637 | 1,534 | 2,904 |
| 1998 | 11,387 | 1,281 | 2,832 |
| 2000 | 13,225 | 1,555 | 2,807 |
| 2002 | 17,872 | 1,346 | 2,765 |
| 2004 | 13,719 | 1,066 | 2,812 |
| 2006 | 13,866 | Not administered | 4,510 |
| 2008 | 18,018 | 2,102 | 2,023 |
| 2010 | 17,504 | Not administered | 2,044 |

*Source:* National exit polls. See the section in Chapter 2 entitled "Creating a Cumulative National Data Set: Selecting Exit Polls" (pp. 28–29).

estimates. The susceptibility of exit polls to any of these four types of errors, though, is no worse than that found in preelection or postelection telephone surveys.

First, exit polls, like all sample surveys, are susceptible to sampling error. Sampling error refers to potential bias in the sample estimates that occurs by chance from selecting a subset of the overall population. Unlike the other forms of error, though, the amount that sample estimates are likely to vary from the population can be calculated. Calculations hinge on the type of sampling, the sample size, and the degree of confidence desired in the calculation. Because the exit polls employ stratified sampling, the sample estimates have more variability than they would if they were truly random. Consequently, sampling error is larger in an exit poll than in a random-digit-dialing telephone survey of equal size once this reduced variability is taken into account.[66] Some of this difference in sampling error is offset by the much greater sample sizes typically found in the exit polls. Nonetheless, exit poll estimates still contain sampling error that must be accounted for when projecting responses to the entire active electorate.

Second, the exit polls can fall prey to coverage error. Coverage error occurs when every individual in the population does not have some probability of being selected. If those who are not covered are systematically different from those who are covered, the results of the poll can be biased. Exit polls have long been susceptible to coverage error from interviewers mistakenly applying interviewing rates by miscounting voters or incorrectly substituting replacements. In recent election cycles, though, a far bigger threat to coverage has emerged from states loosening their rules for early or absentee voting. Research has shown that the characteristics of early/absentee voters can be quite different from election day precinct voters, and this difference is capable of skewing exit poll findings.[67] NEP has confronted the problem by conducting preelection telephone surveys in the states with the highest rates of early/absentee voters, but early/absentee voters in many areas are still missed. To date, though, the coverage error that crept into exit polls has not substantially biased the composition or preferences of voting groups.[68]

Third, exit poll results can be skewed by nonresponse error. Nonresponse error arises when sampled respondents fail to complete the questionnaire. This omission could bias results if certain groups respond at different rates than others. This type of error has been troublesome for the national exit polls in recent years, arguably the most problematic of the four types of survey error.[69] Some sampled voters are missed because of laws requiring interviewers to stand a certain distance from the polls, weather, or evasive voters, whereas others choose not to participate because of time constraints or wariness about some aspect of the process. Regardless of the cause, Republican voters are less likely than their Democratic counterparts to complete exit polls. Fortunately, this differential response among partisan voters does not appear to bias the distribution of vote choices within particular groups, including partisan ones. Nonetheless, exit pollsters have attempted to reduce the threats posed by nonresponse error. They have recruited interviewers possessing characteristics correlated with higher response rates, introduced training techniques to induce greater cooperation, and collected observable information on voters failing to respond that is then used to correct for nonresponse on these factors.

Finally, exit polls can suffer from measurement error like any type of survey. Measurement error results when a question fails to measure what it was intended to measure because either respondents fail to understand the meaning of a question or the context in which it is asked steers them toward an incorrect response. This error can bias the findings of a question if respondents provide answers that are systematically different from their true preferences. National exit pollsters dedicate considerable effort to reducing threats from measurement error. They present questions in a clear, easy-to-read format, employing sparse, simplistic language to enhance understanding of the questions. They use comprehensive, mutually exclusive response options to ensure that one and only one answer is applicable. And, they permit voters to self-administer the questions to limit the interviewer's effect on responses. Moreover, exit pollsters continually undertake experiments designed to expose potential biases in measurement. For example, in 1996, they replaced "grab bag" questions, whereby respondents were asked to choose from a list of characteristics the ones that were applicable to them, with separate yes-no questions for each characteristic after experiments revealed that the incidence of characteristics in the grab bag were being underestimated.

## Design of the Book

Despite the unique insights that exit polls can provide about the composition and preferences of voters, they are seldom used after the days immediately following an election. Once media organizations have tapped the exit polls for explanations of electoral outcomes, they often disappear from the public eye. Some scholars may use them over the next year or two to explore the voting behavior of certain subgroups, such as Hispanics, women, or young people, but for the most part they recede into memory, rarely used beyond the next national election.

Unfortunately, few efforts are made to consider the behavior of voters over time. Historical context typically centers on comparing an election to its most recent predecessor, such as contrasting the 2008 presidential election with the 2004 contest. Rarely are exit poll responses tracked and analyzed over time, leaving many important questions understudied. For example, how have various subgroups in the electorate evolved over time? Have their relative sizes in the active electorate increased or decreased? Have their voting patterns grown increasingly partisan or independent? Which subgroups in the electorate behave similarly through the years?

We suspect that a major reason exit polls are underutilized is that they are largely inaccessible to academics, journalists, or the public. Although each exit poll resides in prominent data archives, such as the Interuniversity Consortium for Political and Social Research at the University of Michigan or the Roper Center for Public Opinion Research at the University of Connecticut, a cumulative data file has not yet been constructed that permits temporal comparisons. Over the years, the seven different media outlets and consortia that have sponsored the thirty-two national exit polls conducted during the last nineteen election cycles have each applied a different coding scheme to the data. They have employed alternative variable labels, assigned different values to the responses, and made use of alternative formatting criteria. As a result, the data cannot be easily merged and analyzed.

We have undertaken the time-consuming effort to arrange the data collected from each exit poll in a standardized format and merged the data across years. As a result, time-ordered observations of every repeated survey question can now be generated and analyzed. In the remainder of this book, we use these time series to derive insights into the presidential and congressional voting behavior of key subgroups in the electorate over the past four decades.

The results of this effort are presented in the next four chapters. In Chapter 2, we discuss how the questions from individual exit polls from different elections were combined and describe the rationale for selecting specific questions for analysis. In the process, we lay out the techniques used to merge the data, detailing how we handled variations in question wording, missing values, and differences in polling organizations. We describe the methods used for computing distributions, generating sampling errors, and producing graphs. And, we explain how the tables and graphs presented in each subsequent chapter should be interpreted.

Chapter 3 focuses on the composition of respondents to the exit polls. Using answers to recurring exit poll questions, we examine the distribution of various groups of respondents from 1972 through 2010. We consider whether different respondent groups have been increasing or decreasing in their relative size in exit polls over time. We detail the results of the most recent exit poll, in 2010, examining how it compares to historical trends. We conclude by considering the differences between respondents in the midterm and presidential exit polls, which is particularly important, considering the differential turnout rates in each election context.

In Chapter 4, we examine the presidential voting preferences of key groups in the exit polls from 1972 through 2008. We examine how partisan preferences have evolved over time. We pay particular attention to the 2008 presidential race, identifying which respondent groups were key supporters of Barack Obama and John McCain and assessing how their choices compare to long-term trends in presidential preferences. We conclude the chapter by considering which groups serve as the party's base, predisposed toward one party's candidates or the other, and which groups are susceptible to swinging their vote from one party to the other.

Chapter 5, the concluding chapter, switches the focus to congressional elections. We examine the congressional voting patterns of prominent groups in the exit polls conducted from 1976 through 2010. We look closely at the Republican takeover of the House in the 2010 election, analyzing how respondent groups deviated from their historical patterns. Again we conclude by differentiating between partisan base groups and swing groups.

## Notes

[1] Warren J. Mitofsky, "A Short History of Exit Polls," in *Polling and Presidential Election Coverage*, ed. Paul J. Lavrakas and Jack K. Holley (Newbury Park, CA: Sage Publications, 1991).

[2] Fritz J. Scheuren and Wendy Alvey, *Elections and Exit Polling* (New York: Wiley, 2008).

[3] David W. Moore, *The Superpollsters* (New York: Four Walls Eight Windows, 1995).

[4] Warren J. Mitofsky and Murray Edelman, "Election Night Estimation," *Journal of Official Statistics* 16 (2002): 165–179.

[5] Mark R. Levy, "The Methodology and Performance of Election Day Polls," *Public Opinion Quarterly* 47, no. 1 (Spring 1983): 54–67.

[6] "Exit Polls Agree on Who Voted for Whom," *National Journal* 16 (1984): 2271.

[7] Harry F. Waters and George Hackett, "Peacock's Night to Crow," *Newsweek,* November 17, 1980, 82.

[8] Kathleen A. Frankovic, "News Organizations' Responses to the Mistakes of Election 2000: Why They Will Continue to Project Elections," *Public Opinion Quarterly* 67 (2003): 19–31.

[9] Jeremy Gerard, "TV Networks May Approve a Pool for Election Exit Polls," *New York Times,* October 31, 1989, C26.

[10] Richard Berke, "Networks Quietly Abandon Competition and Unite to Survey Voters," *New York Times*, November 7, 1990, B1.

[11] Ibid.

[12] Lynne Duke, "Computer Mishap Forces Shift in Election Coverage; Major Newspapers Were Faced with Lack of Exit Poll Data," *Washington Post*, November 7, 1990, A10.

[13] E. J. Dionne Jr. and Richard Morin, "Analysts Debate: Did More Blacks Vote Republican for House This Year? Doubts Arise about Exit Poll That Found Sharp Increase in Support," *Washington Post*, December 10, 1990, A4.

[14] Warren J. Mitofsky, "What Went Wrong with Exit Polling in New Hampshire?" *Public Perspective* 3, no. 3 (March/April 1992): 17.

[15] Daniel M. Merkle and Murray Edelman, "A Review of the 1996 Voter News Service Exit Polls from a Total Survey Error Perspective," in *Election Polls, the News Media, and Democracy,* ed. Paul J. Lavrakas and Michael W. Traugott (New York: Seven Bridges Press, 2000).

[16] Robin Sproul, "Exit Polls: Better or Worse since the 2000 Election?" Joan Shorenstein Center on the Press, Politics and Public Policy, 2008, Discussion Paper Series.

[17] Warren J. Mitofsky and Murray Edelman, "A Review of the 1992 VRS Exit Polls," in *Presidential Polls and the News Media*, ed. Paul J. Lavrakas, Michael W. Traugott, and Peter V. Miller (Boulder, CO: Westview Press, 1995).

[18] Frankovic, "News Organizations' Responses to the Mistakes of Election 2000."

[19] James A. Barnes, "Dueling Exit Polls," *Public Perspective* 5 (1994): 19–20.

[20] Mark Lindeman and Rick Brady, "Behind the Controversy: A Primer on U.S. Presidential Exit Polls," *Public Opinion Pros* (January 2006), http://publicopinionpros.com/from_field/2006/jan/lindeman_1.asp.

[21] Warren J. Mitofsky, "Voter News Service after the Fall," *Public Opinion Quarterly* 67, no. 1 (Spring 2003): 45–58.

[22] Joan Konner, James Risser, and Ben Wattenberg, "Television's Performance on Election Night 2000: A Report for CNN," 2001, http://archives.cnn.com/2001/ALLPOLITICS/stories/02/02/cnn.report/cnn.pdf.

[23] Ibid., 13.

[24] Richard Meyer, "Glitch Led to 'Bush Wins' Call," *USA Today*, November 29, 2000, A15.

[25] Richard Morin, "Bad Call in Florida," *Washington Post*, November 13, 2000, A27.

[26] Konner, Risser, and Wattenberg, "Television's Performance on Election Night 2000."

[27] Martha T. Moore, "TV, Newspapers Get Big One Wrong; Vote Projections Err One Way, Then the Other," *Washington Post*, November 19, 2000, A14.

[28] Charles Laurence, "This Time It's More Important to Be Right Than First; After the Debacle of the 2000 Presidential Elections, the American Television Networks Are Overhauling Their Coverage of This Year's Race for the White House," *Sunday Telegraph* (U.K.), October 31, 2004, 31.

[29] Mitofsky, "Voter News Service after the Fall."

[30] Paul Biemer, Ralph Folsom, Richard Kulka, Judith Lessler, Babu Shah, and Michael Weeks, "An Evaluation of Procedures and Operations Used by the Voter News Service for the 2000 Presidential Election," *Public Opinion Quarterly* 67, no. 1 (Spring 2003): 32–44.

[31] Joan Konner, "The Case for Caution: This System Is Dangerously Flawed," *Public Opinion Quarterly* 67, no. 1 (Spring 2003): 5–18.

[32] Mitofsky, "Voter News Service after the Fall."

[33] Martha T. Moore, "Media Groups Work to Fix Voter News Service," *USA Today*, November 7, 2002, A12.

[34] Richard Morin, "Networks to Dissolve Exit Poll Service; Replacement Sought for Election Surveys," *Washington Post*, January 14, 2003, A3.

[35] Ibid.

[36] Edison Media Research and Mitofsky International, "Evaluation of Edison/Mitofsky Election System 2004," 2005, www.ap.org/media/pdf/evaluationedisonmitofsky.pdf.

[37] Ibid.

[38] Steve Freeman and Josh Mitteldorf, "A Corrupted Election; Despite What You May Have Heard, the Exit Polls Were Right," *In These Times*, March 14, 2005, 14.

[39] Steven F. Freeman, "The Unexplained Exit Poll Discrepancy," Center for Organizational Dynamics, December 29, 2004, www.appliedresearch.us/sf/Documents/ExitPoll.pdf.

[40] Ron Baiman and Kathy Dopp, "The Gun Is Smoking: 2004 Ohio Precinct-Level Exit Poll Data Show Virtually Irrefutable Evidence of Vote Miscount," presented at the 61st Annual Conference of the American Association for Public Opinion Research, Montreal, Canada, May 18–21, 2006.

[41] John Conyers, *What Went Wrong in Ohio: The Conyers Report on the 2004 Presidential Election* (Chicago: Academy Chicago Publishers, 2005).

[42] Edison Media Research and Mitofsky International, "Evaluation of Edison/Mitofsky Election System 2004."

[43] Ibid.

[44] Ibid.

[45] Robert M. Groves, *Survey Errors and Survey Costs* (New York: Wiley, 1989).

[46] Samuel Best, "Sampling Process," in *Polling America: An Encyclopedia of Public Opinion,* ed. Samuel J. Best and Benjamin Radcliff, vol. 1 (A–O) (Westport, CT: Greenwood Press, 2005).

[47] Mark Lindeman and Rick Brady, "Behind the Controversy: A Primer on U.S. Presidential Exit Polls," *Public Opinion Pros* (January 2006), http://publicopinionpros.com/from_field/2006/jan/lindeman_1.asp; Mitofsky, "A Short History of Exit Polls"; Levy, "The Methodology and Performance of Election Day Polls."

[48] Edison Media Research and Mitofsky International, "Evaluation of Edison/Mitofsky Election System 2004."

[49] Lindeman and Brady, "Behind the Controversy."

[50] Steve Karnowski, "Judge Blocks Minn. Law That Hampers Exit Polling," Associated Press, October 15, 2008.

[51] Edison Media Research and Mitofsky International, "Evaluation of Edison/Mitofsky Election System 2004."

[52] Ibid.

[53] Ibid.

[54] Paul Gronke, "Gronke Predicts Early Vote at 33%; McDonald Says 28%," 2010, www.early voting.net/blog/2010/11/gronke-predicts-early-vote-33-mcdonald-says-28.

[55] Lindeman and Brady, "Behind the Controversy"; Edison Media Research and Mitofsky International, "Evaluation of Edison/Mitofsky Election System 2004."

[56] Levy, "The Methodology and Performance of Election Day Polls."

[57] Ibid.

[58] Mark Lindeman, "Beyond Exit Poll Fundamentalism: Surveying the 2004 Election Debate," presented at the 61st Annual Conference of the American Association for Public Opinion Research, Montreal, Canada, May 18–21, 2006.

[59] Benjamin Radcliff, "Exit Polls," in *Polling America*, ed. Best and Radcliff, vol. 1.

[60] Brian D. Silver, P. R. Abramson, and Barbara A. Anderson, "The Presence of Others and Overreporting of Voting in American National Elections," *Public Opinion Quarterly* 50 (1986): 228–239.

[61] Elizabeth Plumb, "Validation of Voter Recall: Time of Electoral Decision Making," *Political Behavior* 8 (1986): 302–312.

[62] Michael W. Traugott and John P. Katosh, "Response Validity in Surveys of Voting Behavior," *Public Opinion Quarterly* 43 (1979): 359–377.

[63] Barry C. Burden, "Voter Turnout and the National Election Studies," *Political Analysis* 8, no. 4 (2000): 389–398.

[64] Alan Abramowitz, "Gallup's Implausible Likely Voter Results," *Huffington Post*, October 15, 2010, www.huffingtonpost.com/alan-abramowitz/gallups-implausible-likel_b_764345.html.

[65] Robert M. Groves, *Survey Errors and Survey Costs* (New York: Wiley, 1989).

[66] Warren J. Mitofsky, "The Latino Vote in 2004," *PS: Political Science and Politics* 38 (2005): 187–188.

[67] Merkle and Edelman, "A Review of the 1996 Voter News Service Exit Polls from a Total Survey Error Perspective."

[68] Edison Media Research and Mitofsky International, "Evaluation of Edison/Mitofsky Election System 2004."

[69] Roper Center for Public Opinion Research, "Exit Polls: Interview with Burns W. Roper and John Brennan," *Public Perspective* 1, no. 6 (September/October 1990): 25–26.

Chapter 2

# Creating and Using Exit Poll Time Series

$S$ ince 1972, the national exit polls have asked voters more than 400 different questions. They have assessed candidate choices in both presidential and congressional elections. They have tapped political preferences, lifestyle choices, and demographic characteristics. They have even recorded contextual information, such as the location and timing of respondents' votes. Together, they are an ideal resource for analyzing the composition and preferences of the active electorate, to understand who voted in particular elections and why.

Despite the important insights the exit polls can offer, they are rarely used to study voters over time. Typically, when exit polls are analyzed, election outcomes are presented in a vacuum, ignoring the long-term dynamics of the active electorate. This short-range approach leaves many important questions unanswered. Are groups increasing or decreasing their share of the active electorate over time? Are groups voting more or less for candidates from the Democratic or Republican Party? Have these changes occurred gradually over time or shifted dramatically during one or two critical elections? Are there emerging groups that could play a greater role in electoral outcomes in the coming years? Researchers simply do not have a way to gauge these comparative temporal questions using exit polls from one or two election years.

Longitudinal research has been problematic because the national exit polls are effectively inaccessible. Although each exit poll resides in prominent data archives, such as the Interuniversity Consortium for Political and Social Research (ICPSR) or the Roper Center for Public Opinion Research, a publicly available cumulative data file has not yet been constructed that permits temporal comparisons. The primary reason is that these data are not configured in a format that can be easily merged and analyzed. Even though the questions themselves demonstrate a great deal of consistency over time, the groups administering the national exit polls during the nineteen different election cycles have changed repeatedly. Not surprisingly, when archiving these data, these organizations employed different coding schemes. Until now, no one has undertaken the time and effort to merge the universe of comparable national exit polls and generate time series of comparable questions.

In this chapter, we discuss the process of constructing a new longitudinal database of exit poll questions for analysis. We begin by describing how we combined the exit poll data over time, dealing with formatting differences across survey organizations. Next, we lay out the rationale for including particular questions in this volume, detailing how we handled wording variation and missing responses. We conclude by discussing the logic underpinning the presentation of these data in this volume, explaining how to read and interpret the information presented in Chapters 3 through 5.

## Creating a Cumulative National Data Set

From 1972 through 2010, seven different media organizations sponsored thirty-two different national exit polls. Each was deposited in archives with little regard for whether the file structure was compatible with previous efforts. As a result, the variable names, values, labels, and properties in these data sets are frequently incompatible.

To construct a cumulative data file, we resolved four key issues. We began by determining which exit polls were the most suitable to be combined. Next, we differentiated between common and unique questions. Then, we developed and applied a uniform format to the common questions. Finally, we merged all the common questions across the selected exit polls into a single data file.

### Selecting Exit Polls

A major concern when combining data collected by different organizations is what statisticians call "house effects." House effects are systematic differences in survey results due to the procedural differences in how various polling organizations administer their polls, including methods of sampling respondents, soliciting their participation, and cataloguing their responses. If the net effects are large enough, they can bias results and produce misleading conclusions about voter preferences over time. What would appear in the data to be a change in voter preferences would really just be an effect of different methodological procedures.

At first glance, this danger might seem especially problematic for the exit polls, considering the turnover in sponsorship over the past four decades. Fortunately, the methodology developed and refined by Warren Mitofsky and his colleagues has influenced the procedures used by at least one of the national exit polls conducted in every election cycle from 1972 through 2010. During the 1970s and 1980s, Mitofsky oversaw the exit polls undertaken by CBS News and CBS News-*New York Times*, where they developed techniques for sampling voters, administering questionnaires, and weighting responses to correct for known survey error. Mitofsky oversaw the first cooperative exit poll unit—VRS—where he implemented the same procedures employed at CBS during the previous two decades. When Mitofsky departed in 1993 after VRS merged with the National Election Service to form VNS, he was succeeded by Murray Edelman, who had served under Mitofsky at CBS and VRS. Edelman retained much of Mitofsky's methodology during his years managing the unit. After the dissolution of VNS in 2002, the latest consortium—NEP—hired Mitofsky's firm, Mitofsky International, to conduct the exit polls with Edison Research. Despite the changes in the organization and leadership of the networks' exit polls, the procedures used to conduct the national exit polls have remained largely stable.

This book leverages the good fortune of having a single basic approach underlie at least one of the national exit polls undertaken biennially since 1972. For each year, we rely on the exit poll that used the Mitofsky methodology—CBS (1972–1978), CBS-*New York Times* (1980–1988), VRS (1990–1992), VNS (1994–2002), and NEP (2004–2010). This emphasis on consistency necessitates that we omit exit poll data collected by ABC, NBC-*Washington Post*, and the *Los Angeles Times*. We lament the omission of this information, but we are buoyed by the fact that potential house effects will be diminished by our reliance on a more consistent methodology.

## Combining Questions

Having selected the exit polls for inclusion in the cumulative data file, we next had to differentiate common from unique questions in each individual exit poll. In many cases, this was a straightforward exercise, as most questions were either identically worded or wholly different in content. However, a subset of questions with different wording but similar intent proved trickier to categorize.

Some minor temporal fluctuations in question wording and response options are natural parts of the survey process. These adjustments, which can be found in other prominent public opinion time series such as the American National Election Studies, typically seek to match the latest vernacular, keep up with changes in objective national conditions, or better correspond with the format of adjacent questions on the exit poll. We used our discretion in classifying these questions but considered them to be the same only if the wording differences were slight or inconsequential to the intent of the questions. Questions deemed to be essentially equivalent were given the same variable name across data sets.

Exit poll questions measuring religious affiliation provide a good example of how wording variations were handled. The 1980 exit poll asked, "What is your religion?" followed by a set of religious categories, such as "Catholic" and "Jewish." From 1982 to 1988, it simply read "Your religion" atop a list of response options. In 1990, the question asked, "Your religious preference today?" followed by the religious categories. From 1992 to 2010, the question wording simply asked, "Are you" with the set of religious categories below. Given the very minor changes to the question wording, we considered each of these to be the same fundamental question. However, from 1972–1978, the exit poll asked about religious affiliation using the following question, "What religion were you brought up in?" Because this question requests information about voters' religious upbringing and not their current religion, we treat it as a separate question and do not include it in the current religious affiliation time series.

So that readers are informed about our decisions regarding which questions to combine, we have included the exact wording used for each question in the tables found at the end of each chapter. Readers can then decide whether to accept our treatment of these questions and data. For example, a reader may decide that he or she is uncomfortable with the combination of religious affiliation questions that have even slightly different wording, preferring to evaluate only the time series starting in 1992, when the current wording first appeared. If so, then as we explain later, the figures and tables are easy to decipher with the unacceptable information omitted.

## Standardizing Response Options

After we identified common questions, response options needed to be standardized to allow the files to be merged. For example, in one exit poll, partisanship might have a coding scheme in which Republican was assigned a value of "1" and Democrat was assigned a value of "2," whereas in another exit poll, Democrat was assigned a value of "1" and Republican was assigned a value of "2." For every comparable question, we established and applied a uniform set of response options.

In some cases, exit poll questions split broad categories into more fine-tuned groups or categories over time. To maintain the comparability of the time series, we recombined these more detailed categories into their original distinctions. The running example about religion provides a good opportunity to consider this issue about response categories. For most of the time series, the response options included "Protestant," "Catholic," "Other Christian," "Jewish," "Something Else," and "None." Beginning in 2002, the exit poll split the "Something Else" category into two groups: "Muslim" and "Something Else." Because only 0.2 percent of respondents declare they are Muslim, the number of cases is too small and the sampling error too large to justify inclusion as a separate group. Therefore, we recombine "Something Else" and "Muslim" into the original "Something Else" category to maintain the consistency of the time series. This decision slightly decreases the detail in information from 2002 to 2010, but it allows for trends to be generated as far back as 1980. We recognize this tradeoff and, in general, choose the trend over the more nuanced information. The precise wording of the response categories for every exit poll question, as well as our decisions on how to combine categories, are listed after each table at the end of the chapters.

One additional issue involving the response options warranted consideration. In the 1980s and 1990s, the exit poll questionnaires used a check-all-that-apply format to identify some voter characteristics. Presumably this check-all-that-apply technique was employed to increase the efficiency of the questionnaire. For example, when assessing whether a voter identified as a "Born Again Christian" between 1980 and 1984, the questionnaire begins, "Are you any of the following?" Next a long series of characteristics is listed, including "Born Again Christian." Voters could then check the "Yes" box next to the term "Born Again Christian" or leave this "Yes" box blank. There were no other options. Starting in 2004 the exit poll began asking voters, "Would you describe yourself as a Born Again or Evangelical Christian?" followed by the options "Yes" or "No."

These two formats are not comparable over time. The reason for this incompatibility is straightforward. The check-all-that-apply format cannot distinguish between voters who are not "Born Again Christians" and voters who refused or could not answer the question for one reason or another. In the check-all-that-apply format, non–Born Again Christians, those refusing to answer the question, those unintentionally skipping the question, and those who did not understand the question would simply leave the "Yes" response box blank. Beginning in 2004, voters explicitly choose either "Yes" or "No" in response to this question, so that those not answering the question are filtered from the analysis. Because of this fundamental challenge to comparability, we exclude all check-all-that-apply questions from the analysis. Although this truncates the time series for some variables, it reduces the measurement error in these data over time.

## Merging Files

The last step in constructing a cumulative national exit poll data set was to merge the individual files. This step is computationally straightforward. As long as common questions have the same labels, numerical coding, and variable properties, the individual data files can be combined seamlessly. After this process was completed, the final cumulative national exit poll data set contained 435 questions, asked from 1972 through 2010. Of these, 133 questions had been asked repeatedly over that time frame. The remaining 302 questions were asked on only one occasion.

For the repeated questions, each variable had a uniform set of response options, with the overwhelming majority ranging between two and five categories. The weights from each individual exit poll were applied to all voters who participated in that particular exit poll. Thus, the estimates generated from any one exit poll match the estimates in the cumulative data set, assuming the response options are formatted in the same manner.

## Analyzing Exit Poll Questions

Once we constructed a cumulative data file, we moved to creating time series for analysis. This process unfolded in three stages. We began by narrowing the repeated questions to a manageable subset, choosing exit poll trends with contemporary relevance. Next, we determined how to handle item nonresponse. Finally, we calculated the sampling error for the response options to each question.

### Selecting Questions

This book does not display and describe the responses to all exit poll questions that have been asked repeatedly since 1972. Instead, we are interested in those questions that can help us understand how recent elections compare with earlier contests. Therefore, we consider only those questions that have been asked both historically and contemporaneously.

Our criteria for selecting series for analysis from the more than 100 repeated exit poll questions were straightforward. We began by identifying those questions that have been asked in the most recent midterm (2010) or presidential (2008) election. Then, we filtered those questions by whether or not they were administered to voters during at least four additional elections. Finally, we screened out items that (1) were related to the interviewing process and not voter preferences, such as which version of the exit poll respondents received or whether respondents completed the Spanish version of the questionnaire, (2) were not asked of respondents in all the states, such as their vote choice for governor or senator, or (3) had too many response categories for it to be practical to report them all, such as respondents' home state or congressional district.

After applying these criteria, we were left with thirty-three time series that serve as the data by which we analyze election results over the past four decades (see Table 2.1). On average, these questions appeared on twelve of the nineteen exit polls administered between 1972 and 2010,

**Table 2.1** Exit Poll Questions Examined In This Book

| | 2010 | 2008 | 2006 | 2004 | 2002 | 2000 | 1998 | 1996 | 1994 | 1992 | 1990 | 1988 | 1986 | 1984 | 1982 | 1980 | 1978 | 1976 | 1972 |
|---|---|---|---|---|---|---|---|---|---|---|---|---|---|---|---|---|---|---|---|
| *Vote Choice* | | | | | | | | | | | | | | | | | | | |
| Presidential Vote | | X | | X | | X | | X | | X | | X | | X | | X | | X | X |
| House Vote | X | X | X | X | X | X | X | X | X | X | X | X | X | X | X | X | X | X | X |
| *Physical Traits* | | | | | | | | | | | | | | | | | | | |
| Race | X | X | X | X | X | X | X | X | X | X | X | X | X | X | X | O | O | O | O |
| Sex | X | X | X | X | X | X | X | X | X | X | X | X | X | X | X | X | X | X | X |
| Age | X | X | X | X | X | X | X | X | X | X | X | X | X | X | X | X | X | X | X |
| Sexual Orientation | X | X | X | X | | X | X | X | X | X | | | | | | | | | |
| *Geographical Location* | | | | | | | | | | | | | | | | | | | |
| Region | X | X | X | X | X | X | X | X | X | X | X | X | O | X | X | X | X | X | X |
| Population Density | X | X | X | X | X | X | X | X | X | X | X | X | X | X | X | X | | | X |
| *Religious Characteristics* | | | | | | | | | | | | | | | | | | | |
| Religious Affiliation | X | X | X | X | X | X | X | | X | X | X | X | X | X | O | O | | | |
| Religious Attendance | X | X | X | X | X | X | | | O | O | O | O | O | O | O | O | | | |
| Evangelical | X | X | X | X | X | | | X | O | O | O | O | O | O | O | O | | | |
| *Lifestyle Choices* | | | | | | | | | | | | | | | | | | | |
| Education | X | X | X | X | X | X | X | X | X | X | X | X | X | O | O | O | | | |
| Employment Status | X | X | | X | X | X | X | X | | | | | | | | | | | |
| Marital Status | X | X | X | X | X | X | X | X | O | | O | | O | O | O | | | | |
| Child in Household | X | X | X | X | X | X | X | X | X | O | | | | | | | | | |
| Union Household | X | X | X | X | X | X | X | X | O | | O | X | X | X | X | X | X | O | |
| *Political Orientations* | | | | | | | | | | | | | | | | | | | |
| Party Identification | X | X | X | X | X | X | X | X | X | X | X | X | X | X | X | X | X | X | X |
| Ideological Identification | X | X | X | X | X | X | X | X | X | X | X | X | X | X | X | X | X | X | X |
| Last Presidential Vote | X | X | X | X | X | X | X | X | X | X | X | X | X | X | X | X | X | X | X |

**Table 2.1** (Continued)

| | 2010 | 2008 | 2006 | 2004 | 2002 | 2000 | 1998 | 1996 | 1994 | 1992 | 1990 | 1988 | 1986 | 1984 | 1982 | 1980 | 1978 | 1976 | 1972 |
|---|---|---|---|---|---|---|---|---|---|---|---|---|---|---|---|---|---|---|---|
| Presidential Approval | X | X | X | X | X | X | X | X | X | X | X | | X | | X | | | X | |
| Congressional Approval | X | X | X | X | X | X | X | X | X | X | X | | | | | | | | |
| Direction of the Country | X | X | X | X | X | X | X | X | X | X | X | | | | | | | | |
| Life of Next Generation | X | X | X | | | | | X | X | X | | | | | | | | | |
| Position on Government Activism | X | X | | X | X | X | X | X | X | X | | | | | | | | | |
| First-Time Voter | X | X | X | X | X | X | X | X | | O | O | O | | | | O | | | |
| Timing of Presidential Vote | X | X | X | X | X | X | X | X | X | X | X | X | | | | X | | | X |
| Presidential Candidates Campaigned Unfairly | X | X | X | X | X | X | X | X | X | X | X | X | | | | | | | |
| Rationale for House Vote | X | | X | | X | O | X | | X | | X | | | | X | | | | |
| *Economic Considerations* | | | | | | | | | | | | | | | | | | | |
| Household Income | X | X | X | X | X | X | X | X | X | X | X | X | X | X | | | | | |
| Current National Economic Conditions | X | X | X | X | X | X | X | X | X | X | X | X | X | X | X | X | X | | |
| Future National Economic Conditions | X | | | X | X | X | | | | X | | X | X | | | | | | |
| Finances in Last Two Years | X | | X | | X | X | X | X | | X | | | | | | | | | |
| Finances in Last Four Years | | X | X | | X | | X | | | X | | | | | | | | | |

X = Exit poll question examined in this book.

O = Exit poll question asked on the topic but excluded from the analysis because it is incompatible with the time series.

including presidential vote choice in every contest since 1972 and House vote choice in every race since 1976. The remaining questions cover a wide range of topics—physical traits, geographical location, religious characteristics, lifestyle choices, political orientations, and economic circumstances. These additional questions offer considerable leverage in understanding the evolution of the active electorate and the dynamics of candidate preferences.

## Handling Item Nonresponse

All survey questions have some degree of item nonresponse, by which certain respondents fail to provide an answer. Some respondents may not want to answer the question. Others may not understand the nature of the question. Still others may simply feel their own view or circumstance cannot be captured sufficiently by the available response options. Unfortunately, exit poll questions do not provide additional categories, such as "don't know" or "refused," which might enable the causes to be determined. As a result, researchers must decide whether to include nonresponse in analyses or whether to analyze only the data based on available response options.

In the exit polls, the extent of nonresponse varies across questions. It is usually quite low on the vote choice questions. Typically, less than 1 percent of respondents fail to indicate how they cast their presidential ballots and less than 5 percent fail to indicate how they cast their House ballots. For the potential explanatory factors, item nonresponse generally ranges from 1 to 10 percent. Questions that tap characteristics of a more sensitive nature—such as household income—tend to yield higher item nonresponse.

The degree of item nonresponse also varies for each question over time. Typically, it fluctuates from election to election by no more than a few percentage points. Our review of the exit poll time series, though, indicates that the degree of intra-item nonresponse generally does not conform to an obvious trend or pattern.

Therefore, we assume that item nonresponse in the exit polls is random and include in the analyses only those respondents who chose one of the available response options. In other words, we exclude from the analyses any respondent who did not answer the question. This decision increases the comparability of items over time by smoothing out any variation due to an increase in the degree of item nonresponse from year to year or question to question.

As a result of this choice, all the response categories reported in this book add to 100 percent, and each category's percentage should be read as the *percent of exit poll respondents who answered the question(s)*. For example, in 2004, the raw percentages for the question soliciting respondents' political ideology are as follows: 19.7 percent "liberal," 42.6 percent "moderate," 31.4 percent "conservative," and 6.4 percent did not answer the question. In the tables and graphs, we remove the respondents who did not answer the question. Thus, in 2004, 21 percent of those answering the ideology question are "liberal," 45.5 percent "moderate," and 33.5 percent "conservative."

## Estimating Sampling Error

Sampling error is the last factor we must take into account when analyzing the exit polls. As we discussed in Chapter 1, exit polls rely on a sample of voters to make inferences about the entire active electorate. Like any sample, the results from the exit polls may not perfectly represent the target population. Sampling error is the error in the distribution of responses to an exit poll question attributed to the use of a sample of voters rather than the entire voting population. Deviations from the population occur by chance, so they cannot be prevented, but the likely margin of sampling error can be calculated.

The margin of sampling error indicates the interval around a sample estimate in which we can say with a certain degree of confidence that the true population parameter is located. This uncertainty must be acknowledged when projecting sample estimates to the overall population. Failing to do so could result in misleading conclusions, which in the context of the exit polls could mean inaccurate understandings of the composition or preferences of the active electorate.

Sampling error varies by statistical estimate, meaning each finding in a poll yields a distinct margin of sampling error. The margin of sampling error hinges on four separate factors. First, it depends on the type of probabilistic sampling used to select respondents. The stratified sampling approach used by the exit polls has more sampling error than polls conducted using simple random sampling because exit polls do not attempt to contact voters at every polling place, but rather they systematically intercept voters in select precincts. Consequently, as characteristics become increasingly clustered in particular precincts, their sampling error increases. Second, sampling error is conditional on the relative distribution of responses. The margin of sampling error decreases as characteristics approach 100 or 0 percent and increases as characteristics approximate 50 percent. Third, sampling error fluctuates by the number of respondents, decreasing as the number of respondents grows and increasing as the number of respondents shrinks. Finally, the margin of sampling error varies by how confident one wishes to be in the projection of the sample result to the overall population. Greater confidence in population estimates increases the margin of sampling error. Because researchers typically want to be very confident in their results to prevent costly errors, 95 percent confidence intervals are usually applied. This means that one can be 95 percent confident that the true population characteristic falls within the margin of sampling error or that the true voter population characteristic will fall outside of the margin of error in only one in twenty cases.

Table 2.2 shows the sampling errors at the 95 percent confidence level for estimates generated by the exit polls. Using it to determine the margin of sampling error for the various statistics presented in the text is generally straightforward. Readers just locate the cell, topped by the column heading "Number of Respondents Asked the Question" (either all the respondents in the exit poll or a subset of respondents such as men or women) and fronted by the row heading "% Respondents with the Characteristic."

For example, in the 1978 exit poll, 7,835 respondents answered a question assessing their political ideology. Of these respondents, 18.0 percent indicated they were "liberal," 48.3 percent "moderate," and 33.7 percent "conservative." To determine the sampling error for any of these values, we locate their position in Table 2.2. Because there were 7,835 total respondents to the question tapping this characteristic, we can use the second-to-last column in the table for all of them, but different relative frequencies for each require us to look at different rows. Because "liberal" respondents comprised 18 percent of the 1978 exit poll sample, the "11–20" percent row is

**Table 2.2**   Percent Error Due to Sampling (+/–) for 95 Percent Confidence Interval

| % Respondents with the Characteristic | Number of Respondents Asked the Question | | | | | | | |
|---|---|---|---|---|---|---|---|---|
| | 100 | 101–200 | 201–500 | 501–950 | 951–2,350 | 2,351–5,250 | 5,251–8,000 | Over 8,000 |
| 0–10 | 6 | 5 | 3 | 2 | 2 | 1 | 1 | 1 |
| 11–20 | 11 | 7 | 5 | 4 | 3 | 2 | 1 | 1 |
| 21–37 | 13 | 9 | 6 | 5 | 3 | 2 | 2 | 1 |
| 38–62 | 15 | 10 | 7 | 5 | 4 | 3 | 2 | 1 |
| 63–79 | 13 | 9 | 6 | 5 | 3 | 2 | 2 | 1 |
| 80–89 | 11 | 7 | 5 | 4 | 3 | 2 | 1 | 1 |
| 90–100 | 6 | 5 | 3 | 2 | 2 | 1 | 1 | 1 |

*Source:* Edison Research, "National Election Poll Exit Poll Methods Statement," 2010, www.cbsnews.com/election2010/pdf/methodsstatement_2010.pdf.

used. Combining these two qualities (18 percent and 7,835 respondents to the question) indicates that the margin of sampling error for the "liberal" characteristic is plus or minus 1 percent. Therefore, in 1978 we can have 95 percent confidence that liberals comprised between 17 and 19 percent of U.S. voters. For "moderate" respondents, we would position ourselves in the same column, but two rows down, where 38–62 percent of respondents with a characteristic are found. There we see the margin of sampling error is plus or minus 2 percent, allowing us to project that moderate voters comprised between 46.3 percent and 50.3 percent of the active electorate. Finally, to determine the sampling error for "conservative" voters, we would use the "21–37" percent row along with the "5,251–8,000" column, which indicates an error of plus or minus 2 percent. Thus, we can be 95 percent confident that conservatives comprised between 31.7 and 35.7 percent of U.S. voters in the 1978 elections.

Note, however, that the sampling error reported with the exit polls does not capture the other three forms of survey error: coverage, nonresponse, or measurement error. As we described in Chapter 1, pollsters go to great effort to limit these other forms of error. They conduct advance research on different methods for effectively sampling respondents, gauging their preferences, and securing their responses as well as apply weights to the aggregated results to correct for observable forms of these errors. Nonetheless, some nonsampling error is introduced to the data. As a result, the range of values around the sample estimate containing the true population value is most certainly larger; how much larger hinges on estimates of the unobservable amounts of nonsampling error, which is rarely agreed upon.

## Presenting and Discussing the Exit Poll Data

We present the time series generated by these procedures throughout the remainder of the book. The data are organized into three empirical chapters, each analyzing a different aspect of the exit polls. Readers may want guidance on interpreting the figures, tables, and prose introduced in the pages that follow. Therefore, we conclude this chapter by providing a "how to" guide for reading each of these chapters.

## Reading Chapter 3: Composition of the Exit Polls

Chapter 3 describes the relative size of various groups in the exit polls over time. It is organized into six sections based on the nature of the questions: physical traits, residential location, religious characteristics, lifestyle choices, political orientations, and economic circumstances. Exit poll questions are presented one at a time, broken down by their respective response categories. The relative frequency distribution for each response option is plotted over time in a figure, providing the reader with a visual account of the changing composition of the active electorate. Text accompanies each figure, explaining changes in the relative frequencies over time as well as the distribution of responses in the most recent election in which the question was asked, either 2008 or 2010. At the end of each chapter, the specific proportions for each year are tabulated and compared with the series average, alongside details about the question wording and number of respondents.

The best way to explain the contents of this chapter is with an example designed to illustrate the features of the book and to show how to make effective use of them. Consider the item tapping voters' ideological self-identifications. The question categorizes voters as "liberal," "moderate," or "conservative," and has appeared on every exit poll from 1976 through 2010.

Figure 2.1 shows the proportion of respondents in each exit poll who identify as "liberal," "moderate," or "conservative." This figure is similar to every other figure appearing in Chapter 3. The horizontal axis indicates the election year, and the vertical axis indicates the percentage of exit poll respondents. Each line corresponds to one of the response categories, represented by the symbol in the legend.

**Figure 2.1** Composition of the Exit Polls by Ideological Identification, 1976–2010

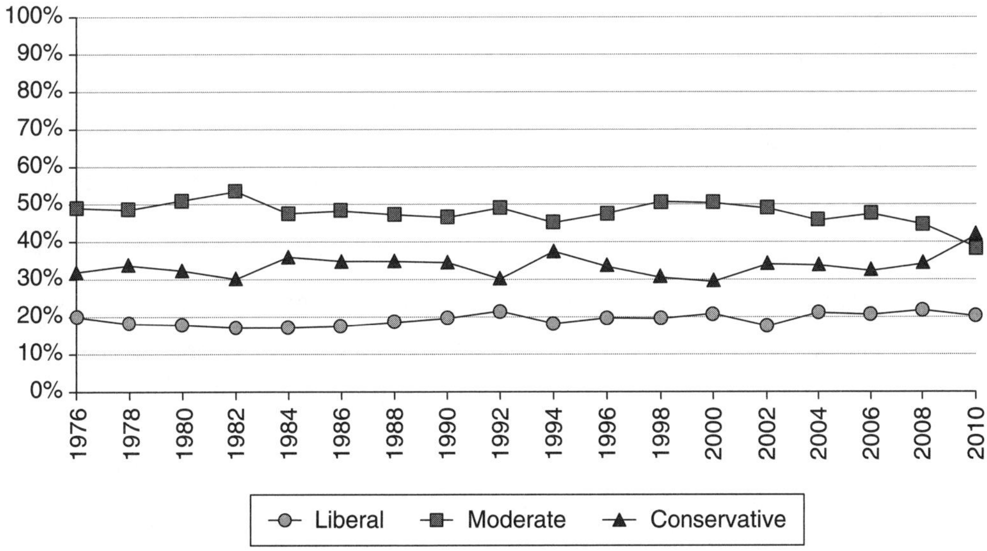

*Source:* National exit polls.

*Note:* When using these results to make inferences about the active electorate, the standard errors should be calculated using Table 2.2 on p. 36.

In this example, the lines represent the percentage of exit poll respondents who identify as "liberal," "moderate," or "conservative." The figure shows that moderates typically comprise slightly less than 50 percent of respondents, though in recent elections the proportion of moderates has declined. It indicates that conservatives filled the void left by moderates in the past two elections. Conservatives typically make up about a third of respondents, but in 2010 they topped 40 percent, making them the largest ideological group in the exit polls for the first time since the question appeared. By contrast, liberals' share of the exit poll has scarcely changed over time, accounting for about 20 percent of respondents.

The figure is useful because it presents a simple visual snapshot of the trends for responses to one exit poll question over time. Readers interested in a finer-grained analysis, though, should use the tables from which the figures are derived. Each exit poll question has a detailed table at the end of the chapter. These tables provide more precise information about the exit poll question itself, such as the number of respondents answering the question, the percentage of respondents selecting each response option for every year in the time series, and the average percentage of respondents selecting each response option across all years. The information in these tables can then be used, along with Table 2.2, to calculate the sampling error for each exit poll estimate, in this case the percentage of each response group's share of the active electorate.

Table 2.3 shows a truncated version of the results for the political ideology exit poll question. For each election year in which the question was asked, it provides the percentage of respondents selecting each of the response categories. The first column is the election year (the bottom row represents the average percentage across all the years and is labeled "Average"). The next columns are the response categories or groups from one exit poll question, in this example, "liberal," "moderate," and "conservative." The final column is the number of exit poll respondents who gave valid answers to the political ideology question.

To clarify how to interpret the table correctly, consider the cell entries alongside 2010 in Table 2.3. Liberals comprised 20.2 percent, moderates 38.2 percent, and conservatives 41.6 percent of the 2010 exit poll respondents. The bottom row indicates the time series average, from 1976 to 2010, of the proportion of liberal (19.1 percent), moderate (47.5 percent), and conservative (33.5 percent) respondents. The final column shows the number of respondents to the ideology question for each year.

**Table 2.3**  Composition of the Exit Polls by Ideological Identification, 1976–2010

| Year | Liberal | Moderate | Conservative | Number of Respondents |
|---|---|---|---|---|
| 2010 | 20.2% | 38.2% | 41.6% | 16,757 |
| ↓ | ↓ | ↓ | ↓ | ↓ |
| 1976 | 19.7% | 48.7% | 31.7% | 11,860 |
| Average | 19.1% | 47.5% | 33.5% | |

*Source:* National exit polls.

*Note:* When using these results to make inferences about the active electorate, the standard errors should be calculated using Table 2.2 on p. 36.

↓ = Election years and data omitted from this example table.

The sampling error for any one of these relative frequencies can be estimated by applying to Table 2.2 the percentage of respondents identifying with one of these orientations and the number of exit poll respondents answering the question. For example, 20.2 percent of respondents reported they were "liberal" in the 2010 exit poll question administered to 16,757 respondents. Locating the joint cell where these two measures meet in Table 2.2 requires shifting our eyes to the last column under the heading "Over 8,000" (which is under the top heading, "Number of Respondents Asked the Question") and the second row after the heading "11–20" (which is fronted by the heading "% Respondents with the Characteristic"). There we find the sampling error for the relative frequency of liberals is plus or minus 1 percent, using a 95 percent confident interval.

Using the sampling error, we can project the proportion of voters in the 2010 electorate who possessed a liberal orientation toward contemporary political issues. Adding and subtracting the 1 percent sampling error to the 20.2 percent of respondents identifying as liberal in the exit poll gives us a range of 19.2 to 21.2 percent. Thus, we can be 95 percent confident that between 19.2 and 21.2 percent of the active electorate was liberal in their 2010 political orientations.

## Reading Chapter 4: Presidential Voting Preferences of Exit Poll Respondents

Chapter 4 describes the presidential voting patterns of various groups in the exit polls. It is organized in the same way as Chapter 3, with similar questions arranged together and then presented individually according to the vote choices of their respective response categories. In the figures, the percentage of the two-party vote given to the Democratic presidential candidate by each group is plotted over time, providing an illustration of the changing support given to the Democratic candidate relative to the Republican candidate over a number of elections. The two-party vote share is used, rather than the actual percentage given to the Democratic candidate, to allow for direct comparison between the parties over time without the confounding influence of third-party presidential voting.

Using our running example, the exit poll question about political ideology is presented in Figure 2.2. The figure shows the two-party Democratic vote, from 1976–2008, for liberals, moderates, and conservatives. The horizontal axis is the presidential election year, whereas the vertical axis is the two-party Democratic presidential vote percentage. Each solid line corresponds to one of the response categories or groups, represented by the symbol in the legend. In this example, the solid lines represent liberals, moderates, and conservatives. As a baseline, the dashed line represents the two-party vote percentage given to the Democratic candidate by the full set of respondents in the exit polls. The figure shows that liberal respondents routinely gave at least 70 percent of their two-party vote to the Democratic presidential candidate and that this percentage has increased over the past three decades. Moderate respondents' two-party Democratic vote typically exceeds the two-party vote shares given to the Democratic presidential candidate by the overall sample, usually coming in between 50 and 60 percent. Conservative respondents' two-party vote for the Democratic presidential candidate dropped from 1976 to 1984 and has fluctuated around 20 percent ever since.

**Figure 2.2**  Democratic Share of Two-Party Presidential Vote by Ideological Identification, 1976–2008

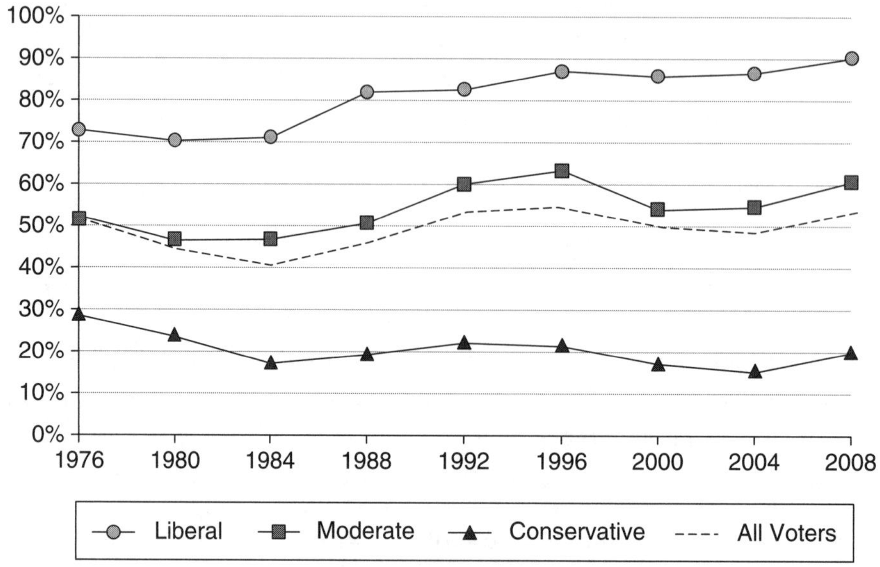

*Source:* National exit polls.

*Note:* When using these results to make inferences about the active electorate, the standard errors should be calculated using Table 2.2 on p. 36.

After the two-party vote over time is illustrated and described, we switch gears and discuss the vote choice of each group in the 2008 presidential election. To do this, we consider the distribution of the actual vote, not the two-party vote, and show the percentage of ballots each group reported casting for Barack Obama and John McCain in the exit poll. Unlike the two-party vote, the shares for Obama, the Democratic candidate, and McCain, the Republican candidate, do not sum to 100 percent because a proportion of the actual vote was reported to be cast for third-party candidates. As a result it will not equal, nor can it be compared to, the two-party vote in 2008 or, for that matter, the two-party vote in any election in the past. However, it does indicate how groups actually reported voting and should be used to detail the outcome of the 2008 presidential election.

In our example, liberal exit poll respondents cast 88.6 percent of their ballots for Obama, 9.6 percent of their ballots for McCain, and the remaining 1.8 percent of their ballots for anyone else. These numbers differ only slightly from the two-party votes for Obama and McCain, which were 90.2 percent and 9.8 percent, respectively. In other years, with stronger third-party candidates (such as 1980 or 1992), the difference between the actual vote and the two-party vote can be considerably larger.

Although information about the actual vote does not appear in the figures accompanying the text, it does appear in the tables at the end of the chapter, which report both the two-party and full presidential vote (with the cumulative third-party share). Table 2.4 shows a truncated version of the presidential vote table for the political ideology exit poll question (see Table 4.23 in Chapter 4

**Table 2.4** Presidential Vote by Ideological Identification, 1976–2008

| Category | Year | Two-Party Presidential Vote | | Full Presidential Vote | | | |
|---|---|---|---|---|---|---|---|
| | | Two-Party Democratic Vote | Difference from Mean Democratic Two-Party Vote | Democratic Vote | Republican Vote | Third-Party Vote | Number of Respondents |
| Liberal | 2008 | 90.2% | 36.5% | 88.6% | 9.6% | 1.8% | 4,314 |
| | ↓ | ↓ | ↓ | ↓ | ↓ | ↓ | ↓ |
| | 1976 | 73.0% | 22.0% | 70.5% | 26.1% | 3.4% | 2,566 |
| | Average | 81.0% | 31.8% | 75.7% | 17.7% | 6.6% | |
| Moderate | 2008 | 60.8% | 7.1% | 59.9% | 38.5% | 1.6% | 7,668 |
| | ↓ | ↓ | ↓ | ↓ | ↓ | ↓ | ↓ |
| | 1976 | 51.7% | 0.7% | 51.0% | 47.7% | 1.4% | 5,653 |
| | Average | 54.4% | 5.2% | 51.2% | 43.2% | 5.5% | |
| Conservative | 2008 | 20.1% | −33.6% | 19.7% | 78.1% | 2.3% | 4,768 |
| | ↓ | ↓ | ↓ | ↓ | ↓ | ↓ | ↓ |
| | 1976 | 29.1% | −21.9% | 28.8% | 70.1% | 1.1% | 3,589 |
| | Average | 20.8% | −28.5% | 19.8% | 75.8% | 4.4% | |

*Source:* National exit polls.

*Note:* When using these results to make inferences about the active electorate, the standard errors should be calculated using Table 2.2 on p. 36.

↓ = Election years and data omitted from this example table.

for the full table). It is grouped by the response categories "liberal," "moderate," and "conservative," which are located in the first column. These groups are then ordered temporally; the second column lists the corresponding election year, save for the bottom cell, which indicates the average percentage across all the years. The next column, labeled "Two-Party Democratic Vote," reports the two-party Democratic presidential vote for the respective response category and year. In this table, liberal exit poll respondents gave the Democratic presidential candidate, Barack Obama, 90.2 percent of the two-party vote in 2008.

The column labeled "Difference from Mean Democratic Two-Party Vote" reports the difference between a group's two-party Democratic presidential vote and the two-party Democratic presidential vote of all respondents in the exit poll. The cell entry for 2008 shows that liberal respondents awarded 36.5 percentage points more of their two-party ballots to the Democratic candidate than did the full sample of respondents in the exit poll. This is an indication of the Democratic vote advantage for a particular group relative to the overall active electorate. One advantage of this measure is that it controls for the closeness of the election. If a Democrat wins an election in a landslide, the percentage of Democratic support among a particular group may jump as well, but the comparison of that group with the general electorate enables the reader to see whether the group's voting really stands out. Take 1984 and 1996 as examples. Walter Mondale captured just over 40 percent of the two-party presidential vote in Ronald Reagan's landslide victory. If a group gave Mondale 50 percent of the two-party vote in 1984, then we would say that even though this group split its vote, it was clearly a Democratic group relative to the rest of the electorate. On the other hand, if a group similarly split its vote for Bill Clinton in 1996, we would not suggest this group was at all Democratic in relative terms, as Clinton won almost 55 percent of the two-party vote in his bid for reelection.

The next three columns under the general heading "Full Presidential Vote" are the Democratic, Republican, and combined third-party vote for the response categories to a given exit poll question. Continuing our example, liberal respondents gave the Democratic candidate 88.6 percent, the Republican candidate 9.6 percent, and all other presidential candidates 1.8 percent of their vote in the 2008 exit poll. The final column is the number of exit poll respondents who answered the presidential vote question and chose one of the valid political ideology response categories ("liberal," "moderate," "conservative"). Of those exit poll respondents answering the presidential vote question in 2008, 4,314 indicated that they were liberal. The numbers of respondents across years are not indicative of changes in the relative size of the group; for that information, readers should consult Chapter 3.

Information about the number of exit poll respondents in a group and their vote share for a given presidential candidate can be used with Table 2.2 to project the group's relative support for the candidate to the overall active electorate. Together, it provides a confidence interval within which we can expect to find the proportion of voters across the country who cast ballots for one of the major-party candidates. Put simply, we can infer from the voting behavior of groups in the exit poll sample to those groups' voting behavior among the population of voters nationwide.

In our example, 88.6 percent of the 4,314 liberal respondents reported that they voted for Obama in the 2008 exit poll. To apply this information to Table 2.2, we treat the number of liberal respondents as the "Number of Respondents Asked the Question," locating the 4,314 respondents in the sixth column under the heading "2,351–5,250." We use the percentage of those respondents who voted for Obama as the "% Respondents with the Characteristic," locating the 88.6 percent in the row headed "80–89." The cell where the row and column meet shows the sampling error for Obama's share of the liberal vote—in this case, plus or minus 2 percent. Applying this computation enables us to project with 95 percent confidence that between 86.6 and 90.6 percent of liberal voters in the electorate cast ballots for Obama in the 2008 presidential election.

If we wish to compute the sampling errors of the two-party vote of a group, we need to make a slight adjustment to the number of respondents before we can use Table 2.2 to determine the sample error. The two-party percentages contain only the individuals who responded "Democrat" or "Republican," whereas the "Number of Respondents" reported in the far-right column of Table 2.4 includes respondents who chose a third party. The number of liberal respondents who chose a major-party candidate, however, is easy to calculate. We simply multiply the group's share of third-party voters by the overall number of exit poll respondents in the group and subtract the amount from the overall number of exit poll respondents in the group. Applying this formula to liberal respondents in 2010, we multiply .018 (the proportion of ballots cast for third-party candidates) by 4,314 (the number of liberal respondents in the exit poll) and find that approximately 78 polled voters chose third-party candidates. We subtract this amount from 4,314 (4,314 − 78 = 4,236) to determine the number of respondents to use with Table 2.2.

To apply this information to Table 2.2, we treat the reduced number of liberal respondents as the "Number of Respondents Asked the Question" and locate the 4,236 respondents under the sixth column heading, "2,351–5,250." We use the two-party percentage of those respondents who voted for Democratic House candidates as "% Respondents with the Characteristic," locating the 90.2 percent within the range headed "90–100." Finding where the column and row meet shows a sampling error of plus or minus 1 percent. Thus, we can be 95 percent confident that the Democratic two-party vote among all liberal voters in the 2010 House elections was between 89.2 and 91.2 percent. The same method can be applied to any other group.

Because the number of liberal respondents is so large, the confidence interval containing the likely population parameter varies little from the vote share found among liberal respondents in the sample. However, with smaller sample sizes, the sampling error and corresponding range of possible population estimates will be much larger, at times large enough to cast doubt on whether the majority of a particular group in the overall electorate cast ballots for the candidate. Take, for example, the full presidential vote choice of respondents who have not completed high school in 2004 (reported in Table 4.16 in Chapter 4). Of the 398 respondents who answered both questions, 50.2 percent indicated that they voted for John Kerry, whereas 48.8 percent indicated that they voted for George W. Bush. Applying this information to Table 2.2 reveals a margin of sampling error of plus or minus 7 percent for the relative proportions for each candidate. Thus, we can be 95 percent confident that between 43.2 and 57.2 percent of voters in the active electorate without a high school diploma cast a ballot for John Kerry and between 41.8 and 55.8 percent cast a ballot for George W. Bush. In such a scenario, we cannot confidently determine which candidate a majority of voters in the active electorate preferred. Therefore, readers should not assume that particular voter groups behaved in the active electorate as they did in the exit polls without first applying a margin of sampling error to the exit poll results.

## Reading Chapter 5: Congressional Voting Preferences of Exit Poll Respondents

Chapter 5 describes how various groups in the exit polls cast ballots in races for the House of Representatives between 1976 and 2010. The chapter parallels Chapter 4 in most respects. Once again, the chapter sections group questions by topic (physical traits, residential location, religious characteristics, lifestyle choices, political orientations, and economic circumstances). Within each section, individual exit poll questions are disaggregated into their respective response categories. For each group, we then discuss how they awarded their two-party House vote to Democratic candidates over time. Figures are used to illustrate these trends, providing a visual account of the changing level of support for Democratic House candidates relative to their Republican counterparts across elections. The two-party vote share is used to describe the long-term trends, rather than the actual percentage given to the Democratic House candidates, to allow for direct comparisons over time without the confounding influence of third-party congressional voting.

In the context of our ongoing example, Figure 2.3 presents the two-party Democratic House vote for liberal, moderate, and conservative exit poll respondents from 1976 to 2010. The horizontal axis indicates the election year, and the vertical axis indicates the percentage of the two-party vote cast for Democratic House candidates by the exit poll respondents. Each solid line

**Figure 2.3** Democratic Share of Two-Party House Vote by Ideological Identification, 1976–2010

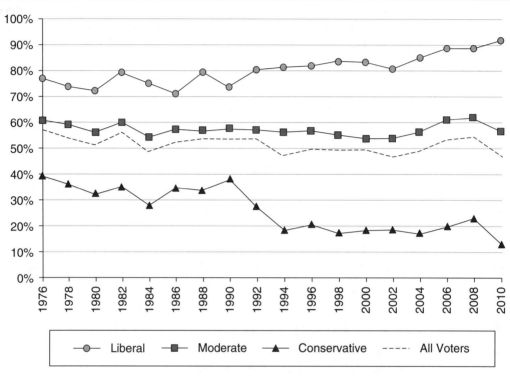

*Source:* National exit polls.

*Note:* When using these results to make inferences about the active electorate, the standard errors should be calculated using Table 2.2 on p. 36.

corresponds to one of the groups, represented by the symbol in the legend. As a baseline, the dashed line represents the two-party vote percentage given to the Democratic House candidates by all exit poll respondents. Much like their presidential voting patterns, liberal respondents routinely gave more than 70 percent of their vote to Democratic House candidates, and as much as 89 percent in the past three elections. The two-party House vote that moderate respondents gave to Democratic House candidates typically exceeded the two-party vote shares awarded to the Democratic House candidates by respondents overall, ranging between 55 and 65 percent. Finally, conservative respondents' two-party vote for the Democratic House candidates hovered between 30 and 40 percent from 1976 to 1990, after which it dropped dramatically. Between 1994 and 2008, it held close to 20 percent until plunging to 13 percent in 2010, its lowest point in the time series.

After describing the two-party Democratic House vote for each group over time, we turn our attention to the recently contested 2010 House races. We provide the actual vote shares received by Democratic and Republican House candidates nationwide. When reporting the outcome of the 2010 elections, these are the results that should be used, as opposed to the two-party shares, which are appropriate when comparing 2010 with past contests. In our example, liberal respondents cast 90.0 percent of their ballots for Democratic House candidates, 7.7 percent for Republican House candidates, and 2.3 percent for independent House candidates in the 2010 elections.

Readers interested in a more detailed breakdown of these data should use the tables located at the end of the chapter. These tables provide more precise information about the exit poll question itself; the number of respondents; the two-party Democratic House vote share for each group; how each group differed from the overall electorate's two-party House vote; and the vote share given to the Democratic, Republican, and third-party House candidates. The tables also provide the averages over time for each of these statistics. The information in these end-of-chapter tables can be used, along with Table 2.2, to calculate the sampling error for the various exit poll estimates.

Walking through our example should clarify the information available in the Chapter 5 tables. Table 2.5 is a truncated version of the House of Representatives vote table for the political ideology exit poll question over time (see Table 5.20 in Chapter 5 for the full table). It is organized by the response categories "liberal," "moderate," and "conservative," which are located in the first column. These groups are ordered secondarily by election year, which is found in the second column. The bottom row at the end of each group represents the average percentage across all the years. The next column is labeled "Two-Party Democratic Vote" and displays the two-party Democratic House vote for the respective response category and year. For example, in this

**Table 2.5**  House Vote by Ideological Identification, 1976–2010

| | | Two-Party House Vote | | Full House Vote | | | |
|---|---|---|---|---|---|---|---|
| Category | Year | Two-Party Democratic Vote | Difference from Mean Democratic Two-Party Vote | Democratic Vote | Republican Vote | Third-Party Vote | Number of Respondents |
| Liberal | 2010 | 92.1% | 45.8% | 90.0% | 7.7% | 2.3% | 3,380 |
| | ↓ | ↓ | ↓ | ↓ | ↓ | ↓ | ↓ |
| | 1976 | 77.1% | 19.5% | 75.9% | 22.5% | 1.6% | 4,034 |
| | Average | 80.6% | 28.7% | 78.4% | 18.9% | 2.8% | |
| Moderate | 2010 | 56.6% | 10.3% | 55.1% | 42.2% | 2.7% | 6,399 |
| | ↓ | ↓ | ↓ | ↓ | ↓ | ↓ | ↓ |
| | 1976 | 60.9% | 3.3% | 60.3% | 38.7% | 1.0% | 5,163 |
| | Average | 57.5% | 5.7% | 56.2% | 41.5% | 2.2% | |
| Conservative | 2010 | 13.4% | −32.9% | 13.0% | 83.9% | 3.0% | 6,978 |
| | ↓ | ↓ | ↓ | ↓ | ↓ | ↓ | ↓ |
| | 1976 | 39.8% | −17.8% | 39.2% | 59.3% | 1.6% | 3,274 |
| | Average | 26.6% | −25.2% | 26.0% | 71.7% | 2.3% | |

*Source:* National exit polls.

*Note:* When using these results to make inferences about the active electorate, the standard errors should be calculated using Table 2.2 on p. 36.

↓ = Elections years and data omitted from this example table.

table, liberals gave the Democratic House candidates 92.1 percent of the two-party vote in 2010. Readers seeking the two-party Republican vote would of course just subtract the Democratic percentage from 100 percent. The column labeled "Difference from Mean Democratic Two-Party Vote" reports the difference between a response category's two-party Democratic House vote and the entire electorate's two-party Democratic House vote. In 2010, liberal respondents gave 45.8 percentage points more of their two-party vote to the Democratic House candidates than did the total sample of respondents in the exit poll.

This information can be used to locate the sampling error for the overall two-party House vote in Table 2.2 in the same way the sampling error for the overall two-party presidential vote was determined. To illustrate, consider the two-party House vote of liberals in the active elector-ate during the 2010 election. First, we need to identify the number of two-party liberal respon-dents, which is done by removing the "Third-Party Vote" from the "Number of Respondents" reported in the table. For our example, this means removing 2.3 percent of the cases from the 3,380 respondents who reported being liberal in 2010. This results in approximately 3,302 liberal two-party respondents [3,380 − (.023)(3,380) = 3,302], placing us in the "2,351–5,250" column of Table 2.2. The 92.1 percent of the two-party vote awarded by liberals to Democrats places us in the last row of Table 2.2, labeled "90–100." The cell where the column and row meet indicates that the margin of sampling error for the liberal two-party Democratic vote is 1 percent. Thus, we can be 95 percent confident that the two-party Democratic House vote for liberals in the active electorate lies between 91.1 and 93.1 percent, leaving little doubt about which party's candidates liberals preferred in the 2010 election.

The next three columns under the general heading "Full House Vote" are the "Democratic Vote," the "Republican Vote," and the combined "Third-Party Vote." In 2010, liberal respon-dents gave the Democratic House candidates 90.0 percent, the Republican House candidates 7.7 percent, and all other House candidates 2.3 percent of the overall vote. The final column shows the number of exit poll respondents who answered the congressional vote question and chose a valid response category to the political ideology question. Of those exit poll respondents answer-ing the House vote question in 2010, 3,380 indicated that they were liberal.

This information, along with the percentage of the vote, can be used with Table 2.2 to deter-mine the sampling error for the full House vote estimates, using the same method described for gen-erating the sampling error for the full presidential vote. The 3,380 cases can be located in the sixth column of Table 2.2, under the heading, "2,351–5,250," and the 90.0 percent of the full House vote for liberals can be located in the row headed "90–100." The cell entry where the row and column meet shows that the margin of sampling error for the proportion of liberals casting their overall ballots for Democratic House candidates is plus or minus 1 percent. Thus, we can be 95 percent confident that between 89.0 and 91.0 percent of liberal voters in the electorate cast ballots for Democratic House candidates in 2010. This same method can be applied to any other group.

## Bringing the Chapters Together

Individually, Chapters 3 through 5 can provide valuable insights into either the composition or the preferences of the voting population. Together, though, they offer a more complete picture of the influence of various groups on the overall vote because the electoral impact of a group on the outcome is a function of both its size in the active electorate *and* the distribution of its vote. Considering one without the other can lead to misleading, if not incorrect, conclusions about the role of various voter groups on election outcomes.

Small groups that award a large share of their votes to the winning candidate may have less of an impact on the results than a large group that awards a smaller share of its vote to the winning candidate. Take, for example, Jewish voters. In 2008, Jewish exit poll respondents preferred Obama nearly as much as any group in the exit poll, awarding 78 percent of their votes to him. On its face, then, Jewish respondents may seem to have been instrumental to Obama's success. Jewish respondents, though, comprised only 2 percent of the exit poll, suggesting Jewish voters likely had little impact on the final result. If every single Jewish respondent had thrown his or her support behind McCain, Obama would still have defeated him by a comfortable, albeit somewhat smaller, margin in the 2008 exit poll.

On the other hand, Catholic voters do not seem critical to either party's success in presidential elections, based on their vote percentages alone. Catholic exit poll respondents have split their votes between the parties on average over the past seven exit polls, casting no more than 54 percent of their ballots for either party's presidential nominee. However, Catholic respondents are a sizable group, comprising roughly a quarter (27 percent) of the respondents to exit polls conducted over this time. Whom they prefer has a major impact on the exit poll results, almost regardless of the size of the margin. In fact, a majority of Catholic respondents have sided with the winner in every presidential election from 1984 through 2008, making them the ultimate battleground group. In the 2008 exit poll, Catholic respondents preferred Obama to McCain 54 percent to 45 percent, likely playing a key role in Obama's victory in the presidential election.

Readers should be mindful, though, that neither the size nor the voting dispositions of groups in the active electorate remain static. Rather, they are evolving constantly over time. As groups change, so does their relative impact on elections. Consider Latino voters. A majority of Latino respondents have supported Democratic candidates in every exit poll since 1984, casting 65 percent of their ballots for them, on average. However, their composition in the exit polls has been growing over time, tripling in little more than two decades, from 2 percent in 1984 to 6 percent in 2008. In 2010, Latinos accounted for 8 percent of all exit poll respondents, suggesting that they may exert an even greater influence in the future. Over the years, Latinos have gone from being a group that parties could largely ignore in the campaign to one that has become a critical voting bloc because their preferences, even at the margins, can now have noticeable effects on the outcome.

Ultimately, understanding the outcomes of elections is a challenging task. The active electorate contains many groups—many more than we present in this book—all with different sizes and dispositions. Moreover, individual voters are members of many groups simultaneously, limiting our ability to directly compare the preferences or behaviors of different groups. This may limit the conclusions that readers can draw about the relative importance of different voter groups in the electorate, but it will ensure that they do not make costly errors, inaccurately projecting their magnitude or stature.

Chapter 3

# Composition of the Exit Polls

W ho votes is a key question to understanding electoral politics in the United States. Answering that question allows us to assess the relative importance of different types of voters, identifying the key groups necessary to build a winning coalition. It enables us to make sense of campaign strategies, dissecting the targets of message marketing, travel schedules, and even the issue positions of competing candidates. It also facilitates our understanding of policymaking, by identifying the types of voter groups that public officials may be responding to when crafting government initiatives.

Election laws in the United States allow all citizens eighteen years of age or older to cast ballots so long as they have met state registration requirements. States, though, can exercise considerable discretion in establishing voting rights provided they are consistent with the federal Constitution, which prohibits suffrage from being denied to individuals on the basis of religion, race, sex, or affluence. Through the years, states have imposed a variety of restrictions limiting the franchise. States' voter qualifications vary on the basis of individuals' immigration status, felony convictions, duration of residency, and mental competence, as well as their registration deadlines and identification requirements.

Figure 3.1 shows the turnout rate for the voting-eligible population from 1972 to 2010 (see Table 3.1 at the end of the chapter for the exact percentages). Turnout seesaws between presidential and midterm elections.[1] In presidential elections, citizens "surge" to the polls in higher numbers than in other political races. In the past ten presidential elections, on average, 56 percent of the voting-eligible population cast ballots. Turnout in presidential elections has expanded of late, increasing 10 points in the past four election cycles.

By comparison, midterm elections witness a "decline" in participation. In the past ten midterm elections, only 40 percent of eligible voters, on average, turned out to the polls, which was 16 percentage points less than those who cast ballots in presidential elections over this period.

**Figure 3.1** Turnout Rate of the Voting-Eligible Population, 1972–2010

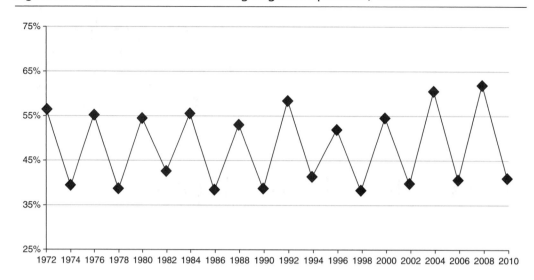

*Source:* Michael McDonald, "United States Elections Project," http://elections.gmu.edu/voter_turnout.htm.

Similar to presidential elections, though, the number of citizens voting has had an upward trend. From 1998 to 2010, the turnout rate of eligible residents has increased steadily by a total of 3 percentage points.

The most recent U.S. elections saw some of the highest turnout rates in decades. In the 2008 presidential election, 62 percent of eligible voters cast ballots, resulting in the highest turnout rate since exit polling began in 1972. In the 2010 midterm election, 41 percent of the voting-eligible population cast ballots. This turnout nearly matched the three-decade-long highs of 41 percent in 1994 and 42 percent in 1982.

In this chapter, we consider the composition of voters in national elections over time by examining questions in the exit polls.[2] We document the proportion of respondents to every question in the national exit polls administered at least five times from 1972 to 2010, including one of the last two exit polls administered in 2008 or 2010. For each question, we first describe how the distribution of respondents offering each response category varies over time, using graphs to facilitate our discussion. Then, we detail the results of the most recent election in which the question was asked, either 2008 or 2010, and explain how this varies, if at all, from the historical pattern. After we analyze each group separately, we conclude the chapter by coming full circle and exploring similarities and differences in the overall composition of respondents in the exit polls conducted in midterm and presidential election years.

Readers can use this information to estimate the distribution of these groups in the active electorate over time. If the response options to a question are mutually exclusive, then we can secure an estimate of the proportion of voters in each category by dividing the number of respondents who chose each response option by the total number of respondents who answered the question and then applying a margin of sampling error (see the section in

Chapter 2 entitled "Reading Chapter 3: Composition of the Exit Polls" for a lengthier discussion of this procedure). Take for example, the exit poll question inquiring whether a respondent's gender is male or female. Say that 10,000 respondents answered the question in the 2010 exit poll, 52 percent of whom indicated they were female. We can apply this information to Table 2.2 to determine the margin of sampling error for the estimate, which in this case is 1 percent. If we wish to project the proportion of voters in the active electorate who are female, we simply add and subtract the sampling error from the exit poll estimate. Thus, we can be 95 percent confident that between 51 and 53 percent of the active electorate was female in the 2010 election.

## Physical Traits

Physical traits play a prominent role in the practice of politics. Individuals with common physical traits are often socialized about politics in similar ways. From sharing the same neighborhoods, schools, and places of worship to encountering the same stereotypes and life experiences, those with similar physical traits frequently adopt common expectations and beliefs about government. This commonality can breed distinctive politics for members of such groups, capable of fostering shared policy preferences, political interests, and partisan orientations.[3]

National exit pollsters have been tapping physical traits since the inception of exit polling. From 1972 through 2010, pollsters repeatedly inquired about respondents' race, gender, age, and sexual orientation. These questions have resulted in some of the longest running time series in the data collection.

### Race

Race perhaps has been the most difficult physical trait for exit pollsters to assess. It is not a biological category, but rather a sociopolitical construct intended to understand how people are viewed and/or view themselves in a particular cultural context. There has been little consensus on how to measure race, in part, because the concept is often confounded with ethnic background in both the academic community and in the general public. These debates have troubled exit pollsters, as well.

Initially, interviewers recorded the race of voters as white, black, or Hispanic. Beginning in 1982, it was included as a standard question on the exit polls, with the same three response options offered through 1988. In the 1990 election, Asian was introduced as a fourth category from which voters could select. In 2004, additional categories were added to the race question—American Indian, Native Alaskan, and Native Hawaiian—to more closely resemble the categories then used by the U.S. Census Bureau. We exclude American Indian, Native Alaskan, and Hawaiian Native from our analysis, though, because their numbers are all well below 1 percent for the years they were included.

The Hispanic category has proved particularly problematic for exit pollsters. Following the lead of the U.S. Census Bureau, they have shifted their interpretation of Hispanic from a race to an ethnicity, in part, because people of Hispanic origin often classified themselves as one of the other racial categories, as well. In 1998, a new permanent item was introduced that asked all respondents regardless of race whether they were of Hispanic descent. However, the national exit polls maintained *Hispanic* as a category in the race question to permit longitudinal comparisons. Our analysis relies on responses to the race question only, even after Hispanic ethnicity is introduced as a separate question, thereby enabling a direct comparison over time.

Figure 3.2 illustrates the distribution of the four most commonly asked categories in the exit polls—white, black, Hispanic/Latino, and Asian—from 1982 through 2010. It shows that the racial composition of respondents has changed gradually over the past three decades. The proportion of white voters in the exit polls has declined fairly steadily since 1990, falling 12 points from the 1990 election to the 2010 election. Conversely, the other racial groupings have inched up over this time frame. The largest change has occurred among Hispanics, whose share of exit poll respondents has quadrupled from 2 to 8 percent in the past twenty years.

The 2010 election witnessed one of the most racially diverse exit polls to date (see Table 3.2 at the end of the chapter). Whites still made up an overwhelming proportion of respondents, but their 78 percent share was smaller than in any midterm election since 1982. African Americans comprised 11 percent of respondents, Hispanics 8 percent, and Asians 2 percent.

**Figure 3.2**   Composition of the Exit Polls by Race, 1982–2010

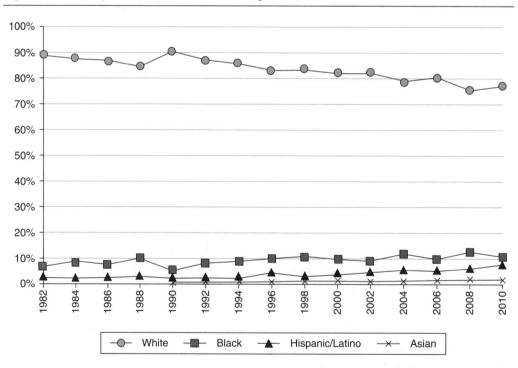

*Source:* National exit polls. See the section in Chapter 2 entitled "Creating a Cumulative National Data Set: Selecting Exit Polls" (pp. 28–29).

*Note:* When using these results to make inferences about the active electorate, the standard errors should be calculated using Table 2.2 (p. 36), which is explained in the adjacent section of Chapter 2, "Analyzing Exit Poll Questions: Estimating Sampling Error" (pp. 34–36). For a guide on how to understand the tables and figures of this chapter, see the section in Chapter 2 entitled "Presenting and Discussing the Exit Poll Data: Reading Chapter 3" (pp. 37–39).

## Gender

Exit pollsters have taken stock of voters' gender since the first national exit poll was administered in 1972. From 1972 to 1980, exit pollsters did not ask respondents directly whether they
were male or female, but had interviewers record it as respondents departed the voting booth.
Beginning in 1982, it was added as a separate question and has been included on every exit poll
administered since.

Figure 3.3 shows the gender split in the exit polls over time. The gender composition of
respondents has shifted decisively over the past several decades. Historically, male voters comprised a larger share of respondents than their female counterparts, much as they did in the general population. In the 1940s, the female share of the population surpassed men as female-leaning
birth rates eventually trumped male-leaning immigration rates. However, it was not until the 1982
midterm election that the political landscape shifted and women finally surpassed men in their
share of the exit polls. Women have maintained this advantage over men ever since.

Since 1982, the gender gap in the exit polls has taken two different trajectories depending
on the type of election. In midterm election years, the gender gap in respondents has remained
remarkably stable, failing to exceed 4 points in the past eight midterm elections. In fact, women
have averaged only a 2-point advantage in the midterm exit polls, virtually identical to their
advantage in the general population over that time span. By contrast, in presidential election
years, the gender gap in exit poll respondents has widened gradually over time. Over the past
seven presidential exit polls, the difference between female and male respondents expanded 5
points, from 2 points in the 1984 election to 7 points in the 2008 election.

**Figure 3.3** Composition of the Exit Polls by Gender, 1972–2010

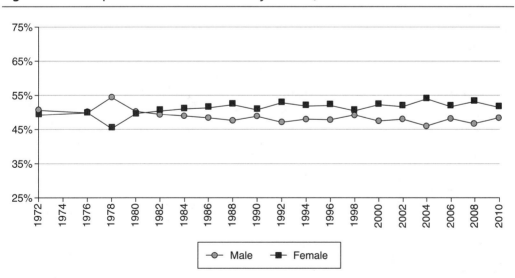

*Source:* National exit polls. See the section in Chapter 2 entitled "Creating a Cumulative National Data Set: Selecting Exit Polls" (pp. 28–29).

*Note:* When using these results to make inferences about the active electorate, the standard errors should be calculated using Table 2.2 (p. 36), which is
explained in the adjacent section of Chapter 2, "Analyzing Exit Poll Questions: Estimating Sampling Error" (pp. 34–36). For a guide on how to understand
the tables and figures of this chapter, see the section in Chapter 2 entitled "Presenting and Discussing the Exit Poll Data: Reading Chapter 3" (pp. 37–39).

In the 2010 midterm election, the gender gap among exit poll respondents was 4 points (see Table 3.3 at the end of the chapter). Men comprised 48 percent of respondents, whereas women comprised 52 percent. This gap was virtually identical in size to those that appeared in the two previous midterm exit polls.

## Age

Age is one of the longest running questions administered to voters. Nonetheless, exit pollsters have changed the response options on numerous occasions, most recently in the 2000 election. Because respondents are asked to place themselves in an age range, rather than provide their exact age or year of birth, pollsters have struggled with both the number of age ranges to provide and their respective endpoints. Since 1972, they have offered as few as four categories to as many as nine categories, with ranges as narrow as four years to as wide as "60 or over." Currently, voters are asked to which of the following nine age groups they belong: "18–24," "25–29," "30–39," "40–44," "45–49," "50–59," "60–64," "65–74," and "75 or over." To permit longitudinal comparisons, we recoded the categories offered into four groupings: 18–29, 30–44, 45–59, and 60 or over.

Figure 3.4 shows the age distribution of respondents in each election from 1972 through 2010. The age composition of the exit polls has shifted repeatedly over the past four decades, with no obvious pattern to most of the changes. A closer look, though, reveals three noteworthy developments underlying the age dynamics of exit poll respondents.

**Figure 3.4**   Composition of the Exit Polls by Age, 1972–2010

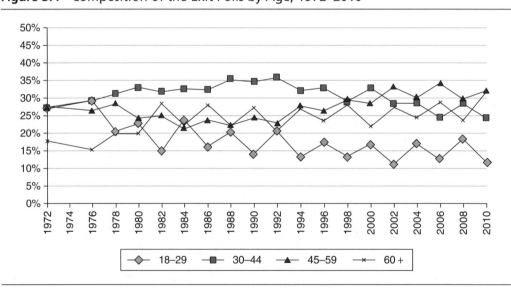

*Source:* National exit polls. See the section in Chapter 2 entitled "Creating a Cumulative National Data Set: Selecting Exit Polls" (pp. 28–29).

*Note:* When using these results to make inferences about the active electorate, the standard errors should be calculated using Table 2.2 (p. 36), which is explained in the adjacent section of Chapter 2, "Analyzing Exit Poll Questions: Estimating Sampling Error" (pp. 34–36). For a guide on how to understand the tables and figures of this chapter, see the section in Chapter 2 entitled "Presenting and Discussing the Exit Poll Data: Reading Chapter 3" (pp. 37–39).

First, the 18–29 age group comprised the greatest proportion of respondents in the exit polls administered immediately after the passage of the Twenty-sixth Amendment, which extended the right to vote to 18- to 21-year-olds. In 1972 and 1976, the 18–29 age group made up, respectively, 28 and 29 percent of respondents. In the elections occurring since, their share has decreased substantially, bottoming out in 2002, when they comprised only 11 percent of exit poll respondents.

Second, many of the changes in the age composition of the exit polls coincide with the maturation of the baby boom generation—the disproportionately sized cohort born between 1946 and 1964. As this cohort has passed from one age group to the next, a surge has typically occurred in the proportion of respondents in the subsequent age group. In fact, the age group containing the baby boomers typically comprises the largest share of respondents in the exit poll. As the baby boomers comprised much of the 18–29 age group in the 1970s and early 1980s, this group saw some of its largest exit poll shares of the past forty years. When baby boomers shifted into early middle age in the late 1980s and early 1990s, the 30–44 age group became the largest group of respondents. During the late 1990s and much of the 2000s, as the baby boom generation transitioned into late middle age, the 45–59 age group exerted the biggest voice in the exit polls. In 2010, the earliest baby boomers began reaching their sixties, corresponding with an increase in the proportion of respondents in the 60 or over age group.

Finally, differences in the age composition of the exit polls can be found in presidential and midterm election years. As the electoral context changes, the mix of younger and older respondents shifts, as well. In presidential election years, younger respondents increase their share at the expense of older voters. In midterm election years, the process reverses itself and the proportion of younger respondents in the exit polls shrinks and the proportion of older respondents grows. Since 1976, the proportion of 18- to 29-year-olds in the exit polls has dropped roughly 6.5 percentage points on average in midterm election years, whereas the proportion of respondents aged 60 or over has grown by roughly 6 percentage points, on average, in midterm election years.

The 2010 midterm election saw the convergence of these trends, leading to one of the oldest exit polls in four decades (see Table 3.4 at the end of the chapter). Respondents aged 45 years or older made up a whopping 64 percent of total exit poll participants, split evenly between voters in the 45–59 and 60 or over age groups. This dwarfed the amount of younger respondents. Respondents under age 30 made up only 12 percent of the exit poll, whereas those in the 30–44 age group made up 24 percent of the exit poll.

## Sexual Orientation

The national exit polls began querying about sexual orientation in the 1990s. The wording of the question changed twice before settling into its current format. Initially, pollsters inquired whether respondents were either gay or lesbian, originally in an all-that-apply and later in a yes-no format. Since 1996, voters have been administered a yes-no question asking whether they are gay, lesbian, or bisexual.

Figure 3.5 shows the ratio of gay, lesbian, or bisexual respondents to those who are not, from 1996 through 2010. The proportion of respondents identifying themselves as gay, lesbian,

**Figure 3.5** Composition of the Exit Polls by Sexual Orientation, 1996–2010

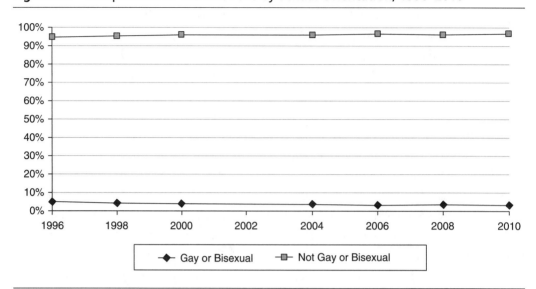

*Source:* National exit polls. See the section in Chapter 2 entitled "Creating a Cumulative National Data Set: Selecting Exit Polls" (pp. 28–29).

*Note:* When using these results to make inferences about the active electorate, the standard errors should be calculated using Table 2.2 (p. 36), which is explained in the adjacent section of Chapter 2, "Analyzing Exit Poll Questions: Estimating Sampling Error" (pp. 34–36). For a guide on how to understand the tables and figures of this chapter, see the section in Chapter 2 entitled "Presenting and Discussing the Exit Poll Data: Reading Chapter 3" (pp. 37–39).

or bisexual has fluctuated between 3 and 5 percent, averaging 4 percent of the total over this time period. Despite gay marriage being a hotly contested political issue in recent years, there has been no discernable change in the proportion of respondents identifying as gay, lesbian, or bisexual either over time or across election types.

In 2010, gays, lesbians, and bisexuals comprised 3 percent of exit poll respondents (see Table 3.5 at the end of the chapter). This rate is virtually unchanged from the 2008 presidential election, when 4 percent of respondents were gay, lesbian, or bisexual.

## Geographic Location

The geographic location of voters is another important factor in American politics. Geographic locales draw together a distinct blend of social groups, natural resources, and institutional arrangements, which, in turn, spawns a unique political culture.[4] Political culture influences which types of individuals become active in politics, what they want and expect out of government, and perceptions about which types of candidates and policies they think are capable of achieving them.[5]

To tap elements of geographically based political cultures, national exit pollsters have assessed two geographic characteristics repeatedly over time: regional location and population density. Regional location identifies the section of the country in which respondents' electoral precincts are found, whereas population density indicates the number of people living in communities containing respondents' electoral precincts. The relative distribution of both measures in the exit polls has evolved over time, changing considerably over the past several decades.

## Regional Location of Voter's Precinct

Exit pollsters classify each respondent's electoral precinct according to one of the four primary regions used by the U.S. Census Bureau. Respondents heading to the polls in Connecticut, Delaware, Maine, Maryland, Massachusetts, New Hampshire, New Jersey, New York, Pennsylvania, Rhode Island, Vermont, Washington, DC, or West Virginia are assigned to the eastern region. Midwestern respondents are defined as those casting a ballot in Illinois, Indiana, Kansas, Michigan, Minnesota, Missouri, Nebraska, North Dakota, Ohio, South Dakota, or Wisconsin. Southern respondents are found in Alabama, Arkansas, Florida, Georgia, Kentucky, Louisiana, Mississippi, North Carolina, Oklahoma, South Carolina, Tennessee, Texas, or Virginia. Finally, western respondents participate in Alaska, Arizona, California, Colorado, Hawaii, Idaho, Montana, Nevada, New Mexico, Oregon, Utah, Washington, or Wyoming.

Figure 3.6 shows the distribution of these groupings in the exit polls over time. Over the past four decades, there have been major shifts in the regional bases of respondents. Southern and western respondents have increased their shares of the exit polls substantially, at the expense of eastern and midwestern respondents. The proportion of southern respondents increased by 8 percentage points since 1972, gradually becoming the largest region represented in the exit polls. The prominence of western respondents also grew as they moved from being the weakest voice in the exit polls to nearly the second strongest. By contrast, the proportion of eastern respondents in the exit polls decreased by more than 7 percentage points over the past four decades, whereas midwestern respondents' share dropped 5 percentage points.

**Figure 3.6**  Composition of the Exit Polls by Region, 1972–2010

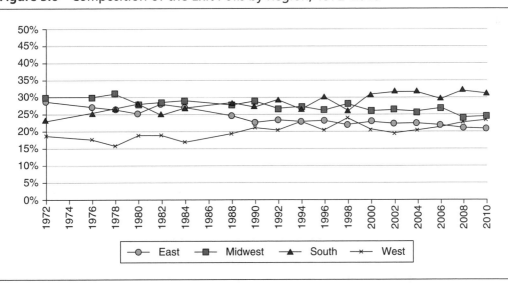

*Source:* National exit polls. See the section in Chapter 2 entitled "Creating a Cumulative National Data Set: Selecting Exit Polls" (pp. 28–29).

*Note:* When using these results to make inferences about the active electorate, the standard errors should be calculated using Table 2.2 (p. 36), which is explained in the adjacent section of Chapter 2, "Analyzing Exit Poll Questions: Estimating Sampling Error" (pp. 34–36). For a guide on how to understand the tables and figures of this chapter, see the section in Chapter 2 entitled "Presenting and Discussing the Exit Poll Data: Reading Chapter 3" (pp. 37–39).

These changes in the regional composition of the exit polls persisted in the 2010 election (see Table 3.6 at the end of the chapter). The South held the most respondents overall, with the region making up 31 percent of the exit poll. Conversely, the East held the smallest share of any region, consisting of only 21 percent of all respondents. Midwestern and western respondents fell in between, comprising 25 percent and 23 percent of the exit poll, respectively.

### Population Density of Voter's Precinct

Since 1984, national exit pollsters have also coded the population density of each respondent's election precinct as urban, suburban, or rural. Urban precincts are located in a central city with a total population of 50,000 or more. Suburban precincts are found in lower-density, autonomous municipalities with easy access to a central city. Rural precincts are found outside metropolitan areas, in communities with populations less than 50,000.

Figure 3.7 shows how the population density of respondents' precincts has varied over time. From 1984 to 1996, suburbanites comprised roughly two-fifths of the exit polls, whereas the proportions of rural and urban respondents each fluctuated at around a third of the exit polls. In the past decade or so, suburbanites have increased their share steadily, comprising nearly one out of two exit poll respondents by 2010. These gains have come primarily at the expense of rural respondents, whose share of the exit polls has dropped by a third over the same period and who now make up only one in five respondents. Meanwhile, the percentage of urban respondents has held steady at around 30 percent of the exit polls, changing little since the start of the series.

**Figure 3.7** Composition of the Exit Polls by Population Density of Precinct, 1984–2010

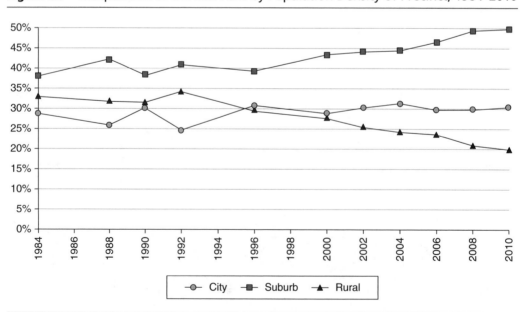

*Source:* National exit polls. See the section in Chapter 2 entitled "Creating a Cumulative National Data Set: Selecting Exit Polls" (pp. 28–29).

*Note:* When using these results to make inferences about the active electorate, the standard errors should be calculated using Table 2.2 (p. 36), which is explained in the adjacent section of Chapter 2, "Analyzing Exit Poll Questions: Estimating Sampling Error" (pp. 34–36). For a guide on how to understand the tables and figures of this chapter, see the section in Chapter 2 entitled "Presenting and Discussing the Exit Poll Data: Reading Chapter 3" (pp. 37–39).

In 2010, the exit poll showed that the population density of respondents' precincts held steady, changing little from 2008. Suburbanites once again dominated the exit poll, comprising nearly half of all respondents (see Table 3.7 at the end of the chapter). Conversely, rural respondents made up only 21 percent of respondents. Meanwhile, urban respondents constituted 31 percent of the exit poll.

## Religious Characteristics

Religion can be a potent force in politics. Religious institutions instill core values and shape a range of beliefs about society. They foster perceptions of right and wrong. They cultivate attitudes toward out groups, promoting tolerance and benevolence in some cases and narrow-mindedness and dogmatism in others. They even advance particular behaviors such as sexual mores or dietary practices. Together these teachings can inform interpretations of politics and ideas about public policies.[6]

National exit pollsters have routinely assessed three different religious characteristics of voters over time. They have asked respondents their religious affiliation, religious attendance, and identification with evangelicalism. Unfortunately, each question has been plagued with measurement issues, limiting the number of response options and time points that can be compared.

### Religious Affiliation

Exit pollsters gauge religious affiliation by querying respondents about whether they identify with one of the main religious traditions found in the United States. The traditions have varied somewhat over time, including affiliations such as Baptist, Muslim, and Mormon at certain points. Pollsters have most frequently asked whether respondents identify themselves as Protestant, Catholic, or Jewish, or whether they do not identify with an organized religion.

Figure 3.8 shows the distribution of these four groups in the exit polls since 1984. The proportion of religious seculars has grown substantially, more than doubling in size in the past quarter-century from roughly one in twenty respondents in the mid-1980s to nearly one in eight respondents by the end of the 2000s. This shift has come at the expense of Judeo-Christian affiliations. The proportion of Christians has fallen roughly 9 percentage points over this period, from 87 percent of the exit poll in 1984 to 78 percent of the exit poll in 2008, with Protestants and Catholics contributing similarly to the decline depending on the election year. Meanwhile, the share of Jews in the exit poll has also declined over the past quarter-century, falling from roughly 4 percent of respondents in the last half of the 1980s to roughly 2 percent of respondents by the end of the 2000s.

The 2010 exit poll had among the smallest shares of religiously affiliated respondents since pollsters first solicited this characteristic in the mid-1980s (see Table 3.8 at the end of the chapter). Seculars comprised 12 percent of respondents in the 2010 election, up 4 percentage points in just the past two midterms. Most of this increase appears to have come at the expense of Catholics, who comprised their smallest share, at 23 percent, of the exit poll since the item first appeared in 1984. Meanwhile, Protestant and Jewish respondents held steady, comprising 55 percent and 2 percent of the exit poll, respectively.

**Figure 3.8**    Composition of the Exit Polls by Religious Affiliation, 1984–2010

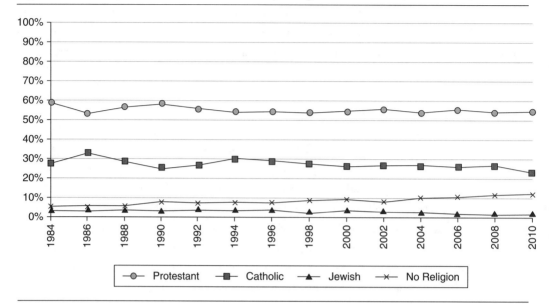

*Source:* National exit polls. See the section in Chapter 2 entitled "Creating a Cumulative National Data Set: Selecting Exit Polls" (pp. 28–29).

*Note:* When using these results to make inferences about the active electorate, the standard errors should be calculated using Table 2.2 (p. 36), which is explained in the adjacent section of Chapter 2, "Analyzing Exit Poll Questions: Estimating Sampling Error" (pp. 34–36). For a guide on how to understand the tables and figures of this chapter, see the section in Chapter 2 entitled "Presenting and Discussing the Exit Poll Data: Reading Chapter 3" (pp. 37–39).

## Religious Attendance

Identifying with a religion does not necessarily mean that voters practice the religion. Therefore, exit pollsters introduced an item tapping how often respondents attend religious services. The wording of the religious attendance question has changed somewhat over time as pollsters have varied both the number and content of the response options administered to exit poll respondents. The question has included as little as one category, such as when respondents were asked if they attended religious services at least once a week, to as many as five categories, such as when respondents were asked whether they attended religious services more than once a week, once a week, a few times a month, a few times a year, or never. To allow for longitudinal comparisons, we recoded comparable questions into two categories differentiating between respondents who attended religious services at least once a week from those who did not attend religious services at least once a week.

Figure 3.9 shows the relative proportion of weekly attendees and non–weekly attendees in the exit polls administered from 2000 through 2010. Over the past decade, a majority of respondents in each election have not attended services at least once a week, comprising 55 percent of the exit polls, on average. Conversely, 45 percent of respondents, on average, have attended religious services at least once a week.

Despite the brevity of the series, the evidence suggests that respondents in midterm election years are more religious than respondents in presidential election years. The three midterm elections this past decade saw upticks in the share of the exit polls comprised of more highly religious

**Figure 3.9** Composition of the Exit Polls by Religious Attendance, 2000–2010

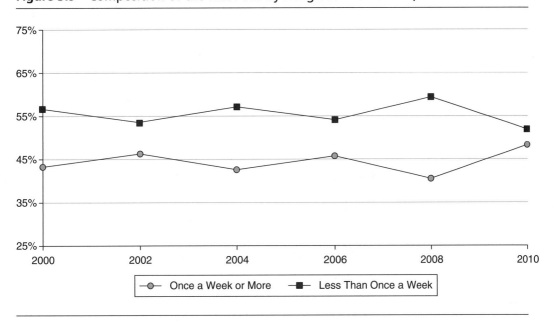

*Source:* National exit polls. See the section in Chapter 2 entitled "Creating a Cumulative National Data Set: Selecting Exit Polls" (pp. 28–29).

*Note:* When using these results to make inferences about the active electorate, the standard errors should be calculated using Table 2.2 (p. 36), which is explained in the adjacent section of Chapter 2, "Analyzing Exit Poll Questions: Estimating Sampling Error" (pp. 34–36). For a guide on how to understand the tables and figures of this chapter, see the section in Chapter 2 entitled "Presenting and Discussing the Exit Poll Data: Reading Chapter 3" (pp. 37–39).

voters. The share of respondents attending church weekly rose 4 percentage points from 2000 to 2002, 3 points from 2004 to 2006, and 7 points from 2008 to 2010. After both 2002 and 2006, the subsequent presidential election saw a decline in the proportion of respondents who were highly religious.

The 2010 election saw the proportion of low-frequency religious attendees fall to its lowest level in the past six elections (see Table 3.9 at the end of the chapter). Fifty-two percent of exit poll respondents reported attending church less than weekly, down 3 points from their decade-long average. By contrast, the proportion of frequent attendees rose to its highest level in the 2000s, reaching 48 percent of the exit poll in 2010.

## Evangelical

After the emergence of evangelical Christian-oriented political organizations in the late 1970s, such as Jerry Falwell's Moral Majority and James Dobson's Focus on the Family, exit pollsters began attempting to capture an affinity for the beliefs underlying such groups. Unfortunately, they have had difficulty settling on question wording for such an amorphous idea. From 1982 to 1994, exit pollsters asked respondents whether they were "born-again Christians" or "evangelical Christians." Sensitive that they might be overstating the numbers in the movement, pollsters began asking voters whether they considered themselves part of the "Religious Right" in 1996. When this descriptor fell out of fashion with newer evangelical political organizations,

**Figure 3.10**   Composition of the Exit Polls by Evangelical, 2004–2010

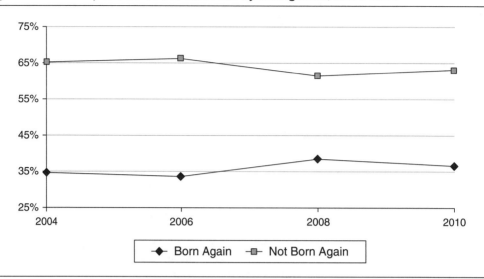

*Source:* National exit polls. See the section in Chapter 2 entitled "Creating a Cumulative National Data Set: Selecting Exit Polls" (pp. 28–29).

*Note:* When using these results to make inferences about the active electorate, the standard errors should be calculated using Table 2.2 (p. 36), which is explained in the adjacent section of Chapter 2, "Analyzing Exit Poll Questions: Estimating Sampling Error" (pp. 34–36). For a guide on how to understand the tables and figures of this chapter, see the section in Chapter 2 entitled "Presenting and Discussing the Exit Poll Data: Reading Chapter 3" (pp. 37–39).

national exit pollsters reverted back to their initial wordings in 2004 and began assessing whether respondents considered themselves "born-again or evangelical Christians." However, the formatting of this most recent version of the question is not comparable with the earlier version.

Figure 3.10 shows the proportion of self-identified evangelicals in the exit polls administered since 2004. On average, evangelicals have comprised 36 percent of respondents in the past four elections. Their share in any given election has remained remarkably stable, fluctuating within a 4-point range.

Despite well-publicized differences in the religious orientations of the incumbent presidents— George W. Bush identified as an evangelical Christian, whereas Barack Obama did not—the proportion of evangelicals in the exit poll changed little from 2006 to 2010 (see Table 3.10 at the end of the chapter). Evangelical Christians made up 37 percent of respondents in the 2010 election. This rate was similar to the 34 percent of evangelicals who completed the midterm exit poll administered four years earlier.

## Lifestyle Characteristics

Another category of questions that pollsters include frequently on national exit polls are those that tap lifestyle choices, such as occupational, consumptive, and recreational decisions. These lifestyle characteristics influence the types of people with which individuals associate and interact. They form the bases of many organizational memberships, from involvement in civic groups to participation in sports leagues. Such social reinforcements of lifestyle choices serve to unify prefer-ences, particularly on issues stemming from these choices.[7]

Political scientists have found that lifestyle decisions are often related to political orientations and behaviors.[8] Laws and regulations frequently aim to constrain lifestyle choices, from licensing requirements to age restrictions. Disagreements on these constraints have prompted numerous electoral debates in recent campaigns over topics such as drug use policy, gun control issues, and environmental practices.

From their inception, national exit polls have included a variety of lifestyle characteristics, from personal vices, such as cigarette smoking and cocaine usage, to mass media practices, such as Internet usage and talk radio listening. Unfortunately, many of these items were included only once or twice, preventing any analysis of their relationship with electoral preferences and behav-iors over time. Over the past several decades, five lifestyle characteristics have appeared on five or more exit polls including either the 2008 or 2010 exit poll: education, employment status, marital status, child in the household, or union member in the household.

## Education

Exit pollsters have surveyed respondents' education in a similar format since the 1986 election. They have measured education as progress toward or completion of particular levels of schooling rather than the number of years of school attendance or knowledge acquired. The five comparable response options administered over time ask whether respondents did not complete high school, completed high school, attended some college, completed a college degree, or undertook graduate study.

During the past quarter-century, exit poll respondents have become increasingly more edu-cated (see Figure 3.11). From 1986 to 2010, the proportion of college-educated respondents grew 20 percentage points, from less than a third in 1986 to more than half in 2010. Conversely, respondents with only a high school diploma or less saw their voice in the exit polls diminish considerably relative to their college-educated counterparts. The proportion of respondents with just a high school education fell 14 percentage points since 1986, whereas the proportion of respondents with less than a high school education dropped 5 points.

By 2010, the exit poll respondents were the most educated they had ever been (see Table 3.11 at the end of the chapter). Ninety-seven percent of respondents had received a high school diploma. Fifty-one percent of respondents had earned a college degree, including 21 percent who had some postgraduate education.

## Employment Status

Exit pollsters have long been interested in the relationship between employment status and vote choice. Since 1996, they have asked respondents whether or not they were employed full time at the time they cast their ballots. Readers should be mindful that those not employed full time may not necessarily be without a job or looking for work, but instead may be employed part time, retired, in school, or acting as a homemaker.

Figure 3.12 shows the share of exit poll respondents employed full time and less than full time over the past two decades. In every election since 1996, respondents employed full time have

**Figure 3.11** Composition of the Exit Polls by Education, 1986–2010

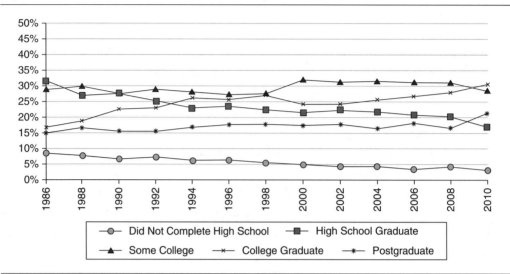

*Source:* National exit polls. See the section in Chapter 2 entitled "Creating a Cumulative National Data Set: Selecting Exit Polls" (pp. 28–29).

*Note:* When using these results to make inferences about the active electorate, the standard errors should be calculated using Table 2.2 (p. 36), which is explained in the adjacent section of Chapter 2, "Analyzing Exit Poll Questions: Estimating Sampling Error" (pp. 34–36). For a guide on how to understand the tables and figures of this chapter, see the section in Chapter 2 entitled "Presenting and Discussing the Exit Poll Data: Reading Chapter 3" (pp. 37–39).

**Figure 3.12** Composition of the Exit Polls by Employment Status, 1996–2008

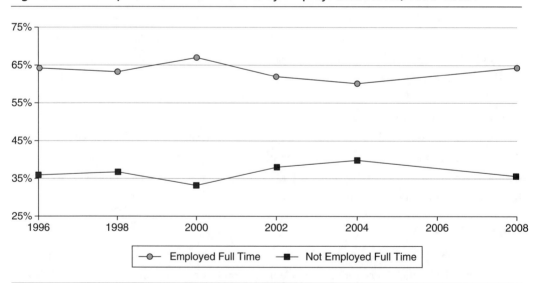

*Source:* National exit polls. See the section in Chapter 2 entitled "Creating a Cumulative National Data Set: Selecting Exit Polls" (pp. 28–29).

*Note:* When using these results to make inferences about the active electorate, the standard errors should be calculated using Table 2.2 (p. 36), which is explained in the adjacent section of Chapter 2, "Analyzing Exit Poll Questions: Estimating Sampling Error" (pp. 34–36). For a guide on how to understand the tables and figures of this chapter, see the section in Chapter 2 entitled "Presenting and Discussing the Exit Poll Data: Reading Chapter 3" (pp. 37–39).

made up a far larger share of the exit poll than voters not employed full time, comprising 63 percent of the exit poll on average and holding at least a 20-point advantage over their counterparts in every election. Their numbers have remained relatively flat over time, fluctuating between 60 and 67 percent and never moving more than 5 points in a single election.

Exit poll respondents were not asked their employment status in the 2010 election. In the 2008 exit poll, a large majority of respondents were once again employed full time (see Table 3.12 at the end of the chapter). Sixty-four percent of exit poll respondents reported that they worked full time, whereas only 36 percent indicated that they worked less than full time.

## Marital Status

Exit pollsters have solicited the marital status of voters in a similar format since 1992. The question asks respondents whether or not they are currently married. It disregards whether respondents have been married in the past or are legally separated in the present.

The composition of married and unmarried respondents in the exit polls can be seen in Figure 3.13. Over the past quarter-century, married respondents have typically comprised a far larger share of the national exit polls than unmarried voters. Married respondents have held a nearly two-to-one advantage over unmarried respondents since 1992. Sixty-six percent of exit poll respondents have been married, fluctuating between 63 and 70 percent over time.

**Figure 3.13**   Composition of the Exit Polls by Marital Status, 1992–2008

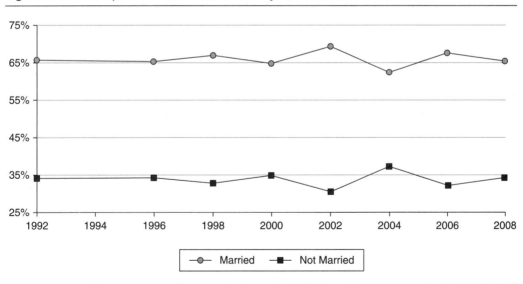

*Source:* National exit polls. See the section in Chapter 2 entitled "Creating a Cumulative National Data Set: Selecting Exit Polls" (pp. 28–29).

*Note:* When using these results to make inferences about the active electorate, the standard errors should be calculated using Table 2.2 (p. 36), which is explained in the adjacent section of Chapter 2, "Analyzing Exit Poll Questions: Estimating Sampling Error" (pp. 34–36). For a guide on how to understand the tables and figures of this chapter, see the section in Chapter 2 entitled "Presenting and Discussing the Exit Poll Data: Reading Chapter 3" (pp. 37–39).

In recent election cycles, married respondents have comprised a somewhat greater share of the exit polls in midterm elections than in presidential elections. In the past three midterms, the proportion of married respondents has increased, with married respondents' share of the exit poll growing 4 points, on average, in the subsequent midterm election before shrinking again in the next presidential election year.

The marital status question did not appear on the exit poll in the 2010 election. In 2008, married respondents comprised 66 percent of the exit poll, down 2 points from the previous midterm election (see Table 3.13 at the end of the chapter). Unmarried respondents made up the remaining third of the survey.

## Child in the Household

Children's issues have played a prominent role in national politics in recent years, from debates over funding for day care centers to educational testing programs. Since 1996, the national exit polls have queried voters in a yes-or-no format on whether they have children under age eighteen living in the household. On average, 37 percent of respondents reported children living at their home over this time span (see Figure 3.14). The proportion of respondents with a child in their household has ranged between 34 and 40 percent with no discernable pattern to the fluctuations.

In the 2010 election, 34 percent of exit poll respondents had children under the age of eighteen living in their household (see Table 3.14 at the end of the chapter). This proportion was down 6 percentage points from 2008 but was identical to the proportion of respondents with children in the household in the previous midterm exit poll.

**Figure 3.14**   Composition of the Exit Polls by Child in Household, 1996–2010

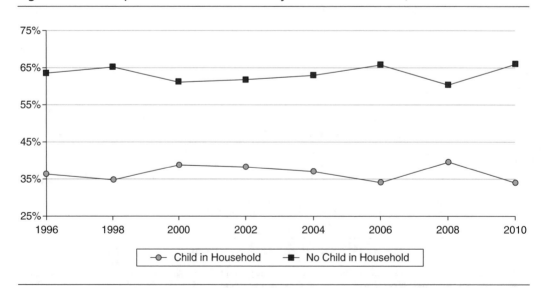

*Source:* National exit polls. See the section in Chapter 2 entitled "Creating a Cumulative National Data Set: Selecting Exit Polls" (pp. 28–29).

*Note:* When using these results to make inferences about the active electorate, the standard errors should be calculated using Table 2.2 (p. 36), which is explained in the adjacent section of Chapter 2, "Analyzing Exit Poll Questions: Estimating Sampling Error" (pp. 34–36). For a guide on how to understand the tables and figures of this chapter, see the section in Chapter 2 entitled "Presenting and Discussing the Exit Poll Data: Reading Chapter 3" (pp. 37–39).

## Union Household

Unions have long had a strong presence in American politics. They promote positions on many campaign issues and direct members toward particular candidates. They also play a vital role in mobilizing voters by organizing registration drives, supplying logistical information, and even providing transportation to the polls.

Exit pollsters have recognized these efforts, assessing union membership in one format or another since the first national exit poll in 1972. The specific wording of the question has varied somewhat over the years. Sometimes pollsters have asked voters whether anyone in the household belongs to a union. On other occasions, pollsters have asked voters to specify whether they were union members or whether some other person in their household fit this description. To ensure the longest series possible, we recoded all versions into a single measure indicating whether or not a union member lived in the respondent's household.

Figure 3.15 shows the proportion of exit poll respondents from union households over the past four decades. Generally speaking, the share of respondents with union connections has been declining over time. The proportion of respondents from union households fell from one-third in the 1970s to less than one-fifth by 2010.

In 2010, only 18 percent of exit poll respondents had a union member in their household (see Table 3.15 at the end of the chapter). This showing was the lowest share of union households represented in the survey since national exit polling began in 1972. Not only was it down 17 points from its high point of the series in the 1976 election, but it was down 9 points in just the past decade alone.

**Figure 3.15**  Composition of the Exit Polls by Union Household, 1972–2010

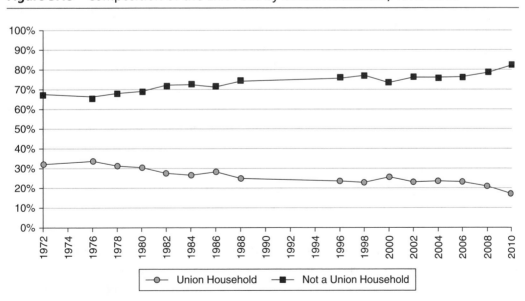

*Source:* National exit polls. See the section in Chapter 2 entitled "Creating a Cumulative National Data Set: Selecting Exit Polls" (pp. 28–29).

*Note:* When using these results to make inferences about the active electorate, the standard errors should be calculated using Table 2.2 (p. 36), which is explained in the adjacent section of Chapter 2, "Analyzing Exit Poll Questions: Estimating Sampling Error" (pp. 34–36). For a guide on how to understand the tables and figures of this chapter, see the section in Chapter 2 entitled "Presenting and Discussing the Exit Poll Data: Reading Chapter 3" (pp. 37–39).

## Political Orientations

The national exit polls routinely solicit information about respondents' political orientations, which are general attitudes about institutions, policy directions, and the general welfare of the country. Rather than specific preferences about a particular policy or event, they are typically conceptualized as comprehensive assessments based on an accumulation of judgments.

Scholars believe political orientations are immediate antecedents of political decisions. They shape individuals' positions on social, economic, and political issues, predisposing them to support particular candidates or policies. Through the years, numerous studies have shown a close correspondence between political orientations and vote choice.[9]

Exit pollsters have assessed a variety of different political orientations over the past four decades. The most commonly asked questions assess party and ideological self-identification, presidential and congressional approval, forecasts about the direction of the country in the immediate future and a generation from now, perceptions about government activism, voting behavior in the prior presidential election, and newness to voting. The exit polls show considerable variation in responses, both within and between items.

### Party Identification

Exit pollsters have inquired about respondents' partisan predispositions since 1972. The question asks respondents whether they usually think of themselves as a Democrat, a Republican, or an independent. In most but not all years, they were also given an option to indicate whether they identified with another unnamed political party. Since there has not been a predominant third political party over the past four decades, we have combined the options for independent and something else to create a category designed to indicate respondents who did not identify with (or were independent from) the two major political parties.

Figure 3.16 illustrates the composition of major-party identifiers in the exit polls conducted from 1972 through 2010. Major-party identifiers—whether Democrats or Republicans—have consistently outnumbered independents by roughly a three-to-one margin. With the exception of an increase in independents immediately following the Watergate scandal, the proportion of independents in each exit poll remained remarkably steady through the 1980s and 1990s. Since 2002, though, the proportion of independents has begun to inch up, gaining 6 percentage points over the past four exit polls.

Among major-party identifiers, Democratic respondents have outnumbered Republican respondents in the exit polls for much of the past four decades. Between 1972 and 2000, Democrats had a 7-point size advantage over Republicans, comprising 40 percent of the exit poll, on average, compared to 33 percent for Republicans. In the 2002 exit poll, the share of self-identified Republicans surpassed the share of self-identified Democrats for the first time in thirty years, topping them 40 percent to 38 percent. In the elections occurring since, the proportion of exit poll respondents identifying with each of the major parties has been roughly equal, with the exception of the 2008 exit poll, when Democratic respondents held a 7-point advantage.

**Figure 3.16**    Composition of the Exit Polls by Party Identification, 1972–2010

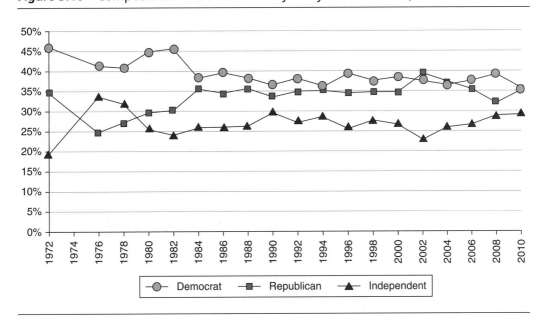

*Source:* National exit polls. See the section in Chapter 2 entitled "Creating a Cumulative National Data Set: Selecting Exit Polls" (pp. 28–29).

*Note:* When using these results to make inferences about the active electorate, the standard errors should be calculated using Table 2.2 (p. 36), which is explained in the adjacent section of Chapter 2, "Analyzing Exit Poll Questions: Estimating Sampling Error" (pp. 34–36). For a guide on how to understand the tables and figures of this chapter, see the section in Chapter 2 entitled "Presenting and Discussing the Exit Poll Data: Reading Chapter 3" (pp. 37–39).

In 2010, Democrats and Republicans appeared in the exit poll in equal numbers. Self-identified Democrats and Republicans each comprised 35 percent of respondents (see Table 3.16 at the end of the chapter). Meanwhile, independents made up 30 percent of exit poll respondents, among their largest shares in the past thirty years.

## Ideological Identification

Exit pollsters have gauged the ideological orientation of respondents' political views since 1976. They have relied exclusively on an item that requests respondents to locate themselves on a unidimensional, liberal-conservative scale. The question asks whether on most political matters respondents consider themselves to be liberal, conservative, or moderate.

Figure 3.17 shows the distribution of ideological self-identification in the exit polls during the past three decades. Generally speaking, the ideological orientation of exit poll respondents has remained relatively stable. From 1976 to 2008, roughly a fifth of respondents identified themselves as liberal, a third identified as conservative, and nearly half identified as moderate. The movement that has occurred in the ideological composition of the exit polls appears to have resulted primarily from fluctuations in the proportion of moderate and conservative identifiers. Upward shifts in the proportion of moderates have typically been mirrored by downward shifts in the proportion of conservatives, and vice versa. Meanwhile, the proportion of liberals has remained essentially the same over the past two-and-a-half decades.

**Figure 3.17** Composition of the Exit Polls by Ideological Identification, 1976–2010

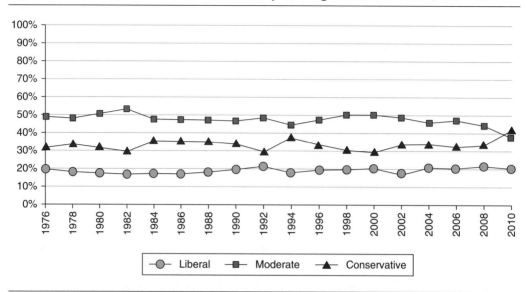

*Source:* National exit polls. See the section in Chapter 2 entitled "Creating a Cumulative National Data Set: Selecting Exit Polls" (pp. 28–29).

*Note:* When using these results to make inferences about the active electorate, the standard errors should be calculated using Table 2.2 (p. 36), which is explained in the adjacent section of Chapter 2, "Analyzing Exit Poll Questions: Estimating Sampling Error" (pp. 34–36). For a guide on how to understand the tables and figures of this chapter, see the section in Chapter 2 entitled "Presenting and Discussing the Exit Poll Data: Reading Chapter 3" (pp. 37–39).

The 2010 exit poll was the most ideologically polarized in at least three decades. Sixty-two percent of respondents indicated an ideological orientation, the first time the number has topped 60 percent since the introduction of the question on the 1976 exit poll (see Table 3.17 at the end of the chapter). Most of this change was due to an increase in the proportion of conservatives, which moved up 7 points from 2008 to 41 percent, and a decrease in the proportion of moderates, which fell 5 points to 39 percent. The 2010 exit poll had the highest share of conservatives and the lowest share of moderates in any election in the series. Meanwhile, the proportion of liberal identifiers remained essentially flat, registering at 20 percent of respondents.

## Last Presidential Vote

To explore the consistency in the electorate's voting behavior, national exit pollsters have queried respondents repeatedly about their presidential vote in the previous election. Since 1972, respondents have been asked in every national exit poll if they voted for the named Democratic nominee (for example, Bill Clinton), the named Republican nominee (for example, Bob Dole), someone else, or if they did not vote in the previous presidential election. We recoded named responses into two categories: Democratic presidential candidates and Republican presidential candidates. Because named third-party candidates were not offered to respondents, we did not recode the response options indicating that respondents had chosen some other candidate or did not vote in the previous presidential election.

Figure 3.18 shows the previous presidential vote for exit poll respondents from 1972 through 2010. At first glance, the distribution of responses appears inexplicable, with the series showing

**Figure 3.18**  Composition of the Exit Polls by Presidential Vote in Last Election, 1972–2010

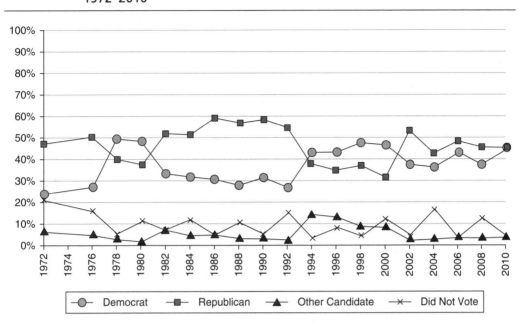

*Source:* National exit polls. See the section in Chapter 2 entitled "Creating a Cumulative National Data Set: Selecting Exit Polls" (pp. 28–29).

*Note:* When using these results to make inferences about the active electorate, the standard errors should be calculated using Table 2.2 (p. 36), which is explained in the adjacent section of Chapter 2, "Analyzing Exit Poll Questions: Estimating Sampling Error" (pp. 34–36). For a guide on how to understand the tables and figures of this chapter, see the section in Chapter 2 entitled "Presenting and Discussing the Exit Poll Data: Reading Chapter 3" (pp. 37–39).

considerable volatility over time. On closer examination, though, several noteworthy patterns stand out.

First, in nearly every exit poll, a greater proportion of respondents supported the winner rather than the loser in the previous presidential election, regardless of the popularity of the sitting president. From 1972 through 2010, 50 percent of exit poll respondents on average recall voting for the winning presidential candidate in the previous election, whereas 35 percent of respondents recall voting for the losing candidate. The proportion of exit poll respondents who supported the winning presidential candidate in the previous election differed from the actual share of the electorate who had voted for the previous winner by 3 points on average, exceeding the winner's share in five exit polls, falling short in nine exit polls, and matching it in five exit polls. By contrast, the proportion of exit poll respondents who supported the losing presidential candidate in the previous election differed from the actual share by 9 points on average, falling short in every exit poll, save one, during the past four decades.

Second, respondents in the subsequent midterm exit poll (two years later) report a previous presidential vote that more closely matches the actual vote than is the case for respondents in the next presidential exit poll (four years later). In the first midterm exit poll conducted after a presidential election, the correlation between the percentage of respondents who voted for the winning candidate in the previous presidential election and the actual vote received by that candidates was .70, whereas the correlation between the percentage of respondents who chose the losing candidate and the actual vote received by that candidate was .74. By the time of the next presidential election, two years after the midterm, the correlation between respondents who voted for the previous winning presidential candidate and the actual vote that candidate received was .38, whereas the correlation between respondents who had voted for the losing candidate and the actual vote the losing candidate received was .21.

Finally, the proportion of respondents who indicated that they had not voted in the previous presidential election was higher in exit polls administered in presidential election years than in exit polls administered in midterm election years. In presidential exit polls, 14 percent of respondents, on average, did not vote in the previous presidential election. That percentage reached as high as 22 percent in the 1972 election, immediately after the Twenty-sixth Amendment gave eighteen- to twenty-one-year-olds the right to vote, and as low as 9 percent in the 1996 election. In midterm exit polls, only 5 percent of respondents, on average, had not voted in the presidential election occurring two years earlier, with the proportion fluctuating in a very small range between 4 and 7 percent.

In the 2010 exit poll, the distribution of respondents' prior presidential votes deviated as much from the aforementioned patterns as at any time in the past (see Table 3.18 at the end of the chapter). For the first time, the proportion of exit poll respondents who chose the winner, Obama, in the previous presidential election did not exceed the proportion of respondents who chose the loser, McCain; each group comprised 46 percent of the exit poll. Finally, the 5 percent of respondents who did not vote in the 2008 election nearly matched the smallest shares of nonvoters found in any of the preceding exit polls.

## Presidential Approval

Exit pollsters have long been interested in the relationship between judgments of presidential performance and vote choice, particularly congressional vote choice. They have included a question tapping presidential approval on surveys administered in midterm election years since 1978. In 2000, they began including the question on exit polls administered in presidential election years, as well. The wording of the question is based on the measure of presidential approval developed by the Gallup Poll and used by the organization since the 1940s. It asks whether respondents approve or disapprove of the way the officeholder is handling his job as president. Beginning in 2002, the response options were expanded to include the intensity of judgment, changing from approve/disapprove to strongly or somewhat approve/disapprove.

Figure 3.19 illustrates exit poll respondents' presidential approval ratings from 1978 through 2010. Judgments of individual presidents appear to move according to their own trajectory, showing few commonalities at similar junctures in their administrations. Jimmy Carter had a weak evaluation in the exit poll conducted at his midterm, securing approval from only 48 percent of respondents. Ronald Reagan received approval from 52 percent of exit poll respondents at his first midterm, and his approval rating only strengthened by his second midterm, when 63 percent of respondents approved of his performance—a greater share in his sixth year than either of his two-term successors received. George H. W. Bush secured 60 percent approval from exit poll respondents during his only midterm election. Bill Clinton's approval rating rose considerably

**Figure 3.19** Composition of the Exit Polls by Presidential Approval, 1978–2010

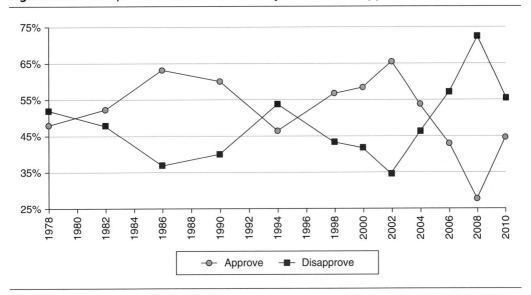

*Source:* National exit polls. See the section in Chapter 2 entitled "Creating a Cumulative National Data Set: Selecting Exit Polls" (pp. 28–29).

*Note:* When using these results to make inferences about the active electorate, the standard errors should be calculated using Table 2.2 (p. 36), which is explained in the adjacent section of Chapter 2, "Analyzing Exit Poll Questions: Estimating Sampling Error" (pp. 34–36). For a guide on how to understand the tables and figures of this chapter, see the section in Chapter 2 entitled "Presenting and Discussing the Exit Poll Data: Reading Chapter 3" (pp. 37–39).

from his first midterm to his second midterm, jumping from 46 percent to 57 percent, where it remained essentially unchanged at the end of his second term in 2000. George W. Bush's approval rating declined steadily in every exit poll conducted while he was in office, falling from 66 percent at his first midterm in 2002 to 54 percent at his reelection in 2004 to 43 percent at his second midterm in 2006 to 28 percent near the end of his second term in 2008.

Barack Obama fared quite badly among exit poll respondents at his first midterm (see Table 3.19 at the end of the chapter). More than half (56 percent) of them disapproved of his performance as president. Only 45 percent of exit poll respondents approved of President Obama, among the lowest midterm approval ratings given to any president in an exit poll administered in the past thirty years.

## Congressional Approval

Since 1990, exit pollsters have asked voters to evaluate the overall performance of Congress in each midterm election. The question used was the same as that used to measure presidential approval. It queried respondents about whether they approve or disapprove of the way Congress is handling its job.

In stark contrast to presidential approval, a majority of exit poll respondents have given Congress negative evaluations in every election in which the question has been asked (see Figure 3.20). In the last seven midterm elections, 70 percent of exit poll respondents, on average, disapproved of the way Congress had been handling its job. Only three in ten respondents approved of its performance.

**Figure 3.20** Composition of the Exit Polls by Congressional Approval, 1990–2010

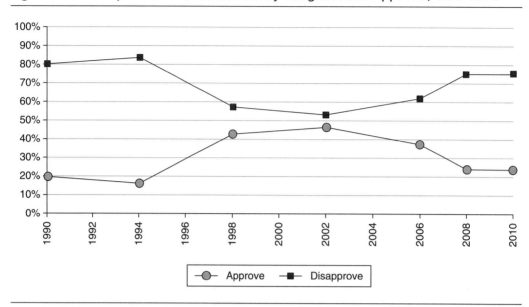

*Source:* National exit polls. See the section in Chapter 2 entitled "Creating a Cumulative National Data Set: Selecting Exit Polls" (pp. 28–29).

*Note:* When using these results to make inferences about the active electorate, the standard errors should be calculated using Table 2.2 (p. 36), which is explained in the adjacent section of Chapter 2, "Analyzing Exit Poll Questions: Estimating Sampling Error" (pp. 34–36). For a guide on how to understand the tables and figures of this chapter, see the section in Chapter 2 entitled "Presenting and Discussing the Exit Poll Data: Reading Chapter 3" (pp. 37–39).

Despite this negative tilt, congressional approval ratings are hardly static, exhibiting considerable variability over time. In the 1990 and 1994 midterm exit polls, respondents' disapproval of Congress topped 80 percent. Respondents' stance on Congress improved considerably over the next decade, as disapproval dropped to 57 percent in the 1998 exit poll and 53 percent in the 2002 exit poll. By 2006, congressional disapproval was again on the rise, reaching 76 percent in the 2008 exit poll.

The 2010 exit poll saw little change in congressional approval, despite a new president from the same political party, capable of working with the majority (see Table 3.20 at the end of the chapter). Three-quarters of the exit poll respondents disapproved of the way Congress was handling its job. A paltry 25 percent of respondents approved of Congress's performance.

### Perceived Direction of the Country

Whereas presidential and congressional approval ratings are retrospective evaluations of two institutions critical to shaping the country's state of affairs, national pollsters have also considered respondents' perceptions about the country's future prospects. Specifically, they have asked respondents whether the country is headed in the right direction or off on the wrong track. The item has appeared on every exit poll administered since 1990, save 1992.

Judgments about the future direction of the country have changed considerably over the past two decades (see Figure 3.21). In 1990 and 1994, only about 40 percent of respondents believed that the country was moving in the right direction. Over the next six years, the proportion of the

**Figure 3.21**   Composition of the Exit Polls by Perceived Direction of the Country, 1990–2010

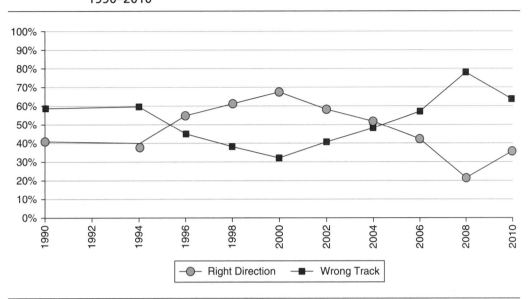

*Source:* National exit polls. See the section in Chapter 2 entitled "Creating a Cumulative National Data Set: Selecting Exit Polls" (pp. 28–29).

*Note:* When using these results to make inferences about the active electorate, the standard errors should be calculated using Table 2.2 (p. 36), which is explained in the adjacent section of Chapter 2, "Analyzing Exit Poll Questions: Estimating Sampling Error" (pp. 34–36). For a guide on how to understand the tables and figures of this chapter, see the section in Chapter 2 entitled "Presenting and Discussing the Exit Poll Data: Reading Chapter 3" (pp. 37–39).

respondents that thought the country was continuing to improve grew by 28 percentage points. By 2000, 68 percent of respondents believed that the country was moving in the right direction.

From 2000 through 2008, though, the tide reversed course, taking the optimism of exit poll respondents away with it. Over the course of the decade, respondents grew increasingly pessimistic about the future of the country. In each of the four elections after 2000, the proportion of respondents believing the country was going off the rails grew by at least 7 percentage points. By 2008, a whopping 79 percent of exit poll respondents thought the country was off on the wrong track, a 47-point increase in only eight years.

The 2010 election found exit poll respondents still quite pessimistic about the country, although decidedly less so than they were in 2008 (see Table 3.21 at the end of the chapter). Optimism increased 14 points since Obama was elected, almost completely mirroring the decline of two years earlier. Nonetheless, an overwhelming 64 percent of respondents thought the country was off on the wrong track, whereas only 36 percent thought the country was moving in the right direction.

## Expected Life for the Next Generation

In recent years, national exit pollsters have extended the outlook about the direction of the country to explore whether the time frame varies respondents' perceptions. Since 1992, the exit polls have asked respondents periodically whether they "expect life for the next generation of Americans to be better than life today, worse than life today, or about the same." The question has been included on half of the past ten exit polls, appearing on three exit polls administered in presidential election years (1992, 1996, 2000) and on two in midterm election years (2006 and 2010).

The response distribution for exit poll respondents can be seen in Figure 3.22. The primary effect of changing the time frame has been to reduce the differences in the proportion of optimists and pessimists about the future. Whereas the difference in the share of respondents believing the country was going in the right direction as opposed to off on the wrong track averaged 23 percentage points and exceeded 15 percentage points on eight of its ten administrations, the difference in the share of respondents believing life for the next generation would be better than today as opposed to worse averaged only 11 points and exceeded 15 points on only one of its five administrations.

The distribution patterns over time, though, are still comparable to those found in the question assessing whether the country is going in the right direction or is off on the wrong track. During the 1990s, pessimists outnumbered optimists for both questions. In 1992, 37 percent of respondents thought the next generation would have it worse than today, compared to 31 percent who thought it would be better. In 1996, the results were quite similar; 34 percent indicated that life would be worse for the next generation, compared to 30 percent who thought it would better. Assessments flipped completely by 2000, just as they they had on the right direction–wrong track question. In the 2000 exit poll, 49 percent of respondents thought the next generation would have it better, whereas only 21 percent thought it would be worse, a change of more than a dozen points in the size of each group. The distribution reversed itself again in the second half of the

**Figure 3.22** Composition of the Exit Polls by Expected Life for the Next Generation, 1992–2010

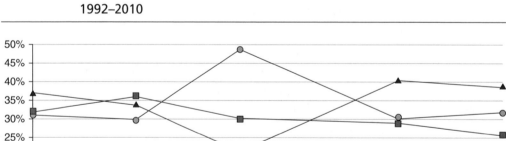

*Source:* National exit polls. See the section in Chapter 2 entitled "Creating a Cumulative National Data Set: Selecting Exit Polls" (pp. 28–29).

*Note:* When using these results to make inferences about the active electorate, the standard errors should be calculated using Table 2.2 (p. 36), which is explained in the adjacent section of Chapter 2, "Analyzing Exit Poll Questions: Estimating Sampling Error" (pp. 34–36). For a guide on how to understand the tables and figures of this chapter, see the section in Chapter 2 entitled "Presenting and Discussing the Exit Poll Data: Reading Chapter 3" (pp. 37–39).

2000s, as it did for responses to the right direction–wrong track question, as well. In the 2006 exit poll, 41 percent of respondents thought life for the next generation would be worse than today, whereas 31 percent of respondents thought it would be better than today, swings of about 19 points, respectively, from six years earlier.

In the 2010 exit polls, forecasts about the future varied little from 2006 (see Table 3.22 at the end of the chapter). A plurality of exit poll respondents (40 percent) felt that life for the next generation would be worse than today. Conversely, 33 percent of respondents believed life would be better in the years to come. The remaining 27 percent of exit poll respondents thought life would be about the same for the next generation.

## Position on Government Activism

The role of government has been a key issue in campaigns for decades, often dividing the parties and their respective candidates. Generally speaking, the Democratic Party promotes government intervention in the marketplace to offset the inequalities and negative externalities generated by it, whereas the Republican Party prefers limited government that does not interfere with the workings of the market, believing the private sector is more effective at helping the less fortunate. Since 1992, exit pollsters have asked respondents whether they think the government should do more to solve problems or is doing too many things better left to businesses and individuals.

A small majority of exit poll respondents typically believes that the government is too active, with 53 percent of respondents, on average, indicating that government does too many

**Figure 3.23**   Composition of the Exit Polls by Position on Government Activism, 1992–2010

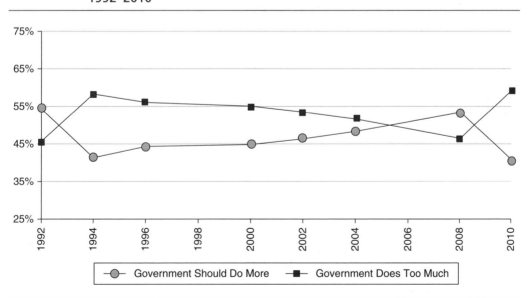

*Source:* National exit polls. See the section in Chapter 2 entitled "Creating a Cumulative National Data Set: Selecting Exit Polls" (pp. 28–29).

*Note:* When using these results to make inferences about the active electorate, the standard errors should be calculated using Table 2.2 (p. 36), which is explained in the adjacent section of Chapter 2, "Analyzing Exit Poll Questions: Estimating Sampling Error" (pp. 34–36). For a guide on how to understand the tables and figures of this chapter, see the section in Chapter 2 entitled "Presenting and Discussing the Exit Poll Data: Reading Chapter 3" (pp. 37–39).

things better left to the private sector (see Figure 3.23). Only twice in the past ten exit polls, both occuring after many years of Republican control of the White House, have a majority of respondents thought the government should do more. In 1992, after twelve years of Ronald Reagan and George H. W. Bush, 55 percent of respondents thought the government should be more active. Again, in 2008, after eight years of George W. Bush, 54 percent of respondents thought the government should do more to solve problems.

The 2010 elections witnessed a dramatic shift in exit poll respondents' perceptions of government activism (see Table 3.23 at the end of the chapter). In the first election since Obama took office, 60 percent of respondents thought the government was doing too much, up 13 points from the 2008 exit poll. This was the highest share of respondents with this opinion since the 1994 exit poll, which was the last time the Democrats lost double-digit seats in the House of Representatives.

### First-Time Voter

In recent years, national exit pollsters have assessed the proportion of new voters in the active electorate. The most commonly used question in the national exit polls asks whether the current election is the first election in which respondents have ever voted. Until recently, though, it has been administered only in exit polls conducted in presidential election years, not in midterm election years.

Figure 3.24 displays the proportion of respondents voting for the first time in exit polls conducted from 1996 through 2010. For the past four exit polls in presidential election years, one out of ten respondents, on average, were casting their first ballot. The share of new respondents

**Figure 3.24** Composition of the Exit Polls by First-Time Voter, 1996–2010

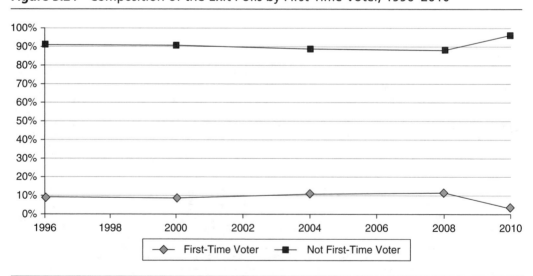

*Source:* National exit polls. See the section in Chapter 2 entitled "Creating a Cumulative National Data Set: Selecting Exit Polls" (pp. 28–29).

*Note:* When using these results to make inferences about the active electorate, the standard errors should be calculated using Table 2.2 (p. 36), which is explained in the adjacent section of Chapter 2, "Analyzing Exit Poll Questions: Estimating Sampling Error" (pp. 34–36). For a guide on how to understand the tables and figures of this chapter, see the section in Chapter 2 entitled "Presenting and Discussing the Exit Poll Data: Reading Chapter 3" (pp. 37–39).

in the presidential exit polls has changed remarkably little over time, fluctuating between 9 and 12 percent, regardless of which candidates were running or what get-out-the-vote strategies were used.

The 2010 exit poll was the first occasion in which pollsters considered whether respondents were participating in a midterm contest for the first time (see Table 3.24 at the end of the chapter). Only 3 percent of exit poll respondents were first-time voters, down from 8 percent in the 2008 exit poll. Without any other midterm elections to consider, conclusions cannot be drawn, but the results are consistent with research that suggests midterms are typically low-stimulus elections, where reduced media coverage, less issue salience, and lower-profile candidates suppress participation from potential voters on the peripheries of politics.[10]

## Economic Considerations

The last group of items included regularly on national exit polls covers economic considerations. Economic traits have long been tied to voters' electoral decisions.[11] They influence citizens' choices to participate by easing some of the costs of voting, such as fees to document eligibility, travel expenses to and from the polls, and lost wages from missing work. They shape individuals' judgments about public policy, particularly initiatives with salient financial elements such as tax rates, public welfare programs, and more recently health care reform. And, they influence voters' candidate preferences.

National exit pollsters have assessed five economic considerations repeatedly over time. Household income is the only item tapping actual individual economic circumstances. The remaining questions—household financial situation compared to two and four years earlier, and judgments about current and future national economic conditions—are based on subjective judgments of financial conditions and as a result tend to show more volatility over time.

### Household Income

Exit pollsters have solicited respondents' household incomes since 1976. Rather than asking respondents to recall the precise income of their households, which they may not know or may refuse to provide, respondents are asked to identify a monetary range within which their household income falls. The number of income ranges offered has varied over time between four and eight. Moreover, the value of each range's endpoints has changed periodically, often in response to inflation in the median income of the population over time. In 1976, the ranges offered to respondents were (1) under $8,000, (2) $8,000–$12,000, (3) $12,001–$20,000, and (4) over $20,000. By 2010, the ranges presented were (1) under $15,000, (2) $15,000–$29,999, (3) $30,000–$49,999, (4) $50,000–$74,999, (5) $75,000–$99,999, (6) $100,000–$149,999, (7) $150,000–$199,999, and (8) $200,000 or more.

These discrepancies make it exceedingly difficult to create uniform ranges that permit comparisons over time. Adjusting the income categories for inflation by converting the nominal dollar values to constant dollar values produces income ranges with little overlap. For example, the $8,000 endpoint of the bottom category in 1976 would be worth roughly $41,000 in 2010, placing it in the middle of the third-highest category for that year. Even recoding the categories into a simple trichotomy that equates one of the ranges with the median household income and then collapses the remaining ones into two categories representing household incomes above and below the median income does not make comparisons any easier because in too many years the median income falls right at the margin of a given range. Instead, we opt to leave the income ranges alone and simply report the distributions for those years in which the ranges remain consistent. Although this avoids the problem of comparing two ranges with different income widths, it ignores price inflation over time. Thus, the exact same income in 2000 can buy less goods and services in 2010.

Figure 3.25 shows the distribution of incomes in the exit polls administered from 1994 through 2010. Exit poll respondents possess increasingly higher incomes over time, as respondents from higher income brackets repeatedly replace those in lower income brackets. This is entirely consistent with changes in the income distribution of the population, where the median household income in the United States was $32,264 in 1994 and has grown to $49,777 in 2010. In the 1994 exit poll, 62 percent of respondents came from households earning less than $50,000, compared to 38 percent who came from households earning $50,000 or more. Within sixteen years, these numbers had flipped entirely. In the 2010 exit poll, 63 percent of respondents came from households earning $50,000 or more, compared to only 37 percent who came from households earning less than $50,000.

**Figure 3.25**  Composition of the Exit Polls by Household Income, 1994–2010

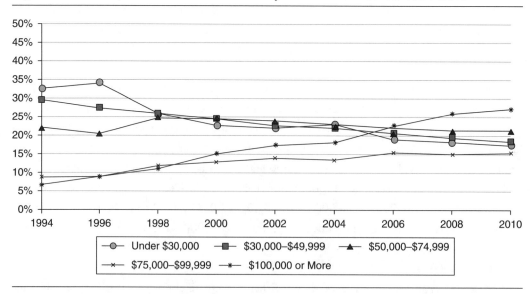

*Source:* National exit polls. See the section in Chapter 2 entitled "Creating a Cumulative National Data Set: Selecting Exit Polls" (pp. 28–29).

*Note:* When using these results to make inferences about the active electorate, the standard errors should be calculated using Table 2.2 (p. 36), which is explained in the adjacent section of Chapter 2, "Analyzing Exit Poll Questions: Estimating Sampling Error" (pp. 34–36). For a guide on how to understand the tables and figures of this chapter, see the section in Chapter 2 entitled "Presenting and Discussing the Exit Poll Data: Reading Chapter 3" (pp. 37–39).

The 2010 exit poll has the highest nominal household incomes to date (see Table 3.25 at the end of the chapter). Respondents from households earning over $100,000 comprised 27 percent of exit poll respondents, whereas respondents from households earning $50,000–$74,999 and $75,000–$100,000 made up 21 percent and 15 percent of exit poll respondents, respectively. Only 37 percent of exit poll respondents came from households earning the median household income or less. Respondents from households earning $30,000–$49,999 comprised 19 percent of the exit poll, and voters from households earning less than $30,000 comprised 18 percent of the exit poll.

## Four-Year Household Financial Situation

Household income does not always give a clear picture of fiscal health, particularly if a voter's income is changing over time. To capture evolving economic circumstances, exit pollsters have queried respondents about their relative financial situation in every presidential year since 1992. Specifically, respondents have been asked whether their household finances have gotten better, gotten worse, or stayed about the same over the previous four years (which is when the last presidential election occurred).

Figure 3.26 shows respondents' perceptions of their four-year household situation in presidential election years occurring from 1992 to 2008. Relative fiscal judgments track with changes in the unemployment rate. As unemployment increased, the ratio of positive to negative financial

**Figure 3.26** Composition of the Exit Polls by Four-Year Household Financial Situation, 1992–2008

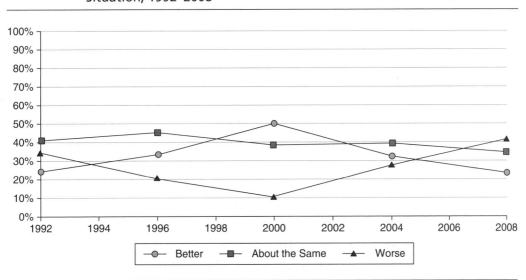

*Source:* National exit polls. See the section in Chapter 2 entitled "Creating a Cumulative National Data Set: Selecting Exit Polls" (pp. 28–29).

*Note:* When using these results to make inferences about the active electorate, the standard errors should be calculated using Table 2.2 (p. 36), which is explained in the adjacent section of Chapter 2, "Analyzing Exit Poll Questions: Estimating Sampling Error" (pp. 34–36). For a guide on how to understand the tables and figures of this chapter, see the section in Chapter 2 entitled "Presenting and Discussing the Exit Poll Data: Reading Chapter 3" (pp. 37–39).

perceptions decreased, whereas when unemployment dropped, the ratio of positive to negative financial perceptions rose. Meanwhile, the proportion of respondents indicating that their financial situation had stayed about the same remained relatively unchanged, fluctuating between 34 and 46 percent over this period.

From 1992 through 2000, the unemployment rate dropped 3.5 points, according to the U.S. Labor Department, moving from 7.4 in November 1992 to 5.4 in November 1996 to 3.9 in November 2000. During this period, the ratio of positive to negative evaluations more than doubled. In 1992, 24 percent of exit poll respondents indicated that their household financial situation had gotten better, whereas 34 percent indicated that it had gotten worse. By 2000, 51 percent of respondents indicated their household finances were improving, whereas 11 percent indicated they were getting worse.

In the past two presidential election cycles, the story flipped completely. The unemployment rate jumped 1.5 points to 5.4 percent in November 2004 and another 1.4 points to 6.8 in November 2008. Meanwhile, the share of exit poll respondents indicating their household finances had gotten better in the past four years dropped 19 points in 2004 and another 8 points in 2008. Conversely, the proportion of respondents who thought that their finances had gotten worse rose 17 points in 2004 and 14 points in 2008.

In the 2008 exit poll, respondents judged the performance of their household finances over the previous four years quite harshly (see Table 3.26 at the end of the chapter). Forty-two percent of respondents indicated that their household financial situation had gotten worse since the 2004 presidential election, which was the most negative that exit poll respondents had been since the question was introduced in 1992. Only 24 percent of respondents said their household finances had gotten better, matching the 1992 election results as the lowest proportion of exit poll respondents to articulate optimism about their finances in the previous four years. The remaining 34 percent of respondents in the 2008 exit poll reported that their household financial situation had remained about the same.

## Two-Year Household Financial Situation

During midterm election years since 1990, to identify a relationship between personal financial situation and congressional vote choice without the confounding role of presidential contests, pollsters have asked exit poll respondents about the performance of their finances in the past two years. The question is identical to that used to gauge perceptions of household finances during the previous four years, save for the change in perspective. Respondents are asked whether their family's financial situation is better today, worse today, or about the same compared to two years earlier.

Similar to the four-year measure, perceptions of household finances over the past two years track with the unemployment rate (see Figure 3.27). Midterm elections yield more negative judgments when the unemployment rate is increasing than when the unemployment rate is declining. From November 1992 to 1994, the unemployment rate dropped 1.8 points to 5.6 percent; from November 1996 to November 1998, it dropped 1 point to 4.4 percent. In the corresponding elections, the share of exit poll respondents indicating that their household finances had gotten worse dropped 3 points and 10 points, respectively.

**Figure 3.27** Composition of the Exit Polls by Two-Year Household Financial Situation, 1990–2010

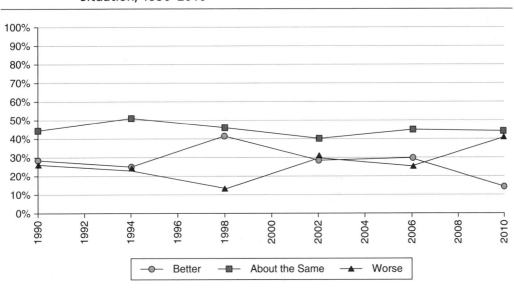

*Source:* National exit polls. See the section in Chapter 2 entitled "Creating a Cumulative National Data Set: Selecting Exit Polls" (pp. 28–29).

*Note:* When using these results to make inferences about the active electorate, the standard errors should be calculated using Table 2.2 (p. 36), which is explained in the adjacent section of Chapter 2, "Analyzing Exit Poll Questions: Estimating Sampling Error" (pp. 34–36). For a guide on how to understand the tables and figures of this chapter, see the section in Chapter 2 entitled "Presenting and Discussing the Exit Poll Data: Reading Chapter 3" (pp. 37–39).

During the 2000s, the two-year financial perceptions of exit poll respondents seesawed up and down, consistent with the dynamics of the unemployment rate. In the 2001–2002 election cycle, the unemployment rate increased 2 points to 5.9 percent, and the proportion of respondents indicating that their finances had worsened grew 17 points and the proportion of respondents indicating that their finances had improved shrunk 12 points. In the 2005–2006 election cycle, the share of those thinking their household situation had improved increased 1 point and the share of those thinking it worsened dropped 6 points, reflecting the roughly 1-point decrease in the unemployment rate. In the 2009–2010 election cycle, the unemployment rate shot up 3 points to 9.8 percent. Similarly, the proportion of exit poll respondents indicating their finances had worsened increased 17 points and the proportion indicating their finances had improved fell 15 points.

The 2010 exit poll saw the harshest judgments of household finances in twenty years (see Table 3.27 at the end of the chapter). Forty-two percent of respondents reported that their household finances had gotten worse, compared to only 15 percent of respondents who reported they had gotten better over the previous two years. Forty-three percent of respondents said that their household finances had remained about the same since the last election.

## Judgments of Current National Economic Conditions

Exit pollsters have also been interested in the relationship between voters' perceptions of the broader economy and their voting decisions. Since 1986, they have solicited judgments of current national economic conditions. Exit poll respondents have been asked whether they think national economic conditions are excellent, good, not so good, or poor. Since the extreme categories attract only a trivial proportion of responses in some years, we have combined "excellent" and "good" as well as "not so good" and "poor" into a pair of categories—performing well and performing badly—to simplify interpretation.

Figure 3.28 shows the distribution of national economic evaluations in the exit polls conducted from 1986 through 2010. Similar to perceptions of household finances, evaluations of the overall economy track with the unemployment rate. As unemployment rises, economic evaluations grow more negative, whereas when unemployment drops, economic evaluations grow more positive. From 1992 to 2000, the October unemployment rate fell each election year, from 7.3 percent to 3.9 percent. At the same time, exit poll respondents became increasingly positive about the economy, with the proportion of respondents judging the economy to be performing well growing from 19 percent to 86 percent. Conversely, the unemployment rate grew during much of the 2000s, reaching 9.8 percent in October 2010. Meanwhile, negative judgments soared. By 2008, more than nine out of ten respondents—nearly the entire exit poll—thought the economy was performing badly.

Judgments of national economic conditions remained overwhelming negative during the 2010 elections (see Table 3.28 at the end of the chapter). A massive 91 percent of exit poll respondents indicated the economy was performing badly. Only 10 percent of respondents thought the economy was performing well.

**Figure 3.28**  Composition of the Exit Polls by Judgments of Current National Economic Conditions, 1986–2010

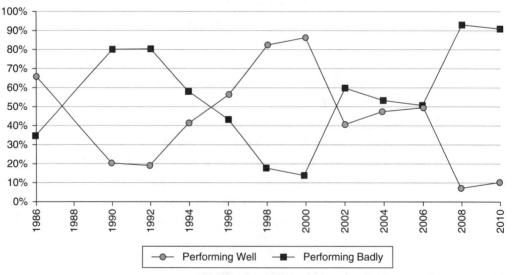

*Source:* National exit polls. See the section in Chapter 2 entitled "Creating a Cumulative National Data Set: Selecting Exit Polls" (pp. 28–29).

*Note:* When using these results to make inferences about the active electorate, the standard errors should be calculated using Table 2.2 (p. 36), which is explained in the adjacent section of Chapter 2, "Analyzing Exit Poll Questions: Estimating Sampling Error" (pp. 34–36). For a guide on how to understand the tables and figures of this chapter, see the section in Chapter 2 entitled "Presenting and Discussing the Exit Poll Data: Reading Chapter 3" (pp. 37–39).

## Judgments of Future National Economic Conditions

Some scholars contend that voters' evaluations of future economic conditions are at least as important to understanding electoral behavior as their judgments of past or present economic conditions.[12] Since 1986, exit pollsters have occasionally included a question tapping respondents' economic forecasts. Specifically, they have asked voters whether they believe the economy will get better, get worse, or stay about the same over the next year.

Figure 3.29 shows exit poll respondents' judgments of future economic conditions in polls conducted from 1986 through 2008. Like perceptions of current economic conditions, their economic forecasts are related to the national unemployment rate. In 1986, 48 percent of respondents thought the economy would remain about the same over next year, consistent with the behavior of the unemployment rate over the preceding year, during which it remained flat, at around 7 percent. In 1990, the majority of respondents thought the economy would likely get worse over the next year, as it had over the previous twelve months, when the unemployment rate increased from 5.3 percent to 5.9 percent. The 1998 and 2000 elections again saw sizable majorities of exit poll respondents speculating that the economy would stay about the same in the next year, as the unemployment rate had in the prior year to each survey, hovering around 4.5 percent throughout 1998 and 4.0 percent throughout 2000.

**Figure 3.29**   Composition of the Exit Polls by Judgments of Future National Economic Conditions, 1986–2008

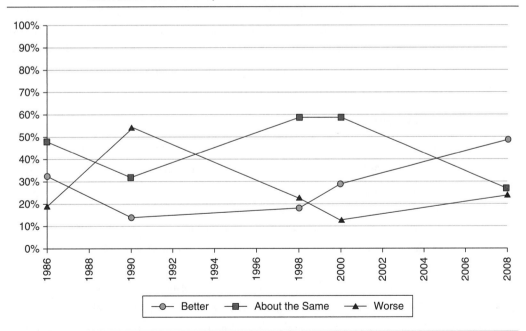

*Source:* National exit polls. See the section in Chapter 2 entitled "Creating a Cumulative National Data Set: Selecting Exit Polls" (pp. 28–29).

*Note:* When using these results to make inferences about the active electorate, the standard errors should be calculated using Table 2.2 (p. 36), which is explained in the adjacent section of Chapter 2, "Analyzing Exit Poll Questions: Estimating Sampling Error" (pp. 34–36). For a guide on how to understand the tables and figures of this chapter, see the section in Chapter 2 entitled "Presenting and Discussing the Exit Poll Data: Reading Chapter 3" (pp. 37–39).

In the 2008 exit poll, respondents diverged from prior behaviors, voicing considerable optimism about future economic conditions in the face of an economic downturn (see Table 3.29 at the end of the chapter). Despite an unemployment rate that had been rising steadily over much of the year, nearly half of the respondents (49 percent) judged the economy would get better over the course of the next year. Only 24 percent of exit poll respondents indicated that the economy would get worse. The remaining 27 percent of respondents thought the economy would stay about the same.

## Comparing the Presidential and Midterm Exit Polls

We conclude this chapter by aggregating all these disparate groups and considering the differences between the exit polls conducted in the presidential and midterm election years. Recall that the turnout rates in midterm and presidential elections are quite distinct (see Figure 3.1 and Table 3.1), differing by 16 percentage points on average. The question remains whether national exit polls are comprised of similar proportions of each group in both presidential and midterm election years or whether the relative distribution of groups varies by election type. Answers to this question are critical to understanding the campaign strategies of the candidates, vote shares, and even policy outcomes.

To assess the relative size of each group participating in the midterm and presidential exit polls over time, we recalculate the average longitudinal share (the figures appearing in the bottom row of each table) of each group analyzed in this chapter by election type. For midterm election years, we average the proportion of responses to each question appearing in the 1978, 1982, 1986, 1990, 1994, 1998, 2002, 2006, and 2010 exit polls. For presidential election years, we use data only from the 1972, 1976, 1980, 1984, 1988, 1992, 1996, 2000, 2004, and 2008 exit polls. Since variability is both extensive and, at times, unpredictable, we omit missing years from the calculation rather than interpolate values for the unavailable data.

### The Presidential Exit Polls

Table 3.30 (at the end of the chapter) reports the average size of each group in the national exit polls conducted in presidential election years from 1972 through 2008. It is rank ordered by magnitude. Topping the chart are the largest groups of respondents in the presidential exit polls, whereas groups at the bottom comprise the smallest share of respondents in the exit polls.

The ten largest groups in the national exit polls each make up at least 58 percent of respondents. Half of the groups are defined by the absence of a politically germane characteristic rather than the presence of one, such as respondents who are *not* gay, not first-time voters, not evangelicals, not living in households with union members, or not living in households with children. The largest groups in the presidential exit polls possessing a noteworthy trait are respondents who are white, are married, work full time, attend religious services less than once a week, or disapprove of Congress.

By comparison, the ten smallest groups in the presidential exit polls each comprise no more than 10 percent of respondents. They are primarily characterized by race—such as black, Hispanic/Latino, Asian, and those of a race other than white, black, Hispanic/Latino, or

Asian—and religious affiliation—such as Jews, those who identify with a religion other than Protestant, Catholic, or Jewish, and those who do not identify with any religion. The remaining groups in the bottom ten are comprised of respondents who are gay, have not completed high school, have voted for a non-major-party candidate in the last presidential election, and are casting ballots for the first time.

Table 3.31 (at the end of the chapter) reports the relative distribution of these groups in the 2008 national exit poll. Comparing groups' shares with their historical averages reveals that the composition of the 2008 presidential exit poll changed only modestly for this historic election. Only a tenth of the seventy-five groups considered in this chapter grew or shrank by more than 10 percentage points from their long-term means; roughly a fifth of the groups changed by more than 5 points.

The groups that changed by more than 10 points from their historical averages were all characterized by their financial judgments or evaluations of the incumbent administration. Respondents who believed current economic conditions were performing badly exceeded their longitudinal average by 36 points, comprising 93 percent of voters in 2008, compared to their average of 57 percent, whereas those who thought that current economic conditions were performing well fell short of their average by 36 points. Respondents who thought the country was off on the wrong track and those who disapproved of the president made up, respectively, 28 points and 20 points more of the exit poll than their long-term average predicted, whereas voters who thought the country was going in the right direction and those who approved of the president comprised, respectively, 27 points and 19 points less than was expected. Finally, respondents who thought future economic conditions would be about the same fell short of their average by 16 points, whereas those whose household finances had gotten worse over the past four years exceeded their average by 15 points.

## The Midterm Exit Polls

The relative distribution of groups in the midterm exit polls is quite comparable to that of the presidential exit polls (see Table 3.32 at the end of the chapter). Nine of the ten largest groups of midterm exit poll respondents are among the ten largest groups of presidential exit poll respondents. Similarly, nine of the ten smallest groups in the midterm exit polls are among the ten smallest groups in the midterm electorate. Moreover, the size of the groups in both electorates is very much alike. The correlation between each group's average share in the midterm exit polls and the presidential exit polls is .95. None of the sixty-five groups for which we have overlapping longitudinal data in both exit polls had an average share in the midterm exit polls that differed by more than 7 percentage points from its average share in the presidential exit polls. In only 14 percent of the groups was their mean composition in the midterm exit poll more than 3 points greater or lesser than it was in the presidential exit poll.

Of the groups that differed the most in their relative sizes between the midterm and presidential electorates, most could be characterized by one of two traits. First, they appear to be differentiated by age. Young respondents (those in the 18–29 age group) had a midterm share 7 points smaller than their presidential share, whereas older respondents (those aged 60 or over) had a 6-point-smaller share in the presidential exit polls than in the midterm exit polls. Similarly, respondents who had not voted in the previous presidential election had a 9-point-smaller share in the midterm exit polls than in the presidential exit polls. Second, they differ by religiosity. Respondents who attended religious services less than once a week had a 5-point-smaller share in the midterm exit polls, and respondents who attended religious services more than once a week had a 5-point-greater share of the midterm exit polls.

The other groups that varied significantly between exit polls were characterized largely by their satisfaction with the incumbent government. Respondents who approved of the incumbent president comprised 6 points more of the midterm exit polls than the presidential exit polls, whereas voters who disapproved of the president comprised 6 points less. Similarly, respondents who thought government does too much comprised 6 points more of the midterm exit polls than the presidential exit polls, and those who thought it does not do enough, therefore, comprised 6 points less. Finally, respondents who voted for a Democrat in the last presidential election comprised 5 points less of the midterm exit polls than the presidential exit polls.

The similarities between the midterm and presidential exit polls extended to the most recent election, in which the 2010 exit poll looked a lot like the 2008 exit poll (see Table 3.33 at the end of the chapter). The size of the groups in the 2010 electorate correlated at .97 with the size of the groups in the 2008 electorate. Only six of the sixty-five groups measured in both elections differed by more than 10 percentage points in their relative size, and all were tied to the presidential transition from Bush to Obama. The proportion of respondents who approved of the president was 17 points higher in the 2010 exit poll than in the 2008 exit poll, whereas the proportion of respondents who disapproved of the president was 17 points lower in 2010 than in 2008. Similarly, the share of respondents in the 2010 exit poll who thought the country was moving in the right direction was 14 points higher than the share of respondents in the 2008 exit poll (and 15 points lower for those who saw it as off on the wrong track). Finally, the proportion of respondents who thought the government was doing too much was 14 points higher in the 2010 exit poll than in the 2008 exit poll, and the proportion of those who thought it should do more was 14 points lower in 2010 than in 2008.

From a historical perspective, the 2010 exit poll deviated from the typical midterm exit poll primarily on economic grounds. Only six groups in the 2010 exit poll differed by more than 10 points from their average share in a midterm electorate, and all the differences were tied to changing economic circumstances. The proportion of respondents who thought current economic conditions were performing badly comprised 35 points more of the 2010 exit poll than their long-term average would predict, and the proportion of respondents who thought current economic conditions were performing well comprised 35 points less of the 2010 exit poll. The share of respondents in the 2010 exit poll whose finances worsened in the previous two years was 15 points higher than their average share, and for those whose finances got better, the share of respondents in 2010 was 14 points lower than the average share. Finally, the share of respondents in the 2010 exit poll who thought the country was off on the wrong track was 11 points higher than their average share, and for those who saw it as moving in the right direction, the share of respondents in 2010 was 11 points lower than the average.

# Notes

[1] Angus Campbell, Philip Converse, Warren E. Miller, and Donald Stokes, *The American Voter* (New York: Wiley, 1960).

[2] All percentages presented in the text have been rounded to the nearest whole number. Any calculations necessary to compute them are also based on rounded whole numbers.

[3] James G. Gimpel and Jason E. Schuknecht, *Cultivating Democracy: Civic Environments and Political Socialization in America* (Washington, DC: Brookings Institution Press, 2003).

[4] Daniel Elazar, *American Federalism: A View from the South* (New York: Crowell, 1966).

[5] James G. Gimpel and Jason E. Schuknecht, *Cultivating Democracy: Civic Environments and Political Socialization in America* (Washington, DC: Brookings Institution Press, 2003); Robert S. Erikson, John P. McIver, and Gerald C. Wright, "State Political Culture and Public Opinion," *American Political Science Review* 81 (1987): 797–813.

[6] David Leege and Lyman A. Kellstedt, *Rediscovering the Religious Factor in American Politics* (New York: M. E. Sharpe, 1993).

[7] Robert D. Putnam, *Bowling Alone* (New York: Simon & Schuster, 2001).

[8] Laura W. Arnold and Herbert Weisberg, "Parenthood, Family Values, and the 1992 Presidential Election," *American Politics Quarterly* 24 (1996): 194–220; Herbert Weisberg, "The Demographics of a New Voting Gap: Marital Differences in American Voting," *Public Opinion Quarterly* 51 (1987): 335–343.

[9] Campbell, Converse, Miller, and Stokes, *The American Voter.*

[10] Ibid.

[11] Gregory B. Markus, "The Impact of Personal and National Economic Conditions on Presidential Voting, 1956–1988," *American Journal of Political Science* 36 (1992): 829–834; Morris P. Fiorina, "Economic Retrospective Voting in American National Elections: A Micro-Analysis," *American Journal of Political Science* 22 (1978): 426–443.

[12] Brad Lockerbie, "Prospective Voting in Presidential Elections, 1956–1988," *American Politics Research* 20 (1992): 308–325.

**Table 3.1**  Turnout Rate of the Voting-Eligible Population, 1972–2010

| Year | Turnout Rate |
| --- | --- |
| 2010 | 41% |
| 2008 | 62% |
| 2006 | 40% |
| 2004 | 60% |
| 2002 | 40% |
| 2000 | 54% |
| 1998 | 38% |
| 1996 | 52% |
| 1994 | 41% |
| 1992 | 58% |
| 1990 | 38% |
| 1988 | 53% |
| 1986 | 38% |
| 1984 | 55% |
| 1982 | 42% |
| 1980 | 54% |
| 1978 | 38% |
| 1976 | 55% |
| 1974 | 39% |
| 1972 | 56% |
| Average | 48% |

*Source:* Michael McDonald, "United States Elections Project," http://elections.gmu.edu/voter_turnout.htm.

**Table 3.2**  Composition of the Exit Polls by Race, 1982–2010

| Year | White | Black | Hispanic/Latino | Asian | Other Race | Number of Respondents |
|------|-------|-------|-----------------|-------|------------|------------------------|
| 2010 | 77.6% | 10.8% | 7.8% | 1.9% | 1.9% | 17,871 |
| 2008 | 75.7% | 13.0% | 6.4% | 2.1% | 2.8% | 17,608 |
| 2006 | 80.6% | 10.2% | 5.6% | 1.7% | 1.9% | 13,560 |
| 2004 | 79.0% | 11.9% | 5.6% | 1.6% | 1.8% | 13,513 |
| 2002 | 82.4% | 9.5% | 4.9% | 1.2% | 2.1% | 17,474 |
| 2000 | 82.2% | 10.2% | 4.1% | 1.8% | 1.6% | 13,035 |
| 1998 | 83.4% | 10.8% | 2.9% | 1.4% | 1.4% | 11,259 |
| 1996 | 83.0% | 10.1% | 4.5% | 1.1% | 1.3% | 16,406 |
| 1994 | 86.0% | 9.1% | 2.7% | 1.2% | 0.9% | 11,205 |
| 1992 | 87.4% | 8.1% | 2.3% | 1.0% | 1.2% | 15,360 |
| 1990 | 90.5% | 5.3% | 2.4% | 1.0% | 0.8% | 19,733 |
| 1988 | 85.1% | 10.2% | 3.2% | | 1.6% | 11,585 |
| 1986 | 87.0% | 7.7% | 2.7% | | 2.5% | 8,964 |
| 1984 | 87.7% | 8.8% | 2.4% | | 1.1% | 9,126 |
| 1982 | 89.1% | 7.1% | 2.7% | | 1.1% | 7,830 |
| Average | 83.8% | 9.5% | 4.0% | 1.5% | 1.6% | |

**Question Wording for Race** (Coded: White = 1; Black = 2; Hispanic/Latino = 3; Asian = 4; Other Race = 5):

**1982–1984 and 1988:** "Are you . . . White (1); Black (2); Hispanic (3); Other (5)"

**1986:** "Are you . . . White (1); Black (2); Hispanic or Latino (3); Other (5)"

**1990 and 1996:** "Are you . . . White (1); Black (2); Hispanic or Latino (3); Asian (4); Other (5)"

**1992–1994 and 1998–2002:** "Are you . . . White (1); Black (2); Hispanic/Latino (3); Asian (4); Other (5)"

**2004–2010:** "Are you . . . White (1); Black (2); Hispanic/Latino (3); Asian (4); Other (5); American Indian (5); Native Alaskan (5)"

*Source:* National exit polls. See the section in Chapter 2 entitled "Creating a Cumulative National Data Set: Selecting Exit Polls" (pp. 28–29).

*Note:* When using these results to make inferences about the active electorate, the standard errors should be calculated using Table 2.2 (p. 36), which is explained in the adjacent section of Chapter 2, "Analyzing Exit Poll Questions: Estimating Sampling Error" (pp. 34–36). For a guide on how to understand the tables and figures of this chapter, see the section in Chapter 2 entitled "Presenting and Discussing the Exit Poll Data: Reading Chapter 3" (pp. 37–39).

**Table 3.3**   Composition of the Exit Polls by Gender, 1972–2010

| Year | Male | Female | Number of Respondents |
|------|------|--------|----------------------|
| 2010 | 48.2% | 51.8% | 18,092 |
| 2008 | 46.7% | 53.3% | 17,937 |
| 2006 | 48.2% | 51.8% | 13,782 |
| 2004 | 46.0% | 54.0% | 13,659 |
| 2002 | 48.1% | 51.9% | 17,682 |
| 2000 | 47.6% | 52.4% | 13,059 |
| 1998 | 49.5% | 50.5% | 11,254 |
| 1996 | 47.9% | 52.1% | 16,416 |
| 1994 | 48.1% | 51.9% | 11,179 |
| 1992 | 47.2% | 52.8% | 14,898 |
| 1990 | 49.1% | 50.9% | 19,519 |
| 1988 | 47.6% | 52.4% | 11,621 |
| 1986 | 48.5% | 51.5% | 8,968 |
| 1984 | 49.0% | 51.0% | 9,149 |
| 1982 | 49.5% | 50.5% | 7,807 |
| 1980 | 50.3% | 49.7% | 15,192 |
| 1978 | 54.6% | 45.4% | 8,794 |
| 1976 | 50.0% | 50.0% | 15,204 |
| 1972 | 50.7% | 49.3% | 17,546 |
| Average | 48.8% | 51.2% | |

**Question Wording for Gender** (Coded: Male = 1; Female = 2):

**1972–1980:** "Interviewer recorded sex of respondent . . . Male (1); Female (2)"

**1982–2010:** "Are you . . . Male (2); Female (2)"

*Source:* National exit polls. See the section in Chapter 2 entitled "Creating a Cumulative National Data Set: Selecting Exit Polls" (pp. 28–29).

*Note:* When using these results to make inferences about the active electorate, the standard errors should be calculated using Table 2.2 (p. 36), which is explained in the adjacent section of Chapter 2, "Analyzing Exit Poll Questions: Estimating Sampling Error" (pp. 34–36). For a guide on how to understand the tables and figures of this chapter, see the section in Chapter 2 entitled "Presenting and Discussing the Exit Poll Data: Reading Chapter 3" (pp. 37–39).

**Table 3.4**  Composition of the Exit Polls by Age, 1972–2010

| Year | 18–29 | 30–44 | 45–59 | 60+ | Number of Respondents |
|------|-------|-------|-------|-----|-----------------------|
| 2010 | 12.0% | 24.3% | 32.1% | 31.7% | 18,035 |
| 2008 | 18.3% | 28.5% | 29.7% | 23.5% | 17,874 |
| 2006 | 12.5% | 24.4% | 34.2% | 28.9% | 13,753 |
| 2004 | 16.9% | 28.6% | 30.0% | 24.5% | 13,639 |
| 2002 | 11.1% | 28.3% | 33.1% | 27.5% | 17,689 |
| 2000 | 16.8% | 32.9% | 28.4% | 22.0% | 13,142 |
| 1998 | 13.4% | 28.9% | 29.6% | 28.1% | 11,312 |
| 1996 | 17.1% | 32.9% | 26.3% | 23.7% | 16,495 |
| 1994 | 13.1% | 32.2% | 27.7% | 27.0% | 11,219 |
| 1992 | 20.7% | 35.8% | 22.9% | 20.6% | 15,256 |
| 1990 | 14.0% | 34.6% | 24.4% | 26.9% | 19,788 |
| 1988 | 20.3% | 35.3% | 22.3% | 22.1% | 11,536 |
| 1986 | 16.0% | 32.3% | 23.8% | 27.8% | 8,945 |
| 1984 | 23.8% | 32.6% | 21.4% | 22.2% | 9,080 |
| 1982 | 14.9% | 31.8% | 25.0% | 28.2% | 7,826 |
| 1980 | 22.9% | 33.0% | 24.3% | 19.8% | 13,918 |
| 1978 | 20.4% | 31.3% | 28.5% | 19.8% | 8,104 |
| 1976 | 29.4% | 29.2% | 26.3% | 15.2% | 12,685 |
| 1972 | 27.5% | 27.1% | 27.8% | 17.6% | 16,510 |
| Average | 18.0% | 30.7% | 27.2% | 24.1% | |

**Question Wording for Age** (Coded: 18–29 = 1; 30–44 = 2; 45–59 = 3; 60+ = 4):

**1972 and 1984–1986:** "To which age group do you belong? . . . 18–24 (1); 25–29 (1); 30–44 (2); 45–59 (3); 60 or over (4)"

**1976 and 1980:** "To which age group do you belong? . . . 18–21 (1); 22–29 (1); 30–44 (2); 45–59 (3); 60 or over (4)"

**1978, 1982, and 1988:** "To which age group do you belong? . . . 18–29 (1); 30–44 (2); 45–59 (3); 60 or over (4)"

**1990:** "To which age group do you belong? . . . 18–29 (1); 30–39 (2); 40–44 (2); 45–49 (3); 50–59 (3); 60 or over (4)"

**1992–1998:** "To which age group do you belong? . . . 18–24 (1); 25–29 (1); 30–39 (2); 40–44 (2); 45–49 (3); 50–59 (3); 60–64 (4); 65 or over (4)"

**2000–2010:** "To which age group do you belong? . . . 18–24 (1); 25–29 (1); 30–39 (2); 40–44 (2); 45–49 (3); 50–59 (3); 60–64 (4); 65–74 (4); 75 or over (4)"

*Source:* National exit polls. See the section in Chapter 2 entitled "Creating a Cumulative National Data Set: Selecting Exit Polls" (pp. 28–29).

*Note:* When using these results to make inferences about the active electorate, the standard errors should be calculated using Table 2.2 (p. 36), which is explained in the adjacent section of Chapter 2, "Analyzing Exit Poll Questions: Estimating Sampling Error" (pp. 34–36). For a guide on how to understand the tables and figures of this chapter, see the section in Chapter 2 entitled "Presenting and Discussing the Exit Poll Data: Reading Chapter 3" (pp. 37–39).

**Table 3.5** Composition of the Exit Polls by Sexual Orientation, 1996–2010

| Year | Gay or Bisexual | Not Gay or Bisexual | Number of Respondents |
|---|---|---|---|
| 2010 | 3.1% | 96.9% | 3,848 |
| 2008 | 3.5% | 96.5% | 4,098 |
| 2006 | 3.1% | 96.9% | 6,063 |
| 2004 | 3.6% | 96.4% | 6,392 |
| 2002 | | | |
| 2000 | 3.8% | 96.2% | 6,082 |
| 1998 | 4.2% | 95.8% | 5,192 |
| 1996 | 5.0% | 95.0% | 3,733 |
| Average | 3.8% | 96.2% | |

**Question Wording for Sexual Orientation** (Coded: Gay or Bisexual = 1; Not Gay or Bisexual = 2):

**1996–2010:** "Are you gay, lesbian, or bisexual? . . . Yes (1); No (2)"

*Source:* National exit polls. See the section in Chapter 2 entitled "Creating a Cumulative National Data Set: Selecting Exit Polls" (pp. 28–29).

*Note:* When using these results to make inferences about the active electorate, the standard errors should be calculated using Table 2.2 (p. 36), which is explained in the adjacent section of Chapter 2, "Analyzing Exit Poll Questions: Estimating Sampling Error" (pp. 34–36). For a guide on how to understand the tables and figures of this chapter, see the section in Chapter 2 entitled "Presenting and Discussing the Exit Poll Data: Reading Chapter 3" (pp. 37–39).

**Table 3.6**   Composition of the Exit Polls by Region, 1972–2010

| Year | East | Midwest | South | West | Number of Respondents |
|------|------|---------|-------|------|----------------------|
| 2010 | 20.8% | 24.9% | 31.1% | 23.2% | 18,132 |
| 2008 | 21.1% | 24.0% | 32.3% | 22.7% | 18,018 |
| 2006 | 22.0% | 27.0% | 29.5% | 21.5% | 13,866 |
| 2004 | 22.4% | 25.5% | 31.6% | 20.4% | 13,719 |
| 2002 | 22.4% | 26.5% | 31.7% | 19.5% | 17,872 |
| 2000 | 22.8% | 25.8% | 30.8% | 20.5% | 13,225 |
| 1998 | 22.0% | 28.0% | 26.0% | 24.0% | 11,387 |
| 1996 | 23.2% | 26.2% | 30.2% | 20.4% | 16,637 |
| 1994 | 23.0% | 27.0% | 27.0% | 23.0% | 11,308 |
| 1992 | 23.5% | 26.7% | 29.4% | 20.4% | 15,490 |
| 1990 | 22.7% | 28.6% | 27.5% | 21.2% | 19,888 |
| 1988 | 24.7% | 27.6% | 28.4% | 19.3% | 11,645 |
| 1986 | | | | | |
| 1984 | 27.0% | 29.0% | 27.0% | 16.9% | 9,174 |
| 1982 | 27.8% | 28.2% | 25.2% | 18.9% | 7,855 |
| 1980 | 25.1% | 28.1% | 28.1% | 18.7% | 15,201 |
| 1978 | 26.5% | 31.1% | 26.7% | 15.8% | 8,808 |
| 1976 | 27.1% | 29.8% | 25.4% | 17.6% | 15,300 |
| 1972 | 28.5% | 29.7% | 23.0% | 18.7% | 17,595 |
| Average | 24.0% | 27.4% | 28.4% | 20.2% | |

**Classification for Region:**

**East:** Connecticut; Delaware; Maine; Maryland; Massachusetts; New Hampshire; New Jersey; New York; Pennsylvania; Rhode Island; Vermont; Washington, DC; West Virginia

**Midwest:** Illinois; Indiana; Iowa; Kansas; Michigan; Minnesota; Missouri; Nebraska; North Dakota; Ohio; South Dakota; Wisconsin

**South:** Alabama; Arkansas; Florida; Georgia; Kentucky; Louisiana; Mississippi; North Carolina; Oklahoma; South Carolina; Tennessee; Texas; Virginia

**West:** Alaska; Arizona; California; Colorado; Hawaii; Idaho; Montana; Nevada; New Mexico; Oregon; Utah; Washington; Wyoming

*Source:* National exit polls. See the section in Chapter 2 entitled "Creating a Cumulative National Data Set: Selecting Exit Polls" (pp. 28–29).

*Note:* When using these results to make inferences about the active electorate, the standard errors should be calculated using Table 2.2 (p. 36), which is explained in the adjacent section of Chapter 2, "Analyzing Exit Poll Questions: Estimating Sampling Error" (pp. 34–36). For a guide on how to understand the tables and figures of this chapter, see the section in Chapter 2 entitled "Presenting and Discussing the Exit Poll Data: Reading Chapter 3" (pp. 37–39).

**Table 3.7**  Composition of the Exit Polls by Population Density of Precinct, 1984–2010

| Year | City | Suburb | Rural | Number of Respondents |
|---|---|---|---|---|
| 2010 | 30.7% | 48.8% | 20.5% | 18,132 |
| 2008 | 29.9% | 49.4% | 20.7% | 18,018 |
| 2006 | 29.8% | 46.6% | 23.5% | 13,866 |
| 2004 | 31.4% | 44.6% | 24.0% | 13,711 |
| 2002 | 30.4% | 44.3% | 25.3% | 17,766 |
| 2000 | 28.8% | 43.4% | 27.8% | 13,022 |
| 1998 | | | | |
| 1996 | 30.9% | 39.2% | 29.9% | 16,637 |
| 1994 | | | | |
| 1992 | 24.7% | 41.0% | 34.3% | 15,490 |
| 1990 | 30.2% | 38.4% | 31.4% | 19,888 |
| 1988 | 26.0% | 42.3% | 31.8% | 11,539 |
| 1986 | | | | |
| 1984 | 28.8% | 38.2% | 33.0% | 9,174 |
| Average | 29.2% | 43.3% | 27.5% | |

**Classification for Population Density:**

**City:** Precinct residing within Census metropolitian statistical area (MSA) containing greater than 50,000 residents

**Suburb:** Precinct residing within Census MSA in close proximity to large urban area

**Rural:** Precinct residing within Census MSA with less than 50,000 residents not in close proximity to large urban area

*Source:* National exit polls. See the section in Chapter 2 entitled "Creating a Cumulative National Data Set: Selecting Exit Polls" (pp. 28–29).

*Note:* When using these results to make inferences about the active electorate, the standard errors should be calculated using Table 2.2 (p. 36), which is explained in the adjacent section of Chapter 2, "Analyzing Exit Poll Questions: Estimating Sampling Error" (pp. 34–36). For a guide on how to understand the tables and figures of this chapter, see the section in Chapter 2 entitled "Presenting and Discussing the Exit Poll Data: Reading Chapter 3" (pp. 37–39).

**Table 3.8**  Composition of the Exit Polls by Religious Affiliation, 1984–2010

| Year | Protestant | Catholic | Jewish | No Religious Affiliation | Other Religion | Number of Respondents |
|------|-----------|----------|--------|--------------------------|----------------|----------------------|
| 2010 | 54.6% | 23.1% | 2.2% | 12.3% | 7.8% | 3,934 |
| 2008 | 54.1% | 26.4% | 2.1% | 11.7% | 5.7% | 4,145 |
| 2006 | 55.3% | 26.0% | 2.1% | 10.7% | 5.9% | 6,445 |
| 2004 | 54.1% | 26.7% | 2.6% | 10.0% | 6.7% | 9,826 |
| 2002 | 55.9% | 26.6% | 3.1% | 8.2% | 6.2% | 8,124 |
| 2000 | 54.7% | 26.0% | 3.5% | 9.3% | 6.5% | 9,251 |
| 1998 | 53.9% | 27.7% | 2.6% | 8.4% | 7.4% | 5,404 |
| 1996 | 54.4% | 28.9% | 3.4% | 7.5% | 5.8% | 7,753 |
| 1994 | 54.4% | 29.6% | 3.6% | 7.6% | 4.9% | 5,364 |
| 1992 | 55.8% | 26.9% | 3.9% | 7.0% | 6.5% | 7,853 |
| 1990 | 58.3% | 25.0% | 3.2% | 7.8% | 5.7% | 8,887 |
| 1988 | 56.8% | 28.3% | 4.2% | 5.3% | 5.4% | 11,004 |
| 1986 | 53.5% | 32.9% | 3.9% | 4.8% | 4.8% | 8,563 |
| 1984 | 58.9% | 27.6% | 3.5% | 5.0% | 5.0% | 8,642 |
| Average | 55.3% | 27.3% | 3.1% | 8.3% | 6.0% | |

**Question Wording for Religious Affiliation** (Coded: Protestant = 1; Catholic = 2; Jewish = 3; No Religious Affiliation = 4; Other Religion = 5):

**1984–1988:** "Your religion . . . Protestant (1); Catholic (2); Other Christian (1); Jewish (3); Something else (5); None (4)"

**1990:** "Your religious preference today? . . . Protestant (1); Catholic (2); Other Christian (1); Jewish (3); Something else (5); None (4)"

**1992–2000:** "Are you . . . Protestant (1); Catholic (2); Other Christian (1); Jewish (3); Something else (5); None (4)"

**2002:** "Are you . . . Protestant (1); Catholic (2); Other Christian (1); Jewish (3); Muslim (5); Something else (5); None (4)"

**2004–2010:** "Are you . . . Protestant (1); Catholic (2); Mormon/LDS (5); Other Christian (1); Jewish (3); Muslim (5); Something else (5); None (4)"

*Source:* National exit polls. See the section in Chapter 2 entitled "Creating a Cumulative National Data Set: Selecting Exit Polls" (pp. 28–29).

*Note:* When using these results to make inferences about the active electorate, the standard errors should be calculated using Table 2.2 (p. 36), which is explained in the adjacent section of Chapter 2, "Analyzing Exit Poll Questions: Estimating Sampling Error" (pp. 34–36). For a guide on how to understand the tables and figures of this chapter, see the section in Chapter 2 entitled "Presenting and Discussing the Exit Poll Data: Reading Chapter 3" (pp. 37–39).

**Table 3.9**  Composition of the Exit Polls by Religious Attendance, 2000–2010

| Year | Once a Week or More | Less Than Once a Week | Number of Respondents |
|---|---|---|---|
| 2010 | 48.1% | 51.9% | 3,957 |
| 2008 | 40.5% | 59.5% | 4,151 |
| 2006 | 45.7% | 54.3% | 6,455 |
| 2004 | 42.7% | 57.3% | 9,853 |
| 2002 | 46.4% | 53.6% | 8,117 |
| 2000 | 43.3% | 56.7% | 6,213 |
| Average | 44.5% | 55.5% | |

**Question Wording for Religious Attendance** (Coded: Once a Week or More = 1; Less Than Once a Week = 2):

**2000–2008:** "How often do you attend religious services? . . . More than once a week (1); Once a week (1); A few times a month (2); A few times a year (2); Never (2)"

**2010:** "Do you attend religious services once a week or more? . . . Yes (1); No (2)"

*Source:* National exit polls. See the section in Chapter 2 entitled "Creating a Cumulative National Data Set: Selecting Exit Polls" (pp. 28–29).

*Note:* When using these results to make inferences about the active electorate, the standard errors should be calculated using Table 2.2 (p. 36), which is explained in the adjacent section of Chapter 2, "Analyzing Exit Poll Questions: Estimating Sampling Error" (pp. 34–36). For a guide on how to understand the tables and figures of this chapter, see the section in Chapter 2 entitled "Presenting and Discussing the Exit Poll Data: Reading Chapter 3" (pp. 37–39).

**Table 3.10**  Composition of the Exit Polls by Evangelical, 2004–2010

| Year | Born Again | Not Born Again | Number of Respondents |
|---|---|---|---|
| 2010 | 36.5% | 63.5% | 3,859 |
| 2008 | 38.5% | 61.5% | 12,992 |
| 2006 | 33.6% | 66.4% | 6,321 |
| 2004 | 34.7% | 65.3% | 9,659 |
| Average | 35.8% | 64.2% | |

**Question Wording for Evangelical** (Coded: Born Again = 1; Not Born Again = 2):

**2004–2010:** "Would you describe yourself as a born again or evangelical Christian? ... Yes (1); No (2)"

*Source:* National exit polls. See the section in Chapter 2 entitled "Creating a Cumulative National Data Set: Selecting Exit Polls" (pp. 28–29).

*Note:* When using these results to make inferences about the active electorate, the standard errors should be calculated using Table 2.2 (p. 36), which is explained in the adjacent section of Chapter 2, "Analyzing Exit Poll Questions: Estimating Sampling Error" (pp. 34–36). For a guide on how to understand the tables and figures of this chapter, see the section in Chapter 2 entitled "Presenting and Discussing the Exit Poll Data: Reading Chapter 3" (pp. 37–39).

**Table 3.11**   Composition of the Exit Polls by Education, 1986–2010

| Year | Did Not Complete High School | High School Graduate | Some College | College Graduate | Postgraduate | Number of Respondents |
|------|------|------|------|------|------|------|
| 2010 | 3.1% | 17.2% | 28.2% | 30.4% | 21.1% | 17,269 |
| 2008 | 4.1% | 20.4% | 31.1% | 27.8% | 16.6% | 17,748 |
| 2006 | 3.2% | 20.7% | 31.1% | 26.8% | 18.2% | 6,345 |
| 2004 | 4.2% | 21.9% | 31.7% | 25.6% | 16.5% | 9,986 |
| 2002 | 4.2% | 22.4% | 31.3% | 24.3% | 17.8% | 8,211 |
| 2000 | 4.8% | 21.4% | 32.0% | 24.2% | 17.5% | 9,360 |
| 1998 | 5.3% | 22.5% | 27.6% | 27.0% | 17.6% | 5,394 |
| 1996 | 6.3% | 23.6% | 27.1% | 25.6% | 17.4% | 8,162 |
| 1994 | 6.1% | 22.8% | 28.1% | 26.2% | 16.8% | 5,317 |
| 1992 | 7.1% | 25.3% | 29.0% | 23.0% | 15.6% | 8,145 |
| 1990 | 6.6% | 27.6% | 27.8% | 22.5% | 15.5% | 10,005 |
| 1988 | 7.6% | 27.0% | 30.1% | 18.8% | 16.5% | 10,955 |
| 1986 | 8.4% | 31.4% | 29.0% | 16.7% | 14.5% | 8,490 |
| Average | 5.5% | 23.4% | 29.5% | 24.5% | 17.1% | |

**Question Wording for Education** (Coded: Did Not Complete High School = 1; High School Graduate = 2; Some College = 3; College Graduate = 4; Postgraduate = 5):

**1986–1988:** "What was the last grade in school you completed? . . . Did not graduate from high school (1); High school graduate (2); Some college but not four years (3); College graduate (4); Postgraduate study (5)"

**1990–1998:** "What was the last grade of school you completed? . . . Did not complete high school (1); High school graduate (2); Some college, but no degree (3); College graduate (4); Postgraduate study (5)"

**2000–2010:** "What was the last grade of school you completed? . . . Did not complete high school (1); High school graduate (2); Some college or associate degree (3); College graduate (4); Postgraduate study (5)"

*Source:* National exit polls. See the section in Chapter 2 entitled "Creating a Cumulative National Data Set: Selecting Exit Polls" (pp. 28–29).

*Note:* When using these results to make inferences about the active electorate, the standard errors should be calculated using Table 2.2 (p. 36), which is explained in the adjacent section of Chapter 2, "Analyzing Exit Poll Questions: Estimating Sampling Error" (pp. 34–36). For a guide on how to understand the tables and figures of this chapter, see the section in Chapter 2 entitled "Presenting and Discussing the Exit Poll Data: Reading Chapter 3" (pp. 37–39).

**Table 3.12**  Composition of the Exit Polls by Employment Status, 1996–2008

| Year | Employed Full Time | Not Employed Full Time | Number of Respondents |
|---|---|---|---|
| 2008 | 64.4% | 35.6% | 4,196 |
| 2006 | | | |
| 2004 | 60.2% | 39.8% | 3,260 |
| 2002 | 61.9% | 38.1% | 8,876 |
| 2000 | 66.8% | 33.2% | 9,760 |
| 1998 | 63.2% | 36.8% | 5,401 |
| 1996 | 64.2% | 35.8% | 11,560 |
| Average | 63.4% | 36.6% | |

Question Wording for Employment Status (Coded: Employed Full Time = 1; Not Employed Full Time = 2):

**1996 and 2000–2008:** "Do you work full time for pay? . . . Yes (1); No (2)"

**1998:** "Do you work for full time pay? . . . Yes (1); No (2)"

*Source:* National exit polls. See the section in Chapter 2 entitled "Creating a Cumulative National Data Set: Selecting Exit Polls" (pp. 28–29).

*Note:* When using these results to make inferences about the active electorate, the standard errors should be calculated using Table 2.2 (p. 36), which is explained in the adjacent section of Chapter 2, "Analyzing Exit Poll Questions: Estimating Sampling Error" (pp. 34–36). For a guide on how to understand the tables and figures of this chapter, see the section in Chapter 2 entitled "Presenting and Discussing the Exit Poll Data: Reading Chapter 3" (pp. 37–39).

**Table 3.13**  Composition of the Exit Polls by Marital Status, 1992–2008

| Year | Married | Not Married | Number of Respondents |
|---|---|---|---|
| 2008 | 65.9% | 34.1% | 4,344 |
| 2006 | 68.0% | 32.0% | 6,460 |
| 2004 | 62.7% | 37.3% | 13,270 |
| 2002 | 69.8% | 30.2% | 8,253 |
| 2000 | 65.2% | 34.8% | 9,357 |
| 1998 | 67.2% | 32.8% | 5,696 |
| 1996 | 65.7% | 34.3% | 11,470 |
| 1994 | | | |
| 1992 | 66.1% | 33.9% | 7,948 |
| Average | 66.3% | 33.7% | |

Question Wording for Marital Status (Coded: Married = 1; Not Married = 2):

**1992:** "Are you . . . Married (1); Single, never married (2); Widowed (2); Divorced/Separated (2)"

**1996–2008:** "Are you currently married? . . . Yes (1); No (2)"

*Source:* National exit polls. See the section in Chapter 2 entitled "Creating a Cumulative National Data Set: Selecting Exit Polls" (pp. 28–29).

*Note:* When using these results to make inferences about the active electorate, the standard errors should be calculated using Table 2.2 (p. 36), which is explained in the adjacent section of Chapter 2, "Analyzing Exit Poll Questions: Estimating Sampling Error" (pp. 34–36). For a guide on how to understand the tables and figures of this chapter, see the section in Chapter 2 entitled "Presenting and Discussing the Exit Poll Data: Reading Chapter 3" (pp. 37–39).

**Table 3.14** Composition of the Exit Polls by Child in Household, 1996–2010

| Year | Child in Household | No Child in Household | Number of Respondents |
|------|--------------------|-----------------------|------------------------|
| 2010 | 34.0% | 66.0% | 4,124 |
| 2008 | 39.7% | 60.3% | 4,348 |
| 2006 | 34.2% | 65.8% | 12,879 |
| 2004 | 37.0% | 63.0% | 10,035 |
| 2002 | 38.2% | 61.8% | 8,255 |
| 2000 | 38.7% | 61.3% | 9,401 |
| 1998 | 34.8% | 65.2% | 5,705 |
| 1996 | 36.4% | 63.6% | 11,617 |
| Average | 36.6% | 63.4% | |

**Question Wording for Child in Household** (Coded: Child in Household = 1; No Child in Household = 2):

**1996:** "Do you have a child under 18 living at home? . . . Yes (1); No (2)"

**1998–2010:** "Do you have any children under 18 living in your household? . . . Yes (1); No (2)"

*Source:* National exit polls. See the section in Chapter 2 entitled "Creating a Cumulative National Data Set: Selecting Exit Polls" (pp. 28–29).

*Note:* When using these results to make inferences about the active electorate, the standard errors should be calculated using Table 2.2 (p. 36), which is explained in the adjacent section of Chapter 2, "Analyzing Exit Poll Questions: Estimating Sampling Error" (pp. 34–36). For a guide on how to understand the tables and figures of this chapter, see the section in Chapter 2 entitled "Presenting and Discussing the Exit Poll Data: Reading Chapter 3" (pp. 37–39).

**Table 3.15**  Composition of the Exit Polls by Union Household, 1972–2010

| Year | Union Household | Not a Union Household | Number of Respondents |
|---|---|---|---|
| 2010 | 17.5% | 82.5% | 3,967 |
| 2008 | 21.1% | 78.9% | 4,170 |
| 2006 | 23.2% | 76.8% | 6,763 |
| 2004 | 23.8% | 76.2% | 9,990 |
| 2002 | 23.2% | 76.8% | 8,194 |
| 2000 | 26.2% | 73.8% | 9,725 |
| 1998 | 22.7% | 77.3% | 5,651 |
| 1996 | 23.6% | 76.4% | 7,731 |
| 1994 | | | |
| 1992 | | | |
| 1990 | | | |
| 1988 | 25.5% | 74.5% | 10,899 |
| 1986 | 28.3% | 71.7% | 8,570 |
| 1984 | 26.8% | 73.2% | 8,665 |
| 1982 | 27.5% | 72.5% | 7,269 |
| 1980 | 30.7% | 69.3% | 13,574 |
| 1978 | 31.5% | 68.5% | 8,009 |
| 1976 | 33.7% | 66.3% | 12,344 |
| 1972 | 32.3% | 67.7% | 16,123 |
| Average | 26.1% | 73.9% | |

Question Wording for Union Household (Coded: Union Household = 1; Not a Union Household = 2):

**1972–1980:** "Are you or is anyone living in your household a union member? . . . Yes (1); No (2)"

**1982:** "Are you or is anyone living in your household a member of a labor union? . . . Yes (1); No (2)"

**1984:** "Are you or is any person in your household a member of a labor union? . . . Yes, I do (1); Yes, other family member (1); No (2)"

**1986–1988:** "Are you or is any person living in your household a member of a labor union? . . . Yes, I do (1); Yes, other family member (1); No (2)"

**1996:** "Do you or someone in your household belong to a labor union? . . . Yes (1); No (2)"

**1998:** "Do you or does someone else in your household belong to a labor union? . . . Yes (1); No (2)"

**2000–2008:** "Do you or does someone in your household belong to a labor union? . . . Yes, I do (1); Yes, someone else does (1); Yes, I do and someone else does (1); No one does (2)"

**2010:** "Does someone in your household belong to a labor union? . . . Yes (1); No (2)"

*Source:* National exit polls. See the section in Chapter 2 entitled "Creating a Cumulative National Data Set: Selecting Exit Polls" (pp. 28–29).

*Note:* When using these results to make inferences about the active electorate, the standard errors should be calculated using Table 2.2 (p. 36), which is explained in the adjacent section of Chapter 2, "Analyzing Exit Poll Questions: Estimating Sampling Error" (pp. 34–36). For a guide on how to understand the tables and figures of this chapter, see the section in Chapter 2 entitled "Presenting and Discussing the Exit Poll Data: Reading Chapter 3" (pp. 37–39).

**Table 3.16**  Composition of the Exit Polls by Party Identification, 1972–2010

| Year | Democrat | Republican | Independent | Number of Respondents |
|------|----------|------------|-------------|-----------------------|
| 2010 | 35.3% | 35.0% | 29.7% | 17,302 |
| 2008 | 39.1% | 32.1% | 28.8% | 17,774 |
| 2006 | 37.7% | 35.5% | 26.8% | 12,850 |
| 2004 | 36.5% | 37.1% | 26.3% | 13,121 |
| 2002 | 37.6% | 39.5% | 22.9% | 16,064 |
| 2000 | 38.6% | 34.7% | 26.7% | 12,432 |
| 1998 | 37.3% | 35.0% | 27.7% | 10,723 |
| 1996 | 39.4% | 34.7% | 25.9% | 15,422 |
| 1994 | 36.0% | 35.4% | 28.7% | 10,575 |
| 1992 | 37.9% | 34.7% | 27.4% | 14,622 |
| 1990 | 36.6% | 33.6% | 29.8% | 19,010 |
| 1988 | 38.1% | 35.5% | 26.4% | 10,936 |
| 1986 | 39.7% | 34.3% | 26.0% | 8,550 |
| 1984 | 38.3% | 35.5% | 26.1% | 9,148 |
| 1982 | 45.6% | 30.3% | 24.2% | 7,695 |
| 1980 | 44.8% | 29.6% | 25.6% | 14,718 |
| 1978 | 40.8% | 27.1% | 32.1% | 7,982 |
| 1976 | 41.4% | 24.9% | 33.7% | 12,556 |
| 1972 | 45.9% | 34.8% | 19.3% | 16,395 |
| Average | 39.3% | 33.6% | 27.1% | |

**Question Wording for Party Identification** (Coded: Democrat = 1; Republican = 2; Independent = 3):

**1972:** "Do you usually think of yourself as a . . . Democrat (1); Republican (2); Independent (3); Other (3)"

**1976–1988:** "Do you usually think of yourself as a . . . Democrat (1); Republican (2); Independent (3)"

**1990–2010:** "No matter how you voted today, do you usually think of yourself as a . . . Democrat (1); Republican (2); Independent (3); Something else (3)"

*Source:* National exit polls. See the section in Chapter 2 entitled "Creating a Cumulative National Data Set: Selecting Exit Polls" (pp. 28–29).

*Note:* When using these results to make inferences about the active electorate, the standard errors should be calculated using Table 2.2 (p. 36), which is explained in the adjacent section of Chapter 2, "Analyzing Exit Poll Questions: Estimating Sampling Error" (pp. 34–36). For a guide on how to understand the tables and figures of this chapter, see the section in Chapter 2 entitled "Presenting and Discussing the Exit Poll Data: Reading Chapter 3" (pp. 37–39).

**Table 3.17**  Composition of the Exit Polls by Ideological Identification, 1976–2010

| Year | Liberal | Moderate | Conservative | Number of Respondents |
|------|---------|----------|--------------|------------------------|
| 2010 | 20.2% | 38.6% | 41.3% | 16,981 |
| 2008 | 21.7% | 44.3% | 34.0% | 16,903 |
| 2006 | 20.4% | 47.4% | 32.2% | 12,667 |
| 2004 | 21.0% | 45.5% | 33.5% | 12,939 |
| 2002 | 17.3% | 48.8% | 34.0% | 15,853 |
| 2000 | 20.4% | 50.2% | 29.4% | 12,250 |
| 1998 | 19.3% | 50.2% | 30.5% | 10,572 |
| 1996 | 19.6% | 47.2% | 33.2% | 15,205 |
| 1994 | 17.9% | 45.0% | 37.1% | 5,276 |
| 1992 | 21.3% | 48.9% | 29.8% | 7,749 |
| 1990 | 19.4% | 46.4% | 34.2% | 9,898 |
| 1988 | 18.3% | 47.1% | 34.7% | 10,815 |
| 1986 | 17.1% | 48.1% | 34.8% | 8,447 |
| 1984 | 17.0% | 47.2% | 35.8% | 8,467 |
| 1982 | 16.8% | 53.2% | 30.0% | 7,613 |
| 1980 | 17.5% | 50.6% | 32.0% | 14,095 |
| 1978 | 18.0% | 48.3% | 33.7% | 7,835 |
| 1976 | 19.7% | 48.7% | 31.7% | 11,860 |
| Average | 19.1% | 47.5% | 33.4% | |

**Question Wording for Ideological Identification** (Coded: Liberal = 1; Moderate = 2; Conservative = 3):

**1976–2010:** "On most political matters, do you consider yourself . . . Liberal (1); Moderate (2); Conservative (3)"

*Source:* National exit polls. See the section in Chapter 2 entitled "Creating a Cumulative National Data Set: Selecting Exit Polls" (pp. 28–29).

*Note:* When using these results to make inferences about the active electorate, the standard errors should be calculated using Table 2.2 (p. 36), which is explained in the adjacent section of Chapter 2, "Analyzing Exit Poll Questions: Estimating Sampling Error" (pp. 34–36). For a guide on how to understand the tables and figures of this chapter, see the section in Chapter 2 entitled "Presenting and Discussing the Exit Poll Data: Reading Chapter 3" (pp. 37–39).

**Table 3.18**  Composition of the Exit Polls by Presidential Vote in Last Election, 1972–2010

| Year | Democrat | Republican | Other Candidate | Did Not Vote | Number of Respondents |
|------|----------|------------|-----------------|--------------|-----------------------|
| 2010 | 45.8% | 46.0% | 3.7% | 4.5% | 8,936 |
| 2008 | 37.6% | 45.9% | 3.7% | 12.8% | 4,178 |
| 2006 | 43.2% | 48.9% | 4.1% | 3.8% | 6,361 |
| 2004 | 36.7% | 43.0% | 3.5% | 16.8% | 3,182 |
| 2002 | 37.9% | 53.8% | 3.8% | 4.5% | 7,886 |
| 2000 | 46.4% | 31.8% | 9.1% | 12.7% | 6,252 |
| 1998 | 48.3% | 37.4% | 9.5% | 4.8% | 5,434 |
| 1996 | 43.4% | 34.8% | 13.3% | 8.5% | 15,400 |
| 1994 | 43.2% | 38.1% | 14.9% | 3.8% | 10,572 |
| 1992 | 27.2% | 54.8% | 2.5% | 15.4% | 14,947 |
| 1990 | 31.7% | 58.7% | 3.9% | 5.7% | 10,033 |
| 1988 | 28.2% | 57.1% | 3.8% | 10.9% | 10,990 |
| 1986 | 31.0% | 59.2% | 4.9% | 4.8% | 8,615 |
| 1984 | 31.9% | 51.1% | 5.0% | 12.0% | 8,653 |
| 1982 | 33.6% | 51.6% | 7.4% | 7.4% | 7,596 |
| 1980 | 48.8% | 37.2% | 2.3% | 11.6% | 13,814 |
| 1978 | 49.9% | 40.6% | 3.9% | 5.6% | 7,962 |
| 1976 | 27.6% | 50.2% | 5.6% | 16.6% | 12,061 |
| 1972 | 23.9% | 47.6% | 7.0% | 21.5% | 16,111 |
| Average | 37.7% | 46.7% | 5.9% | 9.7% | |

**Question Wording for Presidential Vote in Last Election** (Coded: Democrat = 1; Republican = 2; Other Candidate = 3; Did Not Vote = 4):

**1972:** "In 1968, for whom did you vote? . . . Nixon (2); Humphrey (1); Wallace (3); Other (3); Didn't vote (4)"

**1976:** "In 1972, for whom did you vote? . . . Nixon (2); McGovern (1); Someone else (3); Did not vote (4)"

**1978:** "In 1976, for whom did you vote? . . . Carter (1); Ford (2); Someone else (3); Did not vote (4)"

**1980:** "In 1976, for whom did you vote? . . . Jimmy Carter (1); Gerald Ford (2); Someone else (3); Did not vote (4)"

**1982:** "How did you vote in the 1980 election for president? . . . Carter (1); Reagan (2); Anderson (3); Someone else (3); Did not vote for president in [Year] (4)"

**1984:** "Who did you vote for in the 1980 presidential election? . . . Carter (1); Reagan (2); Anderson (3); Didn't vote (4)"

**1986:** "Who did you vote for in the 1984 presidential election? . . . Reagan (2); Mondale (1); Someone else (3); Didn't vote for president (4)"

**1988:** "Who did you vote for in the 1984 presidential election? . . . Reagan (2); Mondale (1); Someone else (3); Didn't vote (4)"

**1990:** "Who did you vote for in the 1988 presidential election? . . . George Bush (2); Michael Dukakis (1); Someone else (3); Didn't happen to vote in [Year] (4)"

**1992:** "Who did you vote for in the 1988 presidential election? . . . George Bush (Rep) (2); Michael Dukakis (Dem) (1); Someone else (3); Did not vote in [Year] (4)"

**1994:** "Who did you vote for in the 1992 presidential election? . . . George Bush (Rep) (2); Bill Clinton (Dem) (1); Ross Perot (Ind) (3); Someone else (3); Did not vote in [Year] (4)"

**1996:** "Who did you vote for in the 1992 presidential election? . . . George Bush (Rep) (2); Bill Clinton (Dem) (1); Ross Perot (Ind) (3); Someone else (3); Did not vote for President (4)"

**1998:** "Who did you vote for in the 1996 presidential election? . . . Bill Clinton (Dem) (1); Bob Dole (Rep) (2); Ross Perot (Ref) (3); Someone else (3); Did not vote for president in [Year] (4)"

**2000:** "In the 1996 election for president, did you vote for . . . Bill Clinton (Dem) (1); Bob Dole (Rep) (2); Ross Perot (Ref) (3); Someone else (3); Did not vote (4)"

**2002:** "In the 2000 election for president, did you vote for . . . Al Gore (Dem) (1); George W. Bush (Rep) (2); Ralph Nader (Gre) (3); Someone else (3); Did not vote (4)"

**2004:** "Did you vote in the 2000 presidential election? . . . Yes, for Al Gore (1); Yes, for George W. Bush (2); Yes, for another candidate (3); No, I did not vote (4)"

**2006–2008:** "In the 2004 election for president, did you vote for . . . George W. Bush (Rep) (2); John Kerry (Dem) (1); Someone else (3); Did not vote (4)"

**2010:** "In the 2008 election for president, did you vote for . . . Obama (D) (1); McCain (2); Other (3); Didn't vote (4)"

*Source:* National exit polls. See the section in Chapter 2 entitled "Creating a Cumulative National Data Set: Selecting Exit Polls" (pp. 28–29).

*Note:* When using these results to make inferences about the active electorate, the standard errors should be calculated using Table 2.2 (p. 36), which is explained in the adjacent section of Chapter 2, "Analyzing Exit Poll Questions: Estimating Sampling Error" (pp. 34–36). For a guide on how to understand the tables and figures of this chapter, see the section in Chapter 2 entitled "Presenting and Discussing the Exit Poll Data: Reading Chapter 3" (pp. 37–39).

**Table 3.19** Composition of the Exit Polls by Presidential Approval, 1978–2010

| Year | Approve | Disapprove | Number of Respondents |
|---|---|---|---|
| 2010 | 44.5% | 55.5% | 4,422 |
| 2008 | 27.5% | 72.5% | 4,282 |
| 2006 | 42.9% | 57.1% | 6,943 |
| 2004 | 53.7% | 46.3% | 6,913 |
| 2002 | 65.6% | 34.4% | 8,738 |
| 2000 | 58.4% | 41.6% | 6,177 |
| 1998 | 56.8% | 43.2% | 11,112 |
| 1996 | | | |
| 1994 | 46.3% | 53.7% | 10,299 |
| 1992 | | | |
| 1990 | 60.1% | 39.9% | 18,491 |
| 1988 | | | |
| 1986 | 63.2% | 36.8% | 8,319 |
| 1984 | | | |
| 1982 | 52.3% | 47.7% | 7,159 |
| 1980 | | | |
| 1978 | 48.0% | 52.0% | 7,576 |
| Average | 51.6% | 48.4% | |

**Question Wording for Presidential Approval** (Coded: Approve = 1; Disapprove = 2):

**1978:** "On most political matters, do you approve or disapprove of the way [President] is handling his job as president? . . . Approve (1); Disapprove (2)"

**1982–2002:** "Do you approve or disapprove of the way [President] is handling his job as president? . . . Approve (1); Disapprove (2)"

**2004–2010:** "Do you approve or disapprove of the way [President] is handling his job as president? . . . Strongly approve (1); Somewhat approve (1); Somewhat disapprove (2); Strongly disapprove (2)"

*Source:* National exit polls. See the section in Chapter 2 entitled "Creating a Cumulative National Data Set: Selecting Exit Polls" (pp. 28–29).

*Note:* When using these results to make inferences about the active electorate, the standard errors should be calculated using Table 2.2 (p. 36), which is explained in the adjacent section of Chapter 2, "Analyzing Exit Poll Questions: Estimating Sampling Error" (pp. 34–36). For a guide on how to understand the tables and figures of this chapter, see the section in Chapter 2 entitled "Presenting and Discussing the Exit Poll Data: Reading Chapter 3" (pp. 37–39).

**Table 3.20** Composition of the Exit Polls by Congressional Approval, 1990–2010

| Year | Approve | Disapprove | Number of Respondents |
|------|---------|------------|----------------------|
| 2010 | 24.2% | 75.8% | 4,392 |
| 2008 | 24.5% | 75.5% | 4,488 |
| 2006 | 37.6% | 62.4% | 6,457 |
| 2004 | | | |
| 2002 | 46.9% | 53.1% | 7,953 |
| 2000 | | | |
| 1998 | 42.6% | 57.4% | 5,482 |
| 1996 | | | |
| 1994 | 16.6% | 83.4% | 5,220 |
| 1992 | | | |
| 1990 | 19.7% | 80.3% | 9,825 |
| Average | 30.3% | 69.7% | |

**Question Wording for Congressional Approval** (Coded: Approve = 1; Disapprove = 2):

**1990–2002:** "Do you approve or disapprove of the way Congress is handling its job? . . . Approve (1); Disapprove (2)"

**2006–2010:** "Do you approve or disapprove of the way Congress is handling its job? . . . Strongly approve (1); Somewhat approve (1); Somewhat disapprove (2); Strongly disapprove (2)"

*Source:* National exit polls. See the section in Chapter 2 entitled "Creating a Cumulative National Data Set: Selecting Exit Polls" (pp. 28–29).

*Note:* When using these results to make inferences about the active electorate, the standard errors should be calculated using Table 2.2 (p. 36), which is explained in the adjacent section of Chapter 2, "Analyzing Exit Poll Questions: Estimating Sampling Error" (pp. 34–36). For a guide on how to understand the tables and figures of this chapter, see the section in Chapter 2 entitled "Presenting and Discussing the Exit Poll Data: Reading Chapter 3" (pp. 37–39).

**Table 3.21** Composition of the Exit Polls by Perceived Direction of the Country, 1990–2010

| Year | Right Direction | Wrong Track | Number of Respondents |
|------|-----------------|-------------|----------------------|
| 2010 | 35.8% | 64.2% | 4,330 |
| 2008 | 21.5% | 78.5% | 4,087 |
| 2006 | 42.4% | 57.6% | 6,215 |
| 2004 | 51.5% | 48.5% | 3,295 |
| 2002 | 58.9% | 41.1% | 8,556 |
| 2000 | 67.8% | 32.2% | 6,099 |
| 1998 | 61.6% | 38.4% | 5,386 |
| 1996 | 54.9% | 45.1% | 3,799 |
| 1994 | 40.3% | 59.7% | 5,400 |
| 1992 | | | |
| 1990 | 40.9% | 59.1% | 9,823 |
| Average | 47.6% | 52.4% | |

**Question Wording for Perceived Direction of the Country** (Coded: Right Direction = 1; Wrong Track = 2):

**1990–2010:** "Do you think things in this country today are: . . . Generally going in the right direction (1); Seriously off on the wrong track (2)"

*Source:* National exit polls. See the section in Chapter 2 entitled "Creating a Cumulative National Data Set: Selecting Exit Polls" (pp. 28–29).

*Note:* When using these results to make inferences about the active electorate, the standard errors should be calculated using Table 2.2 (p. 36), which is explained in the adjacent section of Chapter 2, "Analyzing Exit Poll Questions: Estimating Sampling Error" (pp. 34–36). For a guide on how to understand the tables and figures of this chapter, see the section in Chapter 2 entitled "Presenting and Discussing the Exit Poll Data: Reading Chapter 3" (pp. 37–39).

**Table 3.22**   Composition of the Exit Polls by Expected Life for the Next Generation, 1992–2010

| Year | Better Than Today | About the Same | Worse Than Today | Number of Respondents |
|---|---|---|---|---|
| 2010 | 32.9% | 27.0% | 40.1% | 4,036 |
| 2008 | | | | |
| 2006 | 30.5% | 29.0% | 40.6% | 6,329 |
| 2004 | | | | |
| 2002 | | | | |
| 2000 | 48.8% | 30.0% | 21.2% | 3,187 |
| 1998 | | | | |
| 1996 | 29.9% | 36.2% | 34.0% | 3,912 |
| 1994 | | | | |
| 1992 | 31.1% | 31.8% | 37.1% | 2,832 |
| Average | 34.6% | 30.8% | 34.6% | |

**Question Wording for Expected Life for the Next Generation** (Coded: Better Than Today = 1; About the Same = 2; Worse Than Today = 3):

**1992–2010:** "Do you expect life for the next generation of Americans to be . . . Better than life today (1); Worse than life today (3); About the same (2)"

*Source:* National exit polls. See the section in Chapter 2 entitled "Creating a Cumulative National Data Set: Selecting Exit Polls" (pp. 28–29).

*Note:* When using these results to make inferences about the active electorate, the standard errors should be calculated using Table 2.2 (p. 36), which is explained in the adjacent section of Chapter 2, "Analyzing Exit Poll Questions: Estimating Sampling Error" (pp. 34–36). For a guide on how to understand the tables and figures of this chapter, see the section in Chapter 2 entitled "Presenting and Discussing the Exit Poll Data: Reading Chapter 3" (pp. 37–39).

**Table 3.23** Composition of the Exit Polls by Position on Government Activism, 1992–2010

| Year | Government Should Do More | Government Does Too Much | Number of Respondents |
|---|---|---|---|
| 2010 | 40.5% | 59.5% | 4,256 |
| 2008 | 53.6% | 46.4% | 4,367 |
| 2006 | | | |
| 2004 | 48.2% | 51.8% | 3,142 |
| 2002 | 46.6% | 53.4% | 7,777 |
| 2000 | 44.8% | 55.2% | 6,767 |
| 1998 | | | |
| 1996 | 44.0% | 56.0% | 3,890 |
| 1994 | 41.5% | 58.5% | 5,294 |
| 1992 | 54.6% | 45.4% | 2,735 |
| Average | 46.7% | 53.3% | |

**Question Wording for Position on Government Activism** (Coded: Government Should Do More = 1; Government Does Too Much = 2):

**1992–1994:** "Which comes closest to your view . . . Government should do more to solve national problems (1); Government is doing too many things better left to businesses and individuals (2)"

**1996–2008:** "Which comes closest to your view . . . Government should do more to solve problems (1); Government is doing too many things better left to businesses and individuals (2)"

**2010:** "Which is closer to your view . . . Government should do more to solve problems (1); Government is doing too many things better left to businesses and individuals (2)"

*Source:* National exit polls. See the section in Chapter 2 entitled "Creating a Cumulative National Data Set: Selecting Exit Polls" (pp. 28–29).

*Note:* When using these results to make inferences about the active electorate, the standard errors should be calculated using Table 2.2 (p. 36), which is explained in the adjacent section of Chapter 2, "Analyzing Exit Poll Questions: Estimating Sampling Error" (pp. 34–36). For a guide on how to understand the tables and figures of this chapter, see the section in Chapter 2 entitled "Presenting and Discussing the Exit Poll Data: Reading Chapter 3" (pp. 37–39).

**Table 3.24** Composition of the Exit Polls by First-Time Voter, 1996–2010

| Year | First-Time Voter | Not First-Time Voter | Number of Respondents |
|---|---|---|---|
| 2010 | 3.4% | 96.6% | 4,680 |
| 2008 | 11.5% | 88.5% | 8,586 |
| 2006 | | | |
| 2004 | 11.1% | 88.9% | 6,704 |
| 2002 | | | |
| 2000 | 9.1% | 90.9% | 9,797 |
| 1998 | | | |
| 1996 | 9.3% | 90.7% | 7,719 |
| Average | 8.9% | 91.1% | |

**Question Wording for First-Time Voter** (Coded: First-Time Voter = 1; Not First-Time Voter = 2):

**1996–2004 and 2010:** "Is this the first time you have ever voted? . . . Yes (1); No (2)"

**2008:** "Is this the first year you have ever voted? . . . Yes (1); No (2)"

*Source:* National exit polls. See the section in Chapter 2 entitled "Creating a Cumulative National Data Set: Selecting Exit Polls" (pp. 28–29).

*Note:* When using these results to make inferences about the active electorate, the standard errors should be calculated using Table 2.2 (p. 36), which is explained in the adjacent section of Chapter 2, "Analyzing Exit Poll Questions: Estimating Sampling Error" (pp. 34–36). For a guide on how to understand the tables and figures of this chapter, see the section in Chapter 2 entitled "Presenting and Discussing the Exit Poll Data: Reading Chapter 3" (pp. 37–39).

**Table 3.25**  Composition of the Exit Polls by Household Income, 1994–2010

| Year | Under $30,000 | $30,000–$49,999 | $50,000–$74,999 | $75,000–$99,999 | $100,000 or More | Number of Respondents |
|---|---|---|---|---|---|---|
| 2010 | 17.7% | 18.7% | 21.1% | 15.4% | 27.2% | 12,159 |
| 2008 | 18.2% | 19.4% | 21.3% | 15.0% | 26.1% | 16,129 |
| 2006 | 19.1% | 20.6% | 22.2% | 15.5% | 22.5% | 11,946 |
| 2004 | 23.1% | 22.1% | 23.0% | 13.7% | 18.2% | 12,321 |
| 2002 | 22.0% | 22.5% | 23.8% | 14.0% | 17.6% | 15,188 |
| 2000 | 22.7% | 24.5% | 24.8% | 12.9% | 15.1% | 11,860 |
| 1998 | 26.0% | 25.9% | 24.9% | 11.9% | 11.4% | 9,979 |
| 1996 | 34.1% | 27.4% | 20.6% | 8.9% | 9.0% | 14,724 |
| 1994 | 32.7% | 29.6% | 22.0% | 8.8% | 6.9% | 10,046 |
| Average | 24.0% | 23.4% | 22.6% | 12.9% | 17.1% | |

**Question Wording for Household Income** (Coded: Under $30,000 = 1; $30,000–$49,999 = 2; $50,000–$74,999 = 3; $75,000–$99,999 = 4; $100,000 or More = 5):

**1994–2002:** "[Previous Year] Total family income . . . Under $15,000 (1); $15,000–$29,999 (1); $30,000–$49,999 (2); $50,000–$74,999 (3); $75,000–$99,999 (4); $100,000 or more (5)"

**2004–2010:** "[Previous Year] Total family income . . . Under $15,000 (1); $15,000–$29,999 (1); $30,000–$49,999 (2); $50,000–$74,999 (3); $75,000–$99,999 (4); $100,000–$149,999 (5); $150,000–$199,999 (5); $200,000 or more (5)"

*Source:* National exit polls. See the section in Chapter 2 entitled "Creating a Cumulative National Data Set: Selecting Exit Polls" (pp. 28–29).

*Note:* When using these results to make inferences about the active electorate, the standard errors should be calculated using Table 2.2 (p. 36), which is explained in the adjacent section of Chapter 2, "Analyzing Exit Poll Questions: Estimating Sampling Error" (pp. 34–36). For a guide on how to understand the tables and figures of this chapter, see the section in Chapter 2 entitled "Presenting and Discussing the Exit Poll Data: Reading Chapter 3" (pp. 37–39).

**Table 3.26**  Composition of the Exit Polls by Four-Year Household Financial Situation, 1992–2008

| Year | Better | About the Same | Worse | Number of Respondents |
|---|---|---|---|---|
| 2008 | 23.7% | 34.4% | 42.0% | 4,563 |
| 2006 | | | | |
| 2004 | 32.3% | 39.6% | 28.1% | 6,731 |
| 2002 | | | | |
| 2000 | 50.6% | 38.8% | 10.6% | 6,300 |
| 1998 | | | | |
| 1996 | 33.6% | 45.6% | 20.9% | 15,418 |
| 1994 | | | | |
| 1992 | 24.4% | 41.3% | 34.3% | 7,897 |
| Average | 32.9% | 39.9% | 27.2% | |

**Question Wording for Four-Year Household Financial Situation** (Coded: Better = 1; About the Same = 2; Worse = 3):

**1992–2004:** "Compared to four years ago, is your family's financial situation . . . Better today (1); Worse today (3); About the same (2)"

**2008:** "Compared to four years ago, is your family's financial situation . . . Better (1); Worse (3); About the same (2)"

*Source:* National exit polls. See the section in Chapter 2 entitled "Creating a Cumulative National Data Set: Selecting Exit Polls" (pp. 28–29).

*Note:* When using these results to make inferences about the active electorate, the standard errors should be calculated using Table 2.2 (p. 36), which is explained in the adjacent section of Chapter 2, "Analyzing Exit Poll Questions: Estimating Sampling Error" (pp. 34–36). For a guide on how to understand the tables and figures of this chapter, see the section in Chapter 2 entitled "Presenting and Discussing the Exit Poll Data: Reading Chapter 3" (pp. 37–39).

**Table 3.27** Composition of the Exit Polls by Two-Year Household Financial Situation, 1990–2010

| Year | Better | About the Same | Worse | Number of Respondents |
|------|--------|----------------|-------|----------------------|
| 2010 | 14.8% | 43.3% | 41.9% | 4,513 |
| 2008 | | | | |
| 2006 | 29.8% | 44.8% | 25.4% | 6,947 |
| 2004 | | | | |
| 2002 | 28.8% | 40.6% | 30.6% | 8,231 |
| 2000 | | | | |
| 1998 | 41.2% | 45.4% | 13.5% | 10,762 |
| 1996 | | | | |
| 1994 | 24.9% | 51.1% | 24.0% | 5,410 |
| 1992 | | | | |
| 1990 | 28.6% | 44.9% | 26.5% | 10,038 |
| Average | 28.0% | 45.0% | 27.0% | |

**Question Wording for Two-Year Household Financial Situation** (Coded: Better = 1; About the Same = 2; Worse = 3):

**1990–2010:** "Compared to two years ago, is your family's financial situation . . . Better today (1); Worse today (3); About the same (2)"

*Source:* National exit polls. See the section in Chapter 2 entitled "Creating a Cumulative National Data Set: Selecting Exit Polls" (pp. 28–29).

*Note:* When using these results to make inferences about the active electorate, the standard errors should be calculated using Table 2.2 (p. 36), which is explained in the adjacent section of Chapter 2, "Analyzing Exit Poll Questions: Estimating Sampling Error" (pp. 34–36). For a guide on how to understand the tables and figures of this chapter, see the section in Chapter 2 entitled "Presenting and Discussing the Exit Poll Data: Reading Chapter 3" (pp. 37–39).

**Table 3.28**   Composition of the Exit Polls by Judgments of Current National
Economic Conditions, 1986–2010

| Year | Performing Well | Performing Badly | Number of Respondents |
|------|-----------------|------------------|-----------------------|
| 2010 | 9.5% | 90.5% | 4,509 |
| 2008 | 6.6% | 93.4% | 8,611 |
| 2006 | 49.1% | 50.9% | 6,917 |
| 2004 | 47.6% | 52.4% | 3,386 |
| 2002 | 40.2% | 59.8% | 8,948 |
| 2000 | 86.4% | 13.6% | 6,283 |
| 1998 | 82.8% | 17.2% | 5,580 |
| 1996 | 56.2% | 43.8% | 8,263 |
| 1994 | 41.1% | 58.9% | 5,442 |
| 1992 | 19.1% | 80.9% | 8,190 |
| 1990 | 20.2% | 79.8% | 9,957 |
| 1988 | | | |
| 1986 | 66.1% | 33.9% | 8,465 |
| Average | 43.7% | 56.3% | |

**Question Wording for Judgments of Current National Economic Conditions** (Coded: Performing Well = 1; Perform-ing Badly = 2):

**1986:** "These days, is the condition of the nation's economy . . . Very good (1); Fairly good (1); Fairly bad (2); Very bad (2)"

**1990:** "These days, do you think the condition of the nation's economy is . . . Excellent (1); Good (1); Not so good (2); Poor (2)"

**1992–2010:** "Do you think the condition of the nation's economy is . . . Excellent (1); Good (1); Not so good (2); Poor (2)"

*Source:* National exit polls. See the section in Chapter 2 entitled "Creating a Cumulative National Data Set: Selecting Exit Polls" (pp. 28–29).

*Note:* When using these results to make inferences about the active electorate, the standard errors should be calculated using Table 2.2 (p. 36), which is explained in the adjacent section of Chapter 2, "Analyzing Exit Poll Questions: Estimating Sampling Error" (pp. 34–36). For a guide on how to understand the tables and figures of this chapter, see the section in Chapter 2 entitled "Presenting and Discussing the Exit Poll Data: Reading Chapter 3" (pp. 37–39).

**Table 3.29**   Composition of the Exit Polls by Judgments of Future National Economic Conditions, 1986–2008

| Year | Better | About the Same | Worse | Number of Respondents |
|------|--------|----------------|-------|-----------------------|
| 2008 | 49.0% | 26.7% | 24.3% | 4,224 |
| 2006 | | | | |
| 2004 | | | | |
| 2002 | | | | |
| 2000 | 28.7% | 58.9% | 12.4% | 6,137 |
| 1998 | 18.2% | 58.7% | 23.1% | 5,541 |
| 1996 | | | | |
| 1994 | | | | |
| 1992 | | | | |
| 1990 | 14.0% | 31.7% | 54.3% | 10,365 |
| 1988 | | | | |
| 1986 | 32.5% | 48.3% | 19.2% | 8,571 |
| Average | 28.5% | 44.8% | 26.7% | |

**Question Wording for Judgments of Future National Economic Conditions** (Coded: Better = 1; About the Same = 2; Worse = 3):

**1986:** "A year from now, will the U.S. economy be . . . Better than today (1); Worse than today (3); About the same as today (2)"

**1990–2008:** "During the next year, do you think the nation's economy will . . . Get better (1); Get worse (3); Stay about the same (2)"

*Source:* National exit polls. See the section in Chapter 2 entitled "Creating a Cumulative National Data Set: Selecting Exit Polls" (pp. 28–29).

*Note:* When using these results to make inferences about the active electorate, the standard errors should be calculated using Table 2.2 (p. 36), which is explained in the adjacent section of Chapter 2, "Analyzing Exit Poll Questions: Estimating Sampling Error" (pp. 34–36). For a guide on how to understand the tables and figures of this chapter, see the section in Chapter 2 entitled "Presenting and Discussing the Exit Poll Data: Reading Chapter 3" (pp. 37–39).

**Table 3.30**  Average Size of Groups Responding to Presidential Exit Polls, 1972–2008

| Group | Mean Share |
|---|---|
| Not gay or bisexual | 96% |
| Not first-time voter | 90% |
| White | 83% |
| Disapprove of Congress | 76% |
| Not a union household | 73% |
| Married | 65% |
| Employed full time | 64% |
| Not born again | 63% |
| No child in household | 62% |
| Attend religious services less than once a week | 58% |
| Think current national economic conditions are performing badly | 57% |
| Protestant | 56% |
| Disapprove of the president | 53% |
| Female | 52% |
| Think government does too much | 51% |
| Think country is off on the wrong track | 51% |
| Think country is moving in the right direction | 49% |
| Think government should do more | 49% |
| Male | 48% |
| Moderate | 48% |
| Approve of the president | 47% |
| Voted for Republican candidate in last presidential election | 45% |
| Think future national economic conditions will be about the same | 43% |
| Suburban precinct | 43% |
| Think current national economic conditions are performing well | 43% |
| Attend religious services at least once a week | 42% |
| Household finances have stayed the same in last 4 years | 40% |
| Democrat | 40% |
| Think life will be worse for the next generation (last asked 2000) | 40% |
| Think future national economic conditions will be better | 39% |
| Child in household | 38% |
| Born again | 37% |
| Not employed full time | 36% |
| Not married | 35% |
| Voted for Democratic candidate in last presidential election | 35% |
| Republican | 33% |
| Conservative | 33% |
| Household finances have gotten better in last 4 years | 33% |
| 30–44 age group | 32% |
| Think life will be better for the next generation (last asked in 2000) | 31% |
| Some college education | 30% |
| City precinct | 29% |
| Southerner | 29% |
| Rural precinct | 29% |
| Think life will be about the same for the next generation (last asked in 2000) | 27% |
| Independent | 27% |
| Midwesterner | 27% |
| Household finances have gotten worse in the last 4 years | 27% |
| Catholic | 27% |
| Union household | 27% |

**Table 3.30** *(Continued)*

| Group | Mean Share |
|---|---|
| 45–59 age group | 26% |
| Easterner | 25% |
| Approve of Congress | 25% |
| College graduate | 24% |
| Household earns less than $30,000 annually | 24% |
| High school graduate | 23% |
| Household earns $50,000–$74,999 annually | 23% |
| Household earns $30,000–$49,999 annually | 23% |
| 18–29 age group | 21% |
| 60+ age group | 21% |
| Westerner | 20% |
| Liberal | 20% |
| Think future national economic conditions will be worse | 18% |
| Postgraduate | 17% |
| Household earns $100,000 or more annually | 17% |
| Did not vote in last presidential election | 14% |
| Household earns $75,000–$99,999 annually | 13% |
| Black | 10% |
| First-time voter | 10% |
| No religious affiliation | 8% |
| Religion other than Protestant, Catholic, or Jewish | 6% |
| Did not complete high school | 6% |
| Voted for non-major-party candidate in last presidential election | 6% |
| Hispanic/Latino | 4% |
| Gay or bisexual | 4% |
| Jewish | 3% |
| Race other than white, black, Hispanic/Latino, or Asian | 2% |
| Asian | 2% |

*Source:* National exit polls. See the section in Chapter 2 entitled "Creating a Cumulative National Data Set: Selecting Exit Polls" (pp. 28–29).

*Note:* When using these results to make inferences about the active electorate, the standard errors should be calculated using Table 2.2 (p. 36), which is explained in the adjacent section of Chapter 2, "Analyzing Exit Poll Questions: Estimating Sampling Error" (pp. 34–36). For a guide on how to understand the tables and figures of this chapter, see the section in Chapter 2 entitled "Presenting and Discussing the Exit Poll Data: Reading Chapter 3" (pp. 37–39).

**Table 3.31** Composition of the 2008 Presidential Exit Poll

| Group | 2008 Share |
|---|---|
| Not gay or bisexual | 97% |
| Think current national economic conditions are performing badly | 93% |
| Not first-time voter | 89% |
| Not a union household | 79% |
| Think country is off on the wrong track | 79% |
| White | 76% |
| Disapprove of Congress | 76% |
| Disapprove of the president | 73% |
| Married | 66% |
| Not born again | 62% |
| No child in household | 60% |
| Employed full time | 64% |
| Attend religious services less than once a week | 60% |
| Protestant | 54% |
| Think government should do more | 54% |
| Female | 53% |
| Suburban precinct | 49% |
| Think future national economic conditions will be better | 49% |
| Male | 47% |
| Think government does too much | 46% |
| Voted for Republican candidate in last presidential election | 46% |
| Moderate | 44% |
| Household finances have gotten worse in the last 4 years | 42% |
| Attend religious services at least once a week | 41% |
| Child in household | 40% |
| Democrat | 39% |
| Born again | 39% |
| Voted for Democratic candidate in last presidential election | 38% |
| Not employed full time | 36% |
| Conservative | 34% |
| Household finances have stayed the same in last 4 years | 34% |
| Not married | 34% |
| Southerner | 32% |
| Republican | 32% |
| Some college education | 31% |
| City precinct | 30% |
| 45–59 age group | 30% |
| 30–44 age group | 29% |
| Independent | 29% |
| College graduate | 28% |
| Approve of the president | 28% |
| Think future national economic conditions will be about the same | 27% |
| Household earns $100,000 or more annually | 27% |
| Catholic | 26% |
| Approve of Congress | 25% |
| Household finances have gotten better in last 4 years | 24% |
| Midwesterner | 24% |
| 60+ age group | 24% |
| Think future national economic conditions will be worse | 24% |
| Westerner | 23% |

**Table 3.31** *(Continued)*

| Group | 2008 Share |
| --- | --- |
| Think country is moving in the right direction | 22% |
| Liberal | 22% |
| Union household | 21% |
| Rural precinct | 21% |
| Household earns $50,000–$74,999 annually | 21% |
| Easterner | 21% |
| High school graduate | 20% |
| Household earns $30,000–$49,999 annually | 19% |
| Household earns less than $30,000 annually | 18% |
| 18–29 age group | 18% |
| Postgraduate | 17% |
| Household earns $75,000–$99,999 annually | 15% |
| Did not vote in last presidential election | 13% |
| Black | 13% |
| No religious affiliation | 12% |
| First-time voter | 12% |
| Think current national economic conditions are performing well | 7% |
| Hispanic/Latino | 6% |
| Religion other than Protestant, Catholic, or Jewish | 6% |
| Voted for non-major-party candidate in last presidential election | 4% |
| Did not complete high school | 4% |
| Gay or bisexual | 4% |
| Race other than white, black, Hispanic/Latino, or Asian | 3% |
| Jewish | 2% |
| Asian | 2% |

*Source:* National exit polls. See the section in Chapter 2 entitled "Creating a Cumulative National Data Set: Selecting Exit Polls" (pp. 28–29).

*Note:* When using these results to make inferences about the active electorate, the standard errors should be calculated using Table 2.2 (p. 36), which is explained in the adjacent section of Chapter 2, "Analyzing Exit Poll Questions: Estimating Sampling Error" (pp. 34–36). For a guide on how to understand the tables and figures of this chapter, see the section in Chapter 2 entitled "Presenting and Discussing the Exit Poll Data: Reading Chapter 3" (pp. 37–39).

**Table 3.32**  Average Size of Groups Responding to Midterm Exit Polls, 1978–2010

| Group | Mean Share |
|---|---|
| Not first-time voter (asked only in 2010) | 97% |
| Not gay or bisexual | 97% |
| White | 85% |
| Not a union household | 75% |
| Disapprove of Congress | 69% |
| Married (last asked in 2006) | 68% |
| Not born again | 65% |
| No child in household | 65% |
| Employed full time (last asked in 2002) | 63% |
| Think government does too much | 57% |
| Think current national economic conditions are performing badly | 56% |
| Protestant | 55% |
| Think country is off on the wrong track | 53% |
| Attend religious services less than once a week | 53% |
| Approve of the president | 53% |
| Female | 51% |
| Male | 49% |
| Voted for Republican candidate in last presidential election | 48% |
| Disapprove of the president | 47% |
| Attend religious services at least once a week | 47% |
| Moderate | 47% |
| Think country is moving in the right direction | 47% |
| Think future national economic conditions will be about the same (last asked in 1998) | 46% |
| Suburban precinct | 45% |
| Household finances stayed the same in last 2 years | 45% |
| Think current national economic conditions are performing well | 44% |
| Think government should do more | 43% |
| Voted for Democratic candidate in last presidential election | 40% |
| Think life will be worse for the next generation | 40% |
| Democrat | 39% |
| Not employed full time (last asked in 2002) | 38% |
| Child in household | 35% |
| Born again | 35% |
| Conservative | 34% |
| Republican | 34% |
| Think future national economic conditions will be worse (last asked in 1998) | 32% |
| Not married (last asked in 2006) | 32% |
| Approve of Congress | 31% |
| Think life will be better for the next generation | 31% |
| City precinct | 30% |
| 30–44 age group | 30% |
| Some college education | 29% |
| Household finances have gotten better in last 2 years | 29% |
| 45–59 age group | 29% |
| Southerner | 28% |
| Independent | 28% |
| Midwesterner | 28% |
| Think life will be the same for the next generation | 27% |

**Table 3.32** *(Continued)*

| Group | Mean Share |
| --- | --- |
| 60+ age group | 27% |
| Household finances have gotten worse in the last 2 years | 27% |
| Catholic | 27% |
| College graduate | 25% |
| Union household | 25% |
| Rural precinct | 25% |
| Household earns less than $30,000 annually | 24% |
| High school graduate | 24% |
| Household earns $50,000–$74,999 annually | 23% |
| Easterner | 23% |
| Household earns $30,000–$49,999 annually | 23% |
| Westerner | 21% |
| Think future national economic conditions will be better (last asked in 1998) | 21% |
| Liberal | 19% |
| Postgraduate | 17% |
| Household earns $100,000 or more annually | 17% |
| 18–29 age group | 14% |
| Household earns $75,000–$99,999 annually | 13% |
| No religious affiliation | 9% |
| Black | 9% |
| Religion other than Protestant, Catholic, or Jewish | 6% |
| Voted for non-major-party candidate in last presidential election | 6% |
| Did not complete high school | 5% |
| Did not vote in last presidential election | 5% |
| Hispanic/Latino | 4% |
| Gay or bisexual | 4% |
| First-time voter (asked only in 2010) | 3% |
| Jewish | 3% |
| Race other than white, black, Hispanic/Latino, or Asian | 2% |
| Asian | 1% |

*Source:* National exit polls. See the section in Chapter 2 entitled "Creating a Cumulative National Data Set: Selecting Exit Polls" (pp. 28–29).

*Note:* When using these results to make inferences about the active electorate, the standard errors should be calculated using Table 2.2 (p. 36), which is explained in the adjacent section of Chapter 2, "Analyzing Exit Poll Questions: Estimating Sampling Error" (pp. 34–36). For a guide on how to understand the tables and figures of this chapter, see the section in Chapter 2 entitled "Presenting and Discussing the Exit Poll Data: Reading Chapter 3" (pp. 37–39).

**Table 3.33** Composition of the 2010 Midterm Exit Poll

| Group | 2010 Share |
|---|---|
| Not first-time voter | 97% |
| Not gay or bisexual | 97% |
| Think current national economic conditions are performing badly | 91% |
| Not a union household | 83% |
| White | 78% |
| Disapprove of Congress | 76% |
| No child in household | 66% |
| Think country is off on the wrong track | 64% |
| Not born again | 64% |
| Think government does too much | 60% |
| Disapprove of the president | 56% |
| Protestant | 55% |
| Attend religious services less than once a week | 52% |
| Female | 52% |
| Suburban precinct | 49% |
| Attend religious services at least once a week | 48% |
| Male | 48% |
| Voted for Democratic candidate in last presidential election | 46% |
| Voted for Republican candidate in last presidential election | 46% |
| Approve of the president | 45% |
| Household finances stayed the same in last 2 years | 43% |
| Household finances have gotten worse in the last 2 years | 42% |
| Conservative | 41% |
| Think government should do more | 41% |
| Think life will be worse for the next generation | 40% |
| Moderate | 39% |
| Born again | 37% |
| Think country is moving in the right direction | 36% |
| Democrat | 35% |
| Republican | 35% |
| Child in household | 34% |
| Think life will be better for the next generation | 33% |
| 45–59 age group | 32% |
| 60+ age group | 32% |
| City precinct | 31% |
| Southerner | 31% |
| College graduate | 30% |
| Independent | 30% |
| Some college education | 28% |
| Household earns $100,000 or more annually | 27% |
| Think life will be about the same for the next generation | 27% |
| Midwesterner | 25% |
| Approve of Congress | 24% |
| 30–44 age group | 24% |
| Catholic | 23% |
| Westerner | 23% |
| Easterner | 21% |
| Postgraduate | 21% |
| Household earns $50,000–$74,999 annually | 21% |

**Table 3.33**   *(Continued)*

| Group | 2010 Share |
|---|---|
| Rural precinct | 21% |
| Liberal | 20% |
| Household earns $30,000–$49,999 annually | 19% |
| Household earns less than $30,000 annually | 18% |
| Union household | 18% |
| High school graduate | 17% |
| Household finances have gotten better in last 2 years | 15% |
| Household earns $75,000-$99,999 annually | 15% |
| No religious affiliation | 12% |
| 18–29 age group | 12% |
| Black | 11% |
| Think current national economic conditions are performing well | 10% |
| Hispanic/Latino | 8% |
| Religion other than Protestant, Catholic, or Jewish | 8% |
| Did not vote in last presidential election | 5% |
| Voted for non-major-party candidate in last presidential election | 4% |
| Gay or bisexual | 3% |
| Did not complete high school | 3% |
| First-time voter | 3% |
| Jewish | 2% |
| Race other than white, black, Hispanic/Latino, or Asian | 2% |
| Asian | 2% |

*Source:* National exit polls. See the section in Chapter 2 entitled "Creating a Cumulative National Data Set: Selecting Exit Polls" (pp. 28–29).

*Note:* When using these results to make inferences about the active electorate, the standard errors should be calculated using Table 2.2 (p. 36), which is explained in the adjacent section of Chapter 2, "Analyzing Exit Poll Questions: Estimating Sampling Error" (pp. 34–36). For a guide on how to understand the tables and figures of this chapter, see the section in Chapter 2 entitled "Presenting and Discussing the Exit Poll Data: Reading Chapter 3" (pp. 37–39).

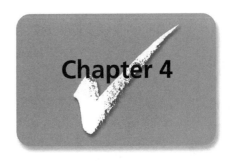

Chapter 4

# Presidential Voting Preferences of Exit Poll Respondents

Over the past four decades, U.S. presidential elections have yielded a wide range of outcomes. Presidential nominees from the two major political parties have been elected and reelected, won by squeakers and landslides, and confronted the challenges of competitive third-party candidates. There was even an instance of an Electoral College winner losing the popular vote, a scenario that has occurred only three times in U.S. history.

This time frame also saw dramatic changes in the political landscape. The economy soared and sunk. The Soviet Union crumbled and the Cold War ended. The United States fought major wars in Vietnam, Iraq, and Afghanistan. And, social issues from abortion to capital punishment to same-sex marriage were hotly contested on the national stage.

Through it all, the two major political parties have remained closely matched in their battles for the White House, with neither party able to dominate electoral outcomes for an extended period of time (see Figure 4.1). The Republicans have won six of the past ten presidential elections, but the Democrats have won three of the past five contests. Similarly, the Republican presidential candidates have won, on average, 60 percent of the electoral votes since 1972, but the Democratic nominees have won 61 percent of the Electoral College votes since 1992 (see Table 4.1 at the end of the chapter for exact percentages).

In this chapter, we examine the presidential voting preferences of different groups of respondents to the exit polls conducted from 1972 through 2008.[1] Examining choices over time, rather than in any particular election, provides several important insights. First, it gives context to election outcomes, allowing us to assess whether results in a given election stem from a long-term trend or a temporary deviation because of an attractive candidate or a distinct issue. Second, it reveals whether particular groups are predisposed to vote for the presidential nominees of the Democratic or Republican Party, enabling us to make better sense of campaign messages and

**Figure 4.1**  Democratic Share of Two-Party Electoral Votes, 1972–2008

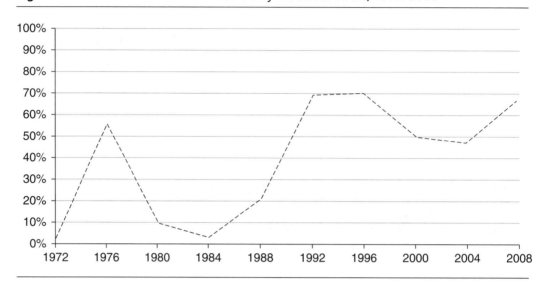

*Source:* Harold W. Stanley and Richard G. Niemi, *Vital Statistics on American Politics, 2011–2012* (Washington, DC: CQ Press, 2011).

mobilizing efforts. Finally, it provides the basis from which to make predictions about future presidential contests.

## Presidential Vote Choice

National exit polls have queried voters about their presidential choice in the ten presidential elections occurring from 1972 through 2008. The wording of the presidential vote question has remained largely unchanged over the years. It features the names of the two major-party candidates, a range of third-party candidates, space to write in the choice of an unnamed candidate, and an option for respondents to indicate that they did not vote in the presidential election. The exact number of third-party candidates has varied from three in 1980, when the names of John Anderson, Ed Clark, and Barry Commoner were included on the questionnaire, to zero in the 1984, 1988, and 2008 elections. Despite the inconsistency in the inclusion of third-party candidates, every third-party candidate securing at least 0.75 percent of the actual vote has appeared on an exit poll questionnaire.

We tabulate the findings of the presidential vote question in two different ways. We report the percentage of the overall presidential vote received by the Democratic and Republican Party nominees as well as the collective percentage received by the third-party candidates. This approach indicates the actual distribution of the vote in the exit poll. It is best suited for describing the outcome of a particular election.

In years when third-party candidates receive a sizable percentage of the vote, such as 1980, 1992, or 1996, the overall vote can distort the relative advantage the parties have over one another, giving the misleading perception that the underlying support for the major political parties had changed rather than deviated temporarily due to an unusually attractive third-party candidate. For example, in the 1992 exit poll, Democrat Bill Clinton received 43 percent of the vote, compared to 38 percent for Republican George H. W. Bush and 19 percent for independent candidate Ross Perot. Taken at face value, it appears that support for the Democratic presidential nominee had dropped from the 1988 exit poll when Democrat Michael Dukakis lost to Republican George H. W. Bush, 46 percent to 53 percent. However, limiting our focus to the share of the vote received by just the two major parties reveals a far different story. From 1988 to 1992, the Democratic share of the two-party vote actually grew from 46 percent to 54 percent, an 8-point increase in relative support for the Democrats, rather than a 3-point decline, as suggested by the overall vote.

Therefore, we also report the vote share awarded only to the two major political party candidates—the Democratic nominee and the Republican nominee—in a given exit poll. It sums to 100 percent and reveals the relative backing that the two major parties had from exit poll respondents over time. Care, though, must be used when interpreting the two-party vote. If a Democratic or Republican nominee receives a majority of the two-party vote from exit poll respondents, it does not necessarily mean the candidate received a majority of the overall vote. In fact, on three separate occasions—1992, 1996, and 2000—the candidate with a majority share of the two-party vote won only a plurality of the overall popular vote. Thus, the two-party vote is more suitable for understanding the dynamics of support for the major political parties in the presidential exit polls over time than the outcome in any particular exit poll.

To identify the voting patterns of different groups in the exit poll, we calculate the joint frequency distribution between the presidential vote and the response options for various questions. We tabulate the results for both the overall and two-party Democratic vote for each exit poll and report them in the tables at the end of the chapter. We also graph the two-party Democratic vote over time for responses to each item and embed them in our substantive discussion of the voting behavior of various groups of exit poll respondents.

Take ideology, for example. The exit poll question tapping the concept offers three options: liberal, moderate, and conservative. For each ideological predisposition, we compute the proportions of the two-party vote the Democratic and Republican nominees received, as well as the total percentage of exit poll respondents who selected each presidential candidate in a given election. We then use the two-party Democratic presidential vote to assess how ideological groups have behaved over time and their actual presidential vote to describe their behavior in the 2008 exit poll. By using both longitudinal and cross-sectional measures, we obtain the fullest picture of the voting patterns of various ideological groups or, for that matter, of any group tapped by the exit polls.

Readers can use this exit poll information to make inferences, with a margin of error and known degree of confidence, about the behavior of all voters in the electorate who fit into one of the categories assessed in this chapter. In other words, these exit poll results can be used to estimate how groups in the active electorate voted over time. This is done, first, by identifying the vote share given by a certain exit poll group to a party's presidential candidate and the number of exit poll respondents from this group who voted for any presidential candidate. Then, this information can be applied to Table 2.2 to determine the margin of sampling error that must be considered when projecting the vote distribution of the group to the active electorate (see the section in Chapter 2 entitled "Reading Chapter 4: Presidential Voting Preferences of Exit Poll Respondents" for a lengthier discussion of this procedure). For example, in 2008, male exit poll respondents gave the Democratic presidential candidate 49 percent of their overall vote (see Table 4.8 at the end of this chapter). Examining the far right-hand column in Table 4.8, we next determine that 7,637 men answered validly the presidential voting question. Applying this information to Table 2.2, we see that the sampling error for male respondents' Democratic vote for president in 2008 is plus or minus 2 percent. Another way to think about this is that we can have 95 percent confidence that between 47 and 51 percent of men in the active electorate voted for Barack Obama in 2008. Readers, though, need to pay special care when calculating the two-party vote sampling errors, as the number of respondents voting for third-party candidates must be removed from the calculation of the total number of exit poll respondents selecting a particular option.

## Overall Presidential Vote

Figure 4.2 shows the Democratic share of the two-party presidential vote of exit poll respondents from 1972 to 2008. Clearly, it has been a very competitive era in American politics, with both major parties faring well over time. Presidential candidates from each political party won a majority of respondents' votes in half of the ten elections. Republican candidates received,

**Figure 4.2** Democratic Share of Two-Party Presidential Vote, 1972–2008

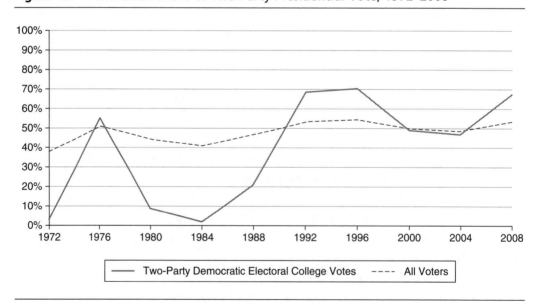

*Source:* National exit polls. See the section in Chapter 2 entitled "Creating a Cumulative National Data Set: Selecting Exit Polls" (pp. 28–29).

*Note:* When using these results to make inferences about the active electorate, the standard errors should be calculated using Table 2.2 (p. 36), which is explained in the adjacent section of Chapter 2, "Analyzing Exit Poll Questions: Estimating Sampling Error" (pp. 34–36). For a guide on how to understand the tables and figures of this chapter, see the section in Chapter 2 entitled "Presenting and Discussing the Exit Poll Data: Reading Chapter 4" (pp. 39–43). The rationale for using two-party percentages to show trends over time is given in this chapter, in the section entitled "Presidential Vote Choice" (pp. 124–131).

on average, 52 percent of respondents' two-party vote during the entire time span, whereas the Democrats averaged 48 percent of the two-party vote.

The two-party presidential vote of exit poll respondents has been a fairly poor gauge of the proportion of electoral votes won by the major political parties. In 2000, Democratic presidential nominee Al Gore won the respondents' vote but lost the electoral vote to Republican nominee George W. Bush. In the remaining nine elections, the proportion of electoral votes secured by the victorious candidate far exceeded the proportion of exit poll respondents won by that candidate. The victorious candidate received 55 percent of the two-party vote between 1972 and 2008 (excluding 2000) but secured a whopping 76 percent of the Electoral College vote.

In the 2008 presidential exit poll, Democratic nominee Barack Obama defeated Republican nominee John McCain, 53 percent to 45 percent (see Table 4.2 at the end of the chapter). It was the largest proportion of the exit poll vote received by a Democratic candidate in the past four decades and the largest share of the two-party vote collected by a Democrat since Bill Clinton in 1996. It translated to 68 percent of the electoral vote, which constituted the largest share of the electoral vote won by a Democratic presidential candidate since Clinton in 1996.

## Tone of the Campaign

On the road to the White House, the campaigning between the major-party nominees can become quite aggressive as the candidates attempt to highlight their strengths and expose their opponents' weaknesses. Since 1992, exit pollsters have inquired about the behavior of the major-party candidates during the campaign. Specifically, they have asked respondents whether either of the candidates attacked the other unfairly. The question enables them to label as unfair one candidate, both, or neither.

Figure 4.3 shows the proportion of exit poll respondents that named the Democratic candidate, the Republican candidate, both of them, or neither of them as behaving unfairly during the presidential campaign. From 1992 through 2008, few respondents believed that the major-party candidates acted appropriately. Only 19 percent of respondents, on average, reported that neither of the candidates campaigned unfairly, and no more than 24 percent approved of both candidates' actions in the past five campaigns.

The overwhelming number of exit poll respondents in each election believed at least one of the candidates acted inappropriately. On average, 41 percent of respondents identified both major-party candidates as behaving unfairly during the campaign, typically the plurality of respondents in a given exit poll. The remaining respondents chose one candidate or the other, with one of the candidates typically receiving the brunt of the blame. In 1992 and 1996, more than twice as many respondents thought Democrat Bill Clinton was treated worse than he treated his opponents. The reverse occurred in 2000 and 2004, when markedly more respondents believed Republican George W. Bush was treated unfairly compared to how he treated his opponents.

During the 2008 presidential campaign, once again a plurality of exit poll respondents—42 percent—thought both candidates behaved inappropriately during the campaign (see Table 4.3 at the end of the chapter). Of those who thought that one major-party nominee acted more unfairly

**Figure 4.3**   Composition of the Exit Polls by the Perceived Unfairness of Candidates' Campaigns, 1992–2008

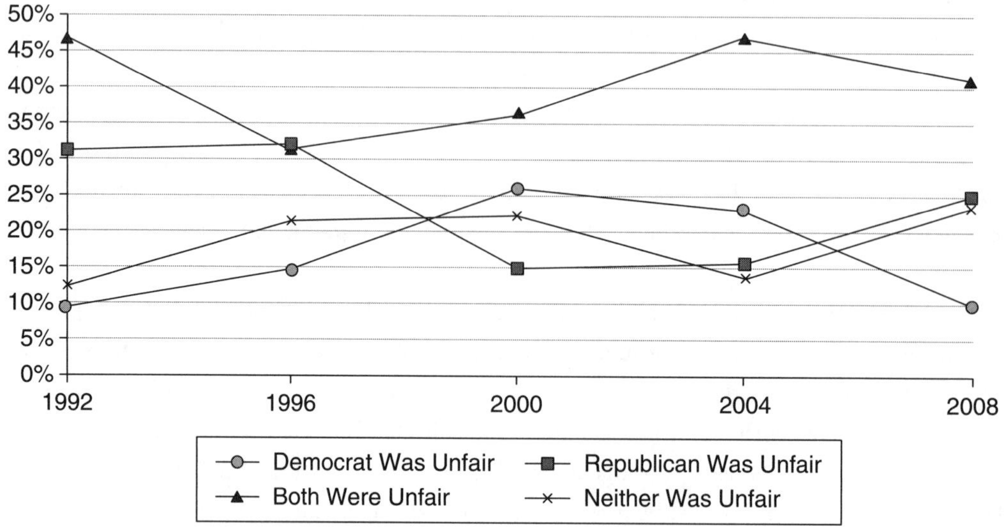

*Source:* National exit polls. See the section in Chapter 2 entitled "Creating a Cumulative National Data Set: Selecting Exit Polls" (pp. 28–29).

*Note:* When using these results to make inferences about the active electorate, the standard errors should be calculated using Table 2.2 (p. 36), which is explained in the adjacent section of Chapter 2, "Analyzing Exit Poll Questions: Estimating Sampling Error" (pp. 34–36). For a guide on how to understand the tables and figures of this chapter, see the section in Chapter 2 entitled "Presenting and Discussing the Exit Poll Data: Reading Chapter 4" (pp. 39–43). The rationale for using two-party percentages to show trends over time is given in this chapter, in the section entitled "Presidential Vote Choice" (pp. 124–131).

than the other, 25 percent selected McCain, compared to only 10 percent who selected Obama. Only 24 percent of respondents reported that neither candidate behaved inappropriately during the campaign.

Judgments about candidates' behavior during the campaign are correlated with exit poll respondents' choices for president. Respondents who thought the candidate from one of the major political parties acted more unfairly than the other overwhelmingly supported the other major-party candidate (see Figure 4.4). Respondents who thought the Democratic nominee alone behaved inappropriately during the campaign cast 88 percent of their two-party ballots for the Republican candidate. Conversely, respondents who thought the Republican nominee alone behaved unfairly during the campaign cast 94 percent of their two-party ballots for the Democratic candidate.

Interestingly, exit poll respondents who did not see a difference between the candidates, regardless of whether they thought they both acted inappropriately, cast a majority of their ballots for candidates from the losing party. Respondents who thought both candidates acted unfairly or neither acted unfairly preferred the Republican nominee during Clinton's victories in 1992 and 1996. In the 2000 and 2004 elections, when Bush won the White House, respondents who did not see a difference in the candidates' campaigns preferred the Democratic nominee.

In the 2008 exit poll, these patterns once again held to form (see Table 4.4 at the end of the chapter). Respondents who thought McCain behaved unfairly during the campaign

**Figure 4.4**   Democratic Share of Two-Party Presidential Vote by the Perceived
Unfairness of Candidates' Campaigns, 1992–2008

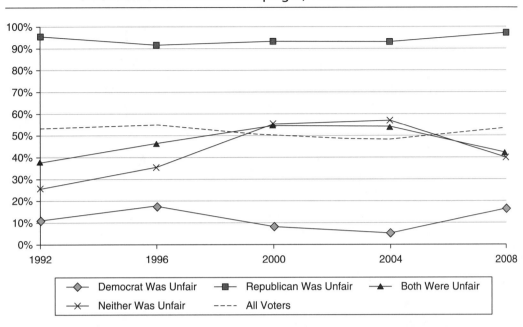

*Source:* National exit polls. See the section in Chapter 2 entitled "Creating a Cumulative National Data Set: Selecting Exit Polls" (pp. 28–29).

*Note:* When using these results to make inferences about the active electorate, the standard errors should be calculated using Table 2.2 (p. 36), which is explained in the adjacent section of Chapter 2, "Analyzing Exit Poll Questions: Estimating Sampling Error" (pp. 34–36). For a guide on how to understand the tables and figures of this chapter, see the section in Chapter 2 entitled "Presenting and Discussing the Exit Poll Data: Reading Chapter 4" (pp. 39–43). The rationale for using two-party percentages to show trends over time is given in this chapter, in the section entitled "Presidential Vote Choice" (pp. 124–131).

overwhelmingly supported Obama over McCain 96 percent to 3 percent. Conversely, respondents who thought Obama behaved unfairly overwhelmingly supported McCain over Obama, 83 percent to 16 percent. Respondents who did not see a difference in the behavior of the candidates during the campaign preferred McCain to Obama, 57 percent to 41 percent, in the case of those who thought both acted unfairly and 58 percent to 39 percent, in the case of those who thought neither acted unfairly.

### Timing of Presidential Vote Decision

Since 1976, national exit pollsters have gauged the timing of respondents' presidential choices. Unfortunately, there has been considerable variation in the response options through the years, ranging from the day of the election to before the party primaries. To allow for longitudinal comparisons, the response options were recoded into two categories representing decisions made during the last week of the campaign and those made before the last week. Despite reducing the variance, this measure still enables us to differentiate between early and late deciders.

Figure 4.5 illustrates the proportion of exit poll respondents over the past three decades making their presidential vote decision in the last week and those making their decision before that. The graph shows clearly that fewer and fewer respondents are making their decision in the waning

**Figure 4.5**   Composition of the Exit Polls by Timing of Presidential Vote Decision,
1976–2008

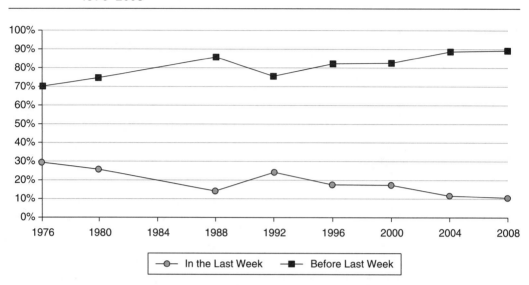

*Source:* National exit polls. See the section in Chapter 2 entitled "Creating a Cumulative National Data Set: Selecting Exit Polls" (pp. 28–29).

*Note:* When using these results to make inferences about the active electorate, the standard errors should be calculated using Table 2.2 (p. 36), which is explained in the adjacent section of Chapter 2, "Analyzing Exit Poll Questions: Estimating Sampling Error" (pp. 34–36). For a guide on how to understand the tables and figures of this chapter, see the section in Chapter 2 entitled "Presenting and Discussing the Exit Poll Data: Reading Chapter 4" (pp. 39–43). The rationale for using two-party percentages to show trends over time is given in this chapter, in the section entitled "Presidential Vote Choice" (pp. 124–131).

moments of the campaign. In 1976, 29 percent of respondents did not make up their mind about which candidate they preferred for president until the last week of the campaign. Over the next three decades, the proportion of late deciders fell by 18 percentage points, hitting 11 percent in 2008 (see Table 4.5 at the end of the chapter).

The timing of vote decisions produces different choices for the White House (see Figure 4.6). Exit poll respondents deciding before the last week typically support the candidate receiving a majority of the popular vote. Since 1976, a majority of early deciders have voted for the popular vote winner, regardless of whether he was Democratic or Republican, in every election. Despite the media attention on undecided voters in the final week of the campaign, the exit polls suggest that early deciders are a bellwether of the election outcome.

By contrast, exit poll respondents determining their presidential preference in the last week gravitate away from the incumbent party's candidates whether or not they ultimately win. Since 1976, a majority of late deciders have voted for the out party's presidential nominee in every exit poll save one. The only exception was the 2000 exit poll, when late deciders opted for the Democrat, Al Gore, by a slim 1-point margin over the Republican nominee, George W. Bush.

In the 2008 exit poll, the early deciders, once again, forecast the winner, whereas the late deciders broke for the out-party candidate (see Table 4.6 at the end of the chapter). Respondents who determined their choice in the last week supported Obama over McCain, 49 percent to 48 percent. Respondents who determined their choice prior to the last week also preferred Obama, but by a larger margin, supporting him 53 percent to 46 percent over McCain.

**Figure 4.6**   Democratic Share of Two-Party Presidential Vote by Timing of
Presidential Vote Decision, 1976–2008

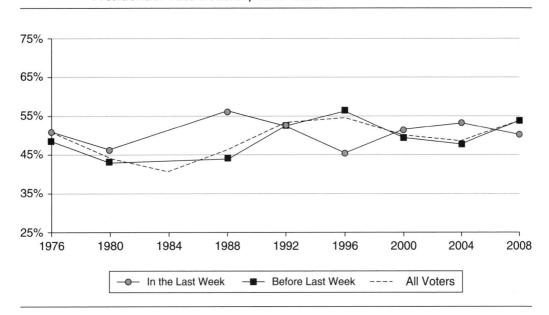

*Source:* National exit polls. See the section in Chapter 2 entitled "Creating a Cumulative National Data Set: Selecting Exit Polls" (pp. 28–29).

*Note:* When using these results to make inferences about the active electorate, the standard errors should be calculated using Table 2.2 (p. 36), which is explained in the adjacent section of Chapter 2, "Analyzing Exit Poll Questions: Estimating Sampling Error" (pp. 34–36). For a guide on how to understand the tables and figures of this chapter, see the section in Chapter 2 entitled "Presenting and Discussing the Exit Poll Data: Reading Chapter 4" (pp. 39–43). The rationale for using two-party percentages to show trends over time is given in this chapter, in the section entitled "Presidential Vote Choice" (pp. 124–131).

## Physical Characteristics

We begin our analysis of the voting behavior of various groups in the exit polls by considering those groups defined by respondents' physical traits. The most commonly assessed physical traits all have strong relationships with presidential preferences. Gender, race, age, and sexual orientation have each served to starkly divide the partisan preferences of exit poll respondents over the past four decades.

### Race

Race yields some of the largest differences in the presidential vote choices of exit poll respondents. Over the past three decades, white respondents have consistently chosen Republican candidates in presidential races, whereas non-white respondents typically preferred Democratic candidates (see Figure 4.7). Although the margins have fluctuated for different racial groups over time, the outcomes, for the most part, have not.

White exit poll respondents have cast a majority of their two-party ballots for Republican presidential nominees in every election from 1984 through 2008. On average, Republican candidates have secured 57 percent of whites' two-party vote. Of any Democrat, Bill Clinton came closest to winning over white respondents but fell a point shy in his 1992 victory.

African American respondents, by contrast, are among the strongest Democratic supporters in the exit polls. In the past seven presidential elections, African American respondents cast an

**Figure 4.7**  Democratic Share of Two-Party Presidential Vote by Race, 1984–2008

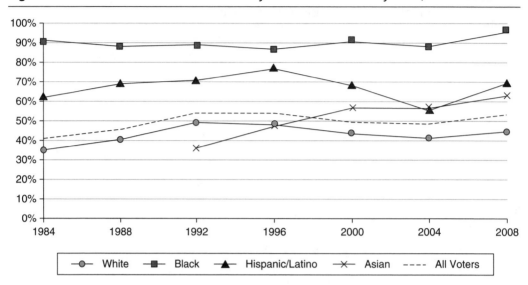

*Source:* National exit polls. See the section in Chapter 2 entitled "Creating a Cumulative National Data Set: Selecting Exit Polls" (pp. 28–29).

*Note:* When using these results to make inferences about the active electorate, the standard errors should be calculated using Table 2.2 (p. 36), which is explained in the adjacent section of Chapter 2, "Analyzing Exit Poll Questions: Estimating Sampling Error" (pp. 34–36). For a guide on how to understand the tables and figures of this chapter, see the section in Chapter 2 entitled "Presenting and Discussing the Exit Poll Data: Reading Chapter 4" (pp. 39–43). The rationale for using two-party percentages to show trends over time is given in this chapter, in the section entitled "Presidential Vote Choice" (pp. 124–131).

average of 90 percent of their two-party ballots for the Democratic nominees. Not once during this period did Republican candidates garner more than 13 percent of the African American vote.

Hispanics also strongly back Democratic presidential candidates, albeit by smaller margins. From 1984 through 2008, Hispanic exit poll respondents cast 68 percent of their two-party ballots for Democratic nominees. Only once did their support for Democrats dip below 60 percent. In 2004, they cast 44 percent of their two-party vote for George W. Bush, before quickly reverting back to historical levels in the subsequent election.

Asian respondents are the only racial group to have switched their party preferences over time. In the 1992 and 1996 exit polls, a majority of Asian respondents cast two-party ballots for Republican candidates, despite Bill Clinton winning the White House in both races. Beginning in 2000, though, Asian respondents switched their support to the Democrats, and a majority have backed the Democratic candidate in the exit polls administered since.

In the 2008 exit poll, these patterns once again held to form (see Table 4.7 at the end of the chapter). Obama easily won all non-white groups, whereas McCain won a majority of white respondents. Obama defeated McCain among African Americans, 95 percent to 4 percent; among Hispanics, 68 percent to 30 percent; and among Asians, 61 percent to 36 percent. McCain bested Obama among whites, 55 percent to 44 percent.

## Gender

Figure 4.8 shows the two-party presidential vote for men and women in the exit polls since 1972. A gender gap in the two-party vote has occurred in every survey since 1980, when female

**Figure 4.8**  Democratic Share of Two-Party Presidential Vote by Gender, 1972–2008

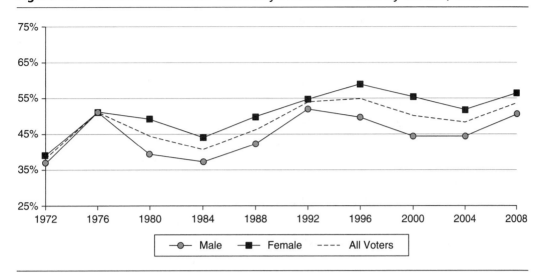

*Source:* National exit polls. See the section in Chapter 2 entitled "Creating a Cumulative National Data Set: Selecting Exit Polls" (pp. 28–29).

*Note:* When using these results to make inferences about the active electorate, the standard errors should be calculated using Table 2.2 (p. 36), which is explained in the adjacent section of Chapter 2, "Analyzing Exit Poll Questions: Estimating Sampling Error" (pp. 34–36). For a guide on how to understand the tables and figures of this chapter, see the section in Chapter 2 entitled "Presenting and Discussing the Exit Poll Data: Reading Chapter 4" (pp. 39–43). The rationale for using two-party percentages to show trends over time is given in this chapter, in the section entitled "Presidential Vote Choice" (pp. 124–131).

respondents were 10 percent more likely than their male counterparts to support Jimmy Carter over Ronald Reagan. From that election forward, female respondents have consistently supported Democratic presidential candidates at higher levels than male respondents. Democratic candidates have received 8 percent more support, on average, from women than men since 1980, ranging from a low of 3 percent in the 1992 election to a high of 11 percent in the 2000 election.

In the 2008 exit poll, the gender gap in the two-party presidential vote shrunk to 6 percent, the smallest disparity between the sexes since Bill Clinton's defeat of George H. W. Bush in the 1992 presidential election. Compared to men, women were 6 percentage points more likely to vote for Obama and 6 points less likely to vote for McCain. The reduction in the gender gap, though, was not due to any erosion in Democratic support among women but resulted, instead, from a greater relative increase in Democratic support among men.

Obama performed better among women than any Democratic presidential candidate in recent memory (see Table 4.8 at the end of the chapter). Obama attracted 56 percent of the overall female vote, compared to 43 percent for McCain. No Democratic candidate had received the support of a higher percentage of female respondents since the inception of the exit polls in 1972. Compared to previous Democratic nominees, Obama did even better among men. Obama received 49 percent of the male vote, as opposed to 48 percent for McCain. This was 5 percentage points more than John Kerry received in the 2004 exit poll. In fact, it was the first time a Democratic Party candidate had won a plurality of male respondents since the 1976 exit poll, when men preferred Jimmy Carter to Gerald Ford, 50 percent to 48 percent. No Democratic candidate had topped 44 percent support from male respondents in the interim.

## Age

People of varying ages tend to vote differently for president in each election. Figure 4.9 shows the presidential voting dynamics for the four most commonly asked age groups in the exit polls conducted since 1972. Two patterns in the behavior of these age groups are particularly noteworthy.

Generally speaking, all age groups track with the overall vote in the exit polls, but at different rates. With few exceptions, when the two-party share of the overall vote increases (or decreases), each of the individual age groups increases (or decreases) its share of the two-party vote as well, but by different amounts. For example, in the 2000 exit poll, when the Republican share of the two-party vote increased by 5 points overall from the 1996 election, support for George W. Bush increased by 10 points among 18- to 29-year-olds, by 5 points among 30- to 44-year-olds, by 4 points among 45- to 59-year-olds, and by 1 point among respondents aged 60 or over.

Also, there is modest evidence of life cycle effects in the presidential voting of exit poll respondents over the past four decades. Life cycle effects occur when different age groups consistently vote for the same political party over time. The theory of life cycle effects is based on the notion that as voters move through the life cycle their priorities and experiences change, making the platform of one political party more attractive than the other.

Typically, young people gravitate toward Democratic nominees and older people gravitate toward Republican nominees. In seven of the past ten presidential-year exit polls, Democratic candidates have received a majority of the two-party vote from 18- to 29-year-olds, averaging 53 percent of their vote since 1972. Conversely, Republican candidates have received a majority

**Figure 4.9** Democratic Share of Two-Party Presidential Vote by Age, 1972–2008

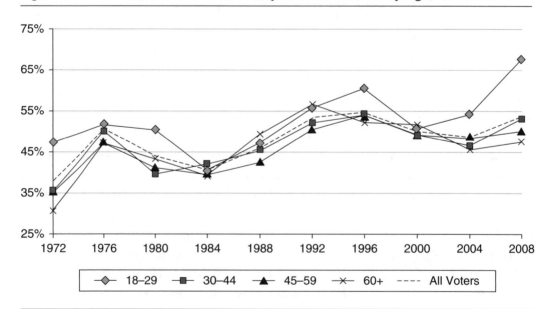

*Source:* National exit polls. See the section in Chapter 2 entitled "Creating a Cumulative National Data Set: Selecting Exit Polls" (pp. 28–29).

*Note:* When using these results to make inferences about the active electorate, the standard errors should be calculated using Table 2.2 (p. 36), which is explained in the adjacent section of Chapter 2, "Analyzing Exit Poll Questions: Estimating Sampling Error" (pp. 34–36). For a guide on how to understand the tables and figures of this chapter, see the section in Chapter 2 entitled "Presenting and Discussing the Exit Poll Data: Reading Chapter 4" (pp. 39–43). The rationale for using two-party percentages to show trends over time is given in this chapter, in the section entitled "Presidential Vote Choice" (pp. 124–131).

of the two-party vote of 45- to 59-year-olds and respondents aged 60 or over in seven of the past ten elections, averaging 54 percent of their two-party vote for each group.

Interestingly, 30- to 44-year-old respondents have behaved more as a swing group. They have voted for the winner in every election since 1972. Younger middle-age respondents gravitated toward Republican candidates in 1972, 1980 through 1988, and 2000 through 2004, contributing to the success of Republican nominees in each of those elections. In 1976, 1992 through 1996, and 2008 they gave Democrats a greater share of the two-party vote, propping up Democratic nominees in those years.

In the 2008 exit poll, Obama won three of the four age groups and improved on Kerry's numbers in all of them (see Table 4.9 at the end of the chapter). Among the 18–29 age group, Obama performed better than any Democratic candidate in four decades, defeating McCain, 66 percent to 32 percent. Obama received 52 percent of the overall vote from the 30–44 age group and 49 percent of the vote from the 45–59 age group, boosting the numbers received by Kerry four years earlier by 6 points and 1 point, respectively. The only age group that Obama lost was the 60 or over group. McCain won the senior vote, 51 percent to 47 percent, although Obama attracted 1 percentage point more from these respondents than Kerry did four years earlier.

## Sexual Orientation

The gay community is a consistently strong supporter of Democratic presidential candidates. They have voted overwhelmingly for Democratic presidential nominees in the past four presidential-year exit polls (see Figure 4.10). Among gays, lesbians, and bisexuals, Democratic nominees have

**Figure 4.10**  Democratic Share of Two-Party Presidential Vote by Sexual Orientation, 1996–2008

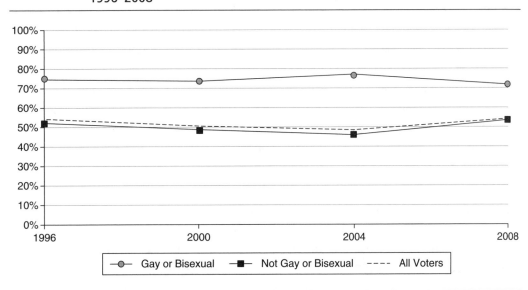

*Source:* National exit polls. See the section in Chapter 2 entitled "Creating a Cumulative National Data Set: Selecting Exit Polls" (pp. 28–29).

*Note:* When using these results to make inferences about the active electorate, the standard errors should be calculated using Table 2.2 (p. 36), which is explained in the adjacent section of Chapter 2, "Analyzing Exit Poll Questions: Estimating Sampling Error" (pp. 34–36). For a guide on how to understand the tables and figures of this chapter, see the section in Chapter 2 entitled "Presenting and Discussing the Exit Poll Data: Reading Chapter 4" (pp. 39–43). The rationale for using two-party percentages to show trends over time is given in this chapter, in the section entitled "Presidential Vote Choice" (pp. 124–131).

received nearly three-quarters of the two-party vote since 1996, with support of at least 72 percent in each of these four exit polls.

In the 2008 exit poll, Obama easily won the support of gay, lesbian, and bisexual respondents (see Table 4.10 at the end of the chapter). Obama received 70 percent of their overall vote. Only 27 percent of gays, lesbians, or bisexuals voted for McCain.

## Geographic Location

The exit polls show that residential location corresponds with partisan differences in presidential voting patterns. The regional location of respondents and the population density of their communities differentiate support for candidates of the major parties. However, neither the partisan preferences of these groups nor the gaps between them have remained constant over time but rather have changed in the face of varying electoral circumstances.

### Region

The presidential preferences of exit poll respondents vary by the regional location of their electoral precinct (see Figure 4.11). Respondents voting in eastern states have predominantly supported Democratic presidential nominees, awarding them, on average, 53 percent of their two-party ballots since 1972. Eastern respondents have preferred Democratic nominees in the past five presidential elections, and the East has been the most Democratic region in nine of the past ten presidential elections.

Conversely, exit poll respondents voting in southern states have consistently supported Republican presidential candidates. Southern respondents cast, on average, 56 percent of their two-party ballots for Republican nominees over the past four decades. They preferred the Republican candidate in every election except 1976, when they voted for Carter, and in 1996, when they were split evenly between Clinton and Bob Dole.

Western states have changed from a Republican stronghold to a Democratic one. From 1972 through 1988, respondents voting in western states preferred the Republican nominee in every exit poll, awarding them, on average, 57 percent of their two-party ballots. Since 1992, western respondents have become decidedly more Democratic. They cast, on average, 54 percent of their two-party ballots for Democratic presidential candidates, giving them a majority of their votes in the past five exit polls.

Unlike other areas of the country, the Midwest is not oriented toward one political party or the other. Rather, it appears to be a bellwether region. Since 1972, exit poll respondents voting in midwestern states have sided with the winning presidential candidate in all but one exit poll. The lone exception was the 1976 election, when midwestern respondents chose former Michigan representative Gerald Ford over Georgian Jimmy Carter, but even then, only by the narrowest of margins.

**Figure 4.11** Democratic Share of Two-Party Presidential Vote by Region of Electoral Precinct, 1972–2008

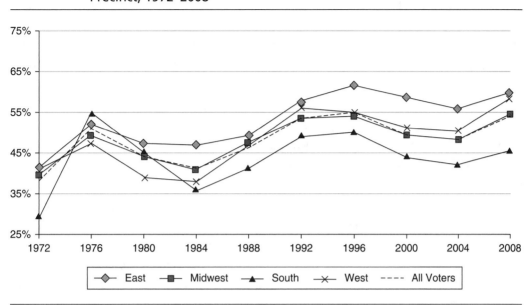

*Source:* National exit polls. See the section in Chapter 2 entitled "Creating a Cumulative National Data Set: Selecting Exit Polls" (pp. 28–29).

*Note:* When using these results to make inferences about the active electorate, the standard errors should be calculated using Table 2.2 (p. 36), which is explained in the adjacent section of Chapter 2, "Analyzing Exit Poll Questions: Estimating Sampling Error" (pp. 34–36). For a guide on how to understand the tables and figures of this chapter, see the section in Chapter 2 entitled "Presenting and Discussing the Exit Poll Data: Reading Chapter 4" (pp. 39–43). The rationale for using two-party percentages to show trends over time is given in this chapter, in the section entitled "Presidential Vote Choice" (pp. 124–131).

Generally speaking, the partisan preference of exit poll respondents in each region moves in unison over time with the overall national vote. When electoral support increases for Democratic (or Republican) presidential candidates in the national exit polls, it typically does so across every geographic region, although at different rates. For instance, support for Democratic candidates grew nationally from Walter Mondale's landslide defeat to Reagan in 1984 to Clinton's reelection in 1996. This shift was a function of increased support for the Democratic candidate in every region, not simply one or two areas of the country.

In the 2008 exit poll, Obama won three of the four regions of the country and improved on Kerry's numbers in all of them (see Table 4.11 at the end of the chapter). Obama defeated McCain among eastern respondents, 59 percent to 40 percent, and among western respondents, 57 percent to 40 percent, topping Kerry's total in the regions by 3 and 7 percentage points, respectively. Midwestern respondents switched from supporting Bush, 51 percent to 48 percent, over Kerry to backing Obama over McCain, 54 percent to 44 percent. Obama lost the vote of southern respondents to McCain, 54 percent to 45 percent, but nearly halved the 16-point margin the Republican nominee had in the region in 2004 (when Bush defeated Kerry 58 percent to 42 percent).

## Population Density

Support for presidential candidates also varies by the population density of the electoral precincts in which exit poll respondents are casting their ballots (see Figure 4.12). Urban settings are a Democratic stronghold. Democratic nominees have garnered at least 54 percent of the two-party vote from respondents in every presidential election since 1984, averaging 59 percent of the urban vote.

Conversely, exit poll respondents voting in rural areas predominantly back Republican nominees. Republicans won the two-party vote in rural areas in the past seven elections, save for 1996, when Clinton won the two-party vote by a single percentage point. Typically, rural respondents have supported Republicans over Democrats by double-digit margins, averaging 14 points over this time span.

In recent elections, exit poll respondents voting in suburban precincts have been a key swing group. Since 1984, whichever party has won the suburban vote has won the presidential election. Suburbanites went with Republicans by double-digit margins in 1984 and 1988, propelling Ronald Reagan and George H. W. Bush to victories. Clinton secured a majority of the two-party suburban vote in his electoral victories in 1992 and 1996. Suburbanites swung back to the Republicans in 2000, supporting George W. Bush in his two successful runs for the White House.

**Figure 4.12** Democratic Share of Two-Party Presidential Vote by Population Density of Electoral Precinct, 1984–2008

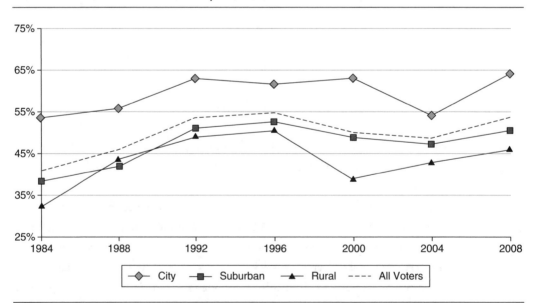

*Source:* National exit polls. See the section in Chapter 2 entitled "Creating a Cumulative National Data Set: Selecting Exit Polls" (pp. 28–29).

*Note:* When using these results to make inferences about the active electorate, the standard errors should be calculated using Table 2.2 (p. 36), which is explained in the adjacent section of Chapter 2, "Analyzing Exit Poll Questions: Estimating Sampling Error" (pp. 34–36). For a guide on how to understand the tables and figures of this chapter, see the section in Chapter 2 entitled "Presenting and Discussing the Exit Poll Data: Reading Chapter 4" (pp. 39–43). The rationale for using two-party percentages to show trends over time is given in this chapter, in the section entitled "Presidential Vote Choice" (pp. 124–131).

In the 2008 exit poll, Obama performed better in all types of communities than Kerry did four years earlier (see Table 4.12 at the end of the chapter). Obama won the vote of suburban respondents, 50 percent to 48 percent, over McCain. Obama garnered 3 percentage points more than Kerry did four years earlier and a greater percentage of the suburban vote than any Democratic candidate received in the exit polls in the past quarter-century.

Obama also prevailed among respondents voting in urban precincts, besting McCain 63 percent to 35 percent. This was a dramatic improvement over Kerry's 54 percent to 45 percent defeat of Bush among urban respondents. In fact, it was the biggest margin of victory for a Democratic candidate among urban respondents since the question was introduced in 1984, besting the previous high of 25 percent when Gore defeated Bush in the 2000 exit poll.

McCain defeated Obama, 53 percent to 45 percent, among exit poll respondents voting in rural precincts, continuing Republicans' winning streak in those areas to seven successive elections. However, McCain performed worse than George W. Bush among rural respondents. McCain's share was 3 percentage points worse than Bush's 56 percent share in 2004, and 6 points off Bush's 59 percent share of the rural vote in 2000.

## Religious Characteristics

Religious characteristics are associated with sizable, longstanding differences in the voting preferences of exit poll respondents. Protestants, frequent attendees of religious services, and evangelicals predominantly support Republican candidates. Conversely, non-Christians, infrequent attendees of religious services, and non-evangelicals predominantly support Democratic candidates. These patterns have held in the exit polls regardless of the candidates running or the campaign context.

### Religious Affiliation

Exit poll respondents with different religious affiliations have steered predominantly toward one or the other of the parties in recent presidential elections (see Figure 4.13). Protestant respondents have voted consistently Republican since 1984. Republican support among Protestants has averaged 58 percent of the two-party vote, with every Republican nominee since 1984 receiving at least 53 percent of the two-party vote.

Democrats, on the other hand, have drawn consistent support from Jewish and secular respondents in the past seven exit polls. More than three out of four Jewish respondents (77 percent), on average, have backed the Democratic nominee. Seculars have been nearly as reliable as Jews for the Democratic Party, with 69 percent of secular respondents, on average, supporting the Democratic nominee over the Republican nominee.

Catholic exit poll respondents have behaved as a swing group over the past quarter-century. Catholics have supported the winner of the overall popular vote in each exit poll since 1984. Catholic respondents preferred Republicans in the 1980s and Clinton in the 1990s. In 2000, they backed Gore, the popular vote winner, before switching their allegiances to George W. Bush in the 2004 presidential exit poll.

**Figure 4.13** Democratic Share of Two-Party Presidential Vote by Religious Affiliation, 1984–2008

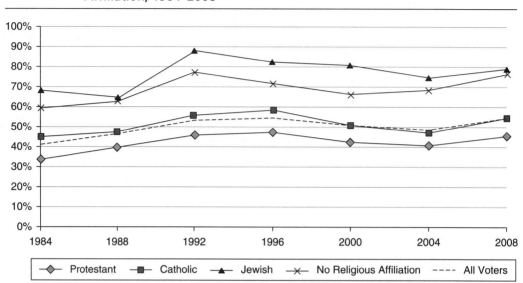

*Source:* National exit polls. See the section in Chapter 2 entitled "Creating a Cumulative National Data Set: Selecting Exit Polls" (pp. 28–29).

*Note:* When using these results to make inferences about the active electorate, the standard errors should be calculated using Table 2.2 (p. 36), which is explained in the adjacent section of Chapter 2, "Analyzing Exit Poll Questions: Estimating Sampling Error" (pp. 34–36). For a guide on how to understand the tables and figures of this chapter, see the section in Chapter 2 entitled "Presenting and Discussing the Exit Poll Data: Reading Chapter 4" (pp. 39–43). The rationale for using two-party percentages to show trends over time is given in this chapter, in the section entitled "Presidential Vote Choice" (pp. 124–131).

In the 2008 exit poll, respondents of different religious affiliations behaved as they had in the past (see Table 4.13 at the end of the chapter). Catholics went with the popular vote winner, gravitating to Obama over McCain, 54 percent to 45 percent, in the overall vote. Obama easily won the support of Jewish and secular respondents, garnering 78 percent and 75 percent of their overall votes, respectively. McCain beat Obama among Protestant respondents, 54 percent to 45 percent; however, Obama performed better among Protestant exit poll respondents than any Democratic presidential nominee in the past quarter-century.

## Religious Attendance

Religious attendance has also served as a polarizing factor in the presidential preferences of exit poll respondents. Exit poll respondents who attend religious services infrequently are more likely to vote for Democratic presidential candidates than their Republican counterparts (see Figure 4.14). Nearly three-fifths (58 percent) of respondents, on average, who attend religious services less than once a week voted for the Democratic nominee in the past three elections. They have awarded Democrats with a majority of their two-party ballots in these races, casting at least 56 percent of their ballots for them.

Conversely, exit poll respondents who regularly attend religious services predominantly support Republican candidates. Among those who attend religious services at least once a week,

**Figure 4.14**   Democratic Share of Two-Party Presidential Vote by Religious Attendance, 2000–2008

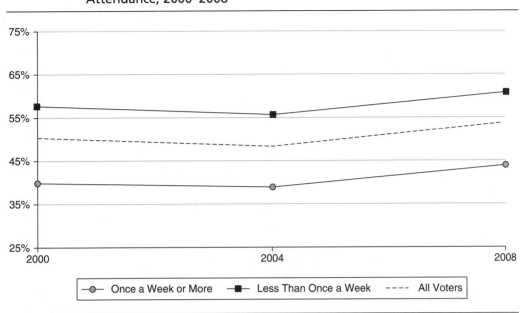

*Source:* National exit polls. See the section in Chapter 2 entitled "Creating a Cumulative National Data Set: Selecting Exit Polls" (pp. 28–29).

*Note:* When using these results to make inferences about the active electorate, the standard errors should be calculated using Table 2.2 (p. 36), which is explained in the adjacent section of Chapter 2, "Analyzing Exit Poll Questions: Estimating Sampling Error" (pp. 34–36). For a guide on how to understand the tables and figures of this chapter, see the section in Chapter 2 entitled "Presenting and Discussing the Exit Poll Data: Reading Chapter 4" (pp. 39–43). The rationale for using two-party percentages to show trends over time is given in this chapter, in the section entitled "Presidential Vote Choice" (pp. 124–131).

Republicans received, on average, 59 percent of their two-party vote since 2000. Support has been consistent over time, fluctuating between 56 and 61 percent over the past three contests.

The 2008 presidential election did not alter the partisan pattern of support among religious attendees (see Table 4.14 at the end of the chapter), although Obama did draw greater support from both exit poll groups than did the last two Democratic nominees. Obama garnered 60 percent support from respondents who attend religious services less than once a week, up 5 points from Kerry's totals in the 2004 exit poll. McCain defeated Obama, 55 percent to 43 percent, among those who attend church at least once a week, but the margin was 5 points smaller than Bush's victory over Kerry in 2004.

### Evangelical

Although most self-identified evangelical Christians also identify as Protestants, the two questions have been asked separately in the exit polls, because not all Protestants identify as evangelical. Evangelical or born-again Christians (the exit poll question uses the two terms synonymously) have long been considered strong Republican supporters in presidential elections.[2] Although longer trends are unavailable due to significant alterations in question wording and format, the last two exit polls demonstrate the hold that Republicans have on evangelical

**Figure 4.15** Democratic Share of Two-Party Presidential Vote by Evangelical, 2004–2008

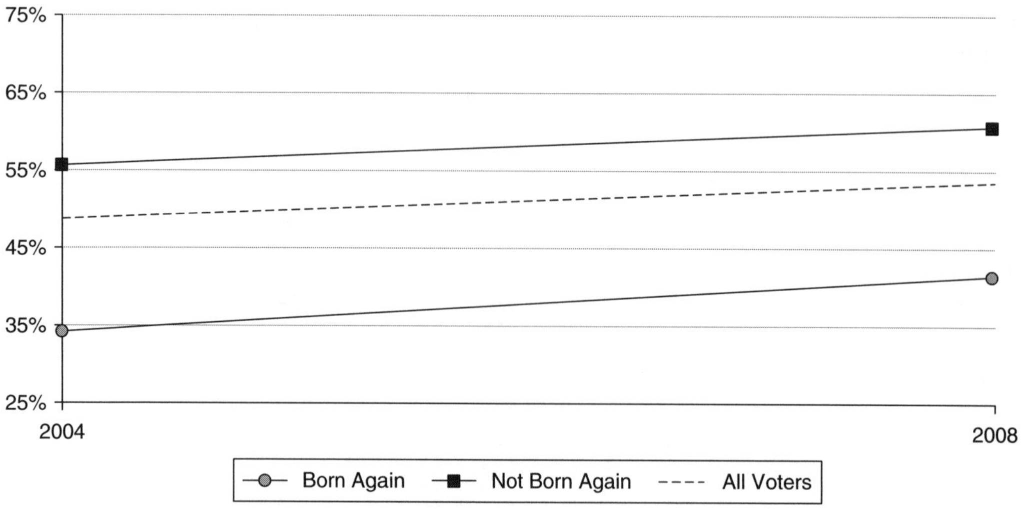

*Source:* National exit polls. See the section in Chapter 2 entitled "Creating a Cumulative National Data Set: Selecting Exit Polls" (pp. 28–29).

*Note:* When using these results to make inferences about the active electorate, the standard errors should be calculated using Table 2.2 (p. 36), which is explained in the adjacent section of Chapter 2, "Analyzing Exit Poll Questions: Estimating Sampling Error" (pp. 34–36). For a guide on how to understand the tables and figures of this chapter, see the section in Chapter 2 entitled "Presenting and Discussing the Exit Poll Data: Reading Chapter 4" (pp. 39–43). The rationale for using two-party percentages to show trends over time is given in this chapter, in the section entitled "Presidential Vote Choice" (pp. 124–131).

Christians in presidential elections (see Figure 4.15). Republican nominees have secured, on average, 62 percent of the two-party vote of born-again exit poll respondents since 2004, surpassing 58 percent of the two-party vote on both occasions.

Just as Obama made substantial gains among respondents attending religious services regularly, he did so with evangelical Christians in the 2008 exit poll (see Table 4.15 at the end of the chapter). McCain decisively won the evangelical vote of exit poll respondents, defeating Obama by a 16-point margin (57 percent to 41 percent). However, Obama improved significantly the Democrats' standing among evangelical Christians, nearly halving Bush's 31-point margin of victory over Kerry in the 2004 exit poll.

## Lifestyle Characteristics

A mixed relationship exists between lifestyle characteristics and presidential voting patterns in the exit polls. Some traits, such as education, marital status, and belonging to a union household, correspond to stark differences in presidential choices. Other traits, such as employment status and having a child in the household, have little association with vote decisions.

### Education

Education corresponds with notable differences in the presidential voting patterns of exit poll respondents. The most highly and lowly educated respondents tend to prefer Democratic presidential candidates (see Figure 4.16). Since 1988, a majority of respondents who have not completed high school have opted for Democratic presidential nominees in each election, awarding them an average of 61 percent of their two-party ballots. Similarly, Democratic candidates have won the support of a majority of respondents who have a postgraduate education in five of the past six elections, receiving an average of 55 percent of their two-party ballots.

By contrast, exit poll respondents with only a college degree generally support Republican presidential candidates. A majority of college graduates in the exit polls have voted for Republicans in five of the past six exit polls. On average, Republicans receive 53 percent of their two-party vote.

Exit poll respondents with only a high school degree or some college behave more like swing groups. Respondents with some college have voted for the winning presidential candidate in the past six elections, whereas respondents with only a high school degree have voted for the winning presidential candidate in five of the past six elections.

In the 2008 exit poll, Obama was preferred to McCain among every educational group, marking the first time a presidential nominee won across all levels of education since the question first appeared in its current form on the 1988 exit poll (see Table 4.16 at the end of the chapter). Obama easily won the support of respondents with less than a high school education, 63 percent to 35 percent, as well as respondents with a postgraduate education, 58 percent to 40 percent. Obama bested McCain among the bellwether groups, defeating him among respondents with

**Figure 4.16**  Democratic Share of Two-Party Presidential Vote by Education, 1988–2008

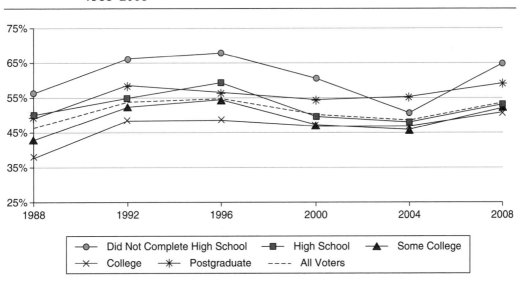

*Source:* National exit polls. See the section in Chapter 2 entitled "Creating a Cumulative National Data Set: Selecting Exit Polls" (pp. 28–29).

*Note:* When using these results to make inferences about the active electorate, the standard errors should be calculated using Table 2.2 (p. 36), which is explained in the adjacent section of Chapter 2, "Analyzing Exit Poll Questions: Estimating Sampling Error" (pp. 34–36). For a guide on how to understand the tables and figures of this chapter, see the section in Chapter 2 entitled "Presenting and Discussing the Exit Poll Data: Reading Chapter 4" (pp. 39–43). The rationale for using two-party percentages to show trends over time is given in this chapter, in the section entitled "Presidential Vote Choice" (pp. 124–131).

a high school degree, 52 percent to 46 percent, and among respondents with some college, 51 percent to 47 percent. Obama even secured a majority of overall ballots among respondents with only a college education, winning 50 percent to 48 percent over McCain.

## Employment Status

Employment status yields few differences in the presidential voting preferences of exit poll respondents (see Figure 4.17). Respondents employed full time cast an average of 52 percent of their two-party ballots for Democratic presidential candidates between 1996 and 2008, whereas respondents employed less than full time cast an average of 51 percent of their two-party ballots for Democratic candidates during the same period. The gap in the two-party vote between those employed full time and less than full time has averaged only 3 percentage points and has not exceeded 5 points in the past four exit polls.

The 2008 exit poll happened to find the largest employment gap in the presidential vote since the item first appeared (see Table 4.17 at the end of the chapter). Respondents employed full time cast 55 percent of their votes for Obama, compared to 44 percent for McCain. Among respondents not employed full time, 50 percent voted for Obama and 48 percent voted for McCain.

## Marital Status

Marriage is associated with a gap in the presidential voting preferences of exit poll respondents (see Figure 4.18). Republican presidential candidates fare better among married respondents,

**Figure 4.17** Democratic Share of Two-Party Presidential Vote by Employment Status, 1996–2008

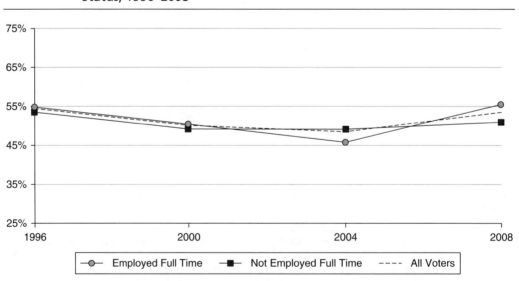

*Source:* National exit polls. See the section in Chapter 2 entitled "Creating a Cumulative National Data Set: Selecting Exit Polls" (pp. 28–29).

*Note:* When using these results to make inferences about the active electorate, the standard errors should be calculated using Table 2.2 (p. 36), which is explained in the adjacent section of Chapter 2, "Analyzing Exit Poll Questions: Estimating Sampling Error" (pp. 34–36). For a guide on how to understand the tables and figures of this chapter, see the section in Chapter 2 entitled "Presenting and Discussing the Exit Poll Data: Reading Chapter 4" (pp. 39–43). The rationale for using two-party percentages to show trends over time is given in this chapter, in the section entitled "Presidential Vote Choice" (pp. 124–131).

**Figure 4.18**   Democratic Share of Two-Party Presidential Vote by Marital Status, 1992–2008

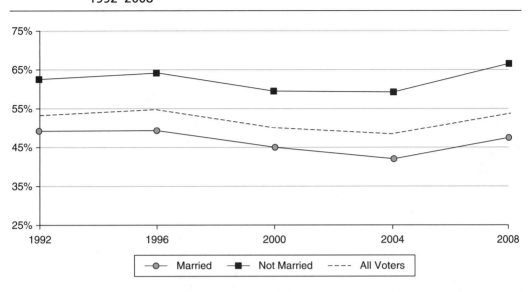

*Source:* National exit polls. See the section in Chapter 2 entitled "Creating a Cumulative National Data Set: Selecting Exit Polls" (pp. 28–29).

*Note:* When using these results to make inferences about the active electorate, the standard errors should be calculated using Table 2.2 (p. 36), which is explained in the adjacent section of Chapter 2, "Analyzing Exit Poll Questions: Estimating Sampling Error" (pp. 34–36). For a guide on how to understand the tables and figures of this chapter, see the section in Chapter 2 entitled "Presenting and Discussing the Exit Poll Data: Reading Chapter 4" (pp. 39–43). The rationale for using two-party percentages to show trends over time is given in this chapter, in the section entitled "Presidential Vote Choice" (pp. 124–131).

whereas unmarried respondents prefer Democratic presidential candidates. In the past five elections occurring since 1992, married respondents cast 53 percent of their two-party ballots on average for Republican nominees, whereas unmarried respondents cast their ballots for the Democratic nominees, with their support amounting to at least 59 percent of the two-party vote in each election.

The marriage gap appears to be expanding gradually over time. The marriage gap in the two-party presidential vote was 14 points in the 1992 exit poll. It has inched upward over the past several elections, despite different candidates and electoral outcomes. By the 2008 exit poll, the marriage gap in the two-party vote had grown to 19 points, producing the biggest disparity between the major-party candidates in the past five elections.

In the 2008 exit poll, married respondents preferred McCain to Obama, 52 percent to 47 percent (see Table 4.18 at the end of the chapter). Obama, by contrast, received 65 percent of the votes cast by unmarried exit poll respondents, compared to only 33 percent received by McCain.

### Child in Household

The presence of children in the household only occasionally serves to divide exit poll respondents, seemingly in years when issues affecting children are prominent in the presidential campaigns (see Figure 4.19). Differences between respondents with and without children in the household emerged in only two of the four presidential exit polls conducted between 1996 and 2008. In

**Figure 4.19**  Democratic Share of Two-Party Presidential Vote by Child in Household, 1996–2008

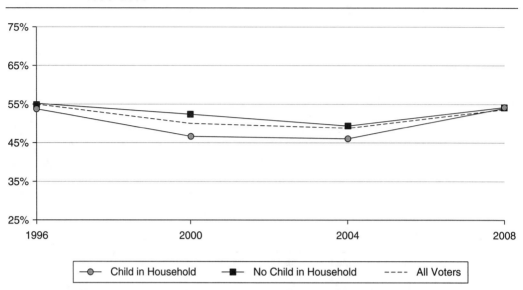

*Source:* National exit polls. See the section in Chapter 2 entitled "Creating a Cumulative National Data Set: Selecting Exit Polls" (pp. 28–29).

*Note:* When using these results to make inferences about the active electorate, the standard errors should be calculated using Table 2.2 (p. 36), which is explained in the adjacent section of Chapter 2, "Analyzing Exit Poll Questions: Estimating Sampling Error" (pp. 34–36). For a guide on how to understand the tables and figures of this chapter, see the section in Chapter 2 entitled "Presenting and Discussing the Exit Poll Data: Reading Chapter 4" (pp. 39–43). The rationale for using two-party percentages to show trends over time is given in this chapter, in the section entitled "Presidential Vote Choice" (pp. 124–131).

2000 and 2004, the gaps in the two-party presidential vote between the groups were 5 points and 3 points, respectively, and the Republican presidential nominee captured more support from respondents with children in the household than did his Democratic counterparts. It so happened that education was featured prominently in these elections. Education reform was a major platform of George W. Bush's campaign in 2000, and the No Child Left Behind Act was highlighted as one of Bush's legislative triumphs during his 2004 reelection campaign. By contrast, in 1996 and 2008, little attention was paid to education or, for that matter, any children's issues.

In the 2008 exit poll, there were no differences in the voting patterns of those with and without children in the household (see Table 4.19 at the end of the chapter). Respondents with and without children in the household both cast 53 percent of their overall ballots for Obama and 45 percent of their ballots for McCain. Not surprisingly, issues germane to children received scant coverage as the economy and foreign policy were at the forefront of the campaign.

### Union Household

Union households strongly support Democratic presidential candidates. In every exit poll from 1976 through 2008, respondents from union households backed Democratic presidential candidates by wide margins (see Figure 4.20). An average of nearly six out of ten union households (59 percent) voted for the Democratic presidential candidate, with their support typically exceeding the mean Democratic two-party vote in the exit poll by more than 10 percentage points.

**Figure 4.20**  Democratic Share of Two-Party Presidential Vote by Union Household, 1972–2008

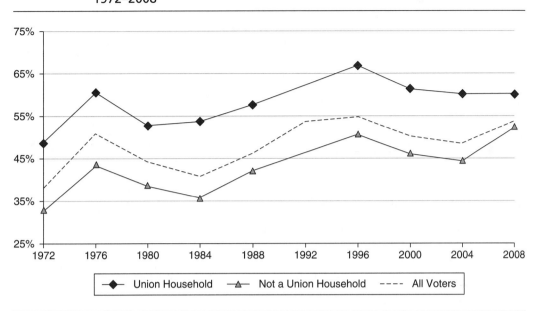

*Source:* National exit polls. See the section in Chapter 2 entitled "Creating a Cumulative National Data Set: Selecting Exit Polls" (pp. 28–29).

*Note:* When using these results to make inferences about the active electorate, the standard errors should be calculated using Table 2.2 (p. 36), which is explained in the adjacent section of Chapter 2, "Analyzing Exit Poll Questions: Estimating Sampling Error" (pp. 34–36). For a guide on how to understand the tables and figures of this chapter, see the section in Chapter 2 entitled "Presenting and Discussing the Exit Poll Data: Reading Chapter 4" (pp. 39–43). The rationale for using two-party percentages to show trends over time is given in this chapter, in the section entitled "Presidential Vote Choice" (pp. 124–131).

Obama continued these trends in 2008 (see Table 4.20 at the end of the chapter). Despite his poor showing among union households in the Democratic primaries, Obama received strong backing from them in the general election.[3] Obama secured 59 percent of the overall union vote, compared to 39 percent for McCain. These numbers are strikingly similar to those received by Kerry and Gore in the previous two elections.

## Political Orientations

Political orientations produce some of the largest differences in the presidential voting preferences of exit poll respondents. Longstanding predispositions, such as party identification and ideology, are associated strongly with vote choices, consistently predicting preferences over time in ways that would be expected. Short-term political evaluations are also tied closely to ballot choices but hinge on the characteristics of the subject being evaluated.

### Party Identification

Party identification, not surprisingly, polarizes the presidential vote choices of exit poll respondents (see Figure 4.21). Respondents identifying with one of the two major parties strongly support their party's respective nominees, whereas independent respondents are more divided in their choices. The electoral tendencies of these groups, however, have not behaved similarly over time.

**Figure 4.21**  Democratic Share of Two-Party Presidential Vote by Party Identification, 1972–2008

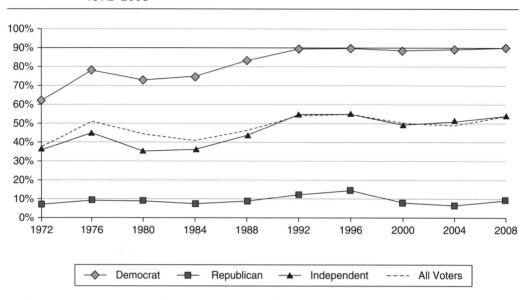

*Source:* National exit polls. See the section in Chapter 2 entitled "Creating a Cumulative National Data Set: Selecting Exit Polls" (pp. 28–29).

*Note:* When using these results to make inferences about the active electorate, the standard errors should be calculated using Table 2.2 (p. 36), which is explained in the adjacent section of Chapter 2, "Analyzing Exit Poll Questions: Estimating Sampling Error" (pp. 34–36). For a guide on how to understand the tables and figures of this chapter, see the section in Chapter 2 entitled "Presenting and Discussing the Exit Poll Data: Reading Chapter 4" (pp. 39–43). The rationale for using two-party percentages to show trends over time is given in this chapter, in the section entitled "Presidential Vote Choice" (pp. 124–131).

Exit poll respondents identifying with the Republican Party have steadily supported their party's nominees at roughly the same rate since 1972. Republican candidates have received, on average, 91 percent of the two-party presidential vote of Republican respondents, with little variation over time. Bill Clinton is the only Democratic nominee in the past four decades to garner more than 10 percent support from Republican respondents, receiving just 12 percent of their two-party vote in the 1992 exit poll and 14 percent in the 1996 exit poll.

By contrast, the preferences of exit poll respondents identifying with the Democratic Party have behaved far less consistently, although they have grown increasingly uniform over time. In the 1972 exit poll, just 62 percent of Democratic identifiers chose the Democratic candidate over the Republican candidate. Over the next five elections, though, Democratic identifiers gave Democratic presidential nominees an increasingly larger share of the vote. By the 1992 exit poll, 89 percent of Democratic identifiers cast their two-party ballots for the Democratic nominee, and that level of support has remained roughly the same ever since.

Exit poll respondents independent of either party have also altered their voting patterns over the past four decades. From 1972 through 1988, independent respondents preferred Republican candidates in every presidential election, giving them an average of 61 percent of their two-party vote. In 1992, independent respondents shifted toward the Democratic Party. Democratic nominees have received a majority of independents' two-party ballots in four of the past five elections, averaging 53 percent of their two-party vote.

In the 2008 exit poll, partisans gravitated to their respective presidential candidates in almost equal proportions (see Table 4.21 at the end of the chapter). Eighty-nine percent of Democrats voted for Obama, roughly the same proportion that supported Kerry in 2004. Ninety percent of Republicans voted for McCain, down nearly 4 percent from the proportion Bush received four years earlier. Independents broke for Obama, supporting him over McCain, 52 percent to 44 percent, in the full presidential vote. This was the largest share of the independent vote that a Democratic nominee had received since national exit polling commenced in 1972.

## Ideological Identification

Ideological identification divides the presidential preferences of exit poll respondents in much the same way as party identification (see Figure 4.22). Liberal respondents overwhelmingly vote for Democratic candidates, whereas conservative respondents overwhelmingly vote for Republican candidates. This ideological gap has widened over time, as the presidential preferences of liberals and conservatives have become more polarized.

In the 1976 exit poll, the gap in the two-party presidential vote between liberal and conservative respondents was 44 points, with Democrats receiving 73 percent of liberals' votes and 29 percent of conservatives' votes. Over the next nine elections, the ideology gap widened considerably, growing to more than 70 points in the past two elections. The increase in the gap is due primarily to the increasing uniformity of liberal respondents. Support for Democratic nominees

**Figure 4.22** Democratic Share of Two-Party Presidential Vote by Ideological Identification, 1976–2008

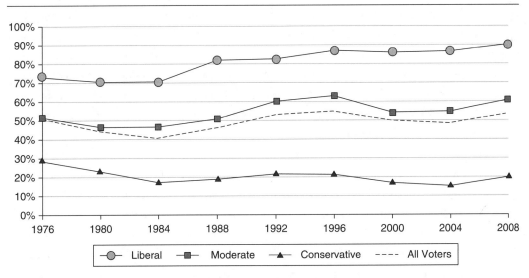

*Source:* National exit polls. See the section in Chapter 2 entitled "Creating a Cumulative National Data Set: Selecting Exit Polls" (pp. 28–29).

*Note:* When using these results to make inferences about the active electorate, the standard errors should be calculated using Table 2.2 (p. 36), which is explained in the adjacent section of Chapter 2, "Analyzing Exit Poll Questions: Estimating Sampling Error" (pp. 34–36). For a guide on how to understand the tables and figures of this chapter, see the section in Chapter 2 entitled "Presenting and Discussing the Exit Poll Data: Reading Chapter 4" (pp. 39–43). The rationale for using two-party percentages to show trends over time is given in this chapter, in the section entitled "Presidential Vote Choice" (pp. 124–131).

among liberals averaged 72 percent from 1976 to 1984. Since then, support for Democratic nominees has increased, reaching 90 percent of the two-party vote in 2008.

The polarization of conservative voting preferences occurred earlier than that of liberals, and to a lesser extent. From 1976 to 1984, the share of conservative exit poll respondents casting ballots for the Republican presidential nominee grew from 71 percent to 82 percent. Since 1984, Republicans have averaged 80 percent of conservatives' votes, with support fluctuating between 78 and 84 percent.

Moderate exit poll respondents have also changed their voting patterns over time. From 1976 to 1988, their votes were almost evenly split between the two major parties, with Republicans receiving 51 percent of the two-party vote. In the past five elections, moderates have become decidedly more Democratic in their presidential voting preferences. From 1992 to 2008, moderates have sided with the Democratic nominees, giving Democratic candidates 59 percent of their two-party vote.

In the 2008 exit poll, the voting orientations of each ideological group remained largely consistent, with Obama drawing greater support in the exit poll from each of the three constituencies than Kerry did four years earlier (see Table 4.22 at the end of the chapter). Liberal respondents went overwhelmingly for Obama, supporting him over McCain, 89 percent to 10 percent, in the overall vote—a margin 7 points greater than Kerry secured in 2004. Moderates also went strongly for Obama. Obama defeated McCain, 60 percent to 39 percent, receiving 5 points more support than Kerry in the exit poll. McCain easily won among conservatives, 78 percent to 20 percent, but even within this group Obama's support grew by 4 points since the last presidential contest.

## Last Presidential Vote

A strong correspondence exists between exit poll respondents' last presidential vote and their current presidential vote choice in the exit polls (see Figure 4.23). An overwhelming majority of respondents stick with the nominee from the party they voted for in the last presidential election. Respondents who voted for the Democratic nominee in the previous presidential election cast, on average, 85 percent of their two-party ballots for the Democratic presidential candidate. Similarly, respondents who voted for the Republican nominee in the previous election cast 85 percent of their two-party ballots for the Republican candidate.

The relationship between exit poll respondents' last presidential vote and current presidential vote is stronger when respondents' current choice wins than when they lose, suggesting that retaining the party's past supporters is vital to a candidate's electoral success. In 1972, 1980, 1984, 1988, 2000, and 2004, respondents who voted for the Republican in the previous election cast an average of 89 percent of their two-party ballots for the successful Republican presidential nominee. In 1976, 1992, 1996, and 2008, respondents who voted for the Republican in the previous election cast, on average, 80 percent of their two-party ballots for the unsuccessful Republican presidential nominee. Prior Democratic supporters showed the same pattern, with respondents who voted for the Democrat in the previous presidential election casting, on average, 89 percent of their two-party ballots for the successful Democratic presidential nominee and 83 percent for the unsuccessful Democratic nominee.

**Figure 4.23**   Democratic Share of Two-Party Presidential Vote by Presidential Vote in Last Election, 1972–2008

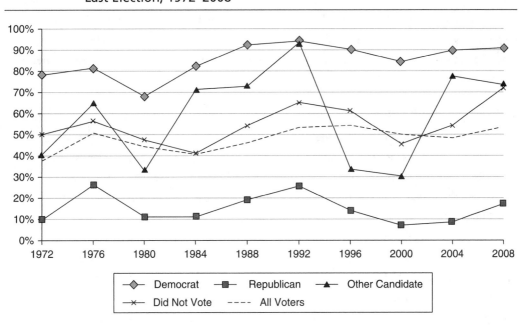

*Source:* National exit polls. See the section in Chapter 2 entitled "Creating a Cumulative National Data Set: Selecting Exit Polls" (pp. 28–29).

*Note:* When using these results to make inferences about the active electorate, the standard errors should be calculated using Table 2.2 (p. 36), which is explained in the adjacent section of Chapter 2, "Analyzing Exit Poll Questions: Estimating Sampling Error" (pp. 34–36). For a guide on how to understand the tables and figures of this chapter, see the section in Chapter 2 entitled "Presenting and Discussing the Exit Poll Data: Reading Chapter 4" (pp. 39–43). The rationale for using two-party percentages to show trends over time is given in this chapter, in the section entitled "Presidential Vote Choice" (pp. 124–131).

Respondents who chose third-party candidates in the previous presidential election typically comprise such a small proportion of exit poll respondents that it is difficult to identify patterns in their contemporary presidential choices. However, on the three occasions in the past four decades in which a particular third-party candidate received a sizeable portion of the vote, respondents who indicated voting for those candidates awarded a majority of their two-party ballots to the party whose candidate lost the popular vote. In 1984, respondents who had cast third-party votes in the past election, many of which were for John Anderson, cast 72 percent of their two-party ballots for the Democratic presidential nominee. In 1996 and 2000, respondents who had cast third-party votes in the 1992 and 1996 elections, many of them for Ross Perot, cast, respectively, 66 and 69 percent of their two-party ballots for the Republican presidential nominee.

Finally, exit poll respondents who did not vote in the previous presidential election typically cast their ballots for the successful presidential nominee. There were three exceptions, all of which occurred in races in which the incumbent party was attempting to secure reelection. In 1972, respondents who did not vote in 1968 cast 50 percent of their two-party ballots for George McGovern. In 1988, respondents who did not vote in the previous election cast 54 percent of their two-party ballots for Michael Dukakis. Finally, in 2004, respondents who did not vote in the 2000 presidential race cast 55 percent of their ballots for John Kerry.

In the 2008 exit poll, respondents once again remained consistent with their past partisan preferences (see Table 4.23 at the end of the chapter). Eighty-nine percent of respondents who voted for John Kerry in 2004 cast ballots for Obama in the 2008 election. Similarly, 82 percent of respondents who voted for George W. Bush in 2004 cast ballots for McCain in 2008. Respondents who did not vote in the 2004 election again sided with the winner, casting 71 percent of their ballots for Obama, compared to only 27 percent for McCain.

### Presidential Approval

Evaluations of the incumbent president's performance are strongly related to presidential vote choice in the exit polls (see Figure 4.24). Respondents who approve of the president's performance overwhelmingly prefer the nominee from the president's party. Conversely, respondents who disapprove of the president's performance predominantly choose the nominee from the party outside the White House.

The relationship between presidential approval and vote choice persists whether the incumbent is running or has been replaced by another member of his party. In the 2000 exit poll, respondents who approved of Bill Clinton gave Al Gore 79 percent of their two-party vote, whereas respondents who disapproved of Bill Clinton awarded George W. Bush 91 percent. The divide was even greater in 2004 with a Republican incumbent running for reelection. President George W. Bush received 91 percent of the two-party vote from those approving of his performance in office and only 6 percent of the two-party vote from those disapproving of his performance.

**Figure 4.24** Democratic Share of Two-Party Presidential Vote by Presidential Approval, 2000–2008

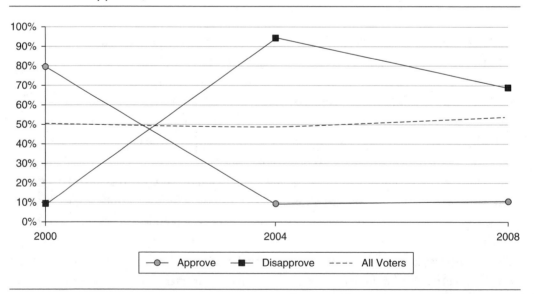

*Source:* National exit polls. See the section in Chapter 2 entitled "Creating a Cumulative National Data Set: Selecting Exit Polls" (pp. 28–29).

*Note:* When using these results to make inferences about the active electorate, the standard errors should be calculated using Table 2.2 (p. 36), which is explained in the adjacent section of Chapter 2, "Analyzing Exit Poll Questions: Estimating Sampling Error" (pp. 34–36). For a guide on how to understand the tables and figures of this chapter, see the section in Chapter 2 entitled "Presenting and Discussing the Exit Poll Data: Reading Chapter 4" (pp. 39–43). The rationale for using two-party percentages to show trends over time is given in this chapter, in the section entitled "Presidential Vote Choice" (pp. 124–131).

The relationship held once again in 2008, even though the incumbent party's nominee came from outside the administration (see Table 4.24 at the end of the chapter). Exit poll respondents who approved of the job George W. Bush was doing preferred McCain to Obama, 89 percent to 10 percent. Respondents who disapproved of George W. Bush's performance awarded Obama 67 percent of their vote, compared to only 31 percent for McCain.

## Perceived Direction of the Country

The relationship between judgments about the direction of the country and presidential vote operates similarly, although not as strongly, as the relationship between presidential approval and presidential vote (see Figure 4.25). In years when a Republican is in the White House, exit poll respondents who believe the country is moving in the right direction tend to vote for the Republican nominee for president, whereas those believing the country is off on the wrong track gravitate toward the Democratic candidate. The opposite is true with a Democratic administration. Respondents believing the country is moving in the right direction under a Democratic president tend to vote for the Democratic nominee, whereas those believing the country is off on the wrong track typically vote for the Republican nominee. This relationship appears to be stronger when an incumbent is running for reelection than when the sitting party has a new nominee for the White House.

In the 1996 exit poll, Bill Clinton received 75 percent of the two-party vote in his bid for reelection from those who thought the country was moving in the right direction under his leadership. He secured only 28 percent of the vote from those who thought the country was off on the wrong track. This gap shrunk somewhat when term limits prevented Clinton from running for

**Figure 4.25**  Democratic Share of Two-Party Presidential Vote by Perceived Direction of the Country, 1996–2008

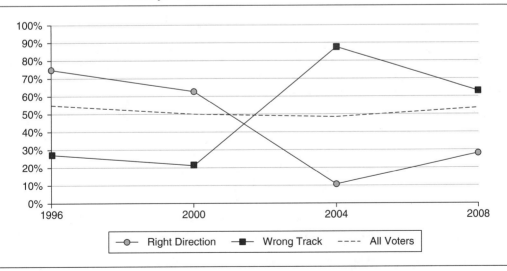

*Source:* National exit polls. See the section in Chapter 2 entitled "Creating a Cumulative National Data Set: Selecting Exit Polls" (pp. 28–29).

*Note:* When using these results to make inferences about the active electorate, the standard errors should be calculated using Table 2.2 (p. 36), which is explained in the adjacent section of Chapter 2, "Analyzing Exit Poll Questions: Estimating Sampling Error" (pp. 34–36). For a guide on how to understand the tables and figures of this chapter, see the section in Chapter 2 entitled "Presenting and Discussing the Exit Poll Data: Reading Chapter 4" (pp. 39–43). The rationale for using two-party percentages to show trends over time is given in this chapter, in the section entitled "Presidential Vote Choice" (pp. 124–131).

a third time. Exit poll respondents who thought the country was moving in the right direction awarded 63 percent of their two-party vote to Al Gore, whereas those who thought the country was off on the wrong track gave him 21 percent of their vote. The 2004 election again saw judgments about the direction of the country act as a referendum on George W. Bush's performance. Among those who thought the country was moving in the right direction, 90 percent voted to reelect him, whereas only 12 percent of those who thought the country was off on the wrong track voted to give him another term.

In the 2008 exit poll, the relationship between judgments of the country's direction and presidential vote once again weakened as the incumbent party nominated a fresh face for the White House (see Table 4.25 at the end of the chapter). Respondents who thought the country was moving in the right direction under the Bush administration preferred McCain to Obama, 71 percent to 27 percent. Conversely, respondents who thought the country was off on the wrong track under the Bush administration preferred Obama to McCain, 62 percent to 36 percent.

### Expected Life for the Next Generation

The impact of long-term forecasts about the direction of the country on the presidential vote choice of exit poll respondents is similar to the impact of short-term forecasts. Respondents who expect life for the next generation to be better than today vote for the incumbent party's

**Figure 4.26** Democratic Share of Two-Party Presidential Vote by Expected Life for the Next Generation, 1992–2000

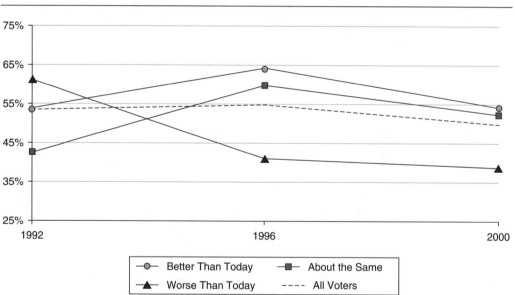

*Source:* National exit polls. See the section in Chapter 2 entitled "Creating a Cumulative National Data Set: Selecting Exit Polls" (pp. 28–29).

*Note:* When using these results to make inferences about the active electorate, the standard errors should be calculated using Table 2.2 (p. 36), which is explained in the adjacent section of Chapter 2, "Analyzing Exit Poll Questions: Estimating Sampling Error" (pp. 34–36). For a guide on how to understand the tables and figures of this chapter, see the section in Chapter 2 entitled "Presenting and Discussing the Exit Poll Data: Reading Chapter 4" (pp. 39–43). The rationale for using two-party percentages to show trends over time is given in this chapter, in the section entitled "Presidential Vote Choice" (pp. 124–131).

presidential nominee at higher rates than respondents who expect life for the next generation to be worse. The difference is that the strength of the relationship between long-term forecasts and vote choice is weaker than the relationship between short-term forecasts and vote choice. The average difference in the two-party Democratic vote between those who think the country is currently moving in the right direction and those who think it is off on the wrong track is 51 percentage points. By contrast, the average difference in the two-party Democratic vote between those who expect life for the next generation to be better and those who expect it to be worse is only 15 percentage points.

In the three presidential exit polls occurring from 1992 through 2000, respondents who expected life for the next generation to be better than today cast 55 percent of their ballots for nominees from the party controlling the presidency. Respondents expecting life to be about the same tended to stick with the party in power, as well, casting 56 percent of their ballots for nominees from the president's party. By contrast, respondents who expected life for the next generation to be worse than today cast 60 percent of their ballots for nominees from the party outside the White House.

National exit pollsters have not asked voters to forecast the long-term direction of the country in the past two presidential elections (see Table 4.26 at the end of the chapter). Instead, they have added it to the midterm exit poll rotation, where the question appears on the past several midterm exit polls. The variable has proven to have the same relationship with congressional vote choice as with presidential vote choice.

## Position on Government Activism

Differing views about government activism also underlie the presidential preferences of exit poll respondents. As Figure 4.27 shows, respondents who think the government should do more overwhelmingly support Democratic presidential candidates, whereas respondents who think the government does too much overwhelmingly support Republican candidates. These relationships have remained stable over time, despite different candidates and issues.

Exit poll respondents who think the federal government does too much have awarded, on average, 70 percent of their two-party ballots to Republican presidential nominees between 1992 and 2008. There has been little change in the preferences of this group through the years. Over the past five elections, support for Republican candidates among respondents preferring smaller government has fluctuated in a narrow 7-point range, not once dipping below two-thirds of the two-party vote.

By contrast, exit poll respondents believing the federal government should do more have cast, on average, 74 percent of their two-party ballots for Democratic presidential nominees. There has been somewhat more variation in support among respondents preferring a more activist government, with the Democratic share of the two-party vote fluctuating within a 12-point range. Nonetheless, respondents who believe the federal government should do more have always matched or surpassed the threshold of two-thirds support achieved by their counterparts.

The 2008 exit poll once again revealed this pattern (see Table 4.27 at the end of the chapter). Among respondents who thought the government should do more, 76 percent overall voted for Obama, compared to the 23 percent who voted for McCain. Among respondents who thought the government does too much, 71 percent voted for McCain, whereas 27 percent voted for Obama.

**Figure 4.27**   Democratic Share of Two-Party Presidential Vote by Position on Government Activism, 1992–2008

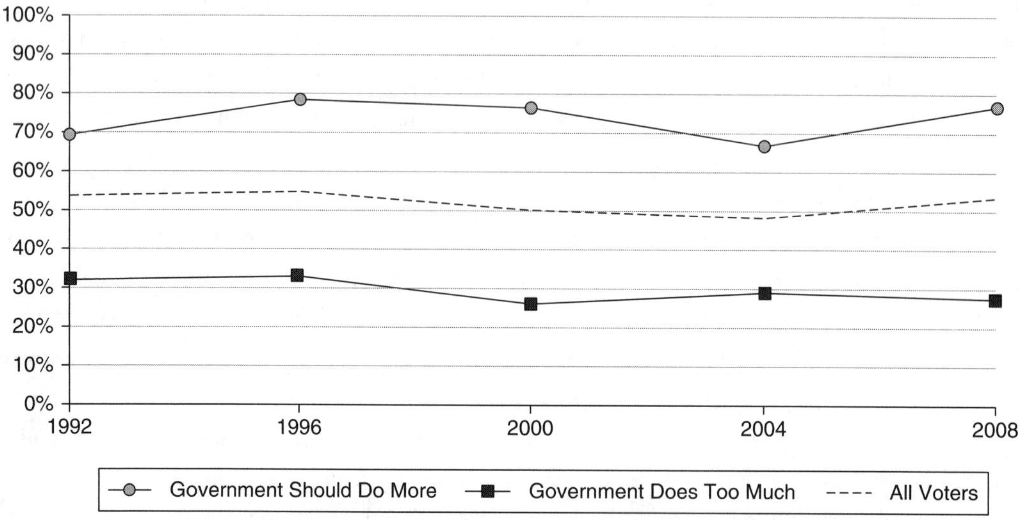

*Source:* National exit polls. See the section in Chapter 2 entitled "Creating a Cumulative National Data Set: Selecting Exit Polls" (pp. 28–29).

*Note:* When using these results to make inferences about the active electorate, the standard errors should be calculated using Table 2.2 (p. 36), which is explained in the adjacent section of Chapter 2, "Analyzing Exit Poll Questions: Estimating Sampling Error" (pp. 34–36). For a guide on how to understand the tables and figures of this chapter, see the section in Chapter 2 entitled "Presenting and Discussing the Exit Poll Data: Reading Chapter 4" (pp. 39–43). The rationale for using two-party percentages to show trends over time is given in this chapter, in the section entitled "Presidential Vote Choice" (pp. 124–131).

### First-Time Voter

Figure 4.28 shows the two-party vote for exit poll respondents casting a ballot for the first time. First-time voters are markedly more Democratic in their candidate preferences than are long-term voters. A majority of first-time voters in the exit polls supported Democratic candidates in every presidential election from 1996 through 2008. They cast an average of 60 percent of their two-party ballots for Democrats, which is 9 points more than Democratic candidates received from long-term voters over this period.

In the 2008 exit poll, respondents casting ballots for the first time again voted overwhelmingly for the Democratic nominee (see Table 4.28 at the end of the chapter). First-time voters cast 69 percent of their ballots overall for Obama, compared to only 31 percent for McCain. This was a 16-point increase from what Kerry secured from first-time voters in the 2004 exit poll and the largest advantage Democrats have had over Republicans among new participants since the question first appeared on the 1996 exit poll.

## Economic Considerations

Economic considerations are strongly associated with presidential preferences in the exit polls. Both respondents' nominal household income and their perceived financial situation correspond with their ballot decisions in expected ways. However, the relationship of each with presidential

**Figure 4.28**   Democratic Share of Two-Party Presidential Vote by First-Time Voter, 1996–2008

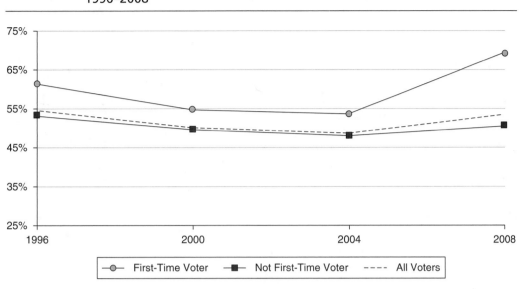

*Source:* National exit polls. See the section in Chapter 2 entitled "Creating a Cumulative National Data Set: Selecting Exit Polls" (pp. 28–29).

*Note:* When using these results to make inferences about the active electorate, the standard errors should be calculated using Table 2.2 (p. 36), which is explained in the adjacent section of Chapter 2, "Analyzing Exit Poll Questions: Estimating Sampling Error" (pp. 34–36). For a guide on how to understand the tables and figures of this chapter, see the section in Chapter 2 entitled "Presenting and Discussing the Exit Poll Data: Reading Chapter 4" (pp. 39–43). The rationale for using two-party percentages to show trends over time is given in this chapter, in the section entitled "Presidential Vote Choice" (pp. 124–131).

preferences varies, with the former tied to partisan predispositions and the latter conditional on the perceived performance of the incumbent presidential administration.

**Household Income**

Household income generally has a linear relationship with presidential vote choice in the exit polls (see Figure 4.29). As the household income of respondents rises, the proportion of respondents casting two-party ballots for Republican candidates increases. The income point at which a majority of respondents shift from supporting Democratic candidates to Republican candidates varies by the value of the dollar. Nonetheless, the extremes of the income scale have behaved similarly over time: respondents from the poorest households vote predominantly for Democratic presidential candidates, whereas respondents from the wealthiest households vote predominantly for Republican presidential candidates.

Over the past four presidential elections, exit poll respondents from households earning less than $50,000 have allotted a majority of their ballots for Democratic candidates. Respondents from households earning less than $30,000 cast an average of 62 percent of their two-party ballots for Democrats, allotting at least 58 percent of their votes for Democrats in each of these elections. Respondents from households earning between $30,000 and $49,999 have also preferred Democrats, albeit by smaller margins. From 1996 through 2008, they cast an average of 53 percent of their ballots for Democratic candidates.

**Figure 4.29**  Democratic Share of Two-Party Presidential Vote by Household Income, 1996–2008

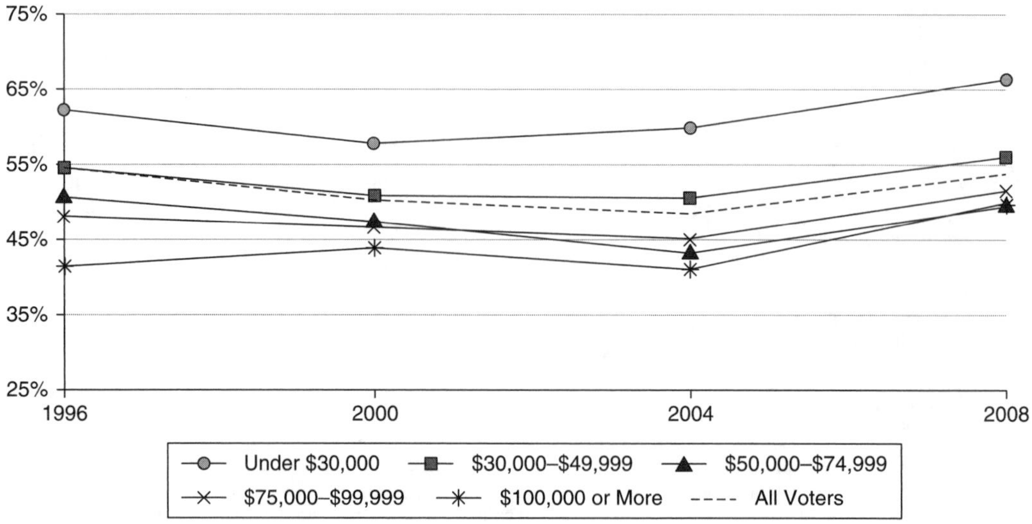

*Source:* National exit polls. See the section in Chapter 2 entitled "Creating a Cumulative National Data Set: Selecting Exit Polls" (pp. 28–29).

*Note:* When using these results to make inferences about the active electorate, the standard errors should be calculated using Table 2.2 (p. 36), which is explained in the adjacent section of Chapter 2, "Analyzing Exit Poll Questions: Estimating Sampling Error" (pp. 34–36). For a guide on how to understand the tables and figures of this chapter, see the section in Chapter 2 entitled "Presenting and Discussing the Exit Poll Data: Reading Chapter 4" (pp. 39–43). The rationale for using two-party percentages to show trends over time is given in this chapter, in the section entitled "Presidential Vote Choice" (pp. 124–131).

At the other end of the income scale, exit poll respondents from households earning $100,000 or more have predominantly supported Republican candidates in the presidential elections occurring since 1996. The wealthiest respondents cast a majority of their ballots for Republican nominees in every contest save 2008. They allotted an average of 56 percent of their vote to Republicans over this time span.

Exit poll respondents between these extremes—earning between $50,000 and $100,000—have not consistently supported one party or the other but have shifted preferences in the past decade and a half. Respondents from households earning between $50,000 and $74,999 cast a majority of their ballots for Clinton in 1996, and Bush in 2000 and 2004, and split their votes nearly evenly between the parties' nominees in 2008. Respondents from households earning between $75,000 and $99,999 cast a majority of their ballots for Dole in 1996 and Bush in 2000 and 2004, before switching sides and voting for Obama in 2008.

Obama did remarkably well across all income groups in the 2008 exit poll, better than any of his three predecessors in every category (see Table 4.29 at the end of the chapter). Obama defeated McCain, 65 percent to 33 percent, in the full presidential vote among respondents from households earning less than $30,000 and 55 percent to 44 percent among respondents from households earning between $30,000 and $49,999. Obama barely lost among respondents earning between $50,000 and $74,999 by a margin of 49 percent to 48 percent, but he bested McCain among respondents from households earning between $75,000 and $99,999 by a margin of 51 percent to 48 percent. Obama even did well among the wealthiest of exit poll respondents, tying McCain, 49 percent to 49 percent, among those from households earning $100,000 or more.

## Four-Year Household Financial Situation

Exit poll respondents' perceptions of their household financial situation are strongly related to their presidential preference. Respondents who report that their household financial condition has gotten better in the past four years prefer to stick with presidential candidates from the party occupying the White House, whereas respondents who indicate that their household financial situation has gotten worse choose candidates from the out party. Those who report that their household financial situation has remained about the same typically split their votes between the parties' nominees.

In the election years when Republicans controlled the White House—1992, 2004, and 2008—exit poll respondents who said their household financial situation had gotten better in the past four years cast, on average, 65 percent of their ballots for Republican presidential candidates, whereas respondents who said that their household financial situation had worsened cast, on average, 70 percent of their ballots for Democratic nominees. Conversely, in the elections occurring during a Democratic administration—1996 and 2000—respondents who said their household financial situation had gotten better in the past four years cast 68 percent of their ballots for the

**Figure 4.30**  Democratic Share of Two-Party Presidential Vote by Four-Year Household Financial Situation, 1992–2008

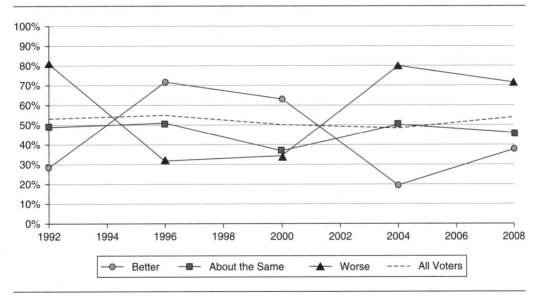

*Source:* National exit polls. See the section in Chapter 2 entitled "Creating a Cumulative National Data Set: Selecting Exit Polls" (pp. 28–29).

*Note:* When using these results to make inferences about the active electorate, the standard errors should be calculated using Table 2.2 (p. 36), which is explained in the adjacent section of Chapter 2, "Analyzing Exit Poll Questions: Estimating Sampling Error" (pp. 34–36). For a guide on how to understand the tables and figures of this chapter, see the section in Chapter 2 entitled "Presenting and Discussing the Exit Poll Data: Reading Chapter 4" (pp. 39–43). The rationale for using two-party percentages to show trends over time is given in this chapter, in the section entitled "Presidential Vote Choice" (pp. 124–131).

Democratic nominee, and respondents who said their financial situation had worsened cast 67 percent of their votes for the Republican nominee.

Exit poll respondents who report that their household finances remained about the same over the prior four years typically split their votes between the two parties' nominees. Only once in the past five elections has the margin between the two major parties exceeded 8 percentage points (in 2000, George W. Bush defeated Al Gore, 63 percent to 37 percent, among respondents whose household incomes stayed the same from the previous presidential election). In the 1992, 1996, and 2004 elections, the gap in the two-party vote was 2 points or less.

With George W. Bush in the White House, the 2008 exit poll again held to form (see Table 4.30 at the end of the chapter). Respondents who thought their household financial situation had improved over the past four years strongly supported McCain over Obama, 60 percent to 37 percent, in the full presidential vote. Respondents who thought that their household finances had gotten worse strongly supported Obama over McCain, 71 percent to 28 percent. Respondents who thought their finances had stayed about the same fell in between, preferring Obama to McCain, 53 percent to 45 percent.

## Perception of Current National Economic Conditions

The relationship between exit poll respondents' perceptions of national economic conditions and their presidential preference operates similarly to their perceptions of their own financial situation. Respondents who perceive the national economy to be performing well tend to prefer candidates from the party controlling the White House, whereas respondents who perceive the national economy is performing badly typically choose candidates from the out party. During the 1992, 2004, and 2008 elections, in which George H. W. Bush and George W. Bush were in the White House, respondents who thought the economy was performing well cast, on average, 83 percent of their two-party ballots for the Republican presidential nominee, whereas respondents who thought the economy was performing badly cast, on average, 67 percent of their two-party ballots for the Democratic presidential nominee. During the 1996 and 2000 elections, the opposite occurred. With Bill Clinton in the White House, respondents who thought the economy was doing well cast, on average, 60 percent of their two-party ballots for the Democratic presidential nominee, and respondents who thought the economy was doing badly cast, on average, 64 percent of their ballots for the Republican presidential nominee.

In 2008, George W. Bush was the face of the government's economic policy. Exit poll respondents who thought the economy was doing well chose to stick with the party in the White House, preferring McCain to Obama, 72 percent to 26 percent, in the full presidential vote (see Table 4.31 at the end of the chapter). Respondents who thought the economy was doing badly opted for a new direction, preferring Obama to McCain, 54 percent to 44 percent.

## Judgments of Future National Economic Conditions

The impact of judgments about future national economic conditions on vote choice does not appear to be conditional on which party controls the White House. With only two time points,

**Figure 4.31**   Democratic Share of Two-Party Presidential Vote by Judgments of Current National Economic Conditions, 1992–2008

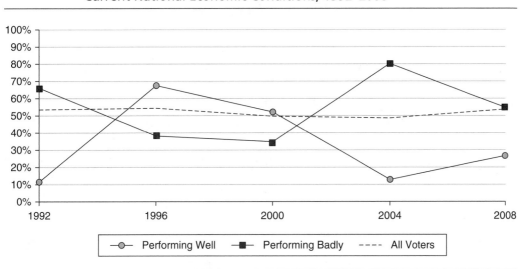

*Source:* National exit polls. See the section in Chapter 2 entitled "Creating a Cumulative National Data Set: Selecting Exit Polls" (pp. 28–29).

*Note:* When using these results to make inferences about the active electorate, the standard errors should be calculated using Table 2.2 (p. 36), which is explained in the adjacent section of Chapter 2, "Analyzing Exit Poll Questions: Estimating Sampling Error" (pp. 34–36). For a guide on how to understand the tables and figures of this chapter, see the section in Chapter 2 entitled "Presenting and Discussing the Exit Poll Data: Reading Chapter 4" (pp. 39–43). The rationale for using two-party percentages to show trends over time is given in this chapter, in the section entitled "Presidential Vote Choice" (pp. 124–131).

it is difficult to draw conclusions from the data. Nonetheless, exit poll respondents who were optimistic about the future direction of the national economy supported Democratic presidential nominees, whereas respondents pessimistic about the future direction of the national economy supported Republican presidential nominees (see Figure 4.32).

In the 2000 exit poll, with Democrat Bill Clinton as president, 53 percent of respondents who thought the economy would be better in the next year voted for Democatic nominee Al Gore (see Table 4.32 at the end of the chapter). Conversely, exit poll respondents who thought the economy would get worse preferred Bush to Gore, 54 percent to 43 percent, in the full presidential vote. Respondents who thought the economy would stay about the same split their votes between the major-party nominees.

Eight years later saw economic optimists continue to gravitate toward the Democratic nominee and pessimists gravitate toward the Republican nominee, even though Republican George W. Bush occupied the White House. Among respondents who thought national economic conditions would get better in the next year, 61 percent voted for Obama, whereas 38 percent voted for McCain. Conversely, respondents who thought the economy would get worse preferred McCain to Obama, 54 percent to 43 percent. Respondents who thought the economy would be about the same fell in between, casting 52 percent of their ballots for Obama and 46 percent for McCain.

**Figure 4.32**  Democratic Share of Two-Party Presidential Vote by Judgments of Future National Economic Conditions, 2000–2008

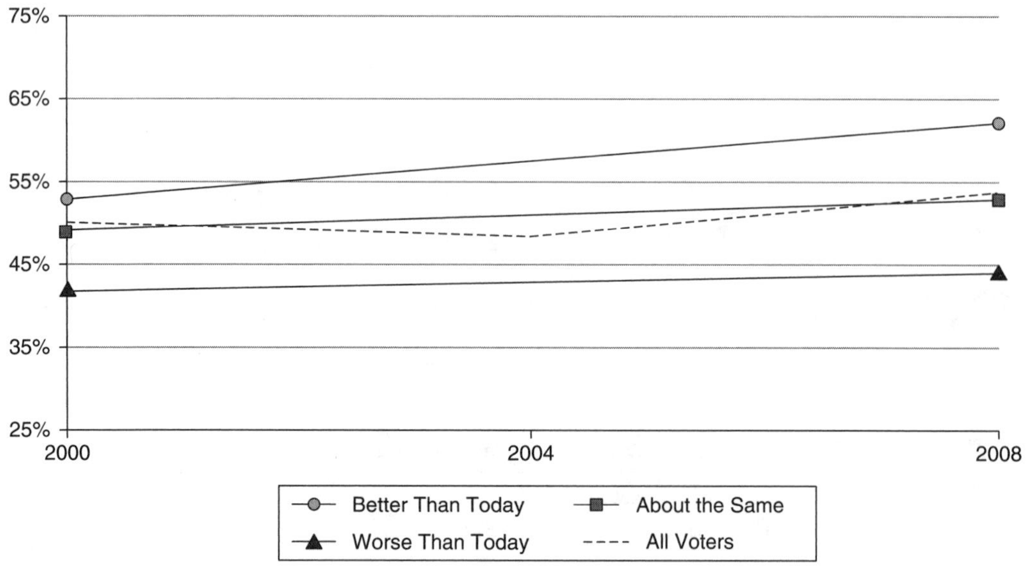

*Source:* National exit polls. See the section in Chapter 2 entitled "Creating a Cumulative National Data Set: Selecting Exit Polls" (pp. 28–29).

*Note:* When using these results to make inferences about the active electorate, the standard errors should be calculated using Table 2.2 (p. 36), which is explained in the adjacent section of Chapter 2, "Analyzing Exit Poll Questions: Estimating Sampling Error" (pp. 34–36). For a guide on how to understand the tables and figures of this chapter, see the section in Chapter 2 entitled "Presenting and Discussing the Exit Poll Data: Reading Chapter 4" (pp. 39–43). The rationale for using two-party percentages to show trends over time is given in this chapter, in the section entitled "Presidential Vote Choice" (pp. 124–131).

## Partisan Predispositions of the Presidential Exit Polls

Elections are not won or lost by attracting the support of a single group of voters, but by assembling and mobilizing a combination of groups from across the electorate. To craft winning coalitions, candidates not only must satisfy like-minded rank-and-file members of the party, but also must attract voters of differing political orientations, some of whom may disagree with numerous positions in the party platform. Identifying both types of voters—those predisposed toward a party's candidate and those susceptible to changing their vote from one party to the other—is often an initial step in determining campaign strategies and formulating campaign messages.

There has been considerable debate over how best to identify groups predisposed toward one party or those that are up for grabs in the electorate. It typically hinges on answers to particular questions.[4] What types of groups should be considered—those defined by demographic characteristics, political preferences, or environmental conditions? What type of support should be considered—past vote decisions or current evaluations of the candidates or parties? How much support is necessary to confidently predict future ballot choices? What time frame of support should be considered? We answer these questions by making use of all the information available in this chapter and presenting it to readers in a way that allows them to reorganize it using their own criteria if they disagree with our choices.

To determine the predispositions of various groups in the presidential exit polls, we categorized each group according to its long-term partisan voting patterns, regardless of the type of characteristic from which it was derived. We began by rank ordering every group examined in this chapter by the average share of the two-party Democratic and Republican vote over the time period during which the question used to create the group was administered. We then assigned each group to one of five categories along a scale defined by the group's share of the two-party vote: Democratic base groups, Democratic-leaning groups, swing groups, Republican-leaning groups, and Republican base groups.

Base groups are the groups of exit poll respondents that cast at least 67 percent of their two-party ballots, on average, for the Democratic presidential nominees or the Republican presidential nominees over time. They can be viewed as consistently loyal to one party or the other over time, regardless of contextual factors such as the state of the economy, military success, the popularity of the president, or even the performance of the nominees themselves. Theoretically, political parties need not worry about convincing base groups to vote for their respective presidential candidates but can focus their attention instead on getting them to turn out for an election, knowing that they will provide overwhelming support for the party's nominee.

Leaning groups are groups that cast, on average, 56 to 66 percent of their two-party ballots for one political party or the other over time. Generally speaking, they consistently support candidates from one party or the other, deviating only rarely to the other party. Political parties can usually rely on these groups but might pepper them with reinforcing messages to ensure that they stay on board.

Swing groups are the groups of respondents that cast 45 to 55 percent of their two-party ballots for Democratic or Republican presidential candidates. Their tepid backing of one party or the other over time usually manifests itself in their willingness to shift a majority of their support back and forth between the parties over time. In other words, swing groups vote Democratic in some elections and Republican in other elections. Political parties often need to attract a number of these groups if they are to win elections, a feat typically accomplished by identifying a narrow set of concerns or issues that are appealing to them.

Readers need to exercise caution when interpreting these classifications. First, these groups of exit poll respondents do not comprise the universe of groups in the active electorate. They were generated from questions asked repeatedly on the exit polls; however, an infinite number of groups could have been generated by including different questions or alternative response options for the questions considered. Second, the groups of exit poll respondents used in these classifications are not mutually exclusive. Respondents can have membership in one or more of these groups, meaning the cumulative frequency distribution of these groups exceeds 100 percent. Finally, these exit poll groups vary in their duration. The questions used to create them were not included on every survey instrument. Some groups were examined in all ten elections from 1972 to 2008, whereas others were asked in eight or five or even as few as two elections (in the case of evangelical). As a result, some of the groups may have been classified in categories that they would not have found themselves placed in under longer time frames. For example, exit poll groups defined by their reactions to contemporary environmental conditions, such as the state of the economy, may have been categorized differently if the question had been asked at earlier points in time or under different presidential administrations.

Taken together, these shortcomings suggest that readers are best served by considering these groups individually, rather than in combination. The results alert us to commonalities among seemingly dissimilar groups, permitting us to see the different types of voters that might play a role in each party's coalition. However, they do not enable us to determine the structure of winning coalitions or, in other words, the proportion of the vote that must be secured across groups to ensure election. To do so would require a collection of specific mutually exclusive groups that cover the entire active electorate and appear over time. Although we have this exclusivity for groups generated from a single question in a single year, we do not have it for the collection of groups generated from an array of questions administered over time. Nonetheless, many insights can be gained from this classification about the behavior of voter groups in the exit polls.

### Democratic Groups

Thirteen of the eighty-four groups of exit poll respondents examined can be described as the Democratic base (see Table 4.33 at the end of the chapter). Each group preferred Democratic presidential nominees to their Republican counterparts by a two-to-one margin, on average, over time, despite different candidate personalities, issues in the campaign, and economic conditions at the time of the election. Three of the most loyal Democratic groups are defined by physical characteristics—respondents who are black, Hispanic/Latino, or gay or bisexual. Three more are defined by religious characteristics—respondents who are Jewish; those who practice a religion other than Protestantism, Catholicism, or Judaism; or those who do not affiliate with a religion at all. The remaining Democratic base groups comprise respondents who possess similar orientations or preferences as the Democratic Party itself: they identify as Democrats or liberals, voted for the Democratic candidate in the last election, think the government should be more active in solving the nation's problems, approve of Democratic presidents or disapprove of Republican presidents, or thought the Republican candidate campaigned unfairly.

Thirteen of the eighty-four exit poll groups lean toward the Democratic Party, casting, on average, 56 to 66 percent of their two-party ballots for Democratic presidential candidates. These leaning groups are less resolute in their support for Democratic nominees than base groups, even willing to support Republican candidates on rare occasions. Nonetheless, they have proved critical to Democratic efforts to build winning coalitions in presidential elections. They comprise respondents with a wide range of traits, including those who attend church infrequently; are unmarried; failed to complete high school; are from a race other than white, black, Hispanic/Latino, or Asian; are voting in a presidential election for the first time; reside in urban areas; voted for a third party in the previous presidential election; are not born-again Christians; live in union households; and think the future will be better. Also included in the list is the group of respondents who report that their household finances have gotten worse in the last four years, although it has acted like a Democratic base group when a Republican was in the White House (averaging

77 percent of the two-party vote for the Democrats over three elections) and a Republican base group when a Democrat was in the White House (averaging 67 percent of the two-party vote for Republicans over two elections).

## Republican Groups

Seven of the eighty-four groups of exit poll respondents considered in this chapter comprise the Republican base (see Table 4.34 at the end of the chapter). Each awarded Republican nominees at least 67 percent of their two-party vote, on average, over time. All seven of these groups feature political characteristics strongly aligned with the Republican Party: respondents who are Republican, are conservative, voted for a Republican in the last presidential election, thought the Democratic candidate campaigned unfairly, thought that the government intervenes too much in problems best handled by the free-enterprise system, and approve of Republican presidents or disapprove of Democratic presidents. None of these groups have supported Democratic nominees in any election year in which they were examined by the exit polls.

Thirteen of the eighty-four exit poll groups can be identified as Republican-leaning groups—groups that typically support Republican presidential candidates, but by smaller margins. Many of these groups have been popularized in the press as key components of the Republican coalition. They comprise respondents who are white, Protestant, born-again Christian, frequent church attendees, or rural residents, or they come from non–union households, live in households earning more than $100,000 a year, or reside in the South. Also included in the list are respondents whose household finances have gotten better in the last four years, although this group has acted like a Republican base group when a Republican was in the White House (averaging 72 percent of the two-party vote for Republicans over three elections) and a Democratic base group when a Democrat was in the White House (averaging 67 percent of the two-party vote for Democrats over two elections). Similarly, respondents who think the country is on the right track have acted like a Republican base group when a Republican was in the White House (averaging 81 percent of the two-party vote for Republicans), but like a Democratic base group when a Democrat was in the White House (averaging 69 percent of the two-party vote for Democrats).

## Swing Groups

The remaining groups of exit poll respondents can best be described as competitive groups or swing groups (see Table 4.35 at the end of the chapter). The average margin of victory for one party or the other is 10 points or less, making them among the most hotly contested groups of voters. Winning a sizable proportion of them is typically necessary for candidates to assemble a coalition of support capable of propelling them to the White House. Obama won 86 percent of these groups in 2008, including seventeen out of the nineteen groups that Bush had won in 2004.

Swing groups are rooted in almost every type of voter. Generally speaking, though, they comprise voters who fall in the middle of a scale, such as those who come from households earning around the median income, are ideologically moderate, or reside in suburban areas. Some groups swing based on the president in the White House at the time of election. For instance, 75 percent of exit poll respondents who think the country is off on the wrong track have voted against the party of the incumbent president, but because two of the four elections have featured Republican incumbents and two have featured Democratic incumbents, the average for this category is roughly 50 percent. Readers are encouraged not to stop at the basic categorizations, but to delve deeper into the behavior of each group over time.

## Notes

[1] All percentages presented in the text have been rounded to the nearest whole number. Any calculations necessary to compute them are also based on rounded whole numbers.

[2] Richard L. McCormick, "Ethno-Cultural Interpretations of Nineteenth-Century American Voting Behavior," *Political Science Quarterly* 89 (1974): 351–377.

[3] Monika McDermott, "Why Clinton Won Pennsylvania," 2008, www.cbsnews.com/stories/2008/04/22/politics/main4036287.shtml?source=mostpop_story.

[4] William G. Mayer, *The Swing Voter in American Politics* (Washington, DC: Brookings Institution Press, 2008).

**Table 4.1**   Democratic Share of Two-Party Electoral Votes, 1972–2008

| Year | Number of Democratic Electoral College Votes | Two-Party Democratic Electoral College Votes |
|------|-----------------------------------------------|----------------------------------------------|
| 2008 | 365 | 68% |
| 2004 | 251 | 47% |
| 2000 | 266 | 49% |
| 1996 | 379 | 70% |
| 1992 | 370 | 69% |
| 1988 | 111 | 21% |
| 1984 | 13 | 2% |
| 1980 | 49 | 9% |
| 1976 | 297 | 55% |
| 1972 | 17 | 3% |

*Source:* Harold W. Stanley and Richard G. Niemi, *Vital Statistics on American Politics, 2011–2012* (Washington, DC: CQ Press, 2011).

**Table 4.2**   Presidential Vote in the Exit Polls, 1972–2008

| | Year | Two-Party Democratic Presidential Vote | Full Presidential Vote | | | |
|---|---|---|---|---|---|---|
| | | | Democratic Vote | Republican Vote | Third-Party Vote | Number of Respondents |
| All Voters | 2008 | 53.7% | 52.7% | 45.4% | 1.9% | 17,836 |
| | 2004 | 48.5% | 48.0% | 51.0% | 1.0% | 13,660 |
| | 2000 | 50.2% | 48.4% | 48.1% | 3.5% | 13,106 |
| | 1996 | 54.7% | 49.1% | 40.6% | 10.3% | 16,375 |
| | 1992 | 53.6% | 43.4% | 37.6% | 19.1% | 15,237 |
| | 1988 | 46.2% | 45.6% | 53.2% | 1.1% | 11,596 |
| | 1984 | 40.8% | 40.4% | 58.8% | 0.8% | 9,146 |
| | 1980 | 44.3% | 40.6% | 51.1% | 8.3% | 15,168 |
| | 1976 | 51.0% | 50.2% | 48.2% | 1.5% | 15,202 |
| | 1972 | 38.1% | 37.3% | 60.7% | 2.0% | 17,595 |
| | Average | 48.1% | 45.6% | 49.5% | 5.0% | |

**Question Wording for Presidential Vote** (Coded: Democratic Vote = 1; Republican Vote = 2; Third-Party Vote = 3; Did Not Vote = 4):

**1972:** "In the presidential election, who did you just vote for? . . . Nixon (2); McGovern (1); Schmitz (3); Other (3)"

**1976:** "In the presidential election, who did you just vote for? . . . Gerald Ford (2); Jimmy Carter (1); Eugene McCarthy (3); Lester Maddox (3); Other (please specify) (3); Didn't vote for president (4)"

**1980:** "In the presidential election, who did you just vote for? . . . Ronald Reagan (2); John Anderson (3); Ed Clark (3); Barry Commoner (3); Jimmy Carter (1); Other (please specify) (3); Didn't vote for president (4)"

**1984:** "In the presidential election, who did you just vote for? . . . Walter Mondale/Geraldine Ferraro (Dem) (1); Ronald Reagan/George Bush (Rep) (2); Someone else (3); Didn't vote (4)"

**1988:** "In today's election for president, did you just vote for . . . Michael Dukakis/Lloyd Bentsen (Dem) (1); George Bush/Dan Quayle (Rep) (2); Other: Who? (3); Didn't vote for president (4)"

**1992:** "In today's election for president, did you vote for . . . Bill Clinton (Dem) (1); George Bush (Rep) (2); Ross Perot (Ind) (3); Other: Who? (3); Didn't vote for president (4)"

**1996:** "In today's election for president, did you vote for . . . Bill Clinton (Dem) (1); Bob Dole (Rep) (2); Ross Perot (Ref) (3); Other: Who? (3); Didn't vote for president (4)"

**2000:** "In today's election for president, did you just vote for . . . George W. Bush (Rep) (2); Al Gore (Dem) (1); Pat Buchanan (Ref) (3); Ralph Nader (Gre) (3); Other: Who? (3); Did not vote for president (4)"

**2004:** "In today's election for president, did you just vote for . . . John Kerry (Dem) (1); George W. Bush (Rep) (2); Ralph Nader (Ind) (3); Other: Who? (3); Did not vote for president (4)"

**2008:** "In today's election for president, did you just vote for . . . Barack Obama (Dem) (1); John McCain (Rep) (2); Other: Who? (3); Did not vote (4)"

*Source:* National exit polls. See the section in Chapter 2 entitled "Creating a Cumulative National Data Set: Selecting Exit Polls" (pp. 28–29).

*Note:* When using these results to make inferences about the active electorate, the standard errors should be calculated using Table 2.2 (p. 36), which is explained in the adjacent section of Chapter 2, "Analyzing Exit Poll Questions: Estimating Sampling Error" (pp. 34–36). For a guide on how to understand the tables and figures of this chapter, see the section in Chapter 2 entitled "Presenting and Discussing the Exit Poll Data: Reading Chapter 4" (pp. 39–43). The rationale for using two-party percentages to show trends over time is given in this chapter, in the section entitled "Presidential Vote Choice" (pp. 124–131).

**Table 4.3** Composition of the Exit Polls by the Perceived Unfairness of Candidates' Campaigns, 1992–2008

| Year | Democrat Was Unfair | Republican Was Unfair | Both Were Unfair | Neither Was Unfair | Number of Respondents |
|------|------|------|------|------|------|
| 2008 | 9.9% | 25.1% | 41.5% | 23.5% | 8,361 |
| 2004 | 23.1% | 15.7% | 47.4% | 13.8% | 3,161 |
| 2000 | 26.1% | 14.9% | 36.7% | 22.3% | 3,020 |
| 1996 | 14.7% | 32.3% | 31.5% | 21.5% | 3,819 |
| 1992 | 9.4% | 31.3% | 46.9% | 12.4% | 3,833 |
| Average | 16.6% | 23.9% | 40.8% | 18.7% | |

**Question Wording for Perceived Unfairness of Candidates' Campaigns** (Coded: Democrat Was Unfair = 1; Republican Was Unfair = 2; Both Were Unfair = 3; Neither Was Unfair = 4):

**1992:** "Did either of these candidates for president attack the other unfairly? . . . Bill Clinton did (1); George Bush did (2); Both did (3); Neither did (4)"

**1996:** "Did either of these candidates for president attack the other unfairly? . . . Bill Clinton did (1); Bob Dole did (2); Both did (3); Neither did (4)"

**2000:** "Did either of these candidates for president attack the other unfairly? . . . Al Gore did (1); George W. Bush did (2); Both did (3); Neither did (4)"

**2004:** "Did either of these candidates for president attack the other unfairly? . . . Only John Kerry did (1); Only George W. Bush did (2); Both did (3); Neither did (4)"

**2008:** "Did either of these candidates for president attack the other unfairly? . . . Only Barack Obama (1); Only John McCain (2); Both of them (3); Neither of them (4)"

*Source:* National exit polls. See the section in Chapter 2 entitled "Creating a Cumulative National Data Set: Selecting Exit Polls" (pp. 28–29).

*Note:* When using these results to make inferences about the active electorate, the standard errors should be calculated using Table 2.2 (p. 36), which is explained in the adjacent section of Chapter 2, "Analyzing Exit Poll Questions: Estimating Sampling Error" (pp. 34–36). For a guide on how to understand the tables and figures of this chapter, see the section in Chapter 2 entitled "Presenting and Discussing the Exit Poll Data: Reading Chapter 4" (pp. 39–43). The rationale for using two-party percentages to show trends over time is given in this chapter, in the section entitled "Presidential Vote Choice" (pp. 124–131).

**Table 4.4**  Presidential Vote by the Perceived Unfairness of Candidates' Campaigns, 1992–2008

| | | Two-Party Presidential Vote | | Full Presidential Vote | | | |
|---|---|---|---|---|---|---|---|
| Category | Year | Two-Party Democratic Vote | Difference from Mean Democratic Two-Party Vote | Democratic Vote | Republican Vote | Third-Party Vote | Number of Respondents |
| Democrat | 2008 | 15.9% | −37.8% | 15.8% | 83.3% | 0.9% | 739 |
| Was | 2004 | 5.4% | −43.1% | 5.3% | 94.4% | 0.3% | 686 |
| Unfair | 2000 | 8.3% | −41.9% | 8.2% | 90.5% | 1.3% | 741 |
| | 1996 | 17.8% | −36.9% | 17.1% | 79.1% | 3.8% | 520 |
| | 1992 | 10.9% | −42.7% | 9.9% | 80.6% | 9.6% | 350 |
| | Average | 11.7% | −40.5% | 11.3% | 85.6% | 3.2% | |
| Republican | 2008 | 97.0% | 43.3% | 96.2% | 3.0% | 0.8% | 2,419 |
| Was | 2004 | 92.9% | 44.5% | 92.7% | 7.1% | 0.2% | 525 |
| Unfair | 2000 | 93.6% | 43.4% | 91.7% | 6.3% | 2.0% | 454 |
| | 1996 | 91.7% | 36.9% | 86.5% | 7.9% | 5.7% | 1,316 |
| | 1992 | 95.6% | 42.0% | 86.6% | 4.0% | 9.4% | 1,230 |
| | Average | 94.1% | 42.0% | 90.7% | 5.6% | 3.6% | |
| Both Were | 2008 | 41.9% | −11.8% | 40.9% | 56.7% | 2.4% | 3,204 |
| Unfair | 2004 | 53.9% | 5.4% | 53.2% | 45.6% | 1.2% | 1,506 |
| | 2000 | 54.4% | 4.2% | 51.6% | 43.2% | 5.2% | 1,112 |
| | 1996 | 46.1% | −8.6% | 39.7% | 46.4% | 13.9% | 1,155 |
| | 1992 | 37.9% | −15.7% | 27.6% | 45.2% | 27.2% | 1,740 |
| | Average | 46.8% | −5.3% | 42.6% | 47.4% | 10.0% | |
| Neither | 2008 | 40.4% | −13.3% | 39.2% | 57.8% | 3.0% | 1,925 |
| Was | 2004 | 56.9% | 8.5% | 55.6% | 42.1% | 2.3% | 431 |
| Unfair | 2000 | 55.3% | 5.2% | 54.0% | 43.6% | 2.4% | 682 |
| | 1996 | 35.3% | −19.4% | 32.0% | 58.6% | 9.4% | 781 |
| | 1992 | 25.6% | −28.0% | 21.0% | 61.1% | 17.8% | 451 |
| | Average | 42.7% | −9.4% | 40.4% | 52.6% | 7.0% | |

**Question Wording for Perceived Unfairness of Candidates' Campaigns** (Coded: Democrat Was Unfair = 1; Republican Was Unfair = 2; Both Were Unfair = 3; Neither Was Unfair = 4):

**1992:** "Did either of these candidates for president attack the other unfairly? . . . Bill Clinton did (1); George Bush did (2); Both did (3); Neither did (4)"

**1996:** "Did either of these candidates for president attack the other unfairly? . . . Bill Clinton did (1); Bob Dole did (2); Both did (3); Neither did (4)"

**2000:** "Did either of these candidates for president attack the other unfairly? . . . Al Gore did (1); George W. Bush did (2); Both did (3); Neither did (4)"

**2004:** "Did either of these candidates for president attack the other unfairly? . . . Only John Kerry did (1); Only George W. Bush did (2); Both did (3); Neither did (4)"

**2008:** "Did either of these candidates for president attack the other unfairly? . . . Only Barack Obama (1); Only John McCain (2); Both of them (3); Neither of them (4)"

*Source:* National exit polls. See the section in Chapter 2 entitled "Creating a Cumulative National Data Set: Selecting Exit Polls" (pp. 28–29).

*Note:* When using these results to make inferences about the active electorate, the standard errors should be calculated using Table 2.2 (p. 36), which is explained in the adjacent section of Chapter 2, "Analyzing Exit Poll Questions: Estimating Sampling Error" (pp. 34–36). For a guide on how to understand the tables and figures of this chapter, see the section in Chapter 2 entitled "Presenting and Discussing the Exit Poll Data: Reading Chapter 4" (pp. 39–43). The rationale for using two-party percentages to show trends over time is given in this chapter, in the section entitled "Presidential Vote Choice" (pp. 124–131).

**Table 4.5**  Composition of the Exit Polls by Timing of Presidential Vote Decision, 1976–2008

| Year | In the Last Week | Before Last Week | Number of Respondents |
|---|---|---|---|
| 2008 | 10.6% | 89.4% | 13,268 |
| 2004 | 11.4% | 88.6% | 8,873 |
| 2000 | 17.3% | 82.7% | 3,240 |
| 1996 | 17.6% | 82.4% | 3,900 |
| 1992 | 24.3% | 75.7% | 2,977 |
| 1988 | 14.6% | 85.4% | 11,002 |
| 1984 | | | |
| 1980 | 25.1% | 74.9% | 14,632 |
| 1976 | 29.3% | 70.7% | 13,376 |
| Average | 18.8% | 81.2% | |

**Question Wording for Timing of Presidential Vote Decision** (Coded: In the Last Week = 1; Before Last Week = 2):

**1976:** "When did you decide who to vote for? . . . During the last few days (1); During the debates (2); After the debates (1); During the convention (2); During the primaries (2); Knew all along (2)"

**1980:** "When did you decide who to vote for? . . . During the last week (1); Since Labor Day (2); Around the conventions (2); During the primaries (2); Knew all along (2)"

**1988:** "When did you decide for sure which presidential candidate you would vote for? . . . Since Saturday (1); In the last week (1); In the last month (2); Earlier (2)"

**1992:** "When did you finally decide who to vote for in the presidential election? . . . Only in the last three days (1); In the last week (1); In the last two weeks, after the debates (2); In early fall, after the conventions (2); Earlier than that (2)"

**1996–2000:** "When did you finally decide who to vote for in the presidential election? . . . In the last three days (1); In the last week (1); In the last month (2); Before that (2)"

**2004:** "When did you finally decide for whom to vote in the presidential election? . . . Just today (1); In the last three days (1); Sometime last week (1); During the last month (2); Before that (2)"

**2008:** "When did you finally decide for whom to vote in the presidential election? . . . Just today (1); In the last three days (1); Sometime last week (1); Earlier in October (2); Sometime in September (2); Before that (2)"

*Source:* National exit polls. See the section in Chapter 2 entitled "Creating a Cumulative National Data Set: Selecting Exit Polls" (pp. 28–29).

*Note:* When using these results to make inferences about the active electorate, the standard errors should be calculated using Table 2.2 (p. 36), which is explained in the adjacent section of Chapter 2, "Analyzing Exit Poll Questions: Estimating Sampling Error" (pp. 34–36). For a guide on how to understand the tables and figures of this chapter, see the section in Chapter 2 entitled "Presenting and Discussing the Exit Poll Data: Reading Chapter 4" (pp. 39–43). The rationale for using two-party percentages to show trends over time is given in this chapter, in the section entitled "Presidential Vote Choice" (pp. 124–131).

**Table 4.6**  Presidential Vote by Timing of Presidential Vote Decision, 1976–2008

| | | Two-Party Presidential Vote | | Full Presidential Vote | | | |
|---|---|---|---|---|---|---|---|
| Category | Year | Two-Party Democratic Vote | Difference from Mean Democratic Two-Party Vote | Democratic Vote | Republican Vote | Third-Party Vote | Number of Respondents |
| In the Last | 2008 | 50.2% | −3.5% | 48.5% | 48.2% | 3.3% | 1,789 |
| Week | 2004 | 53.2% | 4.7% | 51.8% | 45.6% | 2.6% | 1,002 |
| | 2000 | 51.4% | 1.2% | 47.7% | 45.2% | 7.0% | 589 |
| | 1996 | 45.4% | −9.3% | 34.5% | 41.5% | 24.0% | 680 |
| | 1992 | 52.4% | −1.2% | 36.5% | 33.2% | 30.3% | 722 |
| | 1988 | 56.1% | 9.9% | 54.7% | 42.8% | 2.5% | 1,634 |
| | 1984 | | | | | | |
| | 1980 | 46.1% | 1.8% | 39.0% | 45.5% | 15.5% | 3,510 |
| | 1976 | 50.8% | −0.2% | 49.4% | 47.9% | 2.8% | 3,745 |
| | Average | 50.7% | 0.4% | 45.3% | 43.7% | 11.0% | |
| Before Last | 2008 | 53.5% | −0.2% | 52.9% | 45.9% | 1.3% | 11,371 |
| Week | 2004 | 47.6% | −0.9% | 47.3% | 52.1% | 0.6% | 7,834 |
| | 2000 | 49.4% | −0.8% | 48.3% | 49.5% | 2.1% | 2,620 |
| | 1996 | 56.5% | 1.7% | 51.8% | 40.0% | 8.2% | 3,175 |
| | 1992 | 52.5% | −1.1% | 44.6% | 40.4% | 15.0% | 2,219 |
| | 1988 | 44.2% | −2.0% | 43.8% | 55.3% | 0.9% | 9,339 |
| | 1984 | | | | | | |
| | 1980 | 43.0% | −1.3% | 40.6% | 53.7% | 5.8% | 11,096 |
| | 1976 | 48.6% | −2.4% | 48.0% | 50.9% | 1.1% | 9,592 |
| | Average | 49.4% | −0.9% | 47.2% | 48.5% | 4.4% | |

Question Wording for Timing of Presidential Vote Decision (Coded: In the Last Week = 1; Before Last Week = 2):

**1976:** "When did you decide who to vote for? . . . During the last few days (1); During the debates (2); After the debates (1); During the convention (2); During the primaries (2); Knew all along (2)"

**1980:** "When did you decide who to vote for? . . . During the last week (1); Since Labor Day (2); Around the conventions (2); During the primaries (2); Knew all along (2)"

**1988:** "When did you decide for sure which presidential candidate you would vote for? . . . Since Saturday (1); In the last week (1); In the last month (2); Earlier (2)"

**1992:** "When did you finally decide who to vote for in the presidential election? . . . Only in the last three days (1); In the last week (1); In the last two weeks, after the debates (2); In early fall, after the conventions (2); Earlier than that (2)"

**1996–2000:** "When did you finally decide who to vote for in the presidential election? . . . In the last three days (1); In the last week (1); In the last month (2); Before that (2)"

**2004:** "When did you finally decide for whom to vote in the presidential election? . . . Just today (1); In the last three days (1); Sometime last week (1); During the last month (2); Before that (2)"

**2008:** "When did you finally decide for whom to vote in the presidential election? . . . Just today (1); In the last three days (1); Sometime last week (1); Earlier in October (2); Sometime in September (2); Before that (2)"

*Source:* National exit polls. See the section in Chapter 2 entitled "Creating a Cumulative National Data Set: Selecting Exit Polls" (pp. 28–29).

*Note:* When using these results to make inferences about the active electorate, the standard errors should be calculated using Table 2.2 (p. 36), which is explained in the adjacent section of Chapter 2, "Analyzing Exit Poll Questions: Estimating Sampling Error" (pp. 34–36). For a guide on how to understand the tables and figures of this chapter, see the section in Chapter 2 entitled "Presenting and Discussing the Exit Poll Data: Reading Chapter 4" (pp. 39–43). The rationale for using two-party percentages to show trends over time is given in this chapter, in the section entitled "Presidential Vote Choice" (pp. 124–131).

**Table 4.7** Presidential Vote by Race, 1984–2008

| Category | Year | Two-Party Presidential Vote | | Full Presidential Vote | | | |
|---|---|---|---|---|---|---|---|
| | | Two-Party Democratic Vote | Difference from Mean Democratic Two-Party Vote | Democratic Vote | Republican Vote | Third-Party Vote | Number of Respondents |
| White | 2008 | 44.4% | −9.3% | 43.6% | 54.6% | 1.9% | 12,783 |
| | 2004 | 41.4% | −7.1% | 41.1% | 58.1% | 0.8% | 10,785 |
| | 2000 | 43.8% | −6.4% | 42.1% | 54.1% | 3.7% | 10,426 |
| | 1996 | 48.8% | −6.0% | 43.4% | 45.6% | 11.1% | 13,026 |
| | 1992 | 49.1% | −4.5% | 39.0% | 40.5% | 20.5% | 12,830 |
| | 1988 | 40.3% | −5.9% | 39.9% | 59.2% | 1.0% | 9,444 |
| | 1984 | 35.1% | −5.7% | 34.8% | 64.5% | 0.7% | 7,668 |
| | Average | 43.2% | −6.4% | 40.5% | 53.8% | 5.7% | |
| Black | 2008 | 96.2% | 42.5% | 95.3% | 3.7% | 1.0% | 2,596 |
| | 2004 | 88.4% | 40.0% | 88.0% | 11.5% | 0.5% | 1,516 |
| | 2000 | 91.5% | 41.3% | 90.1% | 8.4% | 1.5% | 1,526 |
| | 1996 | 87.4% | 32.7% | 83.7% | 12.0% | 4.3% | 2,060 |
| | 1992 | 89.1% | 35.5% | 83.1% | 10.2% | 6.7% | 1,517 |
| | 1988 | 88.2% | 42.1% | 86.4% | 11.5% | 2.1% | 1,482 |
| | 1984 | 90.7% | 50.0% | 89.6% | 9.2% | 1.3% | 1,104 |
| | Average | 90.2% | 40.6% | 88.0% | 9.5% | 2.5% | |
| Hispanic/Latino | 2008 | 69.6% | 15.9% | 67.7% | 29.6% | 2.7% | 1,085 |
| | 2004 | 55.7% | 7.2% | 54.8% | 43.5% | 1.7% | 712 |
| | 2000 | 68.5% | 18.3% | 66.6% | 30.6% | 2.8% | 529 |
| | 1996 | 77.3% | 22.5% | 71.7% | 21.1% | 7.3% | 706 |
| | 1992 | 70.8% | 17.2% | 60.8% | 25.1% | 14.1% | 430 |
| | 1988 | 69.3% | 23.2% | 68.8% | 30.4% | 0.8% | 441 |
| | 1984 | 62.5% | 21.7% | 61.9% | 37.2% | 0.9% | 226 |
| | Average | 67.7% | 18.0% | 64.6% | 31.1% | 4.3% | |
| Asian | 2008 | 63.1% | 9.4% | 61.0% | 35.7% | 3.4% | 417 |
| | 2004 | 56.6% | 8.1% | 56.3% | 43.2% | 0.5% | 208 |
| | 2000 | 56.5% | 6.3% | 53.8% | 41.5% | 4.7% | 222 |
| | 1996 | 47.6% | −7.2% | 43.3% | 47.8% | 8.9% | 168 |
| | 1992 | 35.9% | −17.7% | 30.7% | 54.7% | 14.7% | 156 |
| | 1988 | | | | | | |
| | 1984 | | | | | | |
| | Average | 51.9% | −0.2% | 49.0% | 44.6% | 6.4% | |
| Other Race | 2008 | 68.9% | 15.2% | 66.5% | 30.0% | 3.4% | 571 |
| | 2004 | 57.0% | 8.5% | 52.4% | 39.5% | 8.2% | 237 |
| | 2000 | 58.6% | 8.4% | 55.0% | 38.9% | 6.2% | 226 |
| | 1996 | 74.9% | 20.1% | 63.7% | 21.4% | 14.9% | 205 |
| | 1992 | 69.6% | 16.0% | 57.0% | 24.8% | 18.2% | 182 |
| | 1988 | 47.9% | 1.7% | 45.7% | 49.7% | 4.6% | 170 |
| | 1984 | 49.0% | 8.2% | 48.0% | 50.0% | 2.0% | 101 |
| | Average | 60.8% | 11.2% | 55.5% | 36.3% | 8.2% | |

**Question Wording for Race** (Coded: White = 1; Black = 2; Hispanic/Latino = 3; Asian = 4; Other Race = 5):

**1984–1988:** "Are you . . . White (1); Black (2); Hispanic (3); Other (5)"

**1992 and 2000:** "Are you . . . White (1); Black (2); Hispanic/Latino (3); Asian (4); Other (5)"

**1996:** "Are you . . . White (1); Black (2); Hispanic or Latino (3); Asian (4); Other (5)"

**Table 4.7** *(Continued)*

**2004–2008:** "Are you . . . White (1); Black (2); Hispanic/Latino (3); Asian (4); Other (5); American Indian (5); Native Alaskan (5)"

*Source:* National exit polls. See the section in Chapter 2 entitled "Creating a Cumulative National Data Set: Selecting Exit Polls" (pp. 28–29).

*Note:* When using these results to make inferences about the active electorate, the standard errors should be calculated using Table 2.2 (p. 36), which is explained in the adjacent section of Chapter 2, "Analyzing Exit Poll Questions: Estimating Sampling Error" (pp. 34–36). For a guide on how to understand the tables and figures of this chapter, see the section in Chapter 2 entitled "Presenting and Discussing the Exit Poll Data: Reading Chapter 4" (pp. 39–43). The rationale for using two-party percentages to show trends over time is given in this chapter, in the section entitled "Presidential Vote Choice" (pp. 124–131).

**Table 4.8**   Presidential Vote by Gender, 1972–2008

| | | Two-Party Presidential Vote | | Full Presidential Vote | | | |
|---|---|---|---|---|---|---|---|
| | | Two-Party Democratic Vote | Difference from Mean Democratic Two-Party Vote | Democratic Vote | Republican Vote | Third-Party Vote | Number of Respondents |
| Male | 2008 | 50.6% | −3.1% | 49.4% | 48.3% | 2.3% | 7,637 |
| | 2004 | 44.5% | −3.9% | 44.0% | 54.8% | 1.3% | 5,957 |
| | 2000 | 44.2% | −6.0% | 42.4% | 53.5% | 4.1% | 6,124 |
| | 1996 | 49.6% | −5.2% | 43.5% | 44.2% | 12.4% | 7,533 |
| | 1992 | 51.9% | −1.7% | 40.9% | 37.9% | 21.2% | 6,828 |
| | 1988 | 42.0% | −4.1% | 41.4% | 57.1% | 1.5% | 5,411 |
| | 1984 | 37.4% | −3.3% | 37.1% | 61.9% | 1.0% | 4,324 |
| | 1980 | 39.5% | −4.8% | 36.2% | 55.5% | 8.3% | 7,291 |
| | 1976 | 51.0% | 0.0% | 50.1% | 48.0% | 1.9% | 7,434 |
| | 1972 | 37.2% | −0.9% | 36.3% | 61.4% | 2.3% | 8,807 |
| | Average | 44.8% | −3.3% | 42.1% | 52.2% | 5.6% | |
| Female | 2008 | 56.5% | 2.8% | 55.5% | 42.8% | 1.6% | 10,136 |
| | 2004 | 51.8% | 3.3% | 51.4% | 47.9% | 0.8% | 7,643 |
| | 2000 | 55.4% | 5.2% | 53.7% | 43.3% | 3.0% | 6,826 |
| | 1996 | 59.0% | 4.2% | 54.0% | 37.6% | 8.4% | 8,632 |
| | 1992 | 54.7% | 1.1% | 45.3% | 37.5% | 17.3% | 7,831 |
| | 1988 | 49.9% | 3.7% | 49.5% | 49.8% | 0.8% | 6,161 |
| | 1984 | 44.0% | 3.2% | 43.7% | 55.7% | 0.6% | 4,798 |
| | 1980 | 49.2% | 4.9% | 45.1% | 46.6% | 8.2% | 7,869 |
| | 1976 | 51.0% | 0.0% | 50.4% | 48.5% | 1.2% | 7,672 |
| | 1972 | 38.9% | 0.9% | 38.3% | 60.1% | 1.6% | 8,739 |
| | Average | 51.0% | 2.9% | 48.7% | 47.0% | 4.3% | |

**Question Wording for Gender** (Coded: Male = 1; Female = 2):

**1972–1980:** "Interviewer recorded sex of respondent . . . Male (1); Female (2)"

**1984–2008:** "Are you . . . Male (2); Female (2)"

*Source:* National exit polls. See the section in Chapter 2 entitled "Creating a Cumulative National Data Set: Selecting Exit Polls" (pp. 28–29).

*Note:* When using these results to make inferences about the active electorate, the standard errors should be calculated using Table 2.2 (p. 36), which is explained in the adjacent section of Chapter 2, "Analyzing Exit Poll Questions: Estimating Sampling Error" (pp. 34–36). For a guide on how to understand the tables and figures of this chapter, see the section in Chapter 2 entitled "Presenting and Discussing the Exit Poll Data: Reading Chapter 4" (pp. 39–43). The rationale for using two-party percentages to show trends over time is given in this chapter, in the section entitled "Presidential Vote Choice" (pp. 124–131).

**Table 4.9** Presidential Vote by Age, 1972–2008

| Category | Year | Two-Party Presidential Vote | | Full Presidential Vote | | | |
| | | Two-Party Democratic Vote | Difference from Mean Democratic Two-Party Vote | Democratic Vote | Republican Vote | Third-Party Vote | Number of Respondents |
|---|---|---|---|---|---|---|---|
| 18–29 | 2008 | 67.6% | 13.9% | 66.0% | 31.6% | 2.4% | 3,630 |
| | 2004 | 54.3% | 5.9% | 53.7% | 45.1% | 1.2% | 2,581 |
| | 2000 | 50.7% | 0.5% | 47.6% | 46.3% | 6.2% | 2,285 |
| | 1996 | 60.6% | 5.8% | 52.8% | 34.4% | 12.8% | 3,101 |
| | 1992 | 55.9% | 2.3% | 43.5% | 34.3% | 22.2% | 3,309 |
| | 1988 | 47.2% | 1.1% | 46.5% | 52.0% | 1.5% | 2,420 |
| | 1984 | 40.6% | −0.2% | 40.2% | 58.9% | 1.0% | 2,293 |
| | 1980 | 50.5% | 6.2% | 44.0% | 43.1% | 12.9% | 3,634 |
| | 1976 | 51.9% | 0.9% | 50.6% | 47.0% | 2.4% | 3,769 |
| | 1972 | 47.4% | 9.3% | 46.5% | 51.6% | 2.0% | 4,575 |
| | Average | 52.7% | 4.6% | 49.1% | 44.4% | 6.5% | |
| 30–44 | 2008 | 53.3% | −0.4% | 52.4% | 45.9% | 1.6% | 5,055 |
| | 2004 | 46.6% | −1.9% | 45.9% | 52.6% | 1.5% | 4,118 |
| | 2000 | 49.3% | −0.9% | 47.7% | 49.1% | 3.3% | 4,567 |
| | 1996 | 54.1% | −0.6% | 48.2% | 40.9% | 10.9% | 5,695 |
| | 1992 | 52.1% | −1.5% | 41.2% | 37.8% | 21.0% | 5,668 |
| | 1988 | 45.6% | −0.6% | 45.1% | 53.7% | 1.2% | 4,301 |
| | 1984 | 42.1% | 1.4% | 41.7% | 57.4% | 0.9% | 3,145 |
| | 1980 | 39.9% | −4.4% | 36.2% | 54.5% | 9.3% | 4,542 |
| | 1976 | 50.1% | −0.9% | 49.3% | 49.1% | 1.7% | 3,731 |
| | 1972 | 35.6% | −2.5% | 34.8% | 63.0% | 2.2% | 4,481 |
| | Average | 46.9% | −1.2% | 44.2% | 50.4% | 5.3% | |
| 45–59 | 2008 | 50.3% | −3.4% | 49.4% | 48.7% | 1.8% | 5,594 |
| | 2004 | 48.5% | 0.0% | 48.1% | 51.1% | 0.8% | 4,247 |
| | 2000 | 49.4% | −0.8% | 47.8% | 49.0% | 3.2% | 3,923 |
| | 1996 | 53.8% | −0.9% | 48.3% | 41.5% | 10.3% | 4,484 |
| | 1992 | 50.8% | −2.8% | 41.1% | 39.8% | 19.1% | 3,649 |
| | 1988 | 42.7% | −3.5% | 42.2% | 56.6% | 1.2% | 2,703 |
| | 1984 | 39.9% | −0.9% | 39.6% | 59.6% | 0.8% | 2,070 |
| | 1980 | 41.2% | −3.1% | 38.6% | 55.1% | 6.3% | 3,386 |
| | 1976 | 47.6% | −3.4% | 47.0% | 51.8% | 1.2% | 3,318 |
| | 1972 | 35.5% | −2.5% | 34.9% | 63.3% | 1.8% | 4,610 |
| | Average | 46.0% | −2.1% | 43.7% | 51.7% | 4.7% | |
| 60+ | 2008 | 47.7% | −6.0% | 46.8% | 51.4% | 1.8% | 3,417 |
| | 2004 | 45.7% | −2.7% | 45.5% | 54.0% | 0.4% | 2,634 |
| | 2000 | 51.7% | 1.5% | 50.5% | 47.1% | 2.3% | 2,253 |
| | 1996 | 52.4% | −2.4% | 48.3% | 44.0% | 7.7% | 2,960 |
| | 1992 | 56.7% | 3.1% | 49.6% | 37.9% | 12.5% | 2,385 |
| | 1988 | 49.4% | 3.2% | 49.0% | 50.3% | 0.6% | 2,063 |
| | 1984 | 39.4% | −1.3% | 39.3% | 60.3% | 0.4% | 1,546 |
| | 1980 | 43.4% | −0.9% | 41.4% | 54.0% | 4.7% | 2,326 |
| | 1976 | 47.2% | −3.8% | 46.7% | 52.4% | 0.9% | 1,811 |
| | 1972 | 30.7% | −7.3% | 30.2% | 68.1% | 1.8% | 2,844 |
| | Average | 46.4% | −1.7% | 44.7% | 51.9% | 3.3% | |

## Table 4.9   *(Continued)*

**Question Wording for Age** (Coded: 18–29 = 1; 30–44 = 2; 45–59 = 3; 60+ = 4):

**1972 and 1984:** "To which age group do you belong? . . . 18–24 (1); 25–29 (1); 30–44 (2); 45–59 (3); 60 or over (4)"

**1976 and 1980:** "To which age group do you belong? . . . 18–21 (1); 22–29 (1); 30–44 (2); 45–59 (3); 60 or over (4)"

**1988:** "To which age group do you belong? . . . 18–29 (1); 30–44 (2); 45–59 (3); 60 or over (4)"

**1992–1996:** "To which age group do you belong? . . . 18–24 (1); 25–29 (1); 30–39 (2); 40–44 (2); 45–49 (3); 50–59 (3); 60–64 (4); 65 or over (4)"

**2000–2008:** "To which age group do you belong? . . . 18–24 (1); 25–29 (1); 30–39 (2); 40–44 (2); 45–49 (3); 50–59 (3); 60–64 (4); 65–74 (4); 75 or over (4)"

*Source:* National exit polls. See the section in Chapter 2 entitled "Creating a Cumulative National Data Set: Selecting Exit Polls" (pp. 28–29).

*Note:* When using these results to make inferences about the active electorate, the standard errors should be calculated using Table 2.2 (p. 36), which is explained in the adjacent section of Chapter 2, "Analyzing Exit Poll Questions: Estimating Sampling Error" (pp. 34–36). For a guide on how to understand the tables and figures of this chapter, see the section in Chapter 2 entitled "Presenting and Discussing the Exit Poll Data: Reading Chapter 4" (pp. 39–43). The rationale for using two-party percentages to show trends over time is given in this chapter, in the section entitled "Presidential Vote Choice" (pp. 124–131).

## Table 4.10   Presidential Vote by Sexual Orientation, 1996–2008

| | | Two-Party Presidential Vote | | Full Presidential Vote | | | |
| | | Two-Party Democratic Vote | Difference from Mean Democratic Two-Party Vote | Democratic Vote | Republican Vote | Third-Party Vote | Number of Respondents |
| Category | Year | | | | | | |
|---|---|---|---|---|---|---|---|
| Gay or Bisexual | 2008 | 71.9% | 18.2% | 69.9% | 27.3% | 2.8% | 151 |
| | 2004 | 77.0% | 28.6% | 76.7% | 22.9% | 0.4% | 227 |
| | 2000 | 73.9% | 23.7% | 70.3% | 24.9% | 4.8% | 246 |
| | 1996 | 74.8% | 20.1% | 66.3% | 22.3% | 11.4% | 194 |
| | Average | 74.4% | 22.6% | 70.8% | 24.3% | 4.9% | |
| Not Gay or Bisexual | 2008 | 53.9% | 0.1% | 52.9% | 45.3% | 1.8% | 3,908 |
| | 2004 | 46.7% | −1.8% | 46.2% | 52.8% | 1.0% | 6,138 |
| | 2000 | 48.4% | −1.7% | 46.7% | 49.7% | 3.6% | 5,798 |
| | 1996 | 52.1% | −2.6% | 47.2% | 43.3% | 9.5% | 3,484 |
| | Average | 50.3% | −1.5% | 48.2% | 47.8% | 4.0% | |

**Question Wording for Sexual Orientation** (Coded: Gay or Bisexual = 1; Not Gay or Bisexual = 2):

**1996–2008:** "Are you gay, lesbian, or bisexual? . . . Yes (1); No (2)"

*Source:* National exit polls. See the section in Chapter 2 entitled "Creating a Cumulative National Data Set: Selecting Exit Polls" (pp. 28–29).

*Note:* When using these results to make inferences about the active electorate, the standard errors should be calculated using Table 2.2 (p. 36), which is explained in the adjacent section of Chapter 2, "Analyzing Exit Poll Questions: Estimating Sampling Error" (pp. 34–36). For a guide on how to understand the tables and figures of this chapter, see the section in Chapter 2 entitled "Presenting and Discussing the Exit Poll Data: Reading Chapter 4" (pp. 39–43). The rationale for using two-party percentages to show trends over time is given in this chapter, in the section entitled "Presidential Vote Choice" (pp. 124–131).

**Table 4.11** Presidential Vote by Region of Electoral Precinct, 1972–2008

| Category | Year | Two-Party Presidential Vote Two-Party Democratic Vote | Difference from Mean Democratic Two-Party Vote | Full Presidential Vote Democratic Vote | Republican Vote | Third-Party Vote | Number of Respondents |
|---|---|---|---|---|---|---|---|
| East | 2008 | 59.8% | 6.1% | 59.0% | 39.6% | 1.3% | 5,319 |
| | 2004 | 56.1% | 7.6% | 55.5% | 43.5% | 1.0% | 2,888 |
| | 2000 | 58.7% | 8.5% | 56.1% | 39.5% | 4.4% | 3,057 |
| | 1996 | 61.6% | 6.9% | 54.9% | 34.2% | 10.8% | 3,957 |
| | 1992 | 57.5% | 3.9% | 47.1% | 34.8% | 18.1% | 3,850 |
| | 1988 | 49.5% | 3.3% | 48.8% | 49.8% | 1.3% | 2,834 |
| | 1984 | 47.0% | 6.3% | 46.7% | 52.6% | 0.7% | 2,473 |
| | 1980 | 47.3% | 2.9% | 42.5% | 47.4% | 10.1% | 4,793 |
| | 1976 | 52.0% | 1.0% | 51.5% | 47.4% | 1.1% | 4,519 |
| | 1972 | 41.4% | 3.4% | 40.9% | 57.7% | 1.4% | 4,846 |
| | Average | 53.1% | 5.0% | 50.3% | 44.7% | 5.0% | |
| Midwest | 2008 | 54.8% | 1.1% | 53.7% | 44.3% | 2.0% | 4,745 |
| | 2004 | 48.4% | −0.1% | 48.0% | 51.2% | 0.8% | 3,676 |
| | 2000 | 49.5% | −0.7% | 48.0% | 49.0% | 3.0% | 3,486 |
| | 1996 | 54.2% | −0.5% | 48.2% | 40.7% | 11.1% | 4,435 |
| | 1992 | 53.5% | −0.1% | 42.5% | 36.9% | 20.7% | 4,008 |
| | 1988 | 47.4% | 1.2% | 46.8% | 52.1% | 1.1% | 3,174 |
| | 1984 | 41.0% | 0.2% | 40.6% | 58.4% | 1.0% | 2,651 |
| | 1980 | 44.1% | −0.2% | 40.5% | 51.4% | 8.1% | 2,934 |
| | 1976 | 49.3% | −1.7% | 48.4% | 49.7% | 1.9% | 3,334 |
| | 1972 | 39.6% | 1.6% | 38.8% | 59.1% | 2.2% | 4,032 |
| | Average | 48.2% | 0.1% | 45.5% | 49.3% | 5.2% | |
| South | 2008 | 45.6% | −8.1% | 44.9% | 53.5% | 1.6% | 4,514 |
| | 2004 | 41.9% | −6.5% | 41.6% | 57.6% | 0.8% | 4,456 |
| | 2000 | 43.9% | −6.3% | 43.0% | 55.0% | 2.0% | 3,884 |
| | 1996 | 50.0% | −4.8% | 46.0% | 46.1% | 7.8% | 4,966 |
| | 1992 | 49.2% | −4.4% | 41.3% | 42.6% | 16.0% | 4,416 |
| | 1988 | 41.6% | −4.6% | 41.3% | 58.0% | 0.7% | 3,344 |
| | 1984 | 36.0% | −4.8% | 35.9% | 63.7% | 0.4% | 2,472 |
| | 1980 | 45.4% | 1.0% | 43.6% | 52.5% | 4.0% | 3,805 |
| | 1976 | 54.4% | 3.4% | 53.9% | 45.2% | 0.9% | 3,550 |
| | 1972 | 29.3% | −8.7% | 29.0% | 69.8% | 1.2% | 4,149 |
| | Average | 43.7% | −4.4% | 42.1% | 54.4% | 3.5% | |
| West | 2008 | 58.5% | 4.8% | 56.7% | 40.3% | 2.9% | 3,258 |
| | 2004 | 50.5% | 2.0% | 49.7% | 48.8% | 1.6% | 2,640 |
| | 2000 | 51.3% | 1.1% | 48.5% | 46.0% | 5.6% | 2,679 |
| | 1996 | 55.0% | 0.3% | 48.4% | 39.5% | 12.1% | 3,017 |

**Table 4.11**   *(Continued)*

| Category | Year | Two-Party Presidential Vote | | Full Presidential Vote | | | |
| | | Two-Party Democratic Vote | Difference from Mean Democratic Two-Party Vote | Democratic Vote | Republican Vote | Third-Party Vote | Number of Respondents |
|---|---|---|---|---|---|---|---|
| West | 1992 | 55.8% | 2.2% | 43.2% | 34.2% | 22.5% | 2,963 |
| | 1988 | 47.0% | 0.9% | 46.3% | 52.1% | 1.6% | 2,244 |
| | 1984 | 38.0% | -2.7% | 37.6% | 61.3% | 1.1% | 1,550 |
| | 1980 | 38.9% | -5.4% | 34.0% | 53.4% | 12.6% | 3,636 |
| | 1976 | 47.3% | -3.7% | 46.0% | 51.4% | 2.6% | 3,799 |
| | 1972 | 41.3% | 3.2% | 39.8% | 56.6% | 3.6% | 4,568 |
| | Average | 48.4% | 0.3% | 45.0% | 48.4% | 6.6% | |

**Classification for Region:**

**East:** Connecticut; Delaware; Maine; Maryland; Massachusetts; New Hampshire; New Jersey; New York; Pennsylvania; Rhode Island; Vermont; Washington, DC; West Virginia

**Midwest:** Illinois; Indiana; Iowa; Kansas; Michigan; Minnesota; Missouri; Nebraska; North Dakota; Ohio; South Dakota; Wisconsin

**South:** Alabama; Arkansas; Florida; Georgia; Kentucky; Louisiana; Mississippi; North Carolina; Oklahoma; South Carolina; Tennessee; Texas; Virginia

**West:** Alaska; Arizona; California; Colorado; Hawaii; Idaho; Montana; Nevada; New Mexico; Oregon; Utah; Washington; Wyoming

*Source:* National exit polls. See the section in Chapter 2 entitled "Creating a Cumulative National Data Set: Selecting Exit Polls" (pp. 28–29).

*Note:* When using these results to make inferences about the active electorate, the standard errors should be calculated using Table 2.2 (p. 36), which is explained in the adjacent section of Chapter 2, "Analyzing Exit Poll Questions: Estimating Sampling Error" (pp. 34–36). For a guide on how to understand the tables and figures of this chapter, see the section in Chapter 2 entitled "Presenting and Discussing the Exit Poll Data: Reading Chapter 4" (pp. 39–43). The rationale for using two-party percentages to show trends over time is given in this chapter, in the section entitled "Presidential Vote Choice" (pp. 124–131).

**Table 4.12** Presidential Vote by Population Density of Electoral Precinct, 1984–2008

| Category | Year | Two-Party Presidential Vote | | Full Presidential Vote | | | |
|---|---|---|---|---|---|---|---|
| | | Two-Party Democratic Vote | Difference from Mean Democratic Two-Party Vote | Democratic Vote | Republican Vote | Third-Party Vote | Number of Respondents |
| City | 2008 | 64.2% | 10.5% | 63.0% | 35.2% | 1.9% | 5,394 |
| | 2004 | 54.2% | 5.7% | 53.5% | 45.3% | 1.2% | 4,300 |
| | 2000 | 63.2% | 13.0% | 60.8% | 35.4% | 3.8% | 4,038 |
| | 1996 | 61.5% | 6.7% | 55.6% | 34.9% | 9.5% | 5,303 |
| | 1992 | 63.0% | 9.4% | 53.5% | 31.5% | 15.1% | 4,275 |
| | 1988 | 56.0% | 9.8% | 55.4% | 43.5% | 1.1% | 3,326 |
| | 1984 | 53.7% | 12.9% | 53.0% | 45.8% | 1.2% | 2,672 |
| | Average | 59.4% | 9.7% | 56.4% | 38.8% | 4.8% | |
| Suburb | 2008 | 50.6% | −3.1% | 49.6% | 48.4% | 1.9% | 8,917 |
| | 2004 | 47.4% | −1.0% | 47.1% | 52.1% | 0.8% | 6,161 |
| | 2000 | 48.8% | −1.3% | 47.2% | 49.4% | 3.3% | 5,110 |
| | 1996 | 52.6% | −2.2% | 47.0% | 42.4% | 10.6% | 6,239 |
| | 1992 | 51.2% | −2.4% | 40.7% | 38.7% | 20.6% | 5,483 |
| | 1988 | 42.1% | −4.1% | 41.5% | 57.2% | 1.3% | 4,547 |
| | 1984 | 38.4% | −2.4% | 38.2% | 61.4% | 0.4% | 3,586 |
| | Average | 47.3% | −2.4% | 44.5% | 50.0% | 5.6% | |
| Rural | 2008 | 46.0% | −7.7% | 45.1% | 52.9% | 2.0% | 3,525 |
| | 2004 | 43.0% | −5.5% | 42.5% | 56.4% | 1.1% | 3,191 |
| | 2000 | 38.8% | −11.4% | 37.5% | 59.1% | 3.4% | 3,755 |
| | 1996 | 50.5% | −4.2% | 45.2% | 44.2% | 10.6% | 4,833 |
| | 1992 | 49.2% | −4.4% | 39.3% | 40.6% | 20.2% | 5,479 |
| | 1988 | 43.6% | −2.6% | 43.2% | 55.9% | 0.9% | 3,617 |
| | 1984 | 32.3% | −8.4% | 32.1% | 67.1% | 0.9% | 2,888 |
| | Average | 43.3% | −6.3% | 40.7% | 53.8% | 5.6% | |

**Classification for Population Density:**

**City:** Precinct residing within Census metropolitan statistical area (MSA) containing greater than 50,000 residents

**Suburb:** Precinct residing within Census MSA in close proximity to large urban area

**Rural:** Precinct residing within Census MSA with less than 50,000 residents not in close proximity to large urban area

*Source:* National exit polls. See the section in Chapter 2 entitled "Creating a Cumulative National Data Set: Selecting Exit Polls" (pp. 28–29).

*Note:* When using these results to make inferences about the active electorate, the standard errors should be calculated using Table 2.2 (p. 36), which is explained in the adjacent section of Chapter 2, "Analyzing Exit Poll Questions: Estimating Sampling Error" (pp. 34–36). For a guide on how to understand the tables and figures of this chapter, see the section in Chapter 2 entitled "Presenting and Discussing the Exit Poll Data: Reading Chapter 4" (pp. 39–43). The rationale for using two-party percentages to show trends over time is given in this chapter, in the section entitled "Presidential Vote Choice" (pp. 124–131).

**Table 4.13**   Presidential Vote by Religious Affiliation, 1984–2008

| Category | Year | Two-Party Presidential Vote | | Full Presidential Vote | | | |
|---|---|---|---|---|---|---|---|
| | | Two-Party Democratic Vote | Difference from Mean Democratic Two-Party Vote | Democratic Vote | Republican Vote | Third-Party Vote | Number of Respondents |
| Protestant | 2008 | 45.3% | −8.4% | 44.7% | 53.9% | 1.4% | 2,083 |
| | 2004 | 40.8% | −7.7% | 40.5% | 58.8% | 0.7% | 5,291 |
| | 2000 | 42.8% | −7.4% | 41.7% | 55.8% | 2.5% | 5,000 |
| | 1996 | 47.3% | −7.4% | 42.4% | 47.2% | 10.4% | 4,144 |
| | 1992 | 46.0% | −7.6% | 37.1% | 43.6% | 19.3% | 4,213 |
| | 1988 | 40.1% | −6.1% | 39.7% | 59.3% | 1.0% | 6,151 |
| | 1984 | 33.6% | −7.2% | 33.4% | 66.0% | 0.5% | 5,064 |
| | Average | 42.3% | −7.4% | 39.9% | 54.9% | 5.1% | |
| Catholic | 2008 | 54.6% | 0.9% | 53.8% | 44.7% | 1.6% | 1,116 |
| | 2004 | 47.3% | −1.1% | 46.9% | 52.2% | 0.9% | 2,517 |
| | 2000 | 51.2% | 1.0% | 49.5% | 47.3% | 3.2% | 2,353 |
| | 1996 | 58.7% | 4.0% | 52.9% | 37.2% | 9.9% | 2,181 |
| | 1992 | 55.6% | 2.0% | 44.3% | 35.4% | 20.4% | 2,136 |
| | 1988 | 47.2% | 1.0% | 46.8% | 52.5% | 0.7% | 3,098 |
| | 1984 | 45.1% | 4.4% | 44.8% | 54.4% | 0.8% | 2,399 |
| | Average | 51.4% | 1.7% | 48.4% | 46.2% | 5.3% | |
| Jewish | 2008 | 79.1% | 25.4% | 78.2% | 20.7% | 1.1% | 102 |
| | 2004 | 74.6% | 26.1% | 74.3% | 25.3% | 0.4% | 267 |
| | 2000 | 81.0% | 30.8% | 79.2% | 18.6% | 2.2% | 306 |
| | 1996 | 82.7% | 27.9% | 77.7% | 16.3% | 6.1% | 264 |
| | 1992 | 87.9% | 34.3% | 79.7% | 11.0% | 9.3% | 278 |
| | 1988 | 64.8% | 18.6% | 64.5% | 35.1% | 0.4% | 421 |
| | 1984 | 68.4% | 27.6% | 66.8% | 30.9% | 2.3% | 235 |
| | Average | 76.9% | 27.2% | 74.3% | 22.6% | 3.1% | |
| No Religious Affiliation | 2008 | 76.6% | 22.9% | 74.8% | 22.9% | 2.3% | 505 |
| | 2004 | 68.4% | 19.9% | 67.3% | 31.1% | 1.6% | 1,063 |
| | 2000 | 66.3% | 16.1% | 60.4% | 30.7% | 9.0% | 889 |
| | 1996 | 71.9% | 17.2% | 59.2% | 23.1% | 17.8% | 572 |
| | 1992 | 77.5% | 23.9% | 61.8% | 17.9% | 20.3% | 552 |
| | 1988 | 63.0% | 16.8% | 61.5% | 36.2% | 2.3% | 613 |
| | 1984 | 59.7% | 18.9% | 58.6% | 39.6% | 1.9% | 450 |
| | Average | 69.1% | 19.4% | 63.4% | 28.8% | 7.9% | |
| Other Religion | 2008 | 77.1% | 23.4% | 72.9% | 21.6% | 5.5% | 297 |
| | 2004 | 76.0% | 27.5% | 74.2% | 23.5% | 2.3% | 645 |
| | 2000 | 68.6% | 18.4% | 61.8% | 28.3% | 9.9% | 635 |
| | 1996 | 72.0% | 17.2% | 59.8% | 23.3% | 16.9% | 476 |

*(Continued)*

**Table 4.13**   Presidential Vote by Religious Affiliation, 1984–2008 *(Continued)*

| Category | Year | Two-Party Presidential Vote | | Full Presidential Vote | | | |
|---|---|---|---|---|---|---|---|
| | | Two-Party Democratic Vote | Difference from Mean Democratic Two-Party Vote | Democratic Vote | Republican Vote | Third-Party Vote | Number of Respondents |
| Other | 1992 | 66.7% | 13.1% | 52.5% | 26.3% | 21.2% | 552 |
| Religion | 1988 | 67.0% | 20.8% | 65.1% | 32.0% | 2.9% | 676 |
| | 1984 | 57.3% | 16.6% | 56.5% | 42.1% | 1.4% | 468 |
| | Average | 69.2% | 19.6% | 63.3% | 28.2% | 8.6% | |

**Question Wording for Religious Affiliation** (Coded: Protestant = 1; Catholic = 2; Jewish = 3; No Religion = 4; Other Religion = 5):

**1984–1988:** " Your religion . . . Protestant (1); Catholic (2); Other Christian (1); Jewish (3); Something else (5); None (4)"

**1992–2000:** "Are you . . . Protestant (1); Catholic (2); Other Christian (1); Jewish (3); Something else (5); None (4)"

**2004–2008:** "Are you . . . Protestant (1); Catholic (2); Mormon/LDS (5); Other Christian (1); Jewish (3); Muslim (5); Something else (5); None (4)"

*Source:* National exit polls. See the section in Chapter 2 entitled "Creating a Cumulative National Data Set: Selecting Exit Polls" (pp. 28–29).

*Note:* When using these results to make inferences about the active electorate, the standard errors should be calculated using Table 2.2 (p. 36), which is explained in the adjacent section of Chapter 2, "Analyzing Exit Poll Questions: Estimating Sampling Error" (pp. 34–36). For a guide on how to understand the tables and figures of this chapter, see the section in Chapter 2 entitled "Presenting and Discussing the Exit Poll Data: Reading Chapter 4" (pp. 39–43). The rationale for using two-party percentages to show trends over time is given in this chapter, in the section entitled "Presidential Vote Choice" (pp. 124–131).

**Table 4.14**  Presidential Vote by Religious Attendance, 2000–2008

| Category | Year | Two-Party Presidential Vote | | Full Presidential Vote | | | |
|---|---|---|---|---|---|---|---|
| | | Two-Party Democratic Vote | Difference from Mean Democratic Two-Party Vote | Democratic Vote | Republican Vote | Third-Party Vote | Number of Respondents |
| Once a Week or More | 2008 | 43.9% | −9.8% | 43.2% | 55.3% | 1.6% | 1,529 |
| | 2004 | 38.9% | −9.6% | 38.6% | 60.5% | 0.9% | 4,030 |
| | 2000 | 39.8% | −10.4% | 38.8% | 58.7% | 2.5% | 2,645 |
| | Average | 40.9% | −9.9% | 40.2% | 58.1% | 1.7% | |
| Less Than Once a Week | 2008 | 60.8% | 7.1% | 59.6% | 38.4% | 1.9% | 2,579 |
| | 2004 | 55.7% | 7.2% | 55.1% | 43.9% | 1.0% | 5,782 |
| | 2000 | 57.5% | 7.3% | 54.9% | 40.5% | 4.6% | 3,530 |
| | Average | 58.0% | 7.2% | 56.5% | 40.9% | 2.5% | |

**Question Wording for Religious Attendance** (Coded: Once a Week or More = 1; Less Than Once a Week = 2):

2000–2008: "How often do you attend religious services? . . . More than once a week (1); Once a week (1); A few times a month (2); A few times a year (2); Never (2)"

*Source:* National exit polls. See the section in Chapter 2 entitled "Creating a Cumulative National Data Set: Selecting Exit Polls" (pp. 28–29).

*Note:* When using these results to make inferences about the active electorate, the standard errors should be calculated using Table 2.2 (p. 36), which is explained in the adjacent section of Chapter 2, "Analyzing Exit Poll Questions: Estimating Sampling Error" (pp. 34–36). For a guide on how to understand the tables and figures of this chapter, see the section in Chapter 2 entitled "Presenting and Discussing the Exit Poll Data: Reading Chapter 4" (pp. 39–43). The rationale for using two-party percentages to show trends over time is given in this chapter, in the section entitled "Presidential Vote Choice" (pp. 124–131).

**Table 4.15**  Presidential Vote by Evangelical, 2004–2008

| Category | Year | Two-Party Presidential Vote | | Full Presidential Vote | | | |
|---|---|---|---|---|---|---|---|
| | | Two-Party Democratic Vote | Difference from Mean Democratic Two-Party Vote | Democratic Vote | Republican Vote | Third-Party Vote | Number of Respondents |
| Born Again | 2008 | 41.5% | −12.2% | 40.7% | 57.4% | 1.9% | 4,608 |
| | 2004 | 34.3% | −14.1% | 34.0% | 65.1% | 0.8% | 3,232 |
| | Average | 37.9% | −13.2% | 37.4% | 61.3% | 1.3% | |
| Not Born Again | 2008 | 60.6% | 6.9% | 59.3% | 38.6% | 2.0% | 8,268 |
| | 2004 | 55.8% | 7.3% | 55.2% | 43.8% | 1.0% | 6,385 |
| | Average | 58.2% | 7.1% | 57.3% | 41.2% | 1.5% | |

**Question Wording for Evangelical** (Coded: Born Again = 1; Not Born Again = 2):

2004–2008: "Would you describe yourself as a born again or evangelical Christian? . . . Yes (1); No (2)"

*Source:* National exit polls. See the section in Chapter 2 entitled "Creating a Cumulative National Data Set: Selecting Exit Polls" (pp. 28–29).

*Note:* When using these results to make inferences about the active electorate, the standard errors should be calculated using Table 2.2 (p. 36), which is explained in the adjacent section of Chapter 2, "Analyzing Exit Poll Questions: Estimating Sampling Error" (pp. 34–36). For a guide on how to understand the tables and figures of this chapter, see the section in Chapter 2 entitled "Presenting and Discussing the Exit Poll Data: Reading Chapter 4" (pp. 39–43). The rationale for using two-party percentages to show trends over time is given in this chapter, in the section entitled "Presidential Vote Choice" (pp. 124–131).

**Table 4.16**   Presidential Vote by Education, 1988–2008

| Category | Year | Two-Party Presidential Vote | | Full Presidential Vote | | | |
| | | Two-Party Democratic Vote | Difference from Mean Democratic Two-Party Vote | Democratic Vote | Republican Vote | Third-Party Vote | Number of Voters |
|---|---|---|---|---|---|---|---|
| Did Not | 2008 | 64.6% | 10.9% | 63.1% | 34.6% | 2.3% | 696 |
| Complete | 2004 | 50.7% | 2.2% | 50.2% | 48.8% | 1.0% | 398 |
| High School | 2000 | 60.5% | 10.3% | 59.1% | 38.6% | 2.3% | 407 |
| | 1996 | 67.9% | 13.1% | 59.3% | 28.1% | 12.6% | 494 |
| | 1992 | 66.0% | 12.4% | 53.9% | 27.7% | 18.4% | 541 |
| | 1988 | 56.2% | 10.1% | 55.7% | 43.3% | 1.0% | 828 |
| | Average | 61.0% | 9.9% | 56.9% | 36.8% | 6.3% | |
| High School | 2008 | 53.0% | −0.7% | 52.2% | 46.3% | 1.5% | 3,419 |
| | 2004 | 47.6% | −0.9% | 47.4% | 52.1% | 0.6% | 2,084 |
| | 2000 | 49.5% | −0.7% | 48.2% | 49.2% | 2.7% | 1,966 |
| | 1996 | 59.4% | 4.6% | 51.5% | 35.2% | 13.4% | 1,872 |
| | 1992 | 54.7% | 1.1% | 43.4% | 35.9% | 20.7% | 2,005 |
| | 1988 | 49.9% | 3.7% | 49.4% | 49.6% | 1.0% | 3,029 |
| | Average | 52.3% | 1.2% | 48.7% | 44.7% | 6.6% | |
| Some College | 2008 | 52.2% | −1.5% | 51.3% | 46.9% | 1.7% | 5,487 |
| | 2004 | 46.0% | −2.5% | 45.6% | 53.6% | 0.8% | 3,205 |
| | 2000 | 46.9% | −3.3% | 45.2% | 51.2% | 3.6% | 2,977 |
| | 1996 | 54.5% | −0.2% | 48.1% | 40.1% | 11.8% | 2,199 |
| | 1992 | 52.5% | −1.1% | 41.3% | 37.4% | 21.3% | 2,298 |
| | 1988 | 42.8% | −3.4% | 42.3% | 56.6% | 1.1% | 3,331 |
| | Average | 49.2% | −2.0% | 45.6% | 47.6% | 6.7% | |
| College | 2008 | 50.7% | −3.0% | 49.5% | 48.1% | 2.3% | 4,778 |
| | 2004 | 46.7% | −1.7% | 46.0% | 52.4% | 1.5% | 2,624 |
| | 2000 | 46.9% | −3.3% | 45.2% | 51.2% | 3.6% | 2,284 |
| | 1996 | 48.6% | −6.2% | 43.6% | 46.2% | 10.2% | 2,085 |
| | 1992 | 48.5% | −5.1% | 39.0% | 41.5% | 19.6% | 1,884 |
| | 1988 | 37.8% | −8.4% | 37.4% | 61.6% | 1.0% | 2,048 |
| | Average | 46.5% | −4.6% | 43.5% | 50.2% | 6.4% | |
| Postgraduate | 2008 | 59.2% | 5.5% | 58.0% | 39.9% | 2.0% | 3,199 |
| | 2004 | 55.3% | 6.8% | 54.7% | 44.2% | 1.2% | 1,637 |
| | 2000 | 54.4% | 4.2% | 52.0% | 43.6% | 4.4% | 1,659 |
| | 1996 | 56.3% | 1.5% | 51.6% | 40.1% | 8.3% | 1,392 |
| | 1992 | 58.3% | 4.7% | 50.2% | 35.9% | 13.9% | 1,290 |
| | 1988 | 49.1% | 3.0% | 48.5% | 50.1% | 1.4% | 1,674 |
| | Average | 55.4% | 4.3% | 52.5% | 42.3% | 5.2% | |

**Question Wording for Education** (Coded: Did Not Complete High School = 1; High School = 2; Some College = 3; College = 4; Postgraduate = 5):

## Table 4.16   *(Continued)*

**1988:** "What was the last grade in school you completed? . . . Did not graduate from high school (1); High school graduate (2); Some college but not four years (3); College graduate (4); Postgraduate study (5)"

**1992–1996:** "What was the last grade of school you completed? . . . Did not complete high school (1); High school graduate (2); Some college, but no degree (3); College graduate (4); Postgraduate study (5)"

**2000–2008:** "What was the last grade of school you completed? . . . Did not complete high school (1); High school graduate (2); Some college or associate degree (3); College graduate (4); Postgraduate study (5)"

*Source:* National exit polls. See the section in Chapter 2 entitled "Creating a Cumulative National Data Set: Selecting Exit Polls" (pp. 28–29).

*Note:* When using these results to make inferences about the active electorate, the standard errors should be calculated using Table 2.2 (p. 36), which is explained in the adjacent section of Chapter 2, "Analyzing Exit Poll Questions: Estimating Sampling Error" (pp. 34–36). For a guide on how to understand the tables and figures of this chapter, see the section in Chapter 2 entitled "Presenting and Discussing the Exit Poll Data: Reading Chapter 4" (pp. 39–43). The rationale for using two-party percentages to show trends over time is given in this chapter, in the section entitled "Presidential Vote Choice" (pp. 124–131).

## Table 4.17   Presidential Vote by Employment Status, 1996–2008

| | | Two-Party Presidential Vote | | Full Presidential Vote | | | |
|---|---|---|---|---|---|---|---|
| Category | Year | Two-Party Democratic Vote | Difference from Mean Two-Party Democratic Vote | Democratic Vote | Republican Vote | Third-Party Vote | Number of Respondents |
| Employed | 2008 | 55.6% | 1.9% | 54.7% | 43.6% | 1.6% | 2,755 |
| Full Time | 2004 | 46.0% | –2.5% | 45.4% | 53.3% | 1.3% | 2,020 |
| | 2000 | 50.5% | 0.3% | 48.7% | 47.8% | 3.5% | 6,710 |
| | 1996 | 54.7% | –0.1% | 48.3% | 40.1% | 11.6% | 7,575 |
| | Average | 51.7% | –0.1% | 49.3% | 46.2% | 4.5% | |
| Not Employed | 2008 | 51.1% | –2.6% | 50.1% | 48.0% | 1.9% | 1,398 |
| Full Time | 2004 | 49.1% | 0.6% | 48.7% | 50.5% | 0.8% | 1,228 |
| | 2000 | 49.3% | –0.8% | 47.2% | 48.4% | 4.4% | 2,972 |
| | 1996 | 53.8% | –0.9% | 48.9% | 42.0% | 9.2% | 3,817 |
| | Average | 50.8% | –1.0% | 48.7% | 47.2% | 4.0% | |

**Question Wording for Employment Status** (Coded: Employed Full Time = 1; Not Employed Full Time = 2):

**1996–2008:** "Do you work full time for pay? . . . Yes (1); No (2)"

*Source:* National exit polls. See the section in Chapter 2 entitled "Creating a Cumulative National Data Set: Selecting Exit Polls" (pp. 28–29).

*Note:* When using these results to make inferences about the active electorate, the standard errors should be calculated using Table 2.2 (p. 36), which is explained in the adjacent section of Chapter 2, "Analyzing Exit Poll Questions: Estimating Sampling Error" (pp. 34–36). For a guide on how to understand the tables and figures of this chapter, see the section in Chapter 2 entitled "Presenting and Discussing the Exit Poll Data: Reading Chapter 4" (pp. 39–43). The rationale for using two-party percentages to show trends over time is given in this chapter, in the section entitled "Presidential Vote Choice" (pp. 124–131).

**Table 4.18**   Presidential Vote by Marital Status, 1992–2008

| Category | Year | Two-Party Presidential Vote | | Full Presidential Vote | | | |
|---|---|---|---|---|---|---|---|
| | | Two-Party Democratic Vote | Difference from Mean Democratic Two-Party Vote | Democratic Vote | Republican Vote | Third-Party Vote | Number of Respondents |
| Married | 2008 | 47.6% | –6.1% | 46.8% | 51.6% | 1.6% | 2,593 |
| | 2004 | 42.0% | –6.4% | 41.7% | 57.5% | 0.8% | 8,076 |
| | 2000 | 45.0% | –5.2% | 43.6% | 53.2% | 3.1% | 5,964 |
| | 1996 | 49.3% | –5.4% | 44.4% | 45.6% | 10.0% | 7,298 |
| | 1992 | 49.4% | –4.2% | 39.6% | 40.6% | 19.8% | 5,104 |
| | Average | 46.7% | –5.5% | 43.2% | 49.7% | 7.1% | |
| Not Married | 2008 | 66.7% | 13.0% | 65.3% | 32.6% | 2.0% | 1,706 |
| | 2004 | 59.0% | 10.5% | 58.3% | 40.5% | 1.2% | 5,139 |
| | 2000 | 59.6% | 9.4% | 56.6% | 38.5% | 4.9% | 3,317 |
| | 1996 | 64.3% | 9.5% | 56.6% | 31.4% | 12.0% | 4,002 |
| | 1992 | 62.7% | 9.1% | 51.1% | 30.3% | 18.5% | 2,720 |
| | Average | 62.5% | 10.3% | 57.6% | 34.7% | 7.7% | |

**Question Wording for Marital Status** (Coded: Married = 1; Not Married = 2):

**1992:** "Are you . . . Married (1); Single, never married (2); Widowed (2); Divorced/Separated (2)"

**1996–2008:** "Are you currently married? . . . Yes (1); No (2)"

*Source:* National exit polls. See the section in Chapter 2 entitled "Creating a Cumulative National Data Set: Selecting Exit Polls" (pp. 28–29).

*Note:* When using these results to make inferences about the active electorate, the standard errors should be calculated using Table 2.2 (p. 36), which is explained in the adjacent section of Chapter 2, "Analyzing Exit Poll Questions: Estimating Sampling Error" (pp. 34–36). For a guide on how to understand the tables and figures of this chapter, see the section in Chapter 2 entitled "Presenting and Discussing the Exit Poll Data: Reading Chapter 4" (pp. 39–43). The rationale for using two-party percentages to show trends over time is given in this chapter, in the section entitled "Presidential Vote Choice" (pp. 124–131).

**Table 4.19**   Presidential Vote by Child in Household, 1996–2008

| Category | Year | Two-Party Presidential Vote | | Full Presidential Vote | | | |
|---|---|---|---|---|---|---|---|
| | | Two-Party Democratic Vote | Difference from Mean Democratic Two-Party Vote | Democratic Vote | Republican Vote | Third-Party Vote | Number of Respondents |
| Child in | 2008 | 54.2% | 0.5% | 53.2% | 45.0% | 1.8% | 1,665 |
| Household | 2004 | 46.1% | −2.4% | 45.5% | 53.2% | 1.3% | 3,842 |
| | 2000 | 46.6% | −3.6% | 45.1% | 51.8% | 3.1% | 3,777 |
| | 1996 | 53.9% | −0.8% | 48.0% | 41.1% | 10.9% | 4,439 |
| | Average | 50.2% | −1.6% | 48.0% | 47.8% | 4.3% | |
| No Child in | 2008 | 54.2% | 0.5% | 53.3% | 45.0% | 1.7% | 2,638 |
| Household | 2004 | 49.4% | 0.9% | 48.9% | 50.2% | 0.9% | 6,154 |
| | 2000 | 52.4% | 2.2% | 50.2% | 45.6% | 4.2% | 5,548 |
| | 1996 | 54.6% | −0.2% | 48.9% | 40.7% | 10.4% | 7,006 |
| | Average | 52.6% | 0.9% | 50.3% | 45.4% | 4.3% | |

**Question Wording for Child in Household** (Coded: Child in Household = 1; No Child in Household = 2):

**1996:** "Do you have a child under 18 living at home? . . . Yes (1); No (2)"

**2000–2008:** "Do you have any children under 18 living in your household? . . . Yes (1); No (2)"

*Source:* National exit polls. See the section in Chapter 2 entitled "Creating a Cumulative National Data Set: Selecting Exit Polls" (pp. 28–29).

*Note:* When using these results to make inferences about the active electorate, the standard errors should be calculated using Table 2.2 (p. 36), which is explained in the adjacent section of Chapter 2, "Analyzing Exit Poll Questions: Estimating Sampling Error" (pp. 34–36). For a guide on how to understand the tables and figures of this chapter, see the section in Chapter 2 entitled "Presenting and Discussing the Exit Poll Data: Reading Chapter 4" (pp. 39–43). The rationale for using two-party percentages to show trends over time is given in this chapter, in the section entitled "Presidential Vote Choice" (pp. 124–131).

**Table 4.20** Presidential Vote by Union Household, 1972–2008

| Category | Year | Two-Party Presidential Vote | | Full Presidential Vote | | | |
|---|---|---|---|---|---|---|---|
| | | Two-Party Democratic Vote | Difference from Mean Democratic Two-Party Vote | Democratic Vote | Republican Vote | Third-Party Vote | Number of Respondents |
| Union | 2008 | 60.1% | 6.4% | 58.9% | 39.0% | 2.0% | 970 |
| Household | 2004 | 60.0% | 11.6% | 59.4% | 39.5% | 1.2% | 2,336 |
| | 2000 | 61.3% | 11.1% | 58.6% | 37.0% | 4.3% | 2,574 |
| | 1996 | 66.7% | 11.9% | 59.1% | 29.5% | 11.4% | 1,873 |
| | 1992 | | | | | | |
| | 1988 | 57.5% | 11.3% | 56.7% | 41.9% | 1.4% | 2,883 |
| | 1984 | 53.7% | 12.9% | 53.2% | 45.9% | 0.9% | 2,406 |
| | 1980 | 52.7% | 8.4% | 48.6% | 43.6% | 7.8% | 4,532 |
| | 1976 | 60.4% | 9.4% | 59.3% | 38.8% | 1.9% | 4,274 |
| | 1972 | 48.6% | 10.5% | 47.4% | 50.2% | 2.4% | 5,398 |
| | Average | 57.9% | 10.4% | 55.7% | 40.6% | 3.7% | |
| Not a Union | 2008 | 52.3% | −1.4% | 51.4% | 46.8% | 1.7% | 3,158 |
| Household | 2004 | 44.4% | −4.1% | 44.0% | 55.0% | 1.0% | 7,614 |
| | 2000 | 46.1% | −4.1% | 44.4% | 52.1% | 3.5% | 7,072 |
| | 1996 | 50.6% | −4.2% | 45.6% | 44.6% | 9.8% | 5,747 |
| | 1992 | | | | | | |
| | 1988 | 42.1% | −4.1% | 41.6% | 57.3% | 1.0% | 7,971 |
| | 1984 | 35.5% | −5.2% | 35.3% | 64.0% | 0.8% | 6,235 |
| | 1980 | 38.6% | −5.7% | 35.2% | 55.9% | 8.9% | 9,015 |
| | 1976 | 43.5% | −7.5% | 42.9% | 55.6% | 1.5% | 8,013 |
| | 1972 | 32.9% | −5.2% | 32.3% | 66.0% | 1.8% | 10,725 |
| | Average | 42.9% | −4.6% | 41.4% | 55.3% | 3.3% | |

**Question Wording for Union Household** (Coded: Union Household = 1; Not a Union Household = 2):

**1972–1980:** "Are you or is anyone living in your household a union member? . . . Yes (1); No (2)"

**1984:** "Are you or is any person in your household a member of a labor union? . . . Yes, I do (1); Yes, Other family member (1); No (2)"

**1988:** "Are you or is any person living in your household a member of a labor union? . . . Yes, I do (1); Yes, Other family member (1); No (2)"

**1996:** "Do you or someone in your household belong to a labor union? . . . Yes (1); No (2)"

**2000–2008:** "Do you or does someone in your household belong to a labor union? . . . Yes, I do (1); Yes, Someone else does (1); Yes, I do and someone else does (1); No one does (2)"

*Source:* National exit polls. See the section in Chapter 2 entitled "Creating a Cumulative National Data Set: Selecting Exit Polls" (pp. 28–29).

*Note:* When using these results to make inferences about the active electorate, the standard errors should be calculated using Table 2.2 (p. 36), which is explained in the adjacent section of Chapter 2, "Analyzing Exit Poll Questions: Estimating Sampling Error" (pp. 34–36). For a guide on how to understand the tables and figures of this chapter, see the section in Chapter 2 entitled "Presenting and Discussing the Exit Poll Data: Reading Chapter 4" (pp. 39–43). The rationale for using two-party percentages to show trends over time is given in this chapter, in the section entitled "Presidential Vote Choice" (pp. 124–131).

**Table 4.21**   Presidential Vote by Party Identification, 1972–2008

| Category | Year | Two-Party Presidential Vote | | Full Presidential Vote | | | |
|---|---|---|---|---|---|---|---|
| | | Two-Party Democratic Vote | Difference from Mean Democratic Two-Party Vote | Democratic Vote | Republican Vote | Third-Party Vote | Number of Respondents |
| Democrat | 2008 | 90.0% | 36.3% | 89.3% | 9.9% | 0.8% | 8,026 |
| | 2004 | 89.2% | 40.7% | 88.8% | 10.8% | 0.4% | 5,004 |
| | 2000 | 88.4% | 38.2% | 86.2% | 11.4% | 2.4% | 4,824 |
| | 1996 | 89.4% | 34.6% | 83.8% | 10.0% | 6.2% | 6,411 |
| | 1992 | 88.9% | 35.3% | 77.3% | 9.6% | 13.1% | 5,763 |
| | 1988 | 83.0% | 36.8% | 82.4% | 16.9% | 0.7% | 4,467 |
| | 1984 | 74.7% | 34.0% | 74.3% | 25.1% | 0.5% | 3,593 |
| | 1980 | 72.5% | 28.2% | 67.4% | 25.6% | 7.0% | 7,239 |
| | 1976 | 77.9% | 26.9% | 77.1% | 21.9% | 1.0% | 5,861 |
| | 1972 | 62.1% | 24.0% | 61.1% | 37.3% | 1.6% | 8,124 |
| | Average | 81.6% | 33.5% | 78.8% | 17.8% | 3.4% | |
| Republican | 2008 | 9.4% | −44.3% | 9.3% | 89.5% | 1.2% | 4,813 |
| | 2004 | 6.4% | −42.1% | 6.3% | 93.4% | 0.3% | 4,516 |
| | 2000 | 7.9% | −42.2% | 7.8% | 90.7% | 1.4% | 4,168 |
| | 1996 | 14.3% | −40.5% | 13.3% | 79.9% | 6.8% | 4,867 |
| | 1992 | 12.2% | −41.4% | 10.1% | 72.8% | 17.1% | 4,591 |
| | 1988 | 8.5% | −37.7% | 8.4% | 90.7% | 0.8% | 3,554 |
| | 1984 | 7.3% | −33.4% | 7.3% | 92.3% | 0.4% | 3,144 |
| | 1980 | 9.1% | −35.2% | 8.7% | 86.3% | 5.1% | 3,808 |
| | 1976 | 9.4% | −41.6% | 9.4% | 89.9% | 0.7% | 2,855 |
| | 1972 | 7.3% | −30.7% | 7.2% | 91.6% | 1.2% | 5,350 |
| | Average | 9.2% | −38.9% | 8.8% | 87.7% | 3.5% | |
| Independent | 2008 | 53.9% | 0.2% | 51.6% | 44.2% | 4.2% | 4,762 |
| | 2004 | 50.9% | 2.4% | 49.5% | 47.8% | 2.8% | 3,547 |
| | 2000 | 49.1% | −1.1% | 45.2% | 46.9% | 8.0% | 3,343 |
| | 1996 | 55.0% | 0.3% | 43.2% | 35.3% | 21.5% | 3,916 |
| | 1992 | 54.4% | 0.8% | 38.1% | 31.9% | 30.0% | 4,046 |
| | 1988 | 43.6% | −2.5% | 42.7% | 55.2% | 2.1% | 2,872 |
| | 1984 | 36.2% | −4.6% | 35.6% | 62.8% | 1.6% | 2,383 |
| | 1980 | 35.4% | −8.9% | 30.2% | 55.2% | 14.6% | 3,640 |
| | 1976 | 44.5% | −6.5% | 43.1% | 53.8% | 3.1% | 3,780 |
| | 1972 | 36.3% | −1.7% | 34.9% | 61.1% | 4.0% | 2,921 |
| | Average | 45.9% | −2.2% | 41.4% | 49.4% | 9.2% | |

**Question Wording for Party Identification** (Coded: Democrat = 1; Republican = 2; Independent = 3):

**1972:** "Do you usually think of yourself as a . . . Democrat (1); Republican (2); Independent (3); Other (3)"

**1976–1988:** "Do you usually think of yourself as a . . . Democrat (1); Republican (2); Independent (3)"

**1992–2008:** "No matter how you voted today, do you usually think of yourself as a . . . Democrat (1); Republican (2); Independent (3); Something else (3)"

*Source:* National exit polls. See the section in Chapter 2 entitled "Creating a Cumulative National Data Set: Selecting Exit Polls" (pp. 28–29).

*Note:* When using these results to make inferences about the active electorate, the standard errors should be calculated using Table 2.2 (p. 36), which is explained in the adjacent section of Chapter 2, "Analyzing Exit Poll Questions: Estimating Sampling Error" (pp. 34–36). For a guide on how to understand the tables and figures of this chapter, see the section in Chapter 2 entitled "Presenting and Discussing the Exit Poll Data: Reading Chapter 4" (pp. 39–43). The rationale for using two-party percentages to show trends over time is given in this chapter, in the section entitled "Presidential Vote Choice" (pp. 124–131).

**Table 4.22**   Presidential Vote by Ideological Identification, 1976–2008

| Category | Year | Two-Party Presidential Vote | | Full Presidential Vote | | | |
|---|---|---|---|---|---|---|---|
| | | Two-Party Democratic Vote | Difference from Mean Democratic Two-Party Vote | Democratic Vote | Republican Vote | Third-Party Vote | Number of Respondents |
| Liberal | 2008 | 90.2% | 36.5% | 88.6% | 9.6% | 1.8% | 4,314 |
| | 2004 | 86.6% | 38.1% | 85.4% | 13.3% | 1.3% | 2,902 |
| | 2000 | 86.1% | 35.9% | 80.3% | 12.9% | 6.8% | 2,598 |
| | 1996 | 87.1% | 32.4% | 77.6% | 11.5% | 10.9% | 3,186 |
| | 1992 | 82.7% | 29.1% | 67.7% | 14.2% | 18.1% | 1,682 |
| | 1988 | 82.0% | 35.8% | 80.9% | 17.7% | 1.3% | 2,104 |
| | 1984 | 71.2% | 30.5% | 70.2% | 28.5% | 1.3% | 1,511 |
| | 1980 | 70.5% | 26.2% | 60.4% | 25.2% | 14.3% | 2,780 |
| | 1976 | 73.0% | 22.0% | 70.5% | 26.1% | 3.4% | 2,566 |
| | Average | 81.0% | 31.8% | 75.7% | 17.7% | 6.6% | |
| Moderate | 2008 | 60.8% | 7.1% | 59.9% | 38.5% | 1.6% | 7,668 |
| | 2004 | 54.8% | 6.3% | 54.3% | 44.8% | 0.9% | 5,936 |
| | 2000 | 54.2% | 4.0% | 52.4% | 44.2% | 3.4% | 6,067 |
| | 1996 | 63.3% | 8.6% | 56.5% | 32.7% | 10.7% | 7,121 |
| | 1992 | 60.2% | 6.6% | 47.5% | 31.4% | 21.1% | 3,823 |
| | 1988 | 50.8% | 4.6% | 50.3% | 48.6% | 1.1% | 5,093 |
| | 1984 | 47.0% | 6.3% | 46.6% | 52.7% | 0.7% | 3,933 |
| | 1980 | 46.7% | 2.4% | 42.5% | 48.5% | 9.0% | 7,139 |
| | 1976 | 51.7% | 0.7% | 51.0% | 47.7% | 1.4% | 5,653 |
| | Average | 54.4% | 5.2% | 51.2% | 43.2% | 5.5% | |
| Conservative | 2008 | 20.1% | −33.6% | 19.7% | 78.1% | 2.3% | 4,768 |
| | 2004 | 15.6% | −32.9% | 15.5% | 83.7% | 0.8% | 4,048 |
| | 2000 | 17.4% | −32.8% | 17.1% | 81.3% | 1.7% | 3,484 |
| | 1996 | 21.7% | −33.0% | 19.7% | 71.1% | 9.2% | 4,679 |
| | 1992 | 22.2% | −31.4% | 18.3% | 64.0% | 17.8% | 2,127 |
| | 1988 | 19.5% | −26.7% | 19.3% | 79.5% | 1.2% | 3,574 |
| | 1984 | 17.6% | −23.2% | 17.4% | 81.8% | 0.8% | 2,999 |
| | 1980 | 23.7% | −20.6% | 22.6% | 72.6% | 4.8% | 4,148 |
| | 1976 | 29.1% | −21.9% | 28.8% | 70.1% | 1.1% | 3,589 |
| | Average | 20.8% | −28.5% | 19.8% | 75.8% | 4.4% | |

**Question Wording for Ideological Identification** (Coded: Liberal = 1; Moderate = 2; Conservative = 3):

**1976–2008:** "On most political matters, do you consider yourself . . . Liberal (1); Moderate (2); Conservative (3)"

*Source:* National exit polls. See the section in Chapter 2 entitled "Creating a Cumulative National Data Set: Selecting Exit Polls" (pp. 28–29).

*Note:* When using these results to make inferences about the active electorate, the standard errors should be calculated using Table 2.2 (p. 36), which is explained in the adjacent section of Chapter 2, "Analyzing Exit Poll Questions: Estimating Sampling Error" (pp. 34–36). For a guide on how to understand the tables and figures of this chapter, see the section in Chapter 2 entitled "Presenting and Discussing the Exit Poll Data: Reading Chapter 4" (pp. 39–43). The rationale for using two-party percentages to show trends over time is given in this chapter, in the section entitled "Presidential Vote Choice" (pp. 124–131).

**Table 4.23**  Presidential Vote by Presidential Vote in Last Election, 1972–2008

| Category | Year | Two-Party Presidential Vote | | Full Presidential Vote | | | |
|---|---|---|---|---|---|---|---|
| | | Two-Party Democratic Vote | Difference from Mean Democratic Two-Party Vote | Democratic Vote | Republican Vote | Third-Party Vote | Number of Respondents |
| Democrat | 2008 | 91.0% | 37.3% | 89.4% | 8.8% | 1.8% | 1,796 |
| | 2004 | 90.1% | 41.6% | 89.7% | 9.9% | 0.4% | 1,219 |
| | 2000 | 84.6% | 34.4% | 81.8% | 14.9% | 3.3% | 2,894 |
| | 1996 | 90.3% | 35.6% | 84.7% | 9.1% | 6.2% | 6,925 |
| | 1992 | 94.4% | 40.7% | 83.0% | 5.0% | 12.0% | 4,231 |
| | 1988 | 92.5% | 46.3% | 91.8% | 7.5% | 0.7% | 3,346 |
| | 1984 | 82.1% | 41.4% | 81.7% | 17.8% | 0.5% | 2,843 |
| | 1980 | 68.2% | 23.9% | 62.8% | 29.2% | 8.0% | 7,244 |
| | 1976 | 81.5% | 30.5% | 79.4% | 18.0% | 2.6% | 3,778 |
| | 1972 | 78.2% | 40.2% | 77.4% | 21.5% | 1.1% | 4,084 |
| | Average | 85.3% | 37.2% | 82.2% | 14.2% | 3.7% | |
| Republican | 2008 | 17.6% | −36.1% | 17.4% | 81.6% | 0.9% | 1,604 |
| | 2004 | 8.9% | −39.6% | 8.8% | 90.6% | 0.6% | 1,250 |
| | 2000 | 7.2% | −43.0% | 7.1% | 91.3% | 1.6% | 1,935 |
| | 1996 | 14.0% | −40.7% | 13.3% | 81.5% | 5.1% | 4,891 |
| | 1992 | 25.8% | −27.8% | 20.6% | 59.3% | 20.1% | 7,735 |
| | 1988 | 19.1% | −27.1% | 18.9% | 80.1% | 1.0% | 5,890 |
| | 1984 | 11.3% | −29.4% | 11.2% | 88.2% | 0.6% | 4,281 |
| | 1980 | 11.2% | −33.1% | 10.5% | 83.1% | 6.4% | 4,453 |
| | 1976 | 26.4% | −24.6% | 26.2% | 73.0% | 0.8% | 5,452 |
| | 1972 | 9.7% | −28.4% | 9.6% | 89.5% | 0.9% | 7,284 |
| | Average | 15.1% | −33.0% | 14.4% | 81.8% | 3.8% | |
| Other Candidate | 2008 | 73.7% | 20.0% | 66.0% | 23.5% | 10.5% | 185 |
| | 2004 | 77.6% | 29.1% | 71.0% | 20.6% | 8.4% | 117 |
| | 2000 | 30.7% | −19.5% | 26.7% | 60.4% | 12.9% | 581 |
| | 1996 | 33.8% | −21.0% | 22.2% | 43.4% | 34.4% | 1,994 |
| | 1992 | 93.4% | 39.8% | 65.7% | 4.7% | 29.7% | 393 |
| | 1988 | 73.1% | 26.9% | 68.8% | 25.4% | 5.9% | 450 |
| | 1984 | 71.5% | 30.7% | 68.8% | 27.5% | 3.8% | 395 |
| | 1980 | 33.2% | −11.1% | 23.4% | 47.2% | 29.4% | 312 |
| | 1976 | 65.0% | 14.0% | 61.9% | 33.3% | 4.8% | 734 |
| | 1972 | 40.7% | 2.7% | 36.4% | 52.9% | 10.7% | 1,178 |
| | Average | 59.3% | 11.2% | 51.1% | 33.9% | 15.0% | |
| Did Not Vote | 2008 | 72.0% | 18.3% | 70.5% | 27.4% | 2.1% | 553 |
| | 2004 | 54.3% | 5.8% | 53.6% | 45.1% | 1.3% | 582 |
| | 2000 | 45.7% | −4.5% | 43.9% | 52.2% | 3.9% | 806 |

*(Continued)*

**Table 4.23** Presidential Vote by Presidential Vote in Last Election, 1972–2008 *(Continued)*

| Category | Year | Two-Party Presidential Vote | | Full Presidential Vote | | | |
|---|---|---|---|---|---|---|---|
| | | Two-Party Democratic Vote | Difference from Mean Democratic Two-Party Vote | Democratic Vote | Republican Vote | Third-Party Vote | Number of Respondents |
| Did Not | 1996 | 61.4% | 6.6% | 52.9% | 33.3% | 13.7% | 1,375 |
| Vote | 1992 | 65.2% | 11.6% | 48.1% | 25.6% | 26.3% | 2,369 |
| | 1988 | 54.3% | 8.1% | 53.5% | 45.1% | 1.4% | 1,258 |
| | 1984 | 41.5% | 0.8% | 41.2% | 58.0% | 0.8% | 1,109 |
| | 1980 | 47.4% | 3.0% | 41.0% | 45.5% | 13.5% | 1,777 |
| | 1976 | 56.7% | 5.7% | 55.8% | 42.6% | 1.5% | 2,044 |
| | 1972 | 50.2% | 12.1% | 49.1% | 48.7% | 2.2% | 3,565 |
| | Average | 54.9% | 6.8% | 51.0% | 42.4% | 6.7% | |

**Question Wording for Presidential Vote in Last Election** (Coded: Democrat = 1; Republican = 2; Other Candidate = 3; Did Not Vote = 4):

**1972:** "In 1968, for whom did you vote? . . . Nixon (2); Humphrey (1); Wallace (3); Other (3); Didn't vote (4)"

**1976:** "In 1972, for whom did you vote? . . . Nixon (2); McGovern (1); Someone else (3); Did not vote (4)"

**1980:** "In 1976, for whom did you vote? . . . Jimmy Carter (1); Gerald Ford (2); Someone else (3); Did not vote (4)"

**1984:** "Who did you vote for in the 1980 presidential election? . . . Carter (1); Reagan (2); Anderson (3); Didn't vote (4)"

**1988:** "Who did you vote for in the 1984 presidential election? . . . Reagan (2); Mondale (1); Someone else (3); Didn't vote (4)"

**1992:** "Who did you vote for in the 1988 presidential election? . . . George Bush (Rep) (2); Michael Dukakis (Dem) (1); Someone else (3); Did not vote in [Year] (4)"

**1996:** "Who did you vote for in the 1992 presidential election? . . . George Bush (Rep) (2); Bill Clinton (Dem) (1); Ross Perot (Ind) (3); Someone else (3); Did not vote for president (4)"

**2000:** "In the 1996 election for president, did you vote for . . . Bill Clinton (Dem) (1); Bob Dole (Rep) (2); Ross Perot (Ref) (3); Someone else (3); Did not vote (4)"

**2004:** "Did you vote in the 2000 presidential election? . . . Yes, for Al Gore (1); Yes, for George W. Bush (2); Yes, for another candidate (3); No, I did not vote (4)"

**2008:** "In the 2004 election for president, did you vote for . . . George W. Bush (Rep) (2); John Kerry (Dem) (1); Someone else (3); Did not vote (4)"

*Source:* National exit polls. See the section in Chapter 2 entitled "Creating a Cumulative National Data Set: Selecting Exit Polls" (pp. 28–29).

*Note:* When using these results to make inferences about the active electorate, the standard errors should be calculated using Table 2.2 (p. 36), which is explained in the adjacent section of Chapter 2, "Analyzing Exit Poll Questions: Estimating Sampling Error" (pp. 34–36). For a guide on how to understand the tables and figures of this chapter, see the section in Chapter 2 entitled "Presenting and Discussing the Exit Poll Data: Reading Chapter 4" (pp. 39–43). The rationale for using two-party percentages to show trends over time is given in this chapter, in the section entitled "Presidential Vote Choice" (pp. 124–131).

**Table 4.24**  Presidential Vote by Presidential Approval, 2000–2008

| Category | Year | Two-Party Presidential Vote | | Full Presidential Vote | | | |
| | | Two-Party Democratic Vote | Difference from Mean Democratic Two-Party Vote | Democratic Vote | Republican Vote | Third-Party Vote | Number of Respondents |
|---|---|---|---|---|---|---|---|
| Approve | 2008 | 10.3% | −43.4% | 10.2% | 88.8% | 1.0% | 976 |
| | 2004 | 9.2% | −39.3% | 9.1% | 90.1% | 0.8% | 3,476 |
| | 2000 | 79.4% | 29.2% | 76.7% | 19.9% | 3.5% | 3,605 |
| | Average | 33.0% | −17.8% | 32.0% | 66.2% | 1.8% | |
| Disapprove | 2008 | 68.6% | 14.9% | 66.8% | 30.6% | 2.5% | 3,257 |
| | 2004 | 94.2% | 45.7% | 93.1% | 5.7% | 1.2% | 3,411 |
| | 2000 | 8.9% | −41.2% | 8.6% | 87.7% | 3.7% | 2,535 |
| | Average | 57.2% | 6.5% | 56.2% | 41.3% | 2.5% | |

**Question Wording for Presidential Approval** (Coded: Approve = 1; Disapprove = 2):

**2000:** " Do you approve or disapprove of the way [President] is handling his job as president? . . . Approve (1); Disapprove (2)"

**2004–2008:** "Do you approve or disapprove of the way [President] is handling his job as president? . . . Strongly approve (1); Somewhat approve (1); Somewhat disapprove (2); Strongly disapprove (2)"

*Source:* National exit polls. See the section in Chapter 2 entitled "Creating a Cumulative National Data Set: Selecting Exit Polls" (pp. 28–29).

*Note:* When using these results to make inferences about the active electorate, the standard errors should be calculated using Table 2.2 (p. 36), which is explained in the adjacent section of Chapter 2, "Analyzing Exit Poll Questions: Estimating Sampling Error" (pp. 34–36). For a guide on how to understand the tables and figures of this chapter, see the section in Chapter 2 entitled "Presenting and Discussing the Exit Poll Data: Reading Chapter 4" (pp. 39–43). The rationale for using two-party percentages to show trends over time is given in this chapter, in the section entitled "Presidential Vote Choice" (pp. 124–131).

**Table 4.25** Presidential Vote by Perceived Direction of the Country, 1996–2008

| Category | Year | Two-Party Presidential Vote | | Full Presidential Vote | | | |
|---|---|---|---|---|---|---|---|
| | | Two-Party Democratic Vote | Difference from Mean Democratic Two-Party Vote | Democratic Vote | Republican Vote | Third-Party Vote | Number of Respondents |
| Right Direction | 2008 | 28.0% | −25.7% | 27.4% | 70.6% | 2.0% | 803 |
| | 2004 | 10.3% | −38.2% | 10.3% | 89.3% | 0.5% | 1,564 |
| | 2000 | 63.0% | 12.8% | 61.5% | 36.2% | 2.4% | 4,078 |
| | 1996 | 74.6% | 19.9% | 69.5% | 23.6% | 6.9% | 2,116 |
| | Average | 44.0% | −7.8% | 42.2% | 54.9% | 2.9% | |
| Wrong Track | 2008 | 62.9% | 9.2% | 61.8% | 36.4% | 1.8% | 3,243 |
| | 2004 | 87.6% | 39.1% | 86.0% | 12.2% | 1.8% | 1,718 |
| | 2000 | 21.4% | −28.8% | 20.0% | 73.6% | 6.4% | 1,985 |
| | 1996 | 27.5% | −27.3% | 23.0% | 60.6% | 16.4% | 1,632 |
| | Average | 49.8% | −1.9% | 47.7% | 45.7% | 6.6% | |

**Question Wording for Perceived Direction of the Country** (Coded: Right Direction = 1; Wrong Track = 2):

**1996–2008:** "Do you think things in this country today are . . . Generally going in the right direction (1); Seriously off on the wrong track (2)"

*Source:* National exit polls. See the section in Chapter 2 entitled "Creating a Cumulative National Data Set: Selecting Exit Polls" (pp. 28–29).

*Note:* When using these results to make inferences about the active electorate, the standard errors should be calculated using Table 2.2 (p. 36), which is explained in the adjacent section of Chapter 2, "Analyzing Exit Poll Questions: Estimating Sampling Error" (pp. 34–36). For a guide on how to understand the tables and figures of this chapter, see the section in Chapter 2 entitled "Presenting and Discussing the Exit Poll Data: Reading Chapter 4" (pp. 39–43). The rationale for using two-party percentages to show trends over time is given in this chapter, in the section entitled "Presidential Vote Choice" (pp. 124–131).

**Table 4.26**   Presidential Vote by Expected Life for the Next Generation, 1992–2000

| Category | Year | Two-Party Presidential Vote | | Full Presidential Vote | | | |
|---|---|---|---|---|---|---|---|
| | | Two-Party Democratic Vote | Difference from Mean Democratic Two-Party Vote | Democratic Vote | Republican Vote | Third-Party Vote | Number of Respondents |
| Better Than Today | 2000 | 54.1% | 3.9% | 52.6% | 44.6% | 2.8% | 1,551 |
| | 1996 | 64.1% | 9.4% | 59.1% | 33.1% | 7.9% | 1,173 |
| | 1992 | 53.8% | 0.2% | 46.4% | 39.9% | 13.7% | 851 |
| | Average | 57.3% | 4.5% | 52.7% | 39.2% | 8.1% | |
| About the Same | 2000 | 52.4% | 2.2% | 50.3% | 45.7% | 4.0% | 932 |
| | 1996 | 59.9% | 5.1% | 54.4% | 36.5% | 9.2% | 1,380 |
| | 1992 | 42.6% | −11.0% | 35.7% | 48.2% | 16.1% | 901 |
| | Average | 51.6% | −1.2% | 46.8% | 43.4% | 9.8% | |
| Worse Than Today | 2000 | 38.8% | −11.4% | 37.0% | 58.3% | 4.7% | 668 |
| | 1996 | 41.1% | −13.7% | 34.4% | 49.3% | 16.3% | 1,296 |
| | 1992 | 61.3% | 7.7% | 45.8% | 28.9% | 25.3% | 1,040 |
| | Average | 47.1% | −5.8% | 39.0% | 45.5% | 15.4% | |

**Question Wording for Expected Life for the Next Generation** (Coded: Better Than Today = 1; About the Same = 2; Worse Than Today = 3):

**1992–2000:** "Do you expect life for the next generation of Americans to be . . . Better than life today (1); Worse than life today (3); About the same (2)"

*Source:* National exit polls. See the section in Chapter 2 entitled "Creating a Cumulative National Data Set: Selecting Exit Polls" (pp. 28–29).

*Note:* When using these results to make inferences about the active electorate, the standard errors should be calculated using Table 2.2 (p. 36), which is explained in the adjacent section of Chapter 2, "Analyzing Exit Poll Questions: Estimating Sampling Error" (pp. 34–36). For a guide on how to understand the tables and figures of this chapter, see the section in Chapter 2 entitled "Presenting and Discussing the Exit Poll Data: Reading Chapter 4" (pp. 39–43). The rationale for using two-party percentages to show trends over time is given in this chapter, in the section entitled "Presidential Vote Choice" (pp. 124–131).

**Table 4.27** Presidential Vote by Position on Government Activism, 1992–2008

| Category | Year | Two-Party Presidential Vote | | Full Presidential Vote | | | |
|---|---|---|---|---|---|---|---|
| | | Two-Party Democratic Vote | Difference from Mean Democratic Two-Party Vote | Democratic Vote | Republican Vote | Third-Party Vote | Number of Respondents |
| Government | 2008 | 77.1% | 23.4% | 76.0% | 22.6% | 1.4% | 2,618 |
| Should Do | 2004 | 66.9% | 18.4% | 66.2% | 32.8% | 1.0% | 1,577 |
| More | 2000 | 76.4% | 26.2% | 73.9% | 22.9% | 3.2% | 3,096 |
| | 1996 | 78.6% | 23.8% | 72.0% | 19.6% | 8.3% | 1,777 |
| | 1992 | 69.2% | 15.6% | 57.5% | 25.5% | 17.0% | 1,533 |
| | Average | 73.6% | 21.5% | 69.1% | 24.7% | 6.2% | |
| Government | 2008 | 27.4% | −26.3% | 26.8% | 70.8% | 2.4% | 1,722 |
| Does Too | 2004 | 29.2% | −19.3% | 28.9% | 70.0% | 1.2% | 1,555 |
| Much | 2000 | 26.2% | −23.9% | 25.3% | 71.1% | 3.7% | 3,628 |
| | 1996 | 33.0% | −21.7% | 29.7% | 60.2% | 10.1% | 2,058 |
| | 1992 | 31.9% | −21.7% | 25.3% | 54.0% | 20.7% | 1,167 |
| | Average | 29.6% | −22.6% | 27.2% | 65.2% | 7.6% | |

**Question Wording for Position on Government Activism** (Coded: Government Should Do More = 1; Government Does Too Much = 2):

**1992:** "Which comes closest to your view . . . Government should do more to solve national problems (1); Government is doing too many things better left to businesses and individuals (2)"

**1996–2008:** "Which comes closest to your view . . . Government should do more to solve problems (1); Government is doing too many things better left to businesses and individuals (2)"

*Source:* National exit polls. See the section in Chapter 2 entitled "Creating a Cumulative National Data Set: Selecting Exit Polls" (pp. 28–29).

*Note:* When using these results to make inferences about the active electorate, the standard errors should be calculated using Table 2.2 (p. 36), which is explained in the adjacent section of Chapter 2, "Analyzing Exit Poll Questions: Estimating Sampling Error" (pp. 34–36). For a guide on how to understand the tables and figures of this chapter, see the section in Chapter 2 entitled "Presenting and Discussing the Exit Poll Data: Reading Chapter 4" (pp. 39–43). The rationale for using two-party percentages to show trends over time is given in this chapter, in the section entitled "Presidential Vote Choice" (pp. 124–131).

**Table 4.28**   Presidential Vote by First-Time Voter, 1996–2008

| Category | Year | Two-Party Presidential Vote | | Full Presidential Vote | | | |
| | | Two-Party Democratic Vote | Difference from Mean Democratic Two-Party Vote | Democratic Vote | Republican Vote | Third-Party Vote | Number of Respondents |
|---|---|---|---|---|---|---|---|
| First-Time | 2008 | 69.3% | 15.6% | 68.7% | 30.5% | 0.8% | 1,057 |
| Voter | 2004 | 53.7% | 5.3% | 52.9% | 45.6% | 1.5% | 810 |
| | 2000 | 54.8% | 4.6% | 51.9% | 42.8% | 5.3% | 929 |
| | 1996 | 61.4% | 6.6% | 54.0% | 34.0% | 11.9% | 762 |
| | Average | 59.8% | 8.0% | 56.9% | 38.2% | 4.9% | |
| Not First- | 2008 | 50.7% | –3.0% | 49.6% | 48.2% | 2.2% | 7,448 |
| Time | 2004 | 48.2% | –0.3% | 47.7% | 51.4% | 0.9% | 5,866 |
| Voter | 2000 | 49.7% | –0.5% | 47.9% | 48.5% | 3.6% | 8,787 |
| | 1996 | 53.4% | –1.3% | 47.9% | 41.8% | 10.3% | 6,851 |
| | Average | 50.5% | –1.3% | 48.3% | 47.5% | 4.2% | |

**Question Wording for First-Time Voter** (Coded: First-Time Voter = 1; Not First-Time Voter = 2):

**1996–2004:** "Is this the first time you have ever voted? . . . Yes (1); No (2)"

**2008:** "Is this the first year you have ever voted? . . . Yes (1); No (2)"

*Source:* National exit polls. See the section in Chapter 2 entitled "Creating a Cumulative National Data Set: Selecting Exit Polls" (pp. 28–29).

*Note:* When using these results to make inferences about the active electorate, the standard errors should be calculated using Table 2.2 (p. 36), which is explained in the adjacent section of Chapter 2, "Analyzing Exit Poll Questions: Estimating Sampling Error" (pp. 34–36). For a guide on how to understand the tables and figures of this chapter, see the section in Chapter 2 entitled "Presenting and Discussing the Exit Poll Data: Reading Chapter 4" (pp. 39–43). The rationale for using two-party percentages to show trends over time is given in this chapter, in the section entitled "Presidential Vote Choice" (pp. 124–131).

**Table 4.29** Presidential Vote by Household Income, 1996–2008

| Category | Year | Two-Party Presidential Vote | | Full Presidential Vote | | | |
|---|---|---|---|---|---|---|---|
| | | Two-Party Democratic Vote | Difference from Mean Democratic Two-Party Vote | Democratic Vote | Republican Vote | Third-Party Vote | Number of Respondents |
| Under $30,000 | 2008 | 66.4% | 12.7% | 64.7% | 32.7% | 2.5% | 3,055 |
| | 2004 | 59.9% | 11.5% | 59.5% | 39.8% | 0.8% | 2,799 |
| | 2000 | 57.8% | 7.6% | 54.7% | 40.0% | 5.2% | 2,653 |
| | 1996 | 62.2% | 7.5% | 55.0% | 33.4% | 11.6% | 4,936 |
| | Average | 61.6% | 9.8% | 58.5% | 36.5% | 5.0% | |
| $30,000–$49,999 | 2008 | 55.9% | 2.2% | 55.0% | 43.5% | 1.5% | 3,074 |
| | 2004 | 50.5% | 2.0% | 50.1% | 49.2% | 0.7% | 2,647 |
| | 2000 | 50.8% | 0.6% | 49.0% | 47.5% | 3.5% | 2,961 |
| | 1996 | 54.5% | −0.2% | 48.1% | 40.2% | 11.7% | 3,962 |
| | Average | 52.9% | 1.1% | 50.6% | 45.1% | 4.4% | |
| $50,000–$74,999 | 2008 | 49.6% | −4.1% | 48.3% | 49.1% | 2.6% | 3,393 |
| | 2004 | 43.3% | −5.1% | 42.9% | 56.1% | 1.0% | 2,838 |
| | 2000 | 47.4% | −2.8% | 46.1% | 51.2% | 2.7% | 2,915 |
| | 1996 | 51.0% | −3.8% | 46.6% | 44.8% | 8.6% | 3,030 |
| | Average | 47.8% | −3.9% | 46.0% | 50.3% | 3.7% | |
| $75,000–$99,999 | 2008 | 51.6% | −2.1% | 50.9% | 47.8% | 1.3% | 2,289 |
| | 2004 | 45.1% | −3.4% | 44.7% | 54.5% | 0.8% | 1,717 |
| | 2000 | 46.6% | −3.6% | 45.3% | 51.9% | 2.8% | 1,510 |
| | 1996 | 47.9% | −6.8% | 43.8% | 47.5% | 8.7% | 1,331 |
| | Average | 47.8% | −4.0% | 46.2% | 50.4% | 3.4% | |
| $100,000 or More | 2008 | 49.8% | −3.9% | 49.1% | 49.4% | 1.5% | 4,181 |
| | 2004 | 41.1% | −7.4% | 40.6% | 58.3% | 1.0% | 2,270 |
| | 2000 | 44.0% | −6.2% | 42.5% | 54.2% | 3.3% | 1,733 |
| | 1996 | 41.5% | −13.3% | 38.1% | 53.8% | 8.1% | 1,261 |
| | Average | 44.1% | −7.7% | 42.6% | 53.9% | 3.5% | |

**Question Wording for Household Income** (Coded: Under $30,000 = 1; $30,000–$49,999 = 2; $50,000–$74,999 = 3; $75,000–$99,999 = 4; $100,000 or More = 5):

**1996–2000:** "[Previous Year] Total family income . . . Under $15,000 (1); $15,000–$29,999 (1); $30,000–$49,999 (2); $50,000–$74,999 (3); $75,000–$99,999 (4); $100,000 or more (5)"

**2004–2008:** "[Previous Year] Total family income . . . Under $15,000 (1); $15,000–$29,999 (1); $30,000–$49,999 (2); $50,000–$74,999 (3); $75,000–$99,999 (4); $100,000–$149,999 (5); $150,000–$199,999 (5); $200,000 or more (5)"

*Source:* National exit polls. See the section in Chapter 2 entitled "Creating a Cumulative National Data Set: Selecting Exit Polls" (pp. 28–29).

*Note:* When using these results to make inferences about the active electorate, the standard errors should be calculated using Table 2.2 (p. 36), which is explained in the adjacent section of Chapter 2, "Analyzing Exit Poll Questions: Estimating Sampling Error" (pp. 34–36). For a guide on how to understand the tables and figures of this chapter, see the section in Chapter 2 entitled "Presenting and Discussing the Exit Poll Data: Reading Chapter 4" (pp. 39–43). The rationale for using two-party percentages to show trends over time is given in this chapter, in the section entitled "Presidential Vote Choice" (pp. 124–131).

**Table 4.30** Presidential Vote by Four-Year Household Financial Situation, 1992–2008

| Category | Year | Two-Party Presidential Vote | | Full Presidential Vote | | | |
|---|---|---|---|---|---|---|---|
| | | Two-Party Democratic Vote | Difference from Mean Democratic Two-Party Vote | Democratic Vote | Republican Vote | Third-Party Vote | Number of Respondents |
| Better | 2008 | 37.7% | −16.0% | 36.6% | 60.4% | 3.1% | 1,043 |
| | 2004 | 19.4% | −29.1% | 19.3% | 80.0% | 0.7% | 2,111 |
| | 2000 | 62.9% | 12.8% | 61.0% | 35.9% | 3.1% | 3,200 |
| | 1996 | 71.8% | 17.1% | 66.3% | 26.0% | 7.8% | 5,367 |
| | 1992 | 28.3% | −25.3% | 24.2% | 61.4% | 14.3% | 1,861 |
| | Average | 44.0% | −8.1% | 41.5% | 52.7% | 5.8% | |
| About the Same | 2008 | 45.9% | −7.8% | 44.9% | 52.9% | 2.3% | 1,422 |
| | 2004 | 50.2% | 1.8% | 49.7% | 49.2% | 1.1% | 2,591 |
| | 2000 | 36.8% | −13.4% | 35.2% | 60.5% | 4.3% | 2,398 |
| | 1996 | 50.6% | −4.2% | 45.5% | 44.5% | 9.9% | 6,760 |
| | 1992 | 49.2% | −4.4% | 40.6% | 42.0% | 17.5% | 3,193 |
| | Average | 46.5% | −5.6% | 43.2% | 49.8% | 7.0% | |
| Worse | 2008 | 71.4% | 17.7% | 70.6% | 28.3% | 1.1% | 2,055 |
| | 2004 | 80.1% | 31.7% | 79.2% | 19.6% | 1.2% | 2,002 |
| | 2000 | 34.3% | −15.8% | 32.8% | 62.7% | 4.5% | 661 |
| | 1996 | 32.3% | −22.5% | 27.3% | 57.4% | 15.3% | 3,059 |
| | 1992 | 81.1% | 27.5% | 60.5% | 14.1% | 25.4% | 2,722 |
| | Average | 59.8% | 7.7% | 54.1% | 36.4% | 9.5% | |

**Question Wording for Four-Year Household Financial Situation** (Coded: Better = 1; About the Same = 2; Worse = 3):

**1992–2004:** "Compared to four years ago, is your family's financial situation . . . Better today (1); Worse today (3); About the same (2)"

**2008:** "Compared to four years ago, is your family's financial situation . . . Better (1); Worse (3); About the same (2)"

*Source:* National exit polls. See the section in Chapter 2 entitled "Creating a Cumulative National Data Set: Selecting Exit Polls" (pp. 28–29).

*Note:* When using these results to make inferences about the active electorate, the standard errors should be calculated using Table 2.2 (p. 36), which is explained in the adjacent section of Chapter 2, "Analyzing Exit Poll Questions: Estimating Sampling Error" (pp. 34–36). For a guide on how to understand the tables and figures of this chapter, see the section in Chapter 2 entitled "Presenting and Discussing the Exit Poll Data: Reading Chapter 4" (pp. 39–43). The rationale for using two-party percentages to show trends over time is given in this chapter, in the section entitled "Presidential Vote Choice" (pp. 124–131).

**Table 4.31** Presidential Vote by Judgments of Current National Economic Conditions, 1992–2008

| | | Two-Party Presidential Vote | | Full Presidential Vote | | | |
| | | Two-Party Democratic Vote | Difference from Mean Democratic Two-Party Vote | Democratic Vote | Republican Vote | Third-Party Vote | Number of Respondents |
| Category | Year | | | | | | |
|---|---|---|---|---|---|---|---|
| Performing Well | 2008 | 26.9% | −26.8% | 26.4% | 71.7% | 1.9% | 524 |
| | 2004 | 12.8% | −35.7% | 12.8% | 86.8% | 0.4% | 1,486 |
| | 2000 | 52.3% | 2.1% | 50.5% | 46.0% | 3.5% | 5,367 |
| | 1996 | 67.6% | 12.9% | 62.9% | 30.2% | 6.9% | 4,676 |
| | 1992 | 11.6% | −42.0% | 10.5% | 79.8% | 9.7% | 1,431 |
| | Average | 34.2% | −17.9% | 32.6% | 62.9% | 4.5% | |
| Performing Badly | 2008 | 54.8% | 1.1% | 53.7% | 44.3% | 2.0% | 8,004 |
| | 2004 | 80.1% | 31.6% | 78.6% | 19.5% | 1.8% | 1,886 |
| | 2000 | 34.7% | −15.5% | 32.8% | 61.9% | 5.3% | 876 |
| | 1996 | 38.0% | −16.7% | 31.9% | 52.0% | 16.1% | 3,456 |
| | 1992 | 65.9% | 12.3% | 51.6% | 26.7% | 21.7% | 6,628 |
| | Average | 54.7% | 2.6% | 49.7% | 40.9% | 9.4% | |

**Question Wording for Judgments of Current National Economic Conditions** (Coded: Performing Well = 1; Performing Badly = 2):

**1986:** "These days, is the condition of the nation's economy . . . Very good (1); Fairly good (1); Fairly bad (2); Very bad (2)"

**1990:** "These days, do you think the condition of the nation's economy is . . . Excellent (1); Good (1); Not so good (2); Poor (2)"

**1992–2010:** "Do you think the condition of the nation's economy is . . . Excellent (1); Good (1); Not so good (2); Poor (2)"

*Source:* National exit polls. See the section in Chapter 2 entitled "Creating a Cumulative National Data Set: Selecting Exit Polls" (pp. 28–29).

*Note:* When using these results to make inferences about the active electorate, the standard errors should be calculated using Table 2.2 (p. 36), which is explained in the adjacent section of Chapter 2, "Analyzing Exit Poll Questions: Estimating Sampling Error" (pp. 34–36). For a guide on how to understand the tables and figures of this chapter, see the section in Chapter 2 entitled "Presenting and Discussing the Exit Poll Data: Reading Chapter 4" (pp. 39–43). The rationale for using two-party percentages to show trends over time is given in this chapter, in the section entitled "Presidential Vote Choice" (pp. 124–131).

**Table 4.32** Presidential Vote by Judgments of Future National Economic Conditions, 2000–2008

| Category | Year | Two-Party Presidential Vote | | Full Presidential Vote | | | |
|---|---|---|---|---|---|---|---|
| | | Two-Party Democratic Vote | Difference from Mean Democratic Two-Party Vote | Democratic Vote | Republican Vote | Third-Party Vote | Number of Respondents |
| Better | 2008 | 61.8% | 8.1% | 61.1% | 37.8% | 1.1% | 2,144 |
| | 2004 | | | | | | |
| | 2000 | 53.5% | 3.3% | 52.9% | 46.0% | 1.2% | 1,750 |
| | Average | 57.6% | 5.7% | 57.0% | 41.9% | 1.1% | |
| About the Same | 2008 | 52.9% | −0.8% | 52.0% | 46.4% | 1.6% | 1,074 |
| | 2004 | | | | | | |
| | 2000 | 49.1% | −1.0% | 47.3% | 49.0% | 3.7% | 3,571 |
| | Average | 51.0% | −0.9% | 49.7% | 47.7% | 2.7% | |
| Worse | 2008 | 44.3% | −9.4% | 43.0% | 54.0% | 3.0% | 960 |
| | 2004 | | | | | | |
| | 2000 | 41.6% | −8.6% | 37.6% | 52.8% | 9.6% | 778 |
| | Average | 43.0% | −9.0% | 40.3% | 53.4% | 6.3% | |

**Question Wording for Judgments of Future National Economic Conditions** (Coded: Better = 1; About the Same = 2; Worse = 3):

**2000–2008:** "During the next year, do you think the nation's economy will . . . Get Better (1); Get Worse (3); Stay About the Same (2)"

*Source:* National exit polls. See the section in Chapter 2 entitled "Creating a Cumulative National Data Set: Selecting Exit Polls" (pp. 28–29).

*Note:* When using these results to make inferences about the active electorate, the standard errors should be calculated using Table 2.2 (p. 36), which is explained in the adjacent section of Chapter 2, "Analyzing Exit Poll Questions: Estimating Sampling Error" (pp. 34–36). For a guide on how to understand the tables and figures of this chapter, see the section in Chapter 2 entitled "Presenting and Discussing the Exit Poll Data: Reading Chapter 4" (pp. 39–43). The rationale for using two-party percentages to show trends over time is given in this chapter, in the section entitled "Presidential Vote Choice" (pp. 124–131).

**Table 4.33** Democratic Groups in the Presidential Exit Polls, 1972–2008

| Group | Average Share of Exit Polls | Average Two-Party Democratic Vote | Democratic Vote Share in 2008 | Last Year Voted for Other Party |
|---|---|---|---|---|
| *Base (67%+)* | | | | |
| Think the Republican candidate campaigned unfairly | 24% | 94% | 96% | NA |
| Black | 10% | 90% | 95% | NA |
| Voted for Democratic candidate in last presidential election | 35% | 85% | 89% | NA |
| Democrat | 40% | 82% | 89% | NA |
| Disapprove of Republican president | 59% | 81% | 67% | NA |
| Liberal | 20% | 81% | 89% | NA |
| Approve of Democratic president | 58% | 79% | NA | NA |
| Jewish | 3% | 77% | 78% | NA |
| Gay or bisexual | 4% | 74% | 70% | NA |
| Think government should do more | 49% | 74% | 76% | NA |
| No religious affiliation | 8% | 69% | 75% | NA |
| Religion other than Protestant, Catholic, or Jewish | 6% | 69% | 73% | NA |
| Hispanic/Latino | 4% | 68% | 68% | NA |
| *Leaners (56%–66%)* | | | | |
| Not married | 35% | 63% | 65% | NA |
| Household earns less than $30,000 annually | 24% | 62% | 65% | NA |
| Did not complete high school | 6% | 61% | 63% | NA |
| Race other than White, Black, Hispanic/Latino, or Asian | 2% | 61% | 67% | 1988 |
| First-time voter | 10% | 60% | 69% | NA |
| Household finances have gotten worse in the last 4 years | 27% | 60% | 71% | 2000 |
| City precinct | 29% | 59% | 63% | NA |
| Voted for non-major-party candidate in last presidential election | 6% | 59% | 66% | 2000 |
| Attend religious services less than once a week | 58% | 58% | 60% | NA |
| Not born again | 63% | 58% | 59% | NA |
| Union household | 27% | 58% | 59% | 1972 |
| Think future national economic conditions will be better | 39% | 58% | 61% | NA |
| Think life will be better for the next generation (last asked in 2000) | 31% | 57% | NA | NA |

*Source:* National exit polls. See the section in Chapter 2 entitled "Creating a Cumulative National Data Set: Selecting Exit Polls" (pp. 28–29).

*Note:* NA = not applicable. When using these results to make inferences about the active electorate, the standard errors should be calculated using Table 2.2 (p. 36), which is explained in the adjacent section of Chapter 2, "Analyzing Exit Poll Questions: Estimating Sampling Error" (pp. 34–36). For a guide on how to understand the tables and figures of this chapter, see the section in Chapter 2 entitled "Presenting and Discussing the Exit Poll Data: Reading Chapter 4" (pp. 39–43). The rationale for using two-party percentages to show trends over time is given in this chapter, in the section entitled "Presidential Vote Choice" (pp. 124–131).

**Table 4.34**   Republican Groups in the Presidential Exit Polls, 1972–2008

| Group | Average Share of Exit Polls | Average Two-Party Republican Vote | Republican Share of Overall Vote 2008 | Last Year Voted for Other Party |
|---|---|---|---|---|
| *Base (67%+)* | | | | |
| Republican | 33% | 91% | 90% | NA |
| Disapprove of Democratic president | 42% | 91% | NA | NA |
| Approve of Republican president | 41% | 90% | 89% | NA |
| Think the Democratic candidate campaigned unfairly | 17% | 88% | 83% | NA |
| Voted for Republican candidate in last presidential election | 45% | 85% | 82% | NA |
| Conservative | 33% | 79% | 78% | NA |
| Think government does too much | 51% | 70% | 71% | NA |
| | | | | |
| *Leaners (56%–66%)* | | | | |
| Think current national economic conditions are performing well | 43% | 66% | 72% | 2000 |
| Born again | 37% | 62% | 57% | NA |
| Attend religious services at least once a week | 42% | 59% | 55% | NA |
| Protestant | 56% | 58% | 54% | NA |
| White | 83% | 57% | 55% | NA |
| Rural precinct | 29% | 57% | 53% | 1996 |
| Not a union household | 73% | 57% | 47% | 2004 |
| Think neither candidate campaigned unfairly | 19% | 57% | 58% | 2004 |
| Think future national economic conditions will be worse | 18% | 57% | 54% | NA |
| Household earns $100,000 or more annually | 17% | 56% | 49% | NA |
| Southerner | 29% | 56% | 54% | 1976 |
| Household finances have gotten better in last 4 years | 33% | 56% | 60% | 2000 |
| Think country is moving in the right direction | 49% | 56% | 71% | 2000 |

*Source:* National exit polls. See the section in Chapter 2 entitled "Creating a Cumulative National Data Set: Selecting Exit Polls" (pp. 28–29).

*Note:* NA = not applicable. When using these results to make inferences about the active electorate, the standard errors should be calculated using Table 2.2 (p. 36), which is explained in the adjacent section of Chapter 2, "Analyzing Exit Poll Questions: Estimating Sampling Error" (pp. 34–36). For a guide on how to understand the tables and figures of this chapter, see the section in Chapter 2 entitled "Presenting and Discussing the Exit Poll Data: Reading Chapter 4" (pp. 39–43). The rationale for using two-party percentages to show trends over time is given in this chapter, in the section entitled "Presidential Vote Choice" (pp. 124–131).

**Table 4.35** Swing Groups in the Presidential Exit Polls, 1972–2008

| Group | Average Share of Exit Polls | Average Two-Party Democratic Vote | Democratic Share of Overall Vote in 2008 | Last Year Switched Party Vote |
|---|---|---|---|---|
| Postgraduate | 17% | 55% | 58% | 1988 |
| Did not vote in last presidential election | 14% | 55% | 71% | 2000 |
| Think current national economic conditions are performing badly | 57% | 55% | 54% | 2000 |
| Moderate | 48% | 54% | 60% | 1984 |
| Household earns $30,000–$49,999 annually | 23% | 53% | 55% | NA |
| 18–29 age group | 21% | 53% | 66% | 1988 |
| Easterner | 25% | 53% | 59% | 1988 |
| No child in household | 62% | 53% | 53% | 2004 |
| Asian | 2% | 52% | 61% | 1996 |
| Employed full time | 63% | 52% | 55% | 2004 |
| High school graduate | 23% | 52% | 52% | 2004 |
| Not employed full time | 37% | 51% | 50% | 2004 |
| Think life will be about the same for the next generation (last asked in 2000) | 27% | 52% | NA | 1992 |
| Female | 52% | 51% | 56% | 1988 |
| Catholic | 27% | 51% | 54% | 2004 |
| Not first-time voter | 90% | 51% | 50% | 2004 |
| Made presidential choice in last week of campaign | 19% | 51% | 49% | 1996 |
| Think future national economic conditions will be about the same | 43% | 51% | 52% | 2000 |
| Think country is off on the wrong track | 51% | 50% | 62% | 2000 |
| Not gay or bisexual | 96% | 50% | 53% | 2004 |
| Child in household | 38% | 50% | 53% | 2004 |
| Some college education | 30% | 49% | 51% | 2004 |
| Made presidential choice before last week of campaign | 81% | 49% | 53% | 2004 |
| Westerner | 20% | 48% | 50% | 1988 |
| Midwesterner | 27% | 48% | 54% | 2004 |
| Household earns $75,000–$99,999 annually | 13% | 48% | 51% | 2004 |
| Household earns $50,000–$74,999 annually | 23% | 48% | 48% | 1996 |
| Think life will be worse for the next generation (last asked in 2000) | 40% | 47% | NA | 1992 |
| Think both candidates campaigned unfairly | 41% | 47% | 41% | 2004 |

**Table 4.35** *(Continued)*

| Group | Average Share of Exit Polls | Average Two-Party Democratic Vote | Democratic Share of Overall Vote in 2008 | Last Year Switched Party Vote |
|---|---|---|---|---|
| 30–44 age group | 32% | 47% | 52% | 2004 |
| Suburban precinct | 43% | 47% | 50% | 2004 |
| College graduate | 24% | 47% | 50% | 2004 |
| Married | 65% | 47% | 47% | NA |
| Household finances have stayed the same in last 4 years | 40% | 47% | 45% | 2004 |
| Independent | 27% | 46% | 52% | 2000 |
| 45–59 age group | 26% | 46% | 49% | 2004 |
| 60+ age group | 21% | 46% | 47% | 2000 |
| Male | 48% | 45% | 49% | 2004 |

*Source:* National exit polls. See the section in Chapter 2 entitled "Creating a Cumulative National Data Set: Selecting Exit Polls" (pp. 28–29).

*Note:* NA = not applicable. When using these results to make inferences about the active electorate, the standard errors should be calculated using Table 2.2 (p. 36), which is explained in the adjacent section of Chapter 2, "Analyzing Exit Poll Questions: Estimating Sampling Error" (pp. 34–36). For a guide on how to understand the tables and figures of this chapter, see the section in Chapter 2 entitled "Presenting and Discussing the Exit Poll Data: Reading Chapter 4" (pp. 39–43). The rationale for using two-party percentages to show trends over time is given in this chapter, in the section entitled "Presidential Vote Choice" (pp. 124–131).

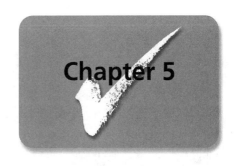

# Chapter 5

# Congressional Voting Preferences of Exit Poll Respondents

The nationwide outcomes of House elections in the United States have proven to be quite dynamic during the past three decades (see Figure 5.1). Each House election[1] produced a net change in the relative number of seats won by the two major political parties, ranging from a single seat in the 1976 election to sixty-four seats in 2010 (see Table 5.1 at the end of the chapter for biennial seat shares). The average net change over this time period has been seventeen seats in each House race. Turnover tended to be greater in midterm election years than in presidential election years. The last nine midterm election years produced an average net change of twenty-four House seats, compared to an average net change of only eleven House seats in the last nine presidential election years.

On three occasions since 1976, turnover in House seats has changed the political party controlling the House of Representatives. From 1976 through 1992, Democrats won a majority of House races in every election, averaging 264 (or 61 percent) of the 435 seats in Congress. In 1994, Republicans swung fifty-four seats in their favor and gained control of the House for the first time in forty years. Republicans won a majority of races in every congressional election through 2004, averaging 227 (or 52 percent) of the House seats.

In the 2006 midterm elections, Democrats regained the majority in the House by winning thirty-one additional seats. These victories gave the Democrats control of 233 (or 54 percent) of the seats in the chamber. They expanded their majority to 257 (or 59 percent) of the seats as a result of the 2008 congressional races.

The tide turned again in 2010, when Republicans seized control of the House by swinging sixty-four seats in their favor. This surge was the largest net pickup by either political party since the 1948 election. Overall, the Republicans won 242 (or 56 percent) of the seats in the

**Figure 5.1**  Democratic Share of Two-Party House Seats, 1976–2010

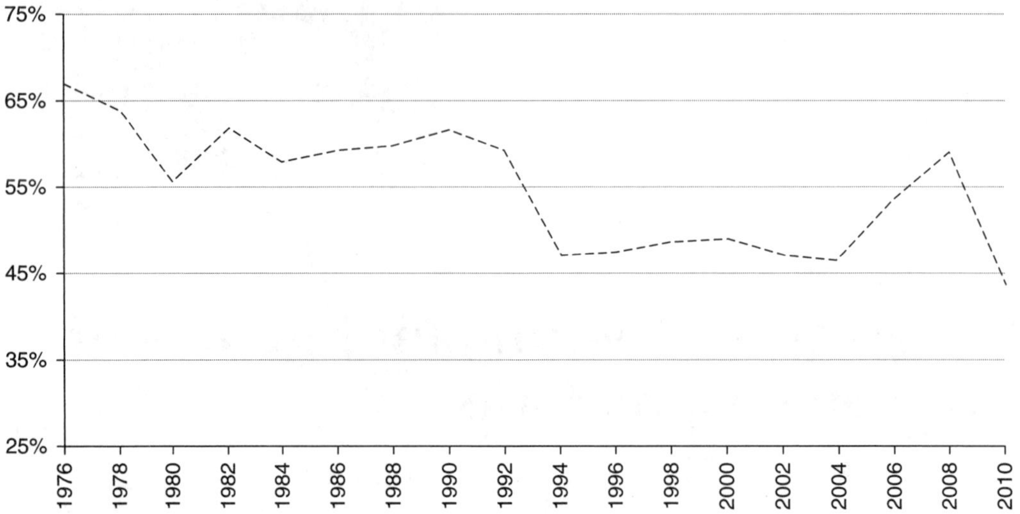

*Source:* Harold W. Stanley and Richard G. Niemi, *Vital Statistics on American Politics,* 2011–2012 (Washington, DC: CQ Press, 2011).

112th Congress, giving them their largest majority since the 1946 elections, in which they held 246 (or 57 percent) of the seats in the 80th Congress.

Party control of the House of Representatives does not simply follow in lockstep with party control of the White House. In only seven of the eighteen congressional elections occurring from 1976 through 2010 was control of the House won by the winning or sitting party of the president. The other eleven House elections produced split-party control. Clearly, other factors influenced the congressional decisions of the electorate.

In the remainder of this chapter, we examine the congressional voting patterns of various groups identified by the exit polls conducted from 1976 through 2010.[2] We tabulate the findings of the congressional vote question in two different ways. We first report the percentage of the vote received by just the two major political party candidates—the Democratic nominee and the Republican nominee—in a given exit poll. The two-party vote allows for comparisons of support for the major political parties over time. It sums to 100 percent and reveals the relative backing that the two major parties had from exit poll respondents. For this reason, we display the "Democratic Share of Two-Party Vote" in the graphs that accompany each section (the Republican share is simply the mirror image of the Democratic share) and base our discussion of each group's longitudinal preferences on them. In the tables at the end of the chapter, we also report the percentage of the overall House vote received by the Democratic and Republican Party nominees from exit poll respondents, as well as the collective percentage received by third-party candidates. This information indicates the actual distribution of the vote in the exit polls. It is best suited for describing the outcome of a particular election. Hence, in each section when we describe the most recent election, we rely on the overall vote rather than the two-party vote.

Readers can use this exit poll information to make inferences, with a margin of error and known degree of confidence, about the behavior of all voters in the electorate who fit into one of the categories assessed in this chapter. In other words, these exit poll results can be used to estimate how groups in the active electorate voted over time. To do this, readers need to identify the percent vote share given by a certain exit poll group to a party's House candidates and the number of exit poll respondents from this group who voted for any House candidate. Then, they need to apply this information to Table 2.2 to determine the margin of sampling error for an exit poll group's vote share given to a party's candidate (see the section in Chapter 2 entitled "Reading Chapter 5: Congressional Voting Preferences of Exit Poll Respondents" for a lengthier discussion of this procedure). For example, in 2010, male exit poll respondents gave Democratic House candidates 42 percent of their overall vote (see Table 5.6 at the end of the chapter). The far right-hand column in Table 5.6 shows that 8,270 men validly answered the House voting question. Applying this information to Table 2.2, we see that the sampling error for male respondents' Democratic House vote in 2010 is plus or minus 1 percent. Another way to think about this is that we can have 95 percent confidence that between 41 and 43 percent of men in the active electorate voted for Democratic House candidates in 2010. Readers must be mindful that when calculating the two-party vote sampling errors, the number of respondents voting for third-party House candidates must be subtracted from the calculation of the total number of respondents before applying this information to the table.

We begin our discussion of congressional voting preferences by describing the two-party congressional vote over time, establishing a baseline by which to compare the performance of the various subgroups in the electorate. Then we document the vote choices for key subgroups in the congressional exit polls, exploring how they have evolved over time. At the end of the chapter, we consider the voting behavior of all these exit poll groups simultaneously by examining the largest partisan voting gaps in an effort to identify congressional base voting groups for the two major political parties.

## Congressional Vote Choice

National exit pollsters have been soliciting voters' choices in their local House races since 1976. Despite the contextual differences across House races, the vote choice question used by exit pollsters has changed little over time or across precinct. It enables respondents to choose between the unnamed Democratic candidate and the unnamed Republican candidate (at times the candidate has been named but not since the 1992 election). It provides a space where voters can write in the name of a candidate for whom they voted that was not a nominee of the two major parties. It also includes an option for voters to indicate if they did not vote in the House election. Partisan preferences are then aggregated across districts to produce nationwide tallies for Democratic, Republican, and third-party candidates in a given congressional election.

### Overall House Vote

Figure 5.2 shows the nationwide two-party House vote derived by the exit polls conducted from 1976 through 2010. Democratic House candidates have won a majority of respondents'

**Figure 5.2**  Democratic Share of Two-Party House Vote, 1976–2010

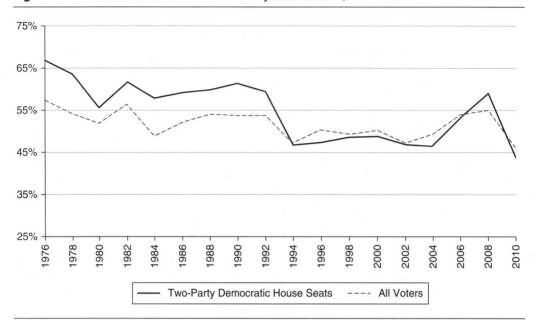

Two-Party Democratic House Seats  ---- All Voters

*Source:* National exit polls. See the section in Chapter 2 entitled "Creating a Cumulative National Data Set: Selecting Exit Polls" (pp. 28–29).

*Note:* When using these results to make inferences about the active electorate, the standard errors should be calculated using Table 2.2 (p. 36), which is explained in the adjacent section of Chapter 2, "Analyzing Exit Poll Questions: Estimating Sampling Error" (pp. 34–36). For a guide on how to understand the tables and figures of this chapter, see the section in Chapter 2 entitled "Presenting and Discussing the Exit Poll Data: Reading Chapter 5" (pp. 43–46). The rationale for using two-party percentages to show trends over time is given in Chapter 4, in the section entitled "Presidential Vote Choice" (pp. 124–131).

two-party congressional vote in eleven of the eighteen elections contested during this time. Democratic House candidates have won, on average, 52 percent of respondents' two-party vote, compared to 48 percent for Republican House candidates. (As explained in the section in Chapter 4 entitled "Presidential Vote Choice," these two-party percentages do not include third parties.)

Exit poll respondents' two-party House vote has proven to be an imperfect indicator of the proportion of seats won by the major parties. The ratio of two-party seat share to two-party vote share typically favors the winning party, meaning that the winning party typically gains a larger percentage of seats in the House than the percentage of votes that it received in the exit poll. From 1976 through 1992, Democrats won an average of 61 percent of the two-party seats in the House, but only an average of 54 percent of exit poll respondents' two-party votes. The balance of power switched in 1994, resulting in a Republican advantage, albeit a much smaller one, over the next decade. From 1994 through 2004, Republicans won an average of 52 percent of the two-party seats in the House, while receiving an average of 51 percent of exit poll respondents' two-party votes. The seat-vote ratio again switched in the Democrats' favor in 2006 and 2008, when they won an average of 56 percent of the two-party seats in the House, compared to an average of 55 percent of exit poll respondents' two-party votes.

In the 2010 midterm elections, the Republican Party regained control of the House of Representatives, winning 56 percent of the seats. In the national exit poll, Republican House candidates defeated their Democratic counterparts nationwide, 52 percent to 45 percent (see Table 5.2 at the end of the chapter). This was the highest percentage of the overall vote received by Republican House candidates since the exit polls began soliciting respondents' congressional vote in 1976.

## House Vote Based on President

National exit pollsters have long been interested in the relationship between exit poll respondents' congressional vote choices and presidential vote choices. Since 1982, they have frequently included a question asking respondents explicitly whether their choice of House candidate was based on their feelings about the sitting president. Respondents could indicate that their vote was intended to express their support for or opposition to the president or that the president was not a factor in their House vote.

Figure 5.3 shows the distribution of responses in the eight exit polls from 1982 through 2010 that contained the question assessing the role of the sitting president in respondents' choice for the House of Representatives. In half of these exit polls, a majority of respondents indicated that the president was not a factor in their House vote decision (1990, 1994, 1998, and 2000). In the other half, a majority of respondents indicated that the president was a factor (1982, 2002, 2006, and 2010).

**Figure 5.3**  Composition of the Exit Polls by House Vote Based on President, 1982–2010

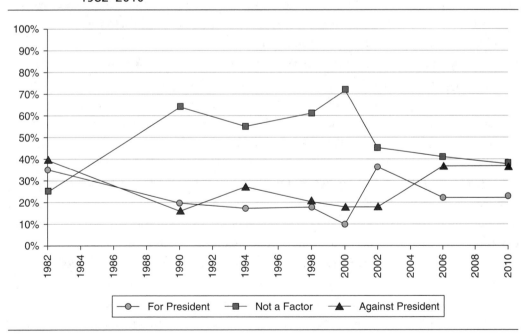

*Source:* National exit polls. See the section in Chapter 2 entitled "Creating a Cumulative National Data Set: Selecting Exit Polls" (pp. 28–29).

*Note:* When using these results to make inferences about the active electorate, the standard errors should be calculated using Table 2.2 (p. 36), which is explained in the adjacent section of Chapter 2, "Analyzing Exit Poll Questions: Estimating Sampling Error" (pp. 34–36). For a guide on how to understand the tables and figures of this chapter, see the section in Chapter 2 entitled "Presenting and Discussing the Exit Poll Data: Reading Chapter 5" (pp. 43–46). The rationale for using two-party percentages to show trends over time is given in Chapter 4, in the section entitled "Presidential Vote Choice" (pp. 124–131).

Among exit poll respondents who indicated the president was a factor (whether or not they constituted a majority), greater numbers typically gravitated toward the party that ultimately won control of the House of Representatives (1990 is the lone exception). In the seven exit polls conducted when the president's party lost the House, 28 percent of respondents overall (and 58 percent of respondents indicating the president was a factor) reported that their vote was intended to express opposition to the sitting president, compared to 21 percent who reported that their vote was intended to express support for the president. In the only exit poll conducted when the president's party won the House (2002), 37 percent of respondents overall (and 67 percent of respondents indicating the president was a factor) reported that their vote was intended to express support for the sitting president, compared to 18 percent who reported that their vote was intended to express opposition to the president.

In the 2010 exit poll, 61 percent of respondents reported that the president was a factor in their congressional vote choice, as opposed to the 39 percent who reported that he was not a factor (see Table 5.3 at the end of the chapter). Of those respondents who indicated that the president was a factor, many more reported that their House vote was designed to show their displeasure with his performance. Specifically, the House vote of 38 percent of respondents (or 62 percent of those indicating the president was a factor) was intended to express opposition to the president, compared to 24 percent of respondents (or 38 percent of those indicating the president was a factor) whose House vote was intended to express support for the president.

Not surprisingly, the exit polls show a strong relationship between respondents' identification of the president as a factor in their congressional vote choices and their actual congressional vote choices (see Figure 5.4). Of those respondents who reported that their House vote was designed to express support for the sitting president, 90 percent, on average, cast their two-party ballots for House candidates from the incumbent's party. When a Democrat was in the White House, respondents who indicated their congressional vote was designed to express support for him cast, on average, 93 percent of their two-party ballots for Democratic House candidates. When a Republican was in the White House, respondents who indicated their congressional vote was designed to express support for him cast 86 percent of their two-party ballots for Republican House candidates.

The nature of the relationship between the two variables flipped when respondents' House vote was intended to show displeasure with the president. Of those respondents who reported that their House vote was designed to express opposition to the president, 91 percent, on average, cast their two-party ballots for House candidates from the party outside the White House. When a Democrat was in the White House, respondents who indicated that their congressional vote was designed to express opposition to him cast 92 percent of their two-party ballots, on average, for Republican House candidates. When a Republican was in the White House, respondents who indicated that their congressional vote was designed to express opposition to him cast 90 percent of their two-party ballots, on average, for Democratic House candidates.

For those exit poll respondents who indicated that the sitting president was not a factor in their congressional vote choice, they tended to split their vote between House candidates from

**Figure 5.4**  Democratic Share of Two-Party House Vote by House Vote Based on President, 1982–2010

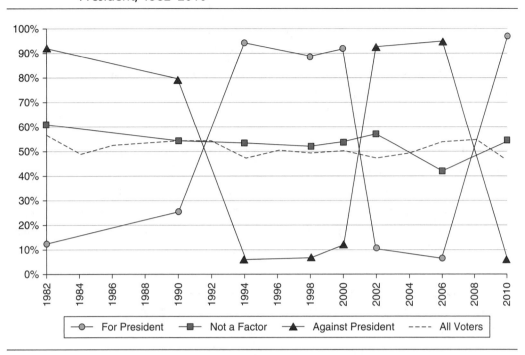

For President    Not a Factor    Against President    All Voters

*Source:* National exit polls. See the section in Chapter 2 entitled "Creating a Cumulative National Data Set: Selecting Exit Polls" (pp. 28–29).

*Note:* When using these results to make inferences about the active electorate, the standard errors should be calculated using Table 2.2 (p. 36), which is explained in the adjacent section of Chapter 2, "Analyzing Exit Poll Questions: Estimating Sampling Error" (pp. 34–36). For a guide on how to understand the tables and figures of this chapter, see the section in Chapter 2 entitled "Presenting and Discussing the Exit Poll Data: Reading Chapter 5" (pp. 43–46). The rationale for using two-party percentages to show trends over time is given in Chapter 4, in the section entitled "Presidential Vote Choice" (pp. 124–131).

the major parties, although they typically gave an edge to the Democrats. Among respondents who indicated that the president was not a factor in the House vote, 53 percent, on average, cast their two-party ballots for Democratic House candidates. When a Democrat was in the White House, respondents who did not base their congressional vote on the president cast 53 percent, on average, of their two-party ballots for Democratic House candidates. When a Republican was in the White House, respondents who did not base their congressional vote on the president cast 54 percent of their two-party ballots, on average, for Democratic House candidates.

In 2010, exit poll respondents once again held to form. Respondents whose House vote was designed to express support for President Barack Obama cast 96 percent of their overall ballots for Democratic House candidates (see Table 5.4 at the end of the chapter). Respondents whose House vote was designed to express opposition to President Obama cast 92 percent of their overall ballots for Republican House candidates. For those respondents whose House vote was not based on judgments of President Obama, 52 percent cast ballots for Democratic House candidates, compared to the 44 percent who cast ballots for Republican House candidates.

## Physical Characteristics

The exit polls show that physical traits differentiate congressional vote choices in much the same way that they do for presidential vote choices. Certain groups consistently prefer Democratic House candidates, whereas other groups consistently prefer Republican House candidates. These relationships are quite resilient, remaining intact despite changes in the candidates running, the popularity of the major parties, and socioeconomic conditions.

### Race

Exit poll respondents' race produces among the largest partisan voting gaps in House elections. White respondents predominantly support Republican House candidates, whereas non-white respondents predominantly support Democratic House candidates (see Figure 5.5). These differences have persisted for much of the past two decades, making each group reliable stalwarts for the two major parties. The voting patterns for House elections are very comparable to those found for presidential elections.

Historically, white exit poll respondents did not consistently support congressional candidates from one party or the other. From 1982 through 1992, white respondents allotted a majority of their two-party vote to Democratic House candidates in two elections (1982 and 1990) and to Republican House candidates in two elections (1984 and 1986), and they split their votes between the two parties' candidates in two elections (1988 and 1992).

**Figure 5.5**  Democratic Share of Two-Party House Vote by Race, 1982–2010

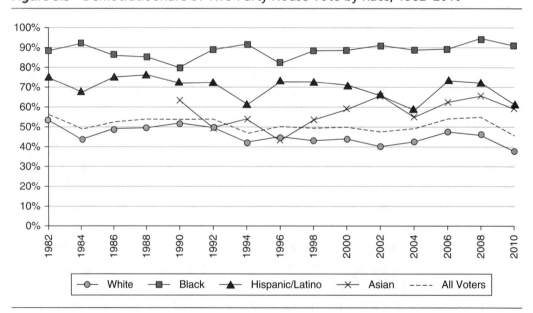

*Source:* National exit polls. See the section in Chapter 2 entitled "Creating a Cumulative National Data Set: Selecting Exit Polls" (pp. 28–29).

*Note:* When using these results to make inferences about the active electorate, the standard errors should be calculated using Table 2.2 (p. 36), which is explained in the adjacent section of Chapter 2, "Analyzing Exit Poll Questions: Estimating Sampling Error" (pp. 34–36). For a guide on how to understand the tables and figures of this chapter, see the section in Chapter 2 entitled "Presenting and Discussing the Exit Poll Data: Reading Chapter 5" (pp. 43–46). The rationale for using two-party percentages to show trends over time is given in Chapter 4, in the section entitled "Presidential Vote Choice" (pp. 124–131).

The Republican "Revolution" of 1994 marked a dramatic shift in the voting preferences of white respondents. White respondents moved sharply in a Republican direction, casting 58 percent of their two-party vote for Republican House candidates. In every election since then, a majority of white respondents have supported Republican candidates nationwide, allotting them an average of 57 percent of their two-party vote.

Conversely, the exit polls show that non-white respondents, regardless of their background, have generally preferred Democratic House candidates nationwide. African American respondents are among the most reliable Democratic supporters in congressional races. An overwhelming majority of African American respondents have supported Democratic House candidates in every exit poll conducted from 1982 through 2010, allotting an average of 88 percent of their two-party vote to them.

Hispanics also have been reliably Democratic voters in House races over the past three decades. Since 1982, Hispanic respondents have voted predominantly Democratic, awarding Democratic House candidates an average of 70 percent of their two-party vote. Only three times in the past fifteen exit polls has Hispanic support for Democrats dipped below 65 percent—in 1994, 2004, and 2010—all years in which the Democrats lost seats, twice by historic proportions.

Asian respondents have been the least Democratic among the minority racial groups considered in the congressional exit polls. Between 1990 and 1996, Asian respondents preferred Republican House candidates nationwide in two out of four elections. Since 1998, Asians have voted consistently Democratic, but by margins far less than African Americans or Hispanics. On average, 60 percent of Asians preferred Democrats in the past seven House elections, although in four of these years their support was only in the mid-to-high fifties.

In the 2010 exit poll, these historical patterns held again, despite Republicans attracting greater support across all racial groups. White respondents preferred Republican House candidates to their Democratic counterparts, 60 percent to 37 percent, in the overall vote, giving Republicans their largest electoral margin among white exit poll respondents in three decades (see Table 5.5 at the end of the chapter). Ninety percent of African American respondents voted for Democratic House candidates, down 3 percentage points from the 2008 exit poll. Sixty percent of Hispanic respondents supported Democrats nationwide, down 11 percentage points from the prior election. Finally, 58 percent of Asian respondents voted for Democrats and 40 percent for Republicans, shrinking the Democratic advantage held in the previous exit poll from 29 to 18 percentage points.

## Gender

Figure 5.6 shows the two-party Democratic House vote for male and female exit poll respondents from 1976 through 2010. A gender gap persists in the House vote over time, similar to that found in the presidential vote. The gender gap in congressional elections emerged clearly in the 1980 election, when Democratic House candidates received 55 percent of the two-party vote among female exit poll respondents and only 49 percent of the two-party vote among male respondents. In the ensuing years, women's support for Democratic House candidates has been 6 percentage points greater, on average, than their male counterparts.

**Figure 5.6**  Democratic Share of Two-Party House Vote by Gender, 1976–2010

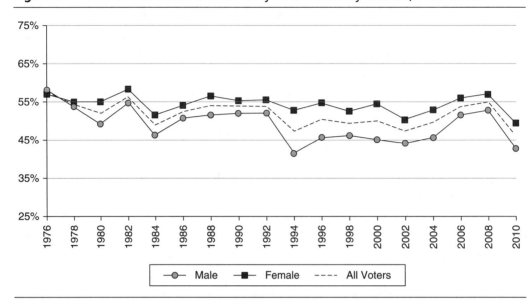

*Source:* National exit polls. See the section in Chapter 2 entitled "Creating a Cumulative National Data Set: Selecting Exit Polls" (pp. 28–29).

*Note:* When using these results to make inferences about the active electorate, the standard errors should be calculated using Table 2.2 (p. 36), which is explained in the adjacent section of Chapter 2, "Analyzing Exit Poll Questions: Estimating Sampling Error" (pp. 34–36). For a guide on how to understand the tables and figures of this chapter, see the section in Chapter 2 entitled "Presenting and Discussing the Exit Poll Data: Reading Chapter 5" (pp. 43–46). The rationale for using two-party percentages to show trends over time is given in Chapter 4, in the section entitled "Presidential Vote Choice" (pp. 124–131).

The magnitude of the gender gap, though, has varied by the relative success of the parties. In elections in which Democrats have secured the most seats, the gender gap in the two-party House vote has averaged a modest 3 percentage points. However, in elections in which the Republicans won control of the House, the gender gap has widened to 8 percentage points, on average. Men have been more responsible for the gender gap than women. Men have accounted for a greater proportion of the net annual change in the two-party vote in nine of the past sixteen elections and have shifted their vote 3 points per year, on average, compared to 2 points for women.

Moreover, support for the major-party candidates among the individual sexes has not followed the same trajectory over time. Female respondents have favored Democratic House candidates in every exit poll since 1976, save 2010, allocating an average of 54 percent of their two-party vote to them. Along the way, women's support of Democratic House candidates has remained remarkably steady over the past three decades of exit polls, deviating more than 3 points from its long-term average on only three occasions.

Male respondents' support for House candidates, by contrast, has been more unpredictable. Men generally supported House Democratic candidates over Republican candidates in exit polls conducted from 1976 through 1992, allocating 52 percent of their two-party ballots to Democrats during those years. Things changed considerably in 1994 when men's support of Republicans soared 10 percentage points, from 48 percent to 58 percent of their two-party vote. Republican House candidates consistently received men's support over the next five elections, securing an average of 55 percent of their two-party vote during that period. Men reversed course again in the 2006 exit poll, allocating a majority of their two-party vote to Democratic House candidates. In 2010, men swung strongly back to the Republicans, altering their preferences as much as they had in any exit poll since 1994.

In 2010, majorities of both genders supported Republican House candidates for the first time since exit polling began tapping congressional vote choice in 1976 (see Table 5.6 at the end of the chapter). Female respondents preferred Republican House candidates to Democratic ones by a margin of 49 percent to 48 percent in the overall vote. This was the first time a majority of female exit poll respondents had supported Republican House candidates nationwide. Male respondents also switched their allegiances from the Democrats, supporting Republican House candidates, 56 percent to 42 percent, over their Democratic counterparts. This was the most support received by Republican House candidates from male voters since the Republican Revolution of 1994.

## Age

The national exit polls show few discernable patterns in the relationship between age and congressional voting preferences (see Figure 5.7). There has been no consistent rank ordering in the partisan preferences of different age groups over time. At various points, each of the different age groups has yielded the greatest proportion of votes for Democratic House candidates.

**Figure 5.7**  Democratic Share of Two-Party House Vote by Age, 1976–2010

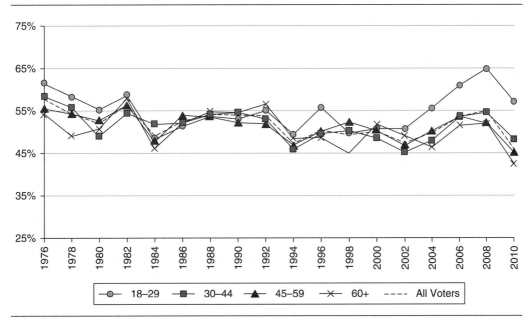

*Source:* National exit polls. See the section in Chapter 2 entitled "Creating a Cumulative National Data Set: Selecting Exit Polls" (pp. 28–29).

*Note:* When using these results to make inferences about the active electorate, the standard errors should be calculated using Table 2.2 (p. 36), which is explained in the adjacent section of Chapter 2, "Analyzing Exit Poll Questions: Estimating Sampling Error" (pp. 34–36). For a guide on how to understand the tables and figures of this chapter, see the section in Chapter 2 entitled "Presenting and Discussing the Exit Poll Data: Reading Chapter 5" (pp. 43–46). The rationale for using two-party percentages to show trends over time is given in Chapter 4, in the section entitled "Presidential Vote Choice" (pp. 124–131).

Also, there has been no consistent variance in the congressional support of different age groups across elections, although House voting patterns among age groups do approximate the patterns found for presidential voting. The age gap between the most Democratic and least Democratic age groups in House elections has been as small as a single point in the 1988 exit poll to as large as 15 points in the 2010 exit poll. The fluctuations in the age gap act unpredictably, failing to correspond to the timing or outcomes of House elections.

Finally, there are few detectable patterns in the behavior of age groups over time. Age group preferences shift in ways that are inconsistent with life cycle or generational effects. They do not even move that tightly in unison over time. In nine of the eighteen exit polls conducted since 1976, at least one age group has moved in the opposite direction of the others from one election to the next.

The only noteworthy pattern in the exit polls appears to be the propensity of young people to vote Democratic in most congressional elections. A majority of 18- to 29-year-olds have cast their two-party vote for Democratic House candidates in fifteen of the eighteen elections held from 1976 to 2010. In the process, they have allotted an average of 55 percent of their two-party vote to Democratic candidates. The remaining age groups exhibited far less consistency in their voting preferences.

In the 2010 exit poll, Republican House candidates won a majority of ballots cast by respondents over 30 years of age and increased their support across all age groups (see Table 5.7 at the end of the chapter). Respondents under 30 years of age once again preferred Democratic House candidates but allotted them their smallest share of the overall vote—55 percent—since 2004. Among respondents aged 30–44, Republicans defeated Democrats, 50 percent to 46 percent, reversing a Democratic advantage over the past two exit polls. Respondents aged 45–59 and those aged 60 or over cast, respectively, 54 percent and 56 percent of their votes for Republican House candidates, both up 7 points or more from the 2008 exit poll.

## Sexual Orientation

Exit poll respondents who are gay, lesbian, or bisexual overwhelmingly support Democratic nominees for Congress, much as they do Democratic presidential nominees. They have cast a majority of their two-party ballots for Democratic candidates in each election for the House of Representatives from 1996 through 2010, averaging 73 percent over these six elections (see Figure 5.8). Despite the best efforts of interest groups, such as the Log Cabin Republicans, to gain support for Republican candidates, gay, lesbian, and bisexual respondents have consistently voted for Democratic House candidates over time. Democrats' share of the two-party vote has always exceeded 66 percent, making them one of the most reliably Democratic groups in the exit polls.

In the 2010 exit poll, gay, lesbian, and bisexual respondents again cast their ballots overwhelmingly for Democratic House candidates, despite a noticeable drop in support (see Table 5.8 at the end of the chapter). Among gay, lesbian, or bisexual respondents, Democratic House candidates received 69 percent of their overall ballots, compared to only 30 percent for Republican House candidates. This number was down 11 points from the 2008 exit poll but still made gays, lesbians, and bisexuals among the strongest supporters of Democratic candidates.

**Figure 5.8** Democratic Share of Two-Party House Vote by Sexual Orientation, 1996–2010

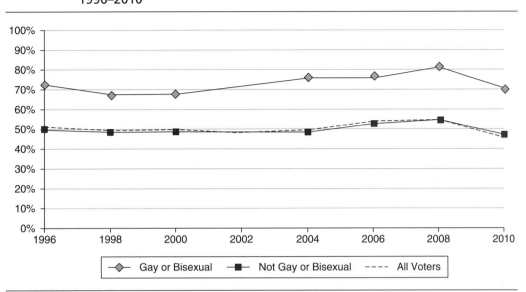

*Source:* National exit polls. See the section in Chapter 2 entitled "Creating a Cumulative National Data Set: Selecting Exit Polls" (pp. 28–29).

*Note:* When using these results to make inferences about the active electorate, the standard errors should be calculated using Table 2.2 (p. 36), which is explained in the adjacent section of Chapter 2, "Analyzing Exit Poll Questions: Estimating Sampling Error" (pp. 34–36). For a guide on how to understand the tables and figures of this chapter, see the section in Chapter 2 entitled "Presenting and Discussing the Exit Poll Data: Reading Chapter 5" (pp. 43–46). The rationale for using two-party percentages to show trends over time is given in Chapter 4, in the section entitled "Presidential Vote Choice" (pp. 124–131).

## Geographic Location

Residential location plays as important a role in the congressional vote choices of exit poll respondents as it does in their presidential vote choices. The geographic region and population density of respondents' precincts tend to orient them toward one or the other major party's congressional candidates. These orientations, though, have not remained constant over time, with several reversing course after the Republican Revolution of 1994.

### Region

Regional differences in exit poll respondents' congressional voting preferences have waxed and waned over the past three decades. Figure 5.9 shows considerable variation in respondents' preferences across geographic regions from 1976 through 1982. Respondents from the South and East strongly backed Democratic House candidates, allocating them, respectively, 59 percent and 58 percent of their two-party vote. Notably, southern respondents remained loyal to Democratic House candidates in the 1980 election, even as they gave Ronald Reagan a majority of their presidential votes in his victory over southerner Jimmy Carter. Conversely, respondents from the West and Midwest were more Republican. They each allotted 52 percent of their two-party vote to Democratic congressional candidates and on two occasions even gave the Republicans majority support.

**Figure 5.9** Democratic Share of Two-Party House Vote by Region, 1976–2010

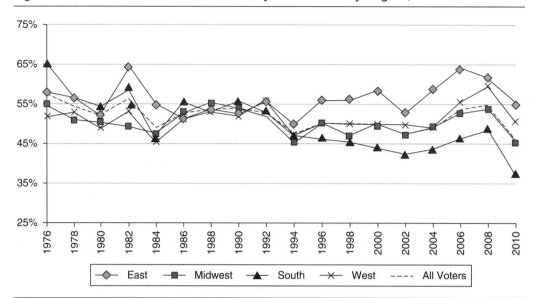

*Source:* National exit polls. See the section in Chapter 2 entitled "Creating a Cumulative National Data Set: Selecting Exit Polls" (pp. 28–29).

*Note:* When using these results to make inferences about the active electorate, the standard errors should be calculated using Table 2.2 (p. 36), which is explained in the adjacent section of Chapter 2, "Analyzing Exit Poll Questions: Estimating Sampling Error" (pp. 34–36). For a guide on how to understand the tables and figures of this chapter, see the section in Chapter 2 entitled "Presenting and Discussing the Exit Poll Data: Reading Chapter 5" (pp. 43–46). The rationale for using two-party percentages to show trends over time is given in Chapter 4, in the section entitled "Presidential Vote Choice" (pp. 124–131).

The 1984 exit poll, which also coincided with Reagan's reelection bid, saw a convergence in regional House voting patterns. That year, southerners, westerners, and midwesterners preferred Republican candidates at roughly the same rate, whereas easterners chose Democratic candidates by about 7 percentage points. By the end of Reagan's second term, even easterners began voting like the rest of the country. From 1988 through 1992, respondents from all regions behaved similarly, casting between 52 percent and 56 percent of their two-party ballots for Democratic House candidates.

The Republican Revolution of 1994 sparked a divergence in the regional voting patterns of exit poll respondents. Eastern respondents became a distinctly Democratic group. From 1994 through 2010, easterners cast an average of 57 percent of their two-party ballots for Democratic House candidates, only twice failing to award them at least 55 percent of their votes. Conversely, southern respondents became solidly Republican. Since 1994, a majority of southerners have preferred Republicans to Democrats in every election, allotting an average of 55 percent of their two-party vote to Republican House candidates.

The battleground in congressional elections appears to center on the Midwest and West, where exit poll respondents now behave like swing voters. From 1994 through 2010, a majority of midwestern respondents preferred candidates from the winning party in eight out of nine elections, splitting their two-party vote, on average, 51 percent to 49 percent between Republicans and Democrats. Similarly, a majority of western respondents have sided with the winning party in five out of nine elections, yielding an average of 51 percent of their votes to Democrats, compared to 49 percent to Republicans. However, in the past three exit polls, western respondents have been trending more Democratic, especially relative to midwestern respondents. Even in the 2010 election, which strongly favored Republican candidates nationwide, western respondents still gave Democrats 51 percent of their two-party vote, 6 points more than midwesterners allocated to Democratic House candidates.

In the 2010 exit poll, Republicans won the support of respondents from two out of four regions and improved their standing across all regions of the country (see Table 5.9 at the end of the chapter). Republican House candidates garnered their highest support from southern respondents, winning 61 percent of southerners' overall votes—the highest proportion secured by either party since the 1976 exit poll. Republican candidates were also the preferred choice among midwesterners, defeating their Democratic counterparts, 53 percent to 44 percent, in the exit poll. By contrast, Democratic House candidates won 54 percent of the overall vote of eastern respondents, although their electoral share shrank 7 percentage points from two years earlier. Democrats also narrowly defeated Republicans among western respondents, 49 percent to 48 percent, in the overall vote, but saw their winning margin shrink from 19 points in 2008 to a single point in 2010.

## Population Density

National exit polls show that voting patterns in congressional elections, like presidential elections, also vary by the population density of respondents' precincts (see Figure 5.10). Urban areas are Democratic strongholds. Democratic House candidates have won by sizable margins the support of respondents from central cities in every election as far back as 1984, even in years when the Democratic Party overall has failed to win a majority of seats. Democratic candidates have received, on average, 60 percent of the two-party vote from urban respondents, with support fluctuating between 55 percent and 65 percent.

Conversely, exit poll respondents from rural areas typically gravitate toward Republican candidates in House elections, particularly in recent years. Since 1996, a majority of rural respondents have preferred Republican candidates in six of the seven elections investigated by exit pollsters. In the process, rural respondents have cast, on average, 54 percent of their two-party ballots for Republican House candidates.

Suburban areas behave more like a harbinger of electoral success in congressional elections. In the past two decades, whichever political party has won the support of suburban exit poll respondents has secured the most seats in Congress. During the 1990 and 1992 elections, Democrats won the support of suburban respondents, averaging 52 percent of the two-party vote. From 1994 through 2004, suburban respondents cast an average of 53 percent of their ballots for Republican candidates, propelling them to majorities in the House over this period. Suburbanites reversed course in 2006 and then again in 2010, corresponding with flips in party control of the House of Representatives.

In the 2010 exit poll, Republican congressional candidates had their best performance across all three types of respondents since 2004. Among respondents living in rural areas, Republican

**Figure 5.10** Democratic Share of Two-Party House Vote by Population Density, 1984–2010

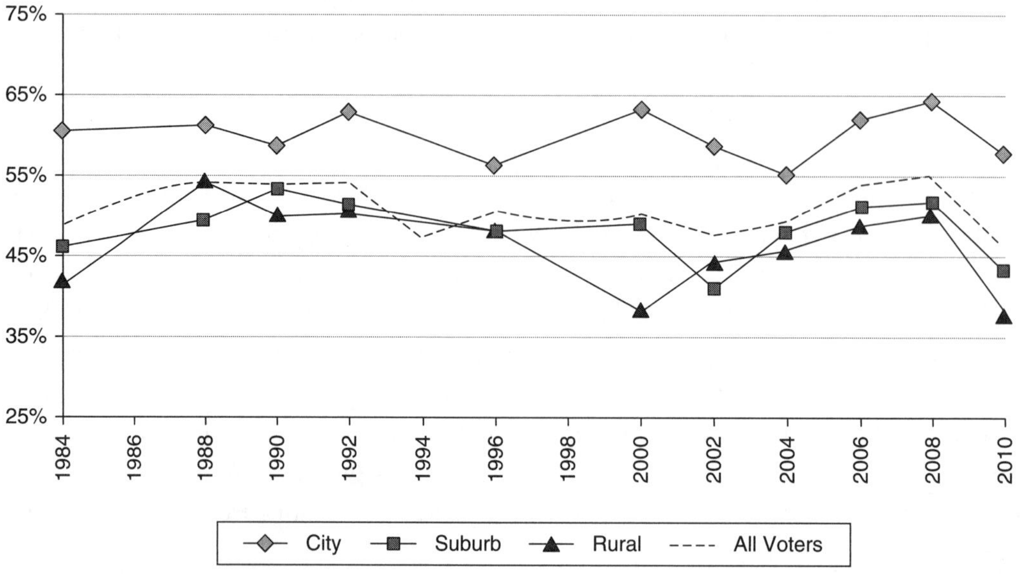

*Source:* National exit polls. See the section in Chapter 2 entitled "Creating a Cumulative National Data Set: Selecting Exit Polls" (pp. 28–29).

*Note:* When using these results to make inferences about the active electorate, the standard errors should be calculated using Table 2.2 (p. 36), which is explained in the adjacent section of Chapter 2, "Analyzing Exit Poll Questions: Estimating Sampling Error" (pp. 34–36). For a guide on how to understand the tables and figures of this chapter, see the section in Chapter 2 entitled "Presenting and Discussing the Exit Poll Data: Reading Chapter 5" (pp. 43–46). The rationale for using two-party percentages to show trends over time is given in Chapter 4, in the section entitled "Presidential Vote Choice" (pp. 124–131).

House nominees defeated their Democratic counterparts, 61 percent to 36 percent, in the overall vote (see Table 5.10 at the end of the chapter). Republican candidates also won, by a 55 percent to 42 percent margin, among suburban respondents. Republicans lost to Democrats among respondents from urban areas, 56 percent to 41 percent, in the overall vote, but narrowed the margin considerably from 2008.

## Religious Characteristics

Exit polls show that religious characteristics create strong partisan divides in congressional elections, just as they do in presidential elections. Protestants, evangelicals, and those who attend religious services frequently gravitate toward Republican congressional candidates, whereas non-Christians, seculars, and infrequent religious attendees gravitate toward Democratic congressional candidates. These orientations have persisted despite varying degrees of electoral success for the major political parties over time.

### Religious Affiliation

Considerable differences exist among the congressional voting preferences of religious groups in the national exit polls (see Figure 5.11). The largest religious group—Protestants—consistently

**Figure 5.11**  Democratic Share of Two-Party House Vote by Religious Affiliation, 1984–2010

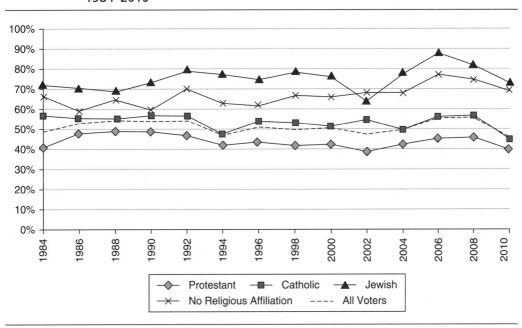

*Source:* National exit polls. See the section in Chapter 2 entitled "Creating a Cumulative National Data Set: Selecting Exit Polls" (pp. 28–29).

*Note:* When using these results to make inferences about the active electorate, the standard errors should be calculated using Table 2.2 (p. 36), which is explained in the adjacent section of Chapter 2, "Analyzing Exit Poll Questions: Estimating Sampling Error" (pp. 34–36). For a guide on how to understand the tables and figures of this chapter, see the section in Chapter 2 entitled "Presenting and Discussing the Exit Poll Data: Reading Chapter 5" (pp. 43–46). The rationale for using two-party percentages to show trends over time is given in Chapter 4, in the section entitled "Presidential Vote Choice" (pp. 124–131).

supports Republican House candidates. Protestants have voted for Republican House candidates in every exit poll since 1984, allocating an average of 56 percent of their two-party vote to them.

By contrast, Democratic congressional candidates have drawn their greatest support in the exit polls from Jewish and secular respondents over the past quarter-century. On average, three-quarters of Jewish respondents have cast two-party ballots for Democratic House candidates, whereas two-thirds of seculars have backed Democratic nominees in their two-party vote. Despite fluctuations in their two-party vote, support from Jewish and secular respondents for Democratic House candidates has not dropped below 59 percent in the thirteen congressional elections over this time span.

Historically, Catholics preferred Democratic House candidates in the exit polls. From 1984 through 2002, a majority of Catholic respondents voted for Democratic House candidates in all but one election, awarding Democratic nominees an average of 54 percent of their two-party vote. Beginning in 2004, though, Catholic respondents began to act more like swing voters in House elections, with the majority gravitating toward the eventual winner. In the 2004 and 2010 elections, when the Republican Party won the House, a majority of Catholic respondents backed Republican congressional candidates. Conversely, when the Democrats won in the House in 2006 and 2008, Catholic respondents predominantly supported Democratic congressional candidates.

Interestingly, Catholics showed signs of swinging in presidential elections prior to House elections. Catholics supported the winning Republican presidential candidates in 1984 and 1988, even as Catholic respondents cast a majority of their ballots for the winning Democrats in the House elections.

In 2010, exit poll respondents of different religious affiliations behaved much like they had in recent congressional elections. Jewish and secular respondents voted overwhelmingly Democratic. They allocated, respectively, 70 percent and 68 percent of their overall votes to Democratic House candidates (see Table 5.11 at the end of the chapter). Conversely, Protestant respondents once again backed Republican House candidates, giving them 59 percent of their vote in the most recent House election. Catholic respondents swung hard toward the Republican Party, casting 55 percent of their ballots for Republican House candidates—a shift of 13 percentage points in the overall vote from 2008.

## Religious Attendance

Exit polls show that Republican House candidates appeal to more religiously active respondents, whereas Democratic House candidates tend to draw less religiously active respondents (see Figure 5.12). This pattern closely follows the trends for presidential voting. Since 2000, respondents attending religious services at least once a week have consistently supported Republicans at much

**Figure 5.12** Democratic Share of Two-Party House Vote by Religious Attendance, 2000–2010

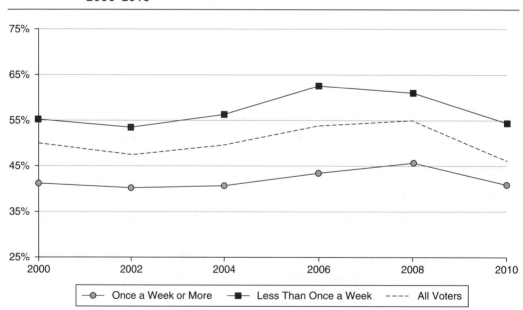

*Source:* National exit polls. See the section in Chapter 2 entitled "Creating a Cumulative National Data Set: Selecting Exit Polls" (pp. 28–29).

*Note:* When using these results to make inferences about the active electorate, the standard errors should be calculated using Table 2.2 (p. 36), which is explained in the adjacent section of Chapter 2, "Analyzing Exit Poll Questions: Estimating Sampling Error" (pp. 34–36). For a guide on how to understand the tables and figures of this chapter, see the section in Chapter 2 entitled "Presenting and Discussing the Exit Poll Data: Reading Chapter 5" (pp. 43–46). The rationale for using two-party percentages to show trends over time is given in Chapter 4, in the section entitled "Presidential Vote Choice" (pp. 124–131).

higher rates than Democrats, awarding 58 percent of their two-party vote, on average, to Republican House candidates in congressional races. Conversely, Democratic candidates have received a majority of votes from those infrequently attending religious services, securing an average of 57 percent of their two-party vote.

In 2010, the national exit polls produced similar results. Respondents attending religious services at least once a week preferred Republican House candidates to their Democratic counterparts, 58 percent to 40 percent, in the overall vote (see Table 5.12 at the end of the chapter). Respondents attending religious services less than weekly chose Democratic House candidates over Republican ones, 53 percent to 44 percent, in the overall vote.

## Evangelicals

Evangelical Christians, or born-again Christians, have been strong supporters of Republican House candidates, much as they have been for Republican presidential candidates. Figure 5.13 shows that Republican candidates have won a sizable majority of evangelical respondents' votes in the past four exit polls. Republican House candidates have received, on average, 60 percent of the evangelical two-party vote, and their advantage over Democratic candidates in House races nationwide has exceeded 10 points on each occasion.

Republican support from evangelicals, though, was not immune to the party's political struggles in House elections toward the end of George W. Bush's second term in office. Republican support among evangelical respondents dropped 7 points from 2004 to 2008. This dip was roughly identical to the drop in the two-party vote for Republican presidential candidates in the exit polls.

**Figure 5.13** Democratic Share of Two-Party House Vote by Evangelical, 2004–2010

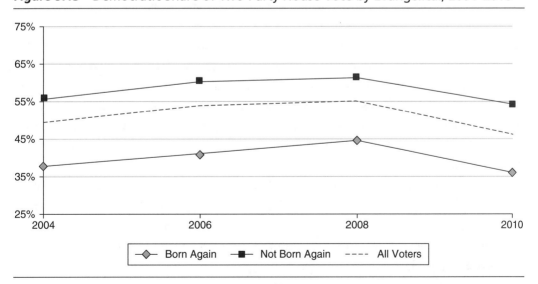

*Source:* National exit polls. See the section in Chapter 2 entitled "Creating a Cumulative National Data Set: Selecting Exit Polls" (pp. 28–29).

*Note:* When using these results to make inferences about the active electorate, the standard errors should be calculated using Table 2.2 (p. 36), which is explained in the adjacent section of Chapter 2, "Analyzing Exit Poll Questions: Estimating Sampling Error" (pp. 34–36). For a guide on how to understand the tables and figures of this chapter, see the section in Chapter 2 entitled "Presenting and Discussing the Exit Poll Data: Reading Chapter 5" (pp. 43–46). The rationale for using two-party percentages to show trends over time is given in Chapter 4, in the section entitled "Presidential Vote Choice" (pp. 124–131).

In the 2010 exit poll, Republican support from evangelical respondents rebounded considerably (see Table 5.13 at the end of the chapter). Evangelicals preferred Republican House candidates to Democratic House candidates, 62 percent to 35 percent, in the overall vote. This was the largest margin of victory for Republicans among evangelicals since the question first appeared in its current form in 2004.

## Lifestyle Characteristics

The exit polls show that lifestyle characteristics play a mixed role in House elections. Some characteristics, such as education and marriage, correspond with stark differences in the support of each party's congressional candidates. Others, such as employment status and children, have little impact, if any, on voting decisions. No obvious differences in the nature of these characteristics allow us to distinguish between those that will exert an electoral impact and those that will not.

### Education

Education has a parabolic relationship with voting preferences in congressional elections, much like it does in presidential elections (see Figure 5.14). As the educational background of exit poll respondents increases, so does their support for Republican House candidates—until they begin to pursue postgraduate degrees, at which point they tend to support Democratic House candidates. This relationship has generally persisted over time, regardless of the timing of the election or the victorious political party.

Since the 1986 exit poll, Democratic congressional candidates have consistently drawn their greatest support from the least and most educated respondents. Democratic House candidates have received, on average, 61 percent of the two-party vote from respondents with less than a high school education. Respondents with only a high school education have also gravitated toward Democrats, but to a lesser extent, awarding them 53 percent of their two-party vote. At the other end of the spectrum, respondents with a postgraduate education have cast, on average, 54 percent of their two-party vote for Democratic House candidates. Support from all three groups has fluctuated in line with the overall vote, but a majority of each group has voted for Democratic congressional candidates in nearly every election (a majority of high school graduate respondents preferred Republicans in 1994 and 2010, and a majority of postgraduate respondents preferred Republicans in 2002).

Republican House candidates, by contrast, have received their greatest support from college graduates in the exit polls. College graduates have allotted a majority of their two-party vote to Republicans in ten of the thirteen exit polls conducted from 1986 to 2010—the exceptions being 1990, 2006, and 2008. On average, Republican candidates have received 54 percent of the vote of college graduates during this time frame.

Exit poll respondents with only some college education are the most independent of the educational groups, behaving more like swing voters than a reliably partisan group. Since 1986, a majority of respondents with some college education have supported congressional candidates from the political party gaining the most House seats in every election except 1996. Respondents

**Figure 5.14**   Democratic Share of Two-Party House Vote by Education, 1986–2010

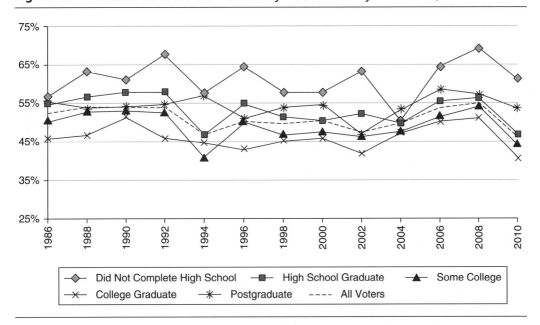

*Source:* National exit polls. See the section in Chapter 2 entitled "Creating a Cumulative National Data Set: Selecting Exit Polls" (pp. 28–29).

*Note:* When using these results to make inferences about the active electorate, the standard errors should be calculated using Table 2.2 (p. 36), which is explained in the adjacent section of Chapter 2, "Analyzing Exit Poll Questions: Estimating Sampling Error" (pp. 34–36). For a guide on how to understand the tables and figures of this chapter, see the section in Chapter 2 entitled "Presenting and Discussing the Exit Poll Data: Reading Chapter 5" (pp. 43–46). The rationale for using two-party percentages to show trends over time is given in Chapter 4, in the section entitled "Presidential Vote Choice" (pp. 124–131).

with some college split their ballots between the major parties, giving Republicans, on average, 51 percent and Democratic candidates 49 percent of their two-party vote.

In the 2010 exit poll, Democrats were again the preferred choice of the least and most educated, but Republicans won every education grouping in between, including high school graduates who typically vote Democratic (see Table 5.14 at the end of the chapter). Democratic House candidates defeated Republican House candidates, 57 percent to 36 percent in the overall vote, among respondents who did not complete high school, and 53 percent to 45 percent among respondents who undertook postgraduate study. However, respondents with only a high school education chose Republicans by a 52 percent to 46 percent margin in the overall vote. Respondents with only some college education preferred Republican congressional candidates to their Democratic counterparts, 54 percent to 43 percent. Finally, respondents with only a college education again sided with Republicans, casting 58 percent of their ballots for them, compared to only 40 percent of the overall vote for Democrats.

## Employment Status

In the exit polls, little difference is seen in the congressional voting patterns of those employed full time and those not employed full time, much like what is found in respondents' choices in presidential elections (see Figure 5.15). The gap in preferences between respondents employed full

**Figure 5.15**   Democratic Share of Two-Party House Vote by Employment Status, 1996–2008

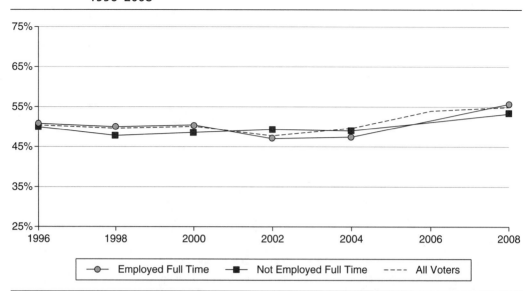

*Source:* National exit polls. See the section in Chapter 2 entitled "Creating a Cumulative National Data Set: Selecting Exit Polls" (pp. 28–29).

*Note:* When using these results to make inferences about the active electorate, the standard errors should be calculated using Table 2.2 (p. 36), which is explained in the adjacent section of Chapter 2, "Analyzing Exit Poll Questions: Estimating Sampling Error" (pp. 34–36). For a guide on how to understand the tables and figures of this chapter, see the section in Chapter 2 entitled "Presenting and Discussing the Exit Poll Data: Reading Chapter 5" (pp. 43–46). The rationale for using two-party percentages to show trends over time is given in Chapter 4, in the section entitled "Presidential Vote Choice" (pp. 124–131).

time and less than full time has averaged only 1 point in the congressional elections from 1996 onward. In four of the six congressional elections in which employment status has been asked, those who were employed full time were somewhat more Democratic in their voting preferences than those employed less than full time, whereas in the other two elections, they were somewhat more Republican.

The national exit polls did not solicit employment status in the 2010 congressional election. In the 2008 House election, there were only modest differences in the congressional voting patterns of those employed full time and those employed less than full time (see Table 5.15 at the end of the chapter). Respondents employed full time preferred Democratic House candidates to Republican House candidates by a margin of 54 percent to 43 percent in the overall vote. Respondents employed less than full time also preferred Democratic House candidates, supporting them 52 percent to 45 percent over their Republican counterparts.

## Marital Status

The national exit polls show that marriage is associated with a sizable gap in congressional voting preferences, similar to that which exists in presidential voting preferences. As Figure 5.16 shows, married respondents typically gravitate toward Republican congressional candidates, whereas unmarried respondents prefer Democratic congressional candidates. Since 1992, Republican nominees have received, on average, 54 percent of the two-party vote from married respondents,

**Figure 5.16**  Democratic Share of Two-Party House Vote by Marital Status, 1992–2008

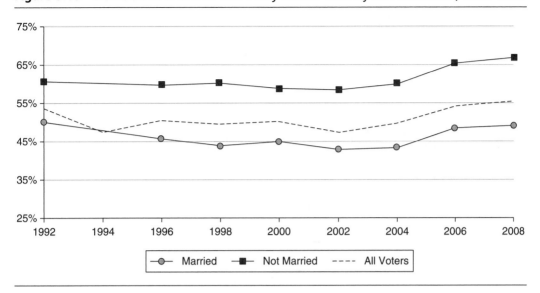

*Source:* National exit polls. See the section in Chapter 2 entitled "Creating a Cumulative National Data Set: Selecting Exit Polls" (pp. 28–29).

*Note:* When using these results to make inferences about the active electorate, the standard errors should be calculated using Table 2.2 (p. 36), which is explained in the adjacent section of Chapter 2, "Analyzing Exit Poll Questions: Estimating Sampling Error" (pp. 34–36). For a guide on how to understand the tables and figures of this chapter, see the section in Chapter 2 entitled "Presenting and Discussing the Exit Poll Data: Reading Chapter 5" (pp. 43–46). The rationale for using two-party percentages to show trends over time is given in Chapter 4, in the section entitled "Presidential Vote Choice" (pp. 124–131).

winning a majority of their support in all but one election. Meanwhile, Democratic nominees have received 61 percent of the two-party vote from unmarried respondents, receiving a majority of support from unmarried voters in every election since 1992.

The marriage gap in congressional voting preferences has widened gradually over time. In the 1992 exit poll, Republican candidates received 10 points more support from married respondents than from unmarried respondents in the two-party vote. Over the next sixteen years, the marriage gap grew, reaching 18 points in the 2008 exit poll.

National exit pollsters did not inquire about marital status in the 2010 congressional elections. In 2008, married respondents cast 50 percent of their overall ballots for Republican candidates, compared to 48 percent for Democratic candidates (see Table 5.16 at the end of the chapter). This result was the best performance by Democratic congressional candidates with married exit poll respondents since the 1992 election. Conversely, unmarried respondents preferred Democratic nominees to Republican nominees nationwide by a margin of 65 percent to 32 percent in the overall vote, which was their highest degree of support for Democratic congressional candidates over this time span.

## Child in Household

According to the national exit polls, respondents with one or more children in their household behave like swing voters in congressional elections (see Figure 5.17). In the eight exit polls since 1996 for which data are available, respondents with children in their household have generally

**Figure 5.17** Democratic Share of Two-Party House Vote by Child in Household, 1996–2010

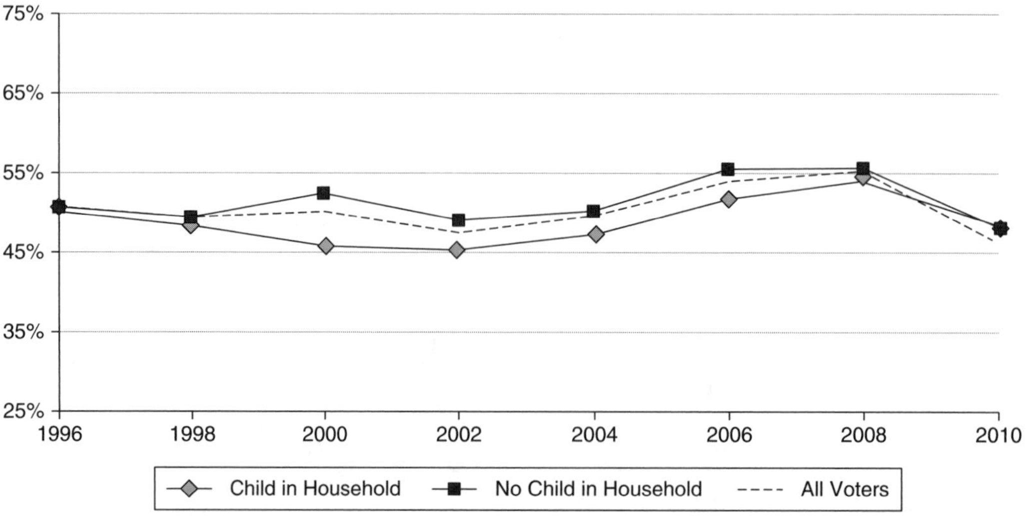

Source: National exit polls. See the section in Chapter 2 entitled "Creating a Cumulative National Data Set: Selecting Exit Polls" (pp. 28–29).

Note: When using these results to make inferences about the active electorate, the standard errors should be calculated using Table 2.2 (p. 36), which is explained in the adjacent section of Chapter 2, "Analyzing Exit Poll Questions: Estimating Sampling Error" (pp. 34–36). For a guide on how to understand the tables and figures of this chapter, see the section in Chapter 2 entitled "Presenting and Discussing the Exit Poll Data: Reading Chapter 5" (pp. 43–46). The rationale for using two-party percentages to show trends over time is given in Chapter 4, in the section entitled "Presidential Vote Choice" (pp. 124–131).

preferred candidates from the political party winning the most seats. This parallels their behavior in presidential elections over the same time span; the winning presidential candidate has won the two-party vote of exit poll respondents with children in their household in each contest since 1996. During Republican control of the House in the late 1990s and early 2000s, respondents with children in their household preferred Republican candidates, giving them, on average, 53 percent of their two-party vote. When the electoral tides swung back to the Democrats in 2006, so did respondents with children in their household, allotting Democratic congressional candidates a majority of their votes in the next two elections.

In the 2010 congressional elections, exit poll respondents from households with children were once again a harbinger of electoral success, favoring Republican congressional candidates in their winning effort (see Table 5.17 at the end of the chapter). Respondents with children in their household preferred Republican House candidates to Democratic ones by a margin of 50 percent to 47 percent in the overall vote. This result represented a 6-point increase in support for Republican candidates, compared with the 2008 exit poll.

## Union Household

The national exit polls show that respondents from union households are among the most reliable Democratic supporters. As Figure 5.18 shows, respondents from union households have cast a majority of their ballots for Democratic House candidates in every election since 1976. They have

**Figure 5.18**   Democratic Share of Two-Party House Vote by Union Household, 1976–2010

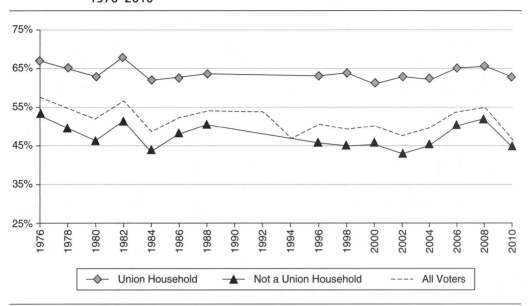

*Source:* National exit polls. See the section in Chapter 2 entitled "Creating a Cumulative National Data Set: Selecting Exit Polls" (pp. 28–29).

*Note:* When using these results to make inferences about the active electorate, the standard errors should be calculated using Table 2.2 (p. 36), which is explained in the adjacent section of Chapter 2, "Analyzing Exit Poll Questions: Estimating Sampling Error" (pp. 34–36). For a guide on how to understand the tables and figures of this chapter, see the section in Chapter 2 entitled "Presenting and Discussing the Exit Poll Data: Reading Chapter 5" (pp. 43–46). The rationale for using two-party percentages to show trends over time is given in Chapter 4, in the section entitled "Presidential Vote Choice" (pp. 124–131).

allocated, on average, 64 percent of their two-party vote to Democratic candidates over the past three decades, never once giving them less than 61 percent of their two-party vote.

Exit poll respondents from union households voted overwhelmingly for Democratic candidates in the 2010 congressional elections (see Table 5.18 at the end of the chapter). Democratic House candidates received 61 percent of the overall vote of respondents from union households, compared to only 37 percent received by Republican House candidates. Despite a substantial drop in support in the electorate as a whole, Democratic congressional candidates received roughly the same level of support from union household respondents as they had in previous years in which the Republicans emerged victorious.

## Political Orientations

Not surprisingly, political orientations have among the strongest associations with congressional voting patterns in the national exit polls. House preferences correlate highly with respondents' party and ideological identifications. Electoral choices also correspond closely with their evaluations of the president, Congress, and the direction of the country. Respondents wish to stick with candidates from the same party when they approve of the performances of members of these institutions, while looking to move in a new direction when they do not.

## Party Identification

The national exit polls show that respondents identifying with the political parties behave as expected in congressional elections (see Figure 5.19). Since 1976, respondents identifying with the Democratic Party have voted overwhelmingly for Democratic House candidates, allotting them an average of 88 percent of their two-party vote. Conversely, respondents identifying with the Republican Party have strongly supported Republican House candidates, giving them 88 percent of their two-party vote over the same time span.

Following a similar pattern found in the presidential elections, the votes of identifiers from both parties have become even more polarized since the 1990 congressional election. In the 1990 exit poll, Democratic identifiers gave Republican congressional candidates 20 percent of their two-party vote, the sixth time in the previous eight elections that Republican candidates had secured at least 15 percent of Democrat identifiers' votes. Beginning with the 1992 exit poll, Democratic identifiers have not awarded Republican candidates a 15 percent share of their two-party vote in a single election, giving them no more than 8 percent of their votes in the past three House contests.

The pattern is comparable for Republicans. From 1976 through 1990, Democratic congressional candidates received double-digit support from Republican identifiers in every election, peaking with 26 percent of Republican identifiers' two-party vote in the 1990 exit poll. In the

**Figure 5.19** Democratic Share of Two-Party House Vote by Party Identification, 1976–2010

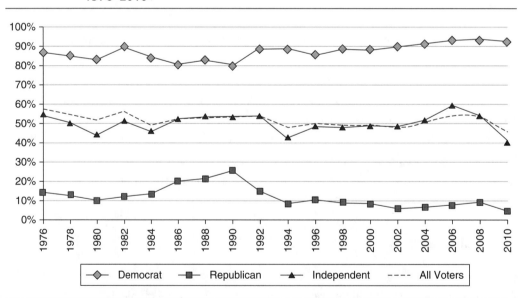

*Source:* National exit polls. See the section in Chapter 2 entitled "Creating a Cumulative National Data Set: Selecting Exit Polls" (pp. 28–29).

*Note:* When using these results to make inferences about the active electorate, the standard errors should be calculated using Table 2.2 (p. 36), which is explained in the adjacent section of Chapter 2, "Analyzing Exit Poll Questions: Estimating Sampling Error" (pp. 34–36). For a guide on how to understand the tables and figures of this chapter, see the section in Chapter 2 entitled "Presenting and Discussing the Exit Poll Data: Reading Chapter 5" (pp. 43–46). The rationale for using two-party percentages to show trends over time is given in Chapter 4, in the section entitled "Presidential Vote Choice" (pp. 124–131).

congressional elections occurring since, Democratic candidates have failed to top 10 percent on a single occasion, receiving as little as 5 percent of their vote in the 2010 exit poll.

Meanwhile, exit poll respondents not identifying with either of the two major political parties have alternated their support between the Democrats and the Republicans over time, typically gravitating toward candidates from the victorious political party. The party securing the most seats in fourteen of the eighteen House elections since 1976 has won the vote of independent exit poll respondents, including all but one election since 1984 (independent respondents preferred Democratic House candidates by a narrow margin in 2004).

The 2010 exit poll saw partisan identifiers hold to form once again. Republican identifiers supported Republican candidates over Democratic candidates, 94 percent to 5 percent, whereas Democratic identifiers preferred Democratic candidates to Republican candidates, 92 percent to 8 percent (see Table 5.19 at the end of the chapter). Independent respondents went with the winning side, preferring Republican candidates to Democratic candidates by a sizable 56 percent to 37 percent margin in the overall vote. The Republicans' 19-point edge among independent respondents was the largest margin either party held over the other among independents since congressional exit polling commenced in 1976, surpassing the 18-point edge the Democrats had in the 2006 exit poll.

## Ideological Identification

Ideology has also produced substantial differences in the congressional voting preferences of exit poll respondents (see Figure 5.20). Liberal respondents have consistently voted Democratic in every House election since 1976, allotting them an average of 81 percent of their two-party vote. Conservative respondents, by contrast, have consistently voted Republican, allotting them an average of 73 percent of their two-party vote.

Contrary to their label, moderates behave more like a reliably Democratic group than like swing voters. Moderate respondents have cast a majority of their ballots with Democratic House candidates in every exit poll since 1976, yielding an average of 58 percent of their two-party vote. Moderates' support for the Democratic candidate in congressional elections has been, on average, 4 points higher than moderates' two-party Democratic vote for president. Moreover, there has been little change in moderate preferences over time in the exit polls. The vote of moderate respondents has fluctuated between 54 percent and 62 percent over the past three decades, changing by more than 3 points from one election to the next on only three occasions since 1976.

Just like presidential elections, the gap between liberals and conservatives has grown over time as the congressional votes of each group have become increasingly polarized. In 1976, the gap in the two-party vote was 37 percentage points. By 2006, the gap had increased to a whopping 69 points. The tipping point was the 1992 election, when the voting patterns of conservatives and liberals began to diverge considerably.

From 1976 through 1990, liberal respondents allotted, on average, 25 percent of their two-party vote to Republican House candidates, giving them at least a fifth of their vote in every exit poll conducted during that time span. Starting with the 1992 exit poll, though, liberals

**Figure 5.20**   Democratic Share of Two-Party House Vote by Ideological
Identification, 1976–2010

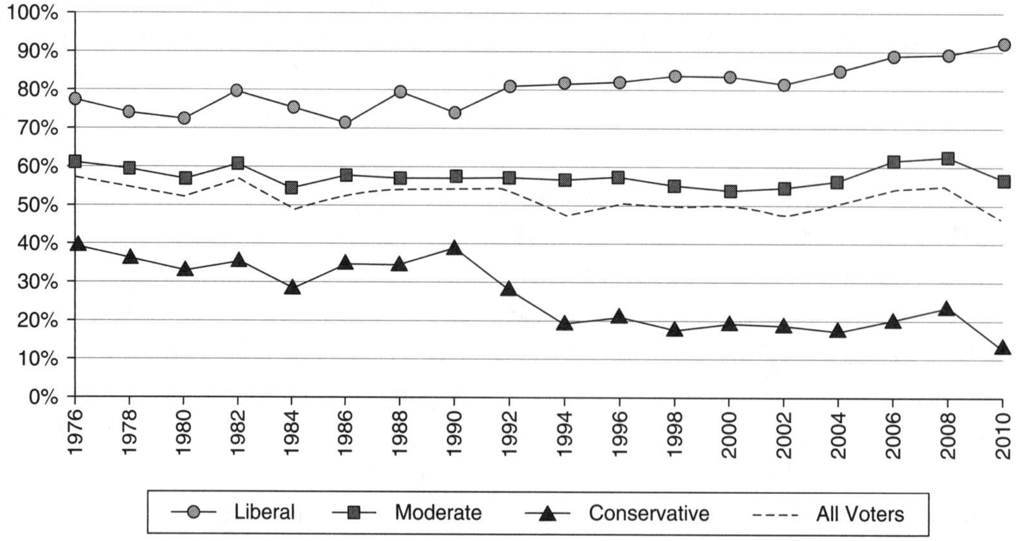

*Source:* National exit polls. See the section in Chapter 2 entitled "Creating a Cumulative National Data Set: Selecting Exit Polls" (pp. 28–29).

*Note:* When using these results to make inferences about the active electorate, the standard errors should be calculated using Table 2.2 (p. 36), which is explained in the adjacent section of Chapter 2, "Analyzing Exit Poll Questions: Estimating Sampling Error" (pp. 34–36). For a guide on how to understand the tables and figures of this chapter, see the section in Chapter 2 entitled "Presenting and Discussing the Exit Poll Data: Reading Chapter 5" (pp. 43–46). The rationale for using two-party percentages to show trends over time is given in Chapter 4, in the section entitled "Presidential Vote Choice" (pp. 124–131).

began voting increasingly Democratic. Republican candidates have not again enjoyed 20 percent support from liberals, and by 2006 Democratic candidates were consistently receiving at least 89 percent of liberals' two-party vote.

Conservatives have behaved much the same way. In the elections occurring through 1990, conservatives gave Democratic candidates 35 percent of their two-party vote, on average, and at least 28 percent of their vote in each election. By 1994, conservatives had shifted substantially to the GOP, awarding Republicans at least 77 percent of their vote in every election thereafter.

In the 2010 exit polls, ideological groups behaved as expected (see Table 5.20 at the end of the chapter). Conservatives strongly supported Republican House candidates, casting 84 percent of their overall ballots for them. Conversely, liberals voted overwhelmingly for Democratic House candidates, awarding them 90 percent of their ballots. Moderates again gravitated toward Democratic candidates, allotting 55 percent of their overall votes for Democratic House candidates, compared to 42 percent for Republican House candidates.

### Presidential Vote in Last Election

The national exit polls show that respondents vote predominantly for House candidates from the same political party as the presidential candidate for whom they voted in the most recent election (see Figure 5.21). Respondents who chose Democratic presidential candidates in the prior election allocated, on average, 85 percent of their two-party vote to Democratic House

**Figure 5.21**  Democratic Share of Two-Party House Vote by Presidential Vote in Last Election, 1976–2010

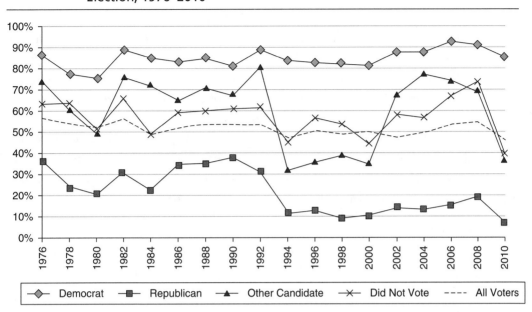

*Source:* National exit polls. See the section in Chapter 2 entitled "Creating a Cumulative National Data Set: Selecting Exit Polls" (pp. 28–29).

*Note:* When using these results to make inferences about the active electorate, the standard errors should be calculated using Table 2.2 (p. 36), which is explained in the adjacent section of Chapter 2, "Analyzing Exit Poll Questions: Estimating Sampling Error" (pp. 34–36). For a guide on how to understand the tables and figures of this chapter, see the section in Chapter 2 entitled "Presenting and Discussing the Exit Poll Data: Reading Chapter 5" (pp. 43–46). The rationale for using two-party percentages to show trends over time is given in Chapter 4, in the section entitled "Presidential Vote Choice" (pp. 124–131).

candidates. Similarly, respondents who voted for Republican presidential candidates cast, on average, 78 percent of their two-party ballots for Republican House candidates.

Over the decades, exit poll respondents have been willing to deviate less and less from the party of their previous presidential vote. In the late 1970s and early 1980s, around a quarter of respondents voted for House candidates from the political party for which they did not vote in the last presidential election. By the 2000s, only around a tenth of voters were willing to vote for House candidates from the opposite political party of their presidential vote.

Exit poll respondents who voted for third-party candidates tend to gravitate toward House candidates from the party that lost its previous bid for the White House. In the 1980s, when Republicans controlled the presidency, a majority of respondents who had voted for independent candidates in the previous presidential election routinely cast their two-party ballots for Democratic House candidates. During the 1990s, when Bill Clinton was president, respondents who had opted for independent candidates in the races he won cast a majority of their two-party ballots for Republican House candidates. The tide shifted again in the naughts. With George W. Bush in the White House, respondents who had chosen third-party candidates in his victorious elections cast their two-party ballots for Democratic House candidates.

Exit poll respondents who did not vote in the prior presidential election typically prefer Democratic House candidates. In all but four elections from 1976 to 2010 (1984, 1994, 2000, and 2010), nonvoters preferred Democratic House candidates by modest margins. Over the entire period, respondents who did not vote for president in the previous presidential election cast an average of 58 percent of their two-party ballots for Democratic House candidates, as opposed to an average of 42 percent for Republican House candidates.

In the 2010 exit poll, the relationship between past presidential vote and House vote largely held to form (see Table 5.21 at the end of the chapter). Respondents who voted for Barack Obama in the 2008 election preferred Democratic House candidates to Republican House candidates, 84 percent to 14 percent. Respondents who voted for John McCain in the 2008 election chose Republican House candidates over Democratic House candidates, 91 percent to 7 percent. Third-party supporters in 2008 cast 58 percent of their ballots for Republican House candidates and 33 percent of their ballots for Democratic House candidates. Contrary to expectations, though, respondents who did not vote in the 2008 presidential election voted for Republican House candidates, 59 percent to 39 percent, over Democratic House candidates.

### Presidential Approval

A strong relationship exists between presidential approval and congressional vote choice in the exit polls, though as expected, it is not quite as strong as the relationship between presidential approval and presidential vote choice (see Figure 5.22). Respondents who approve of the president overwhelmingly select House candidates from the president's party. Respondents who disapprove of the president prefer House candidates from the party out of the White House.

**Figure 5.22**   Democratic Share of Two-Party House Vote by Presidential Approval, 1978–2010

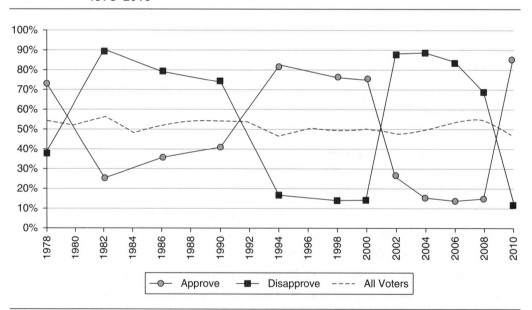

*Source:* National exit polls. See the section in Chapter 2 entitled "Creating a Cumulative National Data Set: Selecting Exit Polls" (pp. 28–29).

*Note:* When using these results to make inferences about the active electorate, the standard errors should be calculated using Table 2.2 (p. 36), which is explained in the adjacent section of Chapter 2, "Analyzing Exit Poll Questions: Estimating Sampling Error" (pp. 34–36). For a guide on how to understand the tables and figures of this chapter, see the section in Chapter 2 entitled "Presenting and Discussing the Exit Poll Data: Reading Chapter 5" (pp. 43–46). The rationale for using two-party percentages to show trends over time is given in Chapter 4, in the section entitled "Presidential Vote Choice" (pp. 124–131).

Democrats controlled the White House from 1978 through 1980, 1994 through 2000, and in 2010. In every exit poll administered during those years, a large majority of respondents who approved of the president supported Democratic House candidates, casting an average of 79 percent of their two-party ballots for Democrats. Conversely, an overwhelming majority of respondents who disapproved of the president supported Republicans in each election, casting 81 percent of their two-party ballots, on average, for Republican House candidates.

This pattern reversed itself when the country had Republican presidents. From 1982 through 1992 and again from 2002 through 2008, a Republican was in the White House. Respondents who approved of the president preferred Republican House candidates by a wide margin in every election, awarding them an average of 75 percent of their two-party ballots. By contrast, respondents who disapproved of the president voted strongly for Democratic House candidates in each election, allotting them 82 percent, on average, of their two-party ballots.

During the 2010 congressional elections, Democrat Barack Obama occupied the White House. Exit poll respondents approving of President Obama overwhelmingly chose Democratic congressional candidates, allotting them 85 percent of their overall ballots, compared to only 14 percent for Republican candidates (see Table 5.22 at the end of the chapter). Conversely, respondents disapproving of President Obama cast 84 percent of their overall ballots for Republican House candidates and only 11 percent for their Democratic counterparts.

## Congressional Approval

The relationship between congressional approval and congressional vote choice is similar to the relationship between presidential approval and congressional vote choice, except that the former hinges on the party controlling Congress rather than the party controlling the presidency. Exit poll respondents evaluating a Democratic Congress positively are more likely to vote for Democratic House candidates, whereas respondents evaluating a Republican Congress positively are more likely to vote for Republican House candidates. Among respondents evaluating Congress negatively, they tend to vote for candidates from the minority party.

Figure 5.23 shows the relationship between evaluations of Congress and congressional vote choice since this question began appearing in exit polls in 1990. Democrats controlled Congress in elections occurring from 1990 through 1994, in 2008, and in 2010. In those elections, respondents who approved of Congress's job performance cast, on average, 70 percent of their two-party ballots for Democratic House candidates. Respondents who disapproved of Congress's performance were more supportive of Republican House candidates, although on two occasions disapproving respondents gave Democratic candidates a majority of their vote—albeit a slim one.

Republicans, by contrast, controlled Congress in elections occurring from 1996 through 2006. During that span, respondents who approved of Congress cast a majority of their ballots for Republican candidates in each election, allotting them an average of 68 percent of their two-party vote. Conversely, respondents who disapproved of Congress gave, on average, 62 percent of their two-party vote to Democratic candidates in these contests.

The 2010 exit poll held to form. Respondents approving of the performance of the Democratic-controlled Congress behaved as expected, supporting Democratic House candidates over

**Figure 5.23**   Democratic Share of Two-Party House Vote by Congressional Approval, 1990–2010

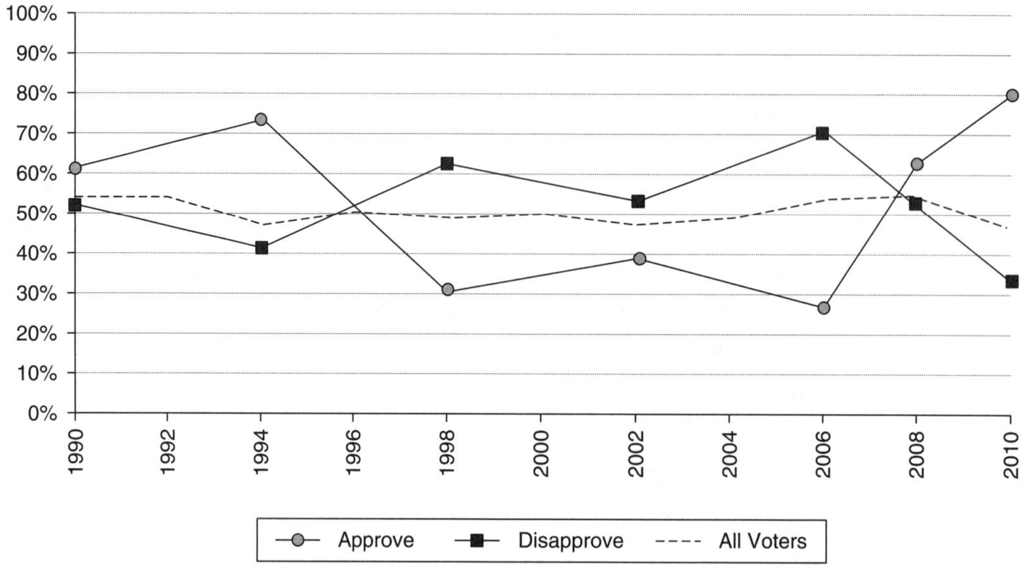

*Source:* National exit polls. See the section in Chapter 2 entitled "Creating a Cumulative National Data Set: Selecting Exit Polls" (pp. 28–29).

*Note:* When using these results to make inferences about the active electorate, the standard errors should be calculated using Table 2.2 (p. 36), which is explained in the adjacent section of Chapter 2, "Analyzing Exit Poll Questions: Estimating Sampling Error" (pp. 34–36). For a guide on how to understand the tables and figures of this chapter, see the section in Chapter 2 entitled "Presenting and Discussing the Exit Poll Data: Reading Chapter 5" (pp. 43–46). The rationale for using two-party percentages to show trends over time is given in Chapter 4, in the section entitled "Presidential Vote Choice" (pp. 124–131).

their Republican rivals by a margin of 79 percent to 20 percent in the overall vote (see Table 5.23 at the end of the chapter). Respondents disapproving of the Democratic-controlled Congress preferred Republican House candidates, 65 percent to 33 percent, over their Democratic counterparts.

## Perceived Direction of the Country

Exit poll respondents' evaluations about the direction of the country closely mirror their presidential approval ratings, resulting in both having a similar relationship with congressional vote choice (see Figure 5.24). During Republican presidential administrations, respondents judging the country to be moving in the right direction prefer Republican House candidates, whereas those judging the country to be off on the wrong track prefer Democratic House candidates. The opposite relationship occurs during Democratic administrations. A very similar pattern occurs in presidential voting (see Chapter 4).

In the exit polls conducted in 1990 as well as 2002 through 2008, Republicans occupied the White House. In congressional elections held in those years, respondents judging the country to be moving in the right direction preferred Republican House candidates, casting an average of 70 percent of their two-party ballots for them. In those same years, respondents who thought the country was on the wrong track supported Democratic House candidates by similar numbers.

**Figure 5.24**    Democratic Share of Two-Party House Vote by Perceived Direction of the Country, 1990–2010

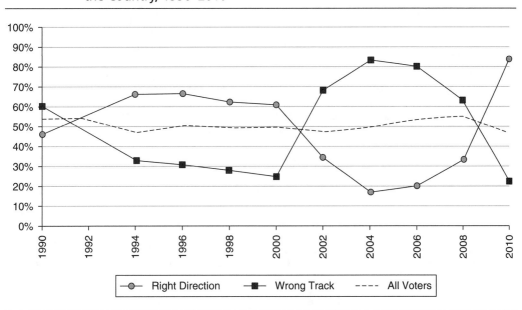

*Source:* National exit polls. See the section in Chapter 2 entitled "Creating a Cumulative National Data Set: Selecting Exit Polls" (pp. 28–29).

*Note:* When using these results to make inferences about the active electorate, the standard errors should be calculated using Table 2.2 (p. 36), which is explained in the adjacent section of Chapter 2, "Analyzing Exit Poll Questions: Estimating Sampling Error" (pp. 34–36). For a guide on how to understand the tables and figures of this chapter, see the section in Chapter 2 entitled "Presenting and Discussing the Exit Poll Data: Reading Chapter 5" (pp. 43–46). The rationale for using two-party percentages to show trends over time is given in Chapter 4, in the section entitled "Presidential Vote Choice" (pp. 124–131).

During the congressional elections held while Democrat Bill Clinton was president, we find the opposite pattern. From 1994 through 2000, exit poll respondents judging the country to be moving in the right direction allotted Democratic candidates at least 60 percent of their two-party vote. Conversely, respondents judging the country to be off on the wrong track predominantly backed Republican candidates.

This pattern held again in the 2010 exit poll (see Table 5.24 at the end of the chapter). With Barack Obama in the White House, respondents judging the country to be moving in the right direction awarded 82 percent of their overall votes to Democratic House candidates and only 16 percent of their votes to Republican candidates. By contrast, Republican House candidates defeated Democratic candidates, 76 percent to 22 percent in the overall vote, among respondents who judged the country to be off on the wrong track.

### Expected Life for the Next Generation

The exit polls show that long-term perceptions about the direction of the country operate similarly to short-term perceptions (see Figure 5.25). During periods of Democratic presidential control, respondents who expect life for the next generation to be better generally prefer Democratic House candidates, whereas those who expect life for the next generation to be worse prefer Republican House candidates. Conversely, during periods of Republican presidential control, respondents

**Figure 5.25**    Democratic Share of Two-Party House Vote by Expected Life for Next Generation, 1992–2010

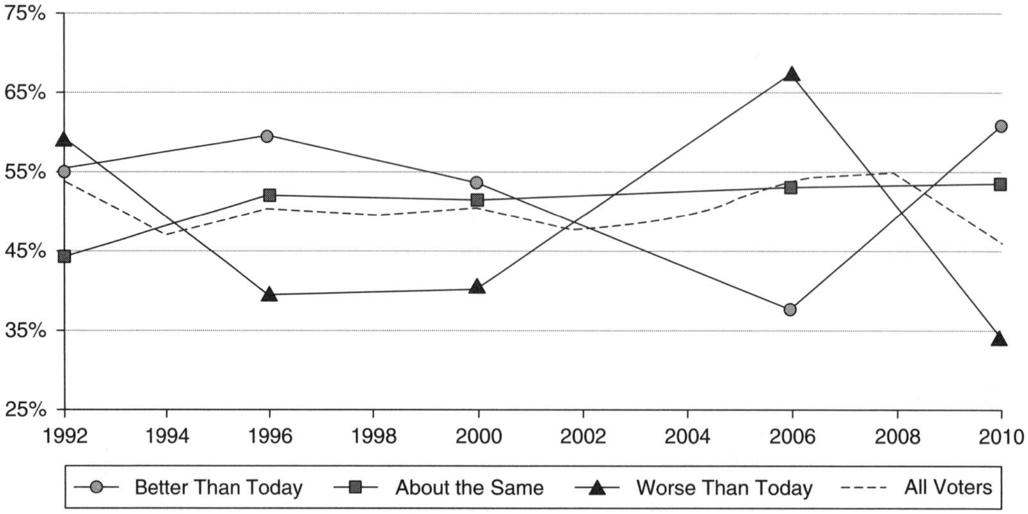

*Source:* National exit polls. See the section in Chapter 2 entitled "Creating a Cumulative National Data Set: Selecting Exit Polls" (pp. 28–29).

*Note:* When using these results to make inferences about the active electorate, the standard errors should be calculated using Table 2.2 (p. 36), which is explained in the adjacent section of Chapter 2, "Analyzing Exit Poll Questions: Estimating Sampling Error" (pp. 34–36). For a guide on how to understand the tables and figures of this chapter, see the section in Chapter 2 entitled "Presenting and Discussing the Exit Poll Data: Reading Chapter 5" (pp. 43–46). The rationale for using two-party percentages to show trends over time is given in Chapter 4, in the section entitled "Presidential Vote Choice" (pp. 124–131).

who expect life for the next generation to be better generally prefer Republican House candidates, whereas those who expect life for the next generation to be worse prefer Democratic House candidates. This pattern for congressional voting is generally analogous to the patterns found in presidential voting, although in 1992 those who expected life for the next generation to be better preferred the Democratic presidential challenger over the Republican incumbent president.

In the 1996, 2000, and 2010 elections, when a Democrat occupied the White House, exit poll respondents who expected life for the next generation to be better cast, on average, 58 percent of their two-party ballots for Democratic House candidates, whereas those who expected life to be worse cast, on average, 62 percent of their two-party ballots for Republican House candidates. In the 2006 election, when Republican George W. Bush was in the White House, the pattern worked in the opposite direction, as 62 percent of respondents who expected life to be better for the next generation preferred Republican House candidates to Democratic ones, whereas 67 percent of respondents who expected life to be worse preferred Democratic House candidates to Republican ones. The only exception to this pattern in the time series was found in the 1992 exit poll, when a majority of respondents who expected life to be better went against the grain and voted for Democratic House candidates (even though Republican George H. W. Bush was president).

Exit poll respondents who fell between these two extremes and expected life for the next generation to be about the same essentially split their two-party ballots. On average, 51 percent of respondents expecting life to be about the same voted for Democratic House candidates, and 49 percent of respondents voted for Republican House candidates. In the five exit polls featuring this question between 1992 and 2010, the difference in the vote for the two parties did not exceed 10 points.

The 2010 exit poll once again showed the same pattern (see Table 5.25 at the end of the chapter). With Obama in the White House, respondents who expected life for the next generation to be better preferred Democratic House candidates to the Republicans, 60 percent to 39 percent. By contrast, respondents who expected life for the next generation to be worse preferred Republican House candidates to the Democrats, 64 percent to 33 percent. Those respondents who expected life for the next generation to be about the same fell in between, preferring the Democrats to the Republicans by a much smaller margin, 52 percent to 45 percent.

## Position on Government Activism

The exit polls reveal that respondents' positions on government activism are tied closely to their congressional preferences, much as they are tied to their presidential preferences (see Figure 5.26). Respondents who think the government should do more have overwhelmingly supported Democratic candidates in each congressional election from 1992 through 2010, allotting them an average of 72 percent of their two-party vote. Conversely, respondents who think the government does too much have consistently preferred Republican House candidates over time, allotting them 70 percent of their two-party vote since 1992.

In the 2010 exit poll, the relationship between government activism and congressional voting preferences was as strong as it has been since its first examination in 1992 (see Table 5.26 at the

**Figure 5.26** Democratic Share of Two-Party House Vote by Position on Government Activism, 1992–2010

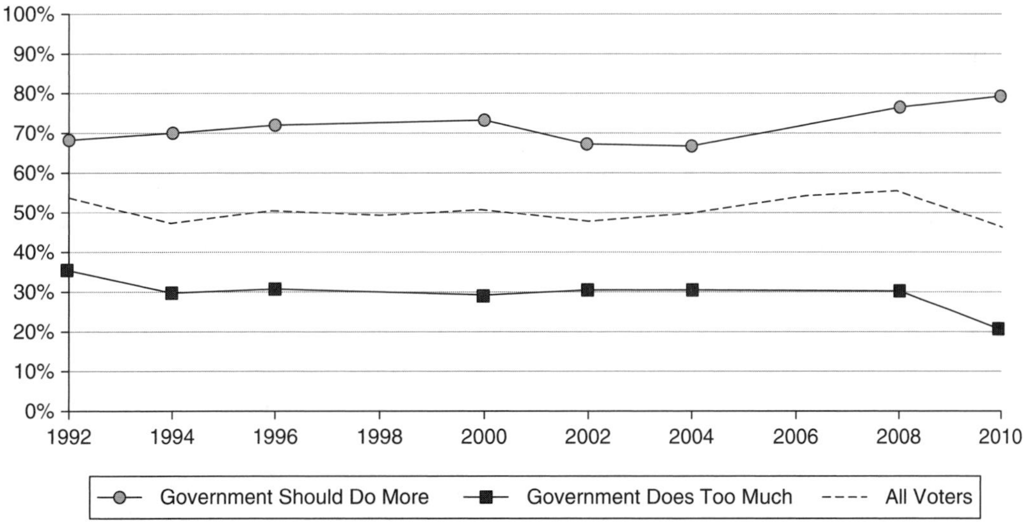

*Source:* National exit polls. See the section in Chapter 2 entitled "Creating a Cumulative National Data Set: Selecting Exit Polls" (pp. 28–29).

*Note:* When using these results to make inferences about the active electorate, the standard errors should be calculated using Table 2.2 (p. 36), which is explained in the adjacent section of Chapter 2, "Analyzing Exit Poll Questions: Estimating Sampling Error" (pp. 34–36). For a guide on how to understand the tables and figures of this chapter, see the section in Chapter 2 entitled "Presenting and Discussing the Exit Poll Data: Reading Chapter 5" (pp. 43–46). The rationale for using two-party percentages to show trends over time is given in Chapter 4, in the section entitled "Presidential Vote Choice" (pp. 124–131).

end of the chapter). Respondents who thought the government should do more overwhelmingly supported Democratic candidates over Republican candidates, 77 percent to 21 percent, in the overall vote. By contrast, respondents who thought the government does too much strongly preferred Republican candidates to Democratic candidates, 76 percent to 20 percent.

## First-Time Voter

Since 1996, exit pollsters have posed a comparable question assessing whether respondents were casting ballots for the first time. Unfortunately, the question has generally been administered in presidential election years, not midterm election years, although it was asked in 2010. Judgments based on these data should take into account differences in the electoral context.

The last four presidential exit polls showed that first-time voters preferred Democratic congressional candidates to Republican ones in each race despite Republican congressional candidates winning a majority of seats in three out of four of these elections (see Figure 5.27). First-time voters have allotted, on average, 56 percent of their two-party ballots to Democrats in House elections nationwide. By comparison, they have given the Democratic presidential candidate 60 percent of their two-party ballots since 1996. However, considerable variability is seen in the House preferences of first-time voters. The 2000 election saw an 8-point drop in support for Democratic House candidates from 1996, before surging 14 points over the next two presidential exit polls.

**Figure 5.27** Democratic Share of Two-Party House Vote by First-Time Voter, 1996–2010

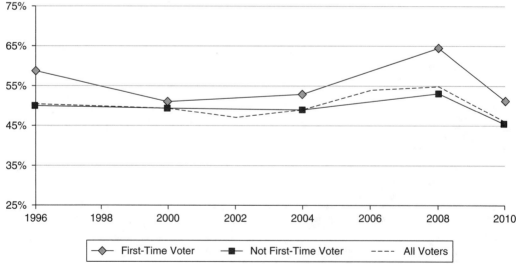

*Source:* National exit polls. See the section in Chapter 2 entitled "Creating a Cumulative National Data Set: Selecting Exit Polls" (pp. 28–29).

*Note:* When using these results to make inferences about the active electorate, the standard errors should be calculated using Table 2.2 (p. 36), which is explained in the adjacent section of Chapter 2, "Analyzing Exit Poll Questions: Estimating Sampling Error" (pp. 34–36). For a guide on how to understand the tables and figures of this chapter, see the section in Chapter 2 entitled "Presenting and Discussing the Exit Poll Data: Reading Chapter 5" (pp. 43–46). The rationale for using two-party percentages to show trends over time is given in Chapter 4, in the section entitled "Presidential Vote Choice" (pp. 124–131).

Democratic congressional candidates were again the preference of first-time voters in the 2010 exit poll, despite respondents overall tilting Republican (see Table 5.27 at the end of the chapter). First-time voters preferred Democratic candidates to Republican candidates, 46 percent to 43 percent, in the overall vote. This was the smallest margin for Democratic House candidates among new voters since the 2000 exit poll.

## Economic Considerations

Economic circumstances are strongly tied to congressional voting patterns in the exit polls. Respondents' incomes correlate with their choices in House races, as do respondents' judgments about their household's past financial situation and the nation's current and future economic conditions. These relationships persist whether the economy is performing well or poorly.

### Household Income

In the exit polls, income has a strong linear relationship with congressional vote choice, just as it does with presidential vote choice (see Figure 5.28). As the household incomes of respondents grow, the likelihood of their supporting Republican House candidates increases and their odds of supporting Democratic House candidates decrease. The precise tipping point changes over time as the value of the dollar inflates. Nonetheless, the rich and the poor have behaved consistently over the past sixteen years, whereas middle-income respondents have swung back and forth toward candidates of the winning party.

**Figure 5.28**  Democratic Share of Two-Party House Vote by Household Income, 1994–2010

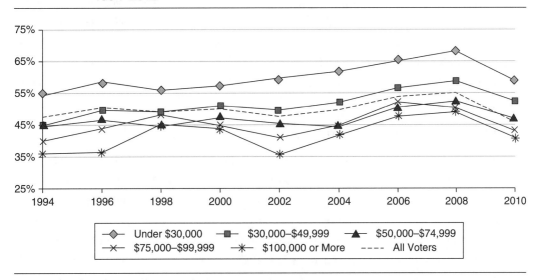

*Source:* National exit polls. See the section in Chapter 2 entitled "Creating a Cumulative National Data Set: Selecting Exit Polls" (pp. 28–29).

*Note:* When using these results to make inferences about the active electorate, the standard errors should be calculated using Table 2.2 (p. 36), which is explained in the adjacent section of Chapter 2, "Analyzing Exit Poll Questions: Estimating Sampling Error" (pp. 34–36). For a guide on how to understand the tables and figures of this chapter, see the section in Chapter 2 entitled "Presenting and Discussing the Exit Poll Data: Reading Chapter 5" (pp. 43–46). The rationale for using two-party percentages to show trends over time is given in Chapter 4, in the section entitled "Presidential Vote Choice" (pp. 124–131).

In the past decade and a half, poor respondents have gravitated consistently toward Democratic House candidates. A majority of respondents who came from households earning less than $30,000 supported Democratic House candidates in every exit poll from 1994 through 2010, casting an average of 60 percent of their two-party ballots for Democrats. Respondents earning between $30,000 and $49,999 have also allotted at least half of their two-party vote to Democratic House candidates in each election since 2000.

Conversely, wealthy respondents have consistently preferred Republican House candidates over time. A majority of respondents from households earning at least $100,000 a year have cast their ballots for Republican House candidates every year since 1994. On average, 58 percent of their two-party vote has been awarded to Republican candidates over the past decade and a half.

Middle-income respondents—those respondents making between $50,000 and $99,999—have fallen between these two extremes, behaving like swing voters in each election. A majority of respondents from households earning between $50,000 and $74,999, as well as those from households earning between $75,000 and $99,999, have allocated their two-party vote to candidates from the party winning the most seats in every House election from 1994 through 2010.

In the 2010 exit poll, the pattern between income and congressional preferences held once again, with the poorest respondents preferring Democratic candidates, the wealthiest respondents preferring Republican candidates, and respondents from middle-income households swinging to the winning Republican side (see Table 5.28 at the end of the chapter). Respondents from households earning less than $30,000 cast 57 percent of their overall ballots for Democratic House candidates, while 51 percent of respondents earning between $30,000 and $49,999 chose Democratic House candidates. Conversely, 58 percent of respondents from households earning $100,000 or more preferred Republican House candidates. Respondents from middle-income households swung toward Republicans, abandoning their Democratic orientations of the previous two election cycles. Republican candidates secured 51 percent of the overall ballots cast by respondents from households earning between $50,000 and $74,999 and 56 percent of the overall ballots cast by respondents from households earning between $75,000 and $99,999, after failing to top 48 percent among either group in the previous exit poll.

## Two-Year Household Financial Situation

Exit poll respondents' perceptions of their two-year household financial situation operate as a referendum on the president rather than on Congress (see Figure 5.29). If the president is a Republican, respondents who believe their household financial situation has gotten better vote for Republican House candidates regardless of which party controls the House, whereas respondents who believe their financial situation has gotten worse vote for Democratic House candidates. The opposite holds true when a Democrat is in the White House. Respondents who believe their household financial situation has remained about the same during the previous two years tend to gravitate toward the party winning the most seats in the congressional election.

During the six midterm elections held from 1990 through 2010, Republicans controlled the White House in half of them. In those elections, respondents who reported that their household

**Figure 5.29**   Democratic Share of Two-Party House Vote by Two-Year Household
Financial Situation, 1990–2010

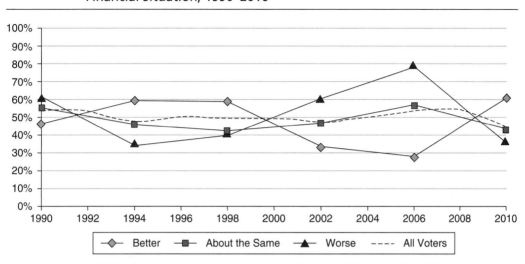

*Source:* National exit polls. See the section in Chapter 2 entitled "Creating a Cumulative National Data Set: Selecting Exit Polls" (pp. 28–29).

*Note:* When using these results to make inferences about the active electorate, the standard errors should be calculated using Table 2.2 (p. 36), which is explained in the adjacent section of Chapter 2, "Analyzing Exit Poll Questions: Estimating Sampling Error" (pp. 34–36). For a guide on how to understand the tables and figures of this chapter, see the section in Chapter 2 entitled "Presenting and Discussing the Exit Poll Data: Reading Chapter 5" (pp. 43–46). The rationale for using two-party percentages to show trends over time is given in Chapter 4, in the section entitled "Presidential Vote Choice" (pp. 124–131).

financial situation had improved in the previous two years cast, on average, 64 percent of their
two-party ballots for Republican House candidates, whereas respondents who reported that their
financial situation had worsened cast 67 percent of their two-party ballots for Democratic House
candidates. Conversely, under Democratic presidents during this time frame, respondents who
reported that their household financial situation had gotten better in the previous two years cast,
on average, 60 percent of their two-party ballots for Democratic House candidates, whereas
respondents who reported that their financial situation had worsened cast 62 percent of their
ballots for Republican House candidates. These patterns occurred despite the opposite political
party controlling the House in a third of the midterm elections held since 1990.

Exit poll respondents who thought their financial situation had remained about the same over
the previous two years behaved like a bellwether in congressional elections, typically gravitating
toward the party that ultimately secured the most seats. In every midterm election from 1990
through 2006, respondents who saw no change in their household financial situation voted for
the winning party in every election. In 1990, respondents whose household financial situation
remained unchanged over the prior two years cast 56 percent of their two-party vote for Democrats, enabling them to pick up the most seats. In the 1994, 1998, and 2002 midterm elections,
respondents from households with static finances cast, on average, 54 percent of their two-party
ballots for Republicans, propelling the GOP to victories in all three elections. In the 2006 midterms, Democrats won 57 percent of the two-party vote of those whose household finances had
remained constant over the previous two years.

In the 2010 congressional elections, these historical patterns held again for exit poll respondents who reported a change in their household finances but deviated somewhat for those respondents who reported no change in their financial situation (see Table 5.29 at the end of the chapter). With a Democrat in the White House, respondents who thought their household financial situation had gotten better in the last two years preferred Democratic House candidates to their Republican counterparts, 60 percent to 37 percent, in the full House vote. Republican House candidates defeated Democratic candidates, 61 percent to 35 percent, among respondents who thought their household financial situation had gotten worse in the past two years. Respondents who thought their financial situation had stayed about the same failed to go with the winning party in the midterm election for the first time since the item was introduced in 1990. Respondents who saw no change in their finances slightly preferred Democratic House candidates to Republican House candidates, 49 percent to 48 percent.

## Judgments of Current National Economic Conditions

Judgments of national economic conditions have a similar influence on congressional voting patterns as perceptions of personal household finances. As Figure 5.30 shows, exit poll respondents reward the president's party in House elections when they believe the national economy is performing well, just as they reward the candidate from the president's party in presidential elections. Similarly, respondents punish the president's party in House elections when they believe the economy is performing badly, just as they do in presidential elections. This occurs regardless of which party controls the House of Representatives.

**Figure 5.30**  Democratic Share of Two-Party House Vote by Judgments of Current National Economic Conditions, 1986–2010

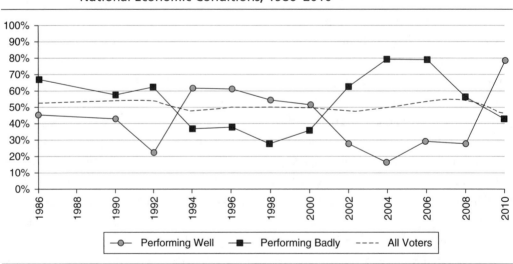

*Source:* National exit polls. See the section in Chapter 2 entitled "Creating a Cumulative National Data Set: Selecting Exit Polls" (pp. 28–29).

*Note:* When using these results to make inferences about the active electorate, the standard errors should be calculated using Table 2.2 (p. 36), which is explained in the adjacent section of Chapter 2, "Analyzing Exit Poll Questions: Estimating Sampling Error" (pp. 34–36). For a guide on how to understand the tables and figures of this chapter, see the section in Chapter 2 entitled "Presenting and Discussing the Exit Poll Data: Reading Chapter 5" (pp. 43–46). The rationale for using two-party percentages to show trends over time is given in Chapter 4, in the section entitled "Presidential Vote Choice" (pp. 124–131).

In the twelve congressional elections from 1986 through 2010 in which exit pollsters assessed national economic conditions, Democrats controlled the White House on five occasions (1994–2000 and 2010). In those five elections, a majority of respondents who thought the national economy was performing well preferred Democrats in each election, casting an average of 61 percent of their two-party ballots for Democratic House candidates. By contrast, respondents who thought the economy was performing badly under a Democratic president predominantly supported Republicans in each congressional election, casting an average of 64 percent of their two-party ballots for Republican House candidates.

The opposite outcome occurred in the seven House elections from 1986 to 2010 in which Republicans controlled the White House. A majority of exit poll respondents who thought the economy was performing well supported the president's party in congressional races, allotting an average of 70 percent of their two-party vote to Republican House candidates. Among those who thought the economy was performing badly, Democratic candidates were the majority preference in each election, receiving an average of 66 percent of the two-party vote.

In the 2010 exit poll, congressional candidates from the president's party were again rewarded or punished based on the perceived performance of the national economy under the incumbent president. Democratic House candidates defeated Republican House candidates, 77 percent to 20 percent overall, among respondents who thought the economy was performing well (see Table 5.30). Conversely, Republican House candidates defeated Democratic House candidates, 56 percent to 41 percent overall, among respondents who thought the economy was performing badly.

## Judgments of Future National Economic Conditions

Judgments of future national economic conditions are related to congressional preferences in much the same way as current national economic conditions (see Figure 5.31). When exit poll respondents think the economy will be better in the next year, they largely stick with candidates from the incumbent president's party. When respondents think the economy will be worse in the future, they gravitate predominantly toward candidates from the party outside the White House.

The 1986 and 1990 exit polls occurred during Republican presidential administrations. Respondents in those years who thought the economy would be better in the next year cast 57 percent of their ballots for Republican House candidates in Reagan's second midterm and 52 percent of their ballots for Republican House candidates in George H. W. Bush's first midterm. Conversely, respondents who thought the economy would be worse cast, respectively, 67 percent and 59 percent of their ballots for Democratic candidates.

When the exit polls were conducted in 1998 and 2000, Democrat Bill Clinton was in the White House and the relationship between future economic conditions and congressional vote choices flipped. In 1998 and 2000, exit poll respondents who thought the economy would get better in the next year cast a majority of their votes for Democratic House candidates. By contrast, a majority of respondents who thought the economy would get worse chose Republican House candidates in the 1998 and 2000 exit poll.

Meanwhile, exit poll respondents who thought that national economic conditions would be about the same in the next year typically split their votes between House candidates from the

**Figure 5.31** Democratic Share of Two-Party House Vote by Judgments of Future National Economic Conditions, 1986–2008

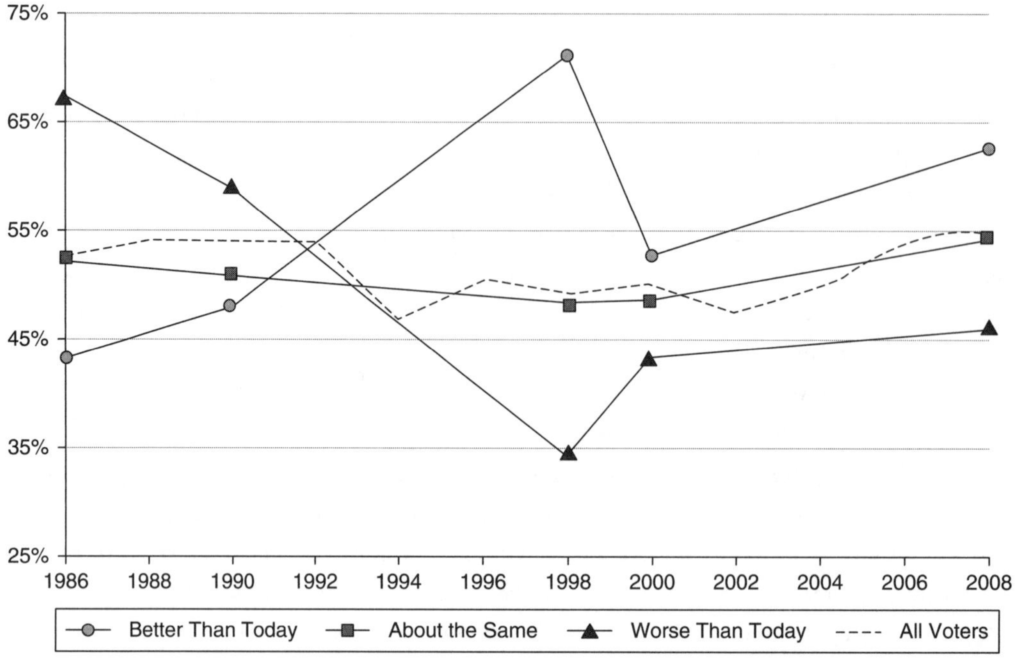

*Source:* National exit polls. See the section in Chapter 2 entitled "Creating a Cumulative National Data Set: Selecting Exit Polls" (pp. 28–29).

*Note:* When using these results to make inferences about the active electorate, the standard errors should be calculated using Table 2.2 (p. 36), which is explained in the adjacent section of Chapter 2, "Analyzing Exit Poll Questions: Estimating Sampling Error" (pp. 34–36). For a guide on how to understand the tables and figures of this chapter, see the section in Chapter 2 entitled "Presenting and Discussing the Exit Poll Data: Reading Chapter 5" (pp. 43–46). The rationale for using two-party percentages to show trends over time is given in Chapter 4, in the section entitled "Presidential Vote Choice" (pp. 124–131).

major parties regardless of which party controlled the White House. In the exit polls conducted between 1986 and 2008, an average of 51 percent of these respondents cast their two-party ballots for Democratic House candidates, whereas an average of 49 percent cast their two-party ballots for Republican House candidates. Only once in the five exit polls conducted during this period did the difference in the two-party vote exceed 4 percentage points for respondents who thought that national economic conditions would be about the same in the next year.

The 2010 exit poll did not ask respondents about future national economic conditions. In 2008, though, exit poll respondents behaved contrary to expectations. Respondents who thought that national economic conditions would be better in the next year voted against the incumbent president's party, allocating 61 percent of their ballots to Democratic House candidates and only 37 percent to Republican House candidates (see Table 5.31). Conversely, respondents who thought that the economy would get worse in the future preferred Republican House candidates to Democratic House candidates, 52 percent to 44 percent. Respondents who thought the economy would be about the same were once again close to an even split, casting 53 percent of their ballots for Democratic House candidates and 45 percent for Republican House candidates.

## Partisan Predispositions of the Congressional Exit Polls

Our analysis of the exit polls in House elections from 1976 to 2010 allows us to distinguish the partisan dispositions of various groups when making congressional choices. We therefore believe it to be helpful to identify base groups for each party in House elections and swing groups that change from election to election.

This process, of course, requires a number of caveats that should lead readers to scrutinize our categorizations, particularly for borderline cases. First, the exit poll groups that we examine should not be viewed as the universe of subgroups in the active congressional electorate. An infinite number of possibilities exist, depending on the information solicited from respondents. Second, these subgroups are not mutually exclusive, meaning that individual respondents can be found in more than one group. As a result, the size and impact of these groups should be considered separately, not cumulatively. Finally, these groups vary in their duration. The exit poll questions used to create the groups were not included on every survey instrument. As a result, some of the groups may have been classified in categories that they would not have found themselves placed in under longer time frames. For example, groups defined by their reactions to contemporary environmental conditions, such as the state of the economy or judgments of the president, may have been categorized differently if the question had been asked at earlier points in time or under different presidential administrations.

Taken together, these shortcomings suggest readers are best served by considering these groups individually, rather than in combination. The results alert us to commonalities between seemingly dissimilar groups, permitting us to see the different types of respondents that might play a role in each party's coalition. However, they do not enable us to determine the structure of winning coalitions or, in other words, what proportion of the vote must be secured from particular groups to ensure election. To do so would require a collection of mutually exclusive groups that cover the entire active electorate and appear over time. Although we have such information for groups generated from a single question in a single year, we do not have it for the collection of groups generated from an array of questions administered over time. Nonetheless, many insights can be gained from this classification about the dynamics of voter groups in the exit polls.

To determine the congressional vote predispositions of various groups in the exit polls, we categorized each group according to its long-term partisan voting patterns, regardless of the type of characteristic from which it was derived. We began by rank ordering every group examined in this chapter by the average share of the two-party vote the group awarded to the major-party candidates over the time period during which the question used to create the group was administered. We then assigned each group to one of five categories along a scale defined by the group's share of the two-party vote: Democratic base groups, Democratic-leaning groups, swing groups, Republican-leaning groups, and Republican base groups.

We categorized base groups as those allotting at least 67 percent of their two-party vote, on average, to Democratic or Republican House candidates over time in the exit polls. Leaners are those subgroups allotting between 56 percent and 66 percent of their two-party vote, on average, to the Democrats or Republicans over time. Finally, swing groups are subgroups that allot less than 56 percent of their two-party vote to either of the major parties over time. Together, this categorization creates a 5-point scale showing the extent to which each subgroup in the exit polls was predisposed to vote for Democratic or Republican House candidates.

Examining the distribution of base, leaning, and swing groups in the congressional exit polls reveals that congressional elections are competitive among most subgroups. The average two-party gap in support over time is 10 percentage points or less for half—forty-one—of the eighty-two subgroups, and 5 percentage points or less for nearly a third—twenty-seven—of them. Only twenty of the subgroups are partisan base groups, overwhelmingly supporting either Democratic or Republican House candidates. The remaining twenty-one groups fall in between, advantaging one party or the other by between 12 and 32 percentage points.

## Democratic Groups

Thirteen of the eighty-two groups analyzed in this chapter comprise the Democratic base—the coalition of voters who consistently prefer Democratic candidates by a two-to-one margin regardless of the electoral context or the candidates on the ballot (see the top section of Table 5.32). Seven of those groups include respondents whose political orientations, attitudes, or past behaviors correspond closely with the Democratic Party: Democratic identifiers, liberals, those who disapprove of the Republican president, those who approve of the Democratic president, those who approve of the Democratic Congress, those who voted for the Democratic presidential nominee in the last election, and respondents who believe government should do more to solve the country's problems. The remaining exit poll subgroups are defined by physical traits or religious characteristics. African Americans, Hispanics, Jews, seculars, affiliates of non-Judeo-Christian religions, and gays or bisexuals are all especially loyal to the Democratic Party. They have voted overwhelmingly for Democratic House candidates in every election in which exit pollsters have assessed their choices.

Another sixteen of the eighty-two exit poll subgroups can be described as Democratic leaners—subgroups that typically prefer Democratic House candidates but by smaller margins than the groups that comprise the Democratic base (see the bottom section of Table 5.32). Many of these groups have been reliably Democratic through the years, such as voters from union households, voters living in urban areas, voters failing to complete a high school education, and voters residing in households earning less than $30,000 a year. However, a few of these groups have deviated from the Democratic Party on occasion, such as easterners in 1994 and Asians in 1992 and 1996.

## Republican Groups

Seven of the eighty-two exit poll subgroups considered in this chapter make up the Republican base (see the top section of Table 5.33). All of them are defined by political orientations that correspond closely with the Republican Party: Republican identifiers, conservatives, those who disapprove of the Democratic president, those who approve of the Republican president, those who approve of the Republican Congress, those who voted for the Republican presidential nominee in the last election, and respondents who believe that government does too much have all allocated, on average, more than two-thirds of their votes to Republican House candidates over the past three decades. In 2010, Republicans' share of these groups' overall vote exceeded 75 percent. Democrats have made little headway with any of these groups over time.

Five of the eighty-two subgroups behave as Republican leaners, allotting Republican House candidates an average of 56 to 66 percent of their two-party vote over time (see the bottom section of Table 5.33). All are defined by religious and economic characteristics. A majority of Protestants, evangelicals, and respondents attending religious services at least once a week have voted for Republican candidates nationwide in every election. Republican House candidates have also had more than a 10-point advantage over time among voters from households earning at least $100,000 a year and among voters who think national economic conditions are good. It should be noted that respondents who think national economic conditions are good have acted like a Republican base group when a Republican is in the White House (averaging 70 percent of the two-party vote for House Republican candidates) but more like a Democratic leaner group when a Democrat is in the White House (averaging 61 percent of the two-party vote for Democrats)—an example of why readers should review the statistical categorizations before making any conclusive judgments.

## Swing Groups

Half of the subgroups in the exit polls split their votes fairly closely between the parties, averaging less than a 10-point gap in their support for the major parties' candidates in House elections over time (see Table 5.34). Winning enough of these groups typically enables one of the parties to build a coalition capable of securing control of the House of Representatives. In 2010, an overwhelming number of these subgroups preferred Republican House candidates nationwide. Two years earlier, many of these same groups had gravitated toward Democratic candidates. Clearly, deciphering the outcomes of congressional elections hinges on understanding what determines candidate preferences and turnout decisions among respondents in these subgroups.

Some groups swing based on the president in the White House at the time of the House election. For example, following a pattern similar to that found in presidential elections, 72 percent of exit poll respondents who think the country is off on the wrong track have voted against the party of the incumbent president in House elections, but because half of the ten elections have featured Republican incumbents and half have featured Democratic incumbents, the average for this category is near 50 percent. Although this base group–swing group categorization offers a useful lens by which to view subgroups in the exit polls, readers are encouraged not to stop at the basic categorizations, but to examine the behavior of each group over time using the detailed figures and tables specifically designed for each group.

## Notes

[1] Because Senate elections are held in only about two-thirds of all states in a given election year, and the mixture of states with a senatorial contest varies from election to election, the exit poll results for Senate elections are not comparable over time. Therefore, we focus solely on House and presidential races.

[2] All percentages presented in the text have been rounded to the nearest whole number. Any calculations necessary to compute them are also based on rounded whole numbers.

**Table 5.1**  Democratic Share of Two-Party House Seats, 1976–2010

| Year | Number of House Seats Won by Democrats | Two-Party Democratic Seat Share |
|------|----------------------------------------|----------------------------------|
| 2010 | 193 | 44% |
| 2008 | 257 | 59% |
| 2006 | 233 | 54% |
| 2004 | 202 | 47% |
| 2002 | 205 | 47% |
| 2000 | 212 | 49% |
| 1998 | 211 | 49% |
| 1996 | 206 | 47% |
| 1994 | 204 | 47% |
| 1992 | 258 | 59% |
| 1990 | 267 | 62% |
| 1988 | 260 | 60% |
| 1986 | 258 | 59% |
| 1984 | 253 | 58% |
| 1982 | 269 | 62% |
| 1980 | 243 | 56% |
| 1978 | 277 | 64% |
| 1976 | 292 | 67% |

*Source:* Harold W. Stanley and Richard G. Niemi, *Vital Statistics on American Politics, 2011–2012* (Washington, DC: CQ Press, 2011).

**Table 5.2**  House Vote in the Exit Polls, 1976–2010

| | Year | Two-Party Democratic House Vote | Full House Vote | | | |
|---|------|---------|-------------------|------------------|-------------------|------------------|
| | | | Democratic Vote | Republican Vote | Third-Party Vote | Number of Respondents |
| All Voters | 2010 | 46.3% | 44.9% | 52.2% | 2.9% | 17,504 |
| | 2008 | 55.0% | 53.7% | 43.9% | 2.4% | 16,521 |
| | 2006 | 54.0% | 52.9% | 45.2% | 1.9% | 13,251 |
| | 2004 | 49.6% | 48.7% | 49.5% | 1.8% | 12,649 |
| | 2002 | 47.4% | 46.2% | 51.1% | 2.7% | 16,428 |
| | 2000 | 50.2% | 49.0% | 48.7% | 2.3% | 11,649 |
| | 1998 | 49.4% | 47.8% | 49.0% | 3.2% | 9,774 |
| | 1996 | 50.5% | 49.5% | 48.5% | 1.9% | 15,354 |
| | 1994 | 47.4% | 46.6% | 51.7% | 1.7% | 10,306 |
| | 1992 | 53.9% | 52.6% | 44.9% | 2.5% | 13,724 |
| | 1990 | 53.8% | 52.2% | 44.8% | 2.9% | 18,713 |
| | 1988 | 54.1% | 51.5% | 43.7% | 4.8% | 10,458 |
| | 1986 | 52.4% | 50.0% | 45.3% | 4.7% | 8,733 |
| | 1984 | 48.9% | 48.3% | 50.5% | 1.2% | 8,537 |
| | 1982 | 56.5% | 55.6% | 42.8% | 1.6% | 7,430 |
| | 1980 | 52.0% | 51.3% | 47.3% | 1.3% | 9,427 |
| | 1978 | 54.4% | 52.9% | 44.4% | 2.6% | 8,238 |
| | 1976 | 57.6% | 56.9% | 41.8% | 1.3% | 12,520 |
| | Average | 51.9% | 50.6% | 47.0% | 2.4% | |

## Table 5.2 *(Continued)*

**Question Wording for House Vote** (Coded: Democratic Vote = 1; Republican Vote = 2; Third-Party Vote = 3; Did Not Vote = 4):

**1976 and 1980:** "Did you vote for the Republican or Democratic candidate for the U.S. House of Representatives? . . . Democratic (1); Republican (2); Some other party (3); Didn't vote for House (4)"

**1978:** "Who did you just vote for in the election for the U.S. House of Representatives? . . . The Democratic candidate (1); The Republican candidate (2); Other candidate (3); Didn't vote for House (4)"

**1982:** "In the election for the U.S. House of Representatives in this district, who did you just vote for? . . . Democratic candidate (1); Republican candidate (2); Other candidate (3); Did not vote for U.S. House (4)"

**1984:** "In the election for the U.S. House of Representatives in this district, who did you just vote for? . . . The Democratic candidate (1); The Republican candidate (2); Other candidate (3); Did not vote for U.S. House (4)"

**1986:** "In the election for the U.S. House of Representatives, who did you just vote for? . . . [Name] (Democrat) (1); [Name] (Republican) (2); Someone else (3); Didn't vote (4)"

**1988:** "In the election for the U.S. House of Representatives in this district, who did you just vote for? . . . [Name] (Dem) (1); [Name] (Rep) (2); Someone else (3); Didn't vote for House (4)"

**1990:** "In today's election to represent your congressional district in the U.S. House of Representatives, did you just vote for . . . [Name] (Dem) (1); [Name] (Rep) (2); [Name] (Ind) (3); Other: Who? (3); Did not vote for U.S. House of Representatives (4)"

**1992:** "In today's election for U.S. House of Representatives, did you just vote for . . . (Dem) (1); (Rep) (2); (Ind) (3); Other: Who? (3); Didn't vote for U.S. House (4)"

**1994:** "In today's election for U.S. House of Representatives, did you just vote for . . . The Democratic candidate (1); The Republican candidate (2); Other: Who? (3); Didn't vote for U.S. House of Representatives (4)"

**1996:** "In today's election for U.S. House of Representatives, did you just vote for . . . The Democratic candidate (1); The Republican candidate (2); Other: Who? (3); Didn't vote for U.S. House (4)"

**1998–2006:** "In today's election for U.S. House of Representatives, did you just vote for . . . The Democratic candidate (1); The Republican candidate (2); Other: Who? (3); Did not vote for U.S. House (4)"

**2008–2010:** "In today's election for U.S. House of Representatives, did you just vote for . . . The Democratic candidate (1); The Republican candidate (2); Other: Who? (3); Did not vote (4)"

*Source:* National exit polls. See the section in Chapter 2 entitled "Creating a Cumulative National Data Set: Selecting Exit Polls" (pp. 28–29).

*Note:* When using these results to make inferences about the active electorate, the standard errors should be calculated using Table 2.2 (p. 36), which is explained in the adjacent section of Chapter 2, "Analyzing Exit Poll Questions: Estimating Sampling Error" (pp. 34–36). For a guide on how to understand the tables and figures of this chapter, see the section in Chapter 2 entitled "Presenting and Discussing the Exit Poll Data: Reading Chapter 5" (pp. 43–46). The rationale for using two-party percentages to show trends over time is given in Chapter 4, in the section entitled "Presidential Vote Choice" (pp. 124–131).

**Table 5.3** Composition of the Exit Polls by House Vote Based on President, 1982–2010

| Year | For President | Not a Factor | Against President | Number of Respondents |
|------|--------------|--------------|-------------------|----------------------|
| 2010 | 23.5% | 39.1% | 37.4% | 4,461 |
| 2008 | | | | |
| 2006 | 22.2% | 40.9% | 36.9% | 6,658 |
| 2004 | | | | |
| 2002 | 36.6% | 45.3% | 18.2% | 8,341 |
| 2000 | 10.0% | 71.9% | 18.1% | 6,467 |
| 1998 | 18.0% | 61.6% | 20.4% | 5,397 |
| 1996 | | | | |
| 1994 | 17.4% | 55.1% | 27.5% | 5,462 |
| 1992 | | | | |
| 1990 | 19.6% | 64.2% | 16.2% | 9,043 |
| 1988 | | | | |
| 1986 | | | | |
| 1984 | | | | |
| 1982 | 35.1% | 24.8% | 40.1% | 7,371 |
| Average | 22.8% | 50.4% | 26.8% | |

**Question Wording for House Vote Based on President** (Coded: For President = 1; Not a Factor = 2; Against President = 3):

**1982:** "Do you think of your vote for U.S. House today as a vote for or against [President] . . . For Reagan (1); Against Reagan (3); Reagan not a factor (2)"

**1990:** "Was one of the reasons for your vote for Congress today . . . To express support for George Bush (1); To express opposition for George Bush (3); Bush was not a factor (2)"

**1994:** "Was one of the reasons for your vote for Congress today . . . To express support for Bill Clinton (1); To express opposition for Bill Clinton (3); Bill Clinton was not a factor in your vote (2)"

**1998:** "Was one reason for your vote for Congress today . . . To express support for Bill Clinton (1); To express opposition for Bill Clinton (3); Clinton was not a factor (2)"

**2000:** "Was one reason for your vote for Congress today . . . To express support for Bill Clinton (1); To express opposition for Bill Clinton (3); Bill Clinton was not a factor (2)"

**2002–2006:** "Was one reason for your vote for Congress today . . . To express support for George W. Bush (1); To express opposition for George W. Bush (3); George W. Bush was not a factor (2)"

**2010:** "Was one reason for your vote for Congress today . . . To express support for Barack Obama (1); To express opposition to Barack Obama (3); Barack Obama was not a factor (2)"

*Source:* National exit polls. See the section in Chapter 2 entitled "Creating a Cumulative National Data Set: Selecting Exit Polls" (pp. 28–29).

*Note:* When using these results to make inferences about the active electorate, the standard errors should be calculated using Table 2.2 (p. 36), which is explained in the adjacent section of Chapter 2, "Analyzing Exit Poll Questions: Estimating Sampling Error" (pp. 34–36). For a guide on how to understand the tables and figures of this chapter, see the section in Chapter 2 entitled "Presenting and Discussing the Exit Poll Data: Reading Chapter 5" (pp. 43–46). The rationale for using two-party percentages to show trends over time is given in Chapter 4, in the section entitled "Presidential Vote Choice" (pp. 124–131).

**Table 5.4**  House Vote by House Vote Based on President, 1982–2010

| Category | Year | Two-Party House Vote | | Full House Vote | | | |
|---|---|---|---|---|---|---|---|
| | | Two-Party Democratic Vote | Difference from Mean Democratic Two-Party Vote | Democratic Vote | Republican Vote | Third-Party Vote | Number of Respondents |
| For President | 2010 | 97.1% | 50.6% | 95.8% | 2.8% | 1.3% | 1,099 |
| | 2008 | | | | | | |
| | 2006 | 6.5% | −47.5% | 6.4% | 92.9% | 0.7% | 1,351 |
| | 2004 | | | | | | |
| | 2002 | 10.4% | −37.0% | 10.3% | 88.6% | 1.1% | 2,757 |
| | 2000 | 92.1% | 41.9% | 90.7% | 7.8% | 1.6% | 582 |
| | 1998 | 88.7% | 39.3% | 87.3% | 11.1% | 1.6% | 901 |
| | 1996 | | | | | | |
| | 1994 | 94.3% | 46.9% | 93.5% | 5.7% | 0.9% | 896 |
| | 1992 | | | | | | |
| | 1990 | 25.5% | −28.3% | 25.2% | 73.6% | 1.2% | 1,704 |
| | 1988 | | | | | | |
| | 1986 | | | | | | |
| | 1984 | | | | | | |
| | 1982 | 12.4% | −44.2% | 12.2% | 86.6% | 1.1% | 2,557 |
| | Average | 53.4% | 2.7% | 52.7% | 46.1% | 1.2% | |
| Not a Factor | 2010 | 54.0% | 7.9% | 51.9% | 44.3% | 3.8% | 1,684 |
| | 2008 | | | | | | |
| | 2006 | 42.3% | −11.6% | 41.4% | 56.3% | 2.3% | 2,535 |
| | 2004 | | | | | | |
| | 2002 | 57.2% | 9.7% | 54.8% | 41.1% | 4.1% | 3,579 |
| | 2000 | 53.7% | 3.6% | 52.4% | 45.1% | 2.6% | 4,077 |
| | 1998 | 52.0% | 2.6% | 50.2% | 46.3% | 3.5% | 2,787 |
| | 1996 | | | | | | |
| | 1994 | 53.2% | 5.8% | 51.9% | 45.7% | 2.5% | 2,736 |
| | 1992 | | | | | | |
| | 1990 | 54.2% | 0.4% | 52.5% | 44.3% | 3.1% | 5,606 |
| | 1988 | | | | | | |
| | 1986 | | | | | | |
| | 1984 | | | | | | |
| | 1982 | 60.4% | 3.9% | 58.7% | 38.4% | 2.8% | 1,827 |
| | Average | 53.4% | 2.8% | 51.7% | 45.2% | 3.1% | |
| Against President | 2010 | 6.1% | −40.2% | 5.9% | 91.9% | 2.2% | 1,551 |
| | 2008 | | | | | | |
| | 2006 | 94.8% | 40.8% | 93.1% | 5.2% | 1.8% | 2,518 |
| | 2004 | | | | | | |
| | 2002 | 92.9% | 45.5% | 89.8% | 6.8% | 3.4% | 1,516 |
| | 2000 | 11.8% | −38.4% | 11.4% | 85.2% | 3.4% | 1,031 |
| | 1998 | 7.1% | −42.3% | 6.9% | 90.1% | 3.0% | 980 |

*(Continued)*

**Table 5.4**  House Vote by House Vote Based on President, 1982–2010 *(Continued)*

| | | Two-Party House Vote | | Full House Vote | | | |
|---|---|---|---|---|---|---|---|
| Category | Year | Two-Party Democratic Vote | Difference from Mean Democratic Two-Party Vote | Democratic Vote | Republican Vote | Third-Party Vote | Number of Respondents |
| Against President | 1996 | | | | | | |
| | 1994 | 6.2% | –41.2% | 6.1% | 92.6% | 1.3% | 1,422 |
| | 1992 | | | | | | |
| | 1990 | 79.6% | 25.7% | 76.1% | 19.6% | 4.3% | 1,271 |
| | 1988 | | | | | | |
| | 1986 | | | | | | |
| | 1984 | | | | | | |
| | 1982 | 92.3% | 35.8% | 91.2% | 7.6% | 1.3% | 2,876 |
| | Average | 48.8% | –1.8% | 47.5% | 49.9% | 2.6% | |

**Question Wording for Rationale for House Vote** (Coded: For President = 1; Not a Factor = 2; Against President = 3):

**1982**: "Do you think of your vote for U.S. House today as a vote for or against [President] . . . For Reagan (1); Against Reagan (3); Reagan not a factor (2)"

**1990**: "Was one of the reasons for your vote for Congress today . . . To express support for George Bush (1); To express opposition for George Bush (3); Bush was not a factor (2)"

**1994**: "Was one of the reasons for your vote for Congress today . . . To express support for Bill Clinton (1); To express opposition for Bill Clinton (3); Bill Clinton was not a factor in your vote (2)"

**1998**: "Was one reason for your vote for Congress today . . . To express support for Bill Clinton (1); To express opposition for Bill Clinton (3); Clinton was not a factor (2)"

**2000**: "Was one reason for your vote for Congress today . . . To express support for Bill Clinton (1); To express opposition for Bill Clinton (3); Bill Clinton was not a factor (2)"

**2002–2006**: "Was one reason for your vote for Congress today . . . To express support for George W. Bush (1); To express opposition for George W. Bush (3); George W. Bush was not a factor (2)"

**2010**: "Was one reason for your vote for Congress today . . . To express support for Barack Obama (1); To express opposition to Barack Obama (3); Barack Obama was not a factor (2)"

*Source:* National exit polls. See the section in Chapter 2 entitled "Creating a Cumulative National Data Set: Selecting Exit Polls" (pp. 28–29).

*Note:* When using these results to make inferences about the active electorate, the standard errors should be calculated using Table 2.2 (p. 36), which is explained in the adjacent section of Chapter 2, "Analyzing Exit Poll Questions: Estimating Sampling Error" (pp. 34–36). For a guide on how to understand the tables and figures of this chapter, see the section in Chapter 2 entitled "Presenting and Discussing the Exit Poll Data: Reading Chapter 5" (pp. 43–46). The rationale for using two-party percentages to show trends over time is given in Chapter 4, in the section entitled "Presidential Vote Choice" (pp. 124–131).

**Table 5.5** House Vote by Race, 1982–2010

| Category | Year | Two-Party House Vote | | Full House Vote | | | |
|---|---|---|---|---|---|---|---|
| | | Two-Party Democratic Vote | Difference from Mean Democratic Two-Party Vote | Democratic Vote | Republican Vote | Third-Party Vote | Number of Respondents |
| White | 2010 | 37.7% | −8.6% | 36.5% | 60.3% | 3.2% | 13,730 |
| | 2008 | 45.8% | −9.3% | 44.7% | 52.9% | 2.4% | 11,796 |
| | 2006 | 47.5% | −6.4% | 46.6% | 51.4% | 2.0% | 10,441 |
| | 2004 | 42.4% | −7.2% | 41.6% | 56.5% | 1.9% | 9,967 |
| | 2002 | 40.2% | −7.3% | 39.1% | 58.1% | 2.8% | 13,068 |
| | 2000 | 44.0% | −6.2% | 42.9% | 54.7% | 2.5% | 9,267 |
| | 1998 | 43.1% | −6.3% | 41.7% | 55.1% | 3.2% | 8,017 |
| | 1996 | 44.9% | −5.6% | 44.0% | 54.0% | 2.0% | 12,191 |
| | 1994 | 42.0% | −5.4% | 41.3% | 57.1% | 1.7% | 8,810 |
| | 1992 | 49.9% | −4.0% | 48.6% | 48.8% | 2.6% | 11,533 |
| | 1990 | 51.6% | −2.2% | 50.1% | 46.9% | 3.0% | 16,869 |
| | 1988 | 49.5% | −4.6% | 47.2% | 48.1% | 4.7% | 8,550 |
| | 1986 | 48.9% | −3.6% | 46.7% | 48.9% | 4.4% | 7,219 |
| | 1984 | 43.7% | −5.2% | 43.1% | 55.6% | 1.2% | 7,130 |
| | 1982 | 53.5% | −3.0% | 52.7% | 45.8% | 1.6% | 6,543 |
| | Average | 45.6% | −5.7% | 44.4% | 52.9% | 2.6% | |
| Black | 2010 | 91.0% | 44.7% | 89.5% | 8.9% | 1.6% | 1,743 |
| | 2008 | 94.3% | 39.2% | 92.6% | 5.6% | 1.8% | 2,486 |
| | 2006 | 89.4% | 35.4% | 88.5% | 10.5% | 1.0% | 1,460 |
| | 2004 | 88.8% | 39.2% | 87.9% | 11.1% | 1.0% | 1,435 |
| | 2002 | 90.9% | 43.4% | 89.5% | 9.0% | 1.5% | 1,789 |
| | 2000 | 88.4% | 38.2% | 87.4% | 11.5% | 1.1% | 1,369 |
| | 1998 | 88.2% | 38.9% | 87.1% | 11.6% | 1.3% | 1,169 |
| | 1996 | 82.1% | 31.6% | 81.4% | 17.7% | 0.9% | 1,950 |
| | 1994 | 91.7% | 44.3% | 90.5% | 8.2% | 1.2% | 897 |
| | 1992 | 88.9% | 35.0% | 87.4% | 10.9% | 1.7% | 1,396 |
| | 1990 | 79.9% | 26.1% | 78.4% | 19.7% | 1.9% | 935 |
| | 1988 | 85.3% | 31.2% | 80.7% | 13.9% | 5.4% | 1,311 |
| | 1986 | 86.2% | 33.8% | 80.3% | 12.8% | 6.9% | 1,151 |
| | 1984 | 92.3% | 43.4% | 91.5% | 7.6% | 0.9% | 1,055 |
| | 1982 | 88.5% | 32.0% | 86.6% | 11.2% | 2.2% | 603 |
| | Average | 88.4% | 37.1% | 86.6% | 11.4% | 2.0% | |
| Hispanic/ Latino | 2010 | 61.2% | 14.9% | 60.0% | 38.1% | 1.9% | 1,218 |
| | 2008 | 72.2% | 17.1% | 71.0% | 27.4% | 1.6% | 991 |
| | 2006 | 73.9% | 19.9% | 73.0% | 25.8% | 1.2% | 612 |
| | 2004 | 58.5% | 8.9% | 58.1% | 41.2% | 0.7% | 656 |
| | 2002 | 65.7% | 18.2% | 64.4% | 33.7% | 2.0% | 741 |
| | 2000 | 71.0% | 20.8% | 70.4% | 28.8% | 0.9% | 460 |
| | 1998 | 72.7% | 23.3% | 68.7% | 25.8% | 5.5% | 242 |
| | 1996 | 72.7% | 22.2% | 71.7% | 27.0% | 1.3% | 667 |

*(Continued)*

**Table 5.5**   House Vote by Race, 1982–2010  *(Continued)*

| Category | Year | Two-Party House Vote | | Full House Vote | | | |
|---|---|---|---|---|---|---|---|
| | | Two-Party Democratic Vote | Difference from Mean Democratic Two-Party Vote | Democratic Vote | Republican Vote | Third-Party Vote | Number of Respondents |
| Hispanic/ | 1994 | 61.2% | 13.8% | 58.9% | 37.3% | 3.8% | 351 |
| Latino | 1992 | 72.1% | 18.2% | 70.3% | 27.2% | 2.6% | 378 |
| | 1990 | 72.3% | 18.5% | 71.0% | 27.1% | 1.9% | 395 |
| | 1988 | 76.3% | 22.2% | 73.0% | 22.7% | 4.3% | 392 |
| | 1986 | 75.2% | 22.8% | 69.7% | 22.9% | 7.4% | 173 |
| | 1984 | 67.6% | 18.7% | 66.0% | 31.6% | 2.4% | 217 |
| | 1982 | 75.4% | 18.8% | 73.8% | 24.1% | 2.1% | 173 |
| | Average | 69.9% | 18.6% | 68.0% | 29.4% | 2.6% | |
| | | | | | | | |
| Asian | 2010 | 59.1% | 12.8% | 57.7% | 39.9% | 2.4% | 248 |
| | 2008 | 65.7% | 10.6% | 62.2% | 32.5% | 5.3% | 369 |
| | 2006 | 62.4% | 8.5% | 61.9% | 37.2% | 0.9% | 209 |
| | 2004 | 55.2% | 5.6% | 53.8% | 43.7% | 2.5% | 196 |
| | 2002 | 65.9% | 18.5% | 64.5% | 33.3% | 2.2% | 210 |
| | 2000 | 59.2% | 9.0% | 57.9% | 40.0% | 2.1% | 191 |
| | 1998 | 53.6% | 4.2% | 50.7% | 43.8% | 5.5% | 129 |
| | 1996 | 43.2% | −7.3% | 40.5% | 53.2% | 6.3% | 150 |
| | 1994 | 54.3% | 6.9% | 52.7% | 44.3% | 3.1% | 98 |
| | 1992 | 49.6% | −4.3% | 48.1% | 48.8% | 3.1% | 134 |
| | 1990 | 63.4% | 9.6% | 62.3% | 36.0% | 1.7% | 192 |
| | 1988 | | | | | | |
| | 1986 | | | | | | |
| | 1984 | | | | | | |
| | 1982 | | | | | | |
| | Average | 57.4% | 6.7% | 55.7% | 41.2% | 3.2% | |
| | | | | | | | |
| Other | 2010 | 54.4% | 8.1% | 52.7% | 44.2% | 3.1% | 325 |
| Race | 2008 | 73.8% | 18.7% | 70.4% | 25.0% | 4.6% | 515 |
| | 2006 | 59.7% | 5.8% | 57.5% | 38.8% | 3.8% | 247 |
| | 2004 | 54.6% | 5.0% | 52.5% | 43.6% | 3.9% | 214 |
| | 2002 | 75.3% | 27.9% | 72.5% | 23.8% | 3.7% | 306 |
| | 2000 | 61.5% | 11.3% | 59.1% | 37.1% | 3.8% | 204 |
| | 1998 | 61.3% | 11.9% | 57.1% | 36.1% | 6.8% | 115 |
| | 1996 | 72.0% | 21.5% | 68.9% | 26.8% | 4.4% | 193 |
| | 1994 | 54.4% | 7.0% | 52.4% | 43.9% | 3.7% | 78 |
| | 1992 | 67.8% | 13.8% | 65.2% | 31.0% | 3.8% | 174 |
| | 1990 | 67.5% | 13.7% | 63.4% | 30.5% | 6.1% | 186 |
| | 1988 | 62.1% | 8.0% | 56.3% | 34.4% | 9.4% | 152 |
| | 1986 | 50.5% | −1.9% | 47.9% | 46.9% | 5.2% | 160 |
| | 1984 | 65.1% | 16.2% | 64.4% | 34.5% | 1.1% | 93 |
| | 1982 | 69.1% | 12.6% | 67.5% | 30.1% | 2.4% | 88 |
| | Average | 63.3% | 12.0% | 60.5% | 35.1% | 4.4% | |

**Table 5.5**   *(Continued)*

**Question Wording for Race** (Coded: White = 1; Black = 2; Hispanic/Latino = 3; Asian = 4; Other Race = 5):

**1982–1984 and 1988:** "Are you . . . White (1); Black (2); Hispanic (3); Other (5)"

**1986:** "Are you . . . White (1); Black (2); Hispanic or Latino (3); Other (5)"

**1990 and 1996:** "Are you . . . White (1); Black (2); Hispanic or Latino (3); Asian (4); Other (5)"

**1992–1994 and 1998–2002:** "Are you . . . White (1); Black (2); Hispanic/Latino (3); Asian (4); Other (5)"

**2004–2010:** "Are you . . . White (1); Black (2); Hispanic/Latino (3); Asian (4); Other (5); American Indian (5); Native Alaskan (5)"

*Source:* National exit polls. See the section in Chapter 2 entitled "Creating a Cumulative National Data Set: Selecting Exit Polls" (pp. 28–29).

*Note:* When using these results to make inferences about the active electorate, the standard errors should be calculated using Table 2.2 (p. 36), which is explained in the adjacent section of Chapter 2, "Analyzing Exit Poll Questions: Estimating Sampling Error" (pp. 34–36). For a guide on how to understand the tables and figures of this chapter, see the section in Chapter 2 entitled "Presenting and Discussing the Exit Poll Data: Reading Chapter 5" (pp. 43–46). The rationale for using two-party percentages to show trends over time is given in Chapter 4, in the section entitled "Presidential Vote Choice" (pp. 124–131).

**Table 5.6**  House Vote by Gender, 1976–2010

| Category | Year | Two-Party House Vote | | Full House Vote | | | |
| | | Two-Party Democratic Vote | Difference from Mean Democratic Two-Party Vote | Democratic Vote | Republican Vote | Third-Party Vote | Number of Respondents |
|---|---|---|---|---|---|---|---|
| Male | 2010 | 42.8% | −3.5% | 41.5% | 55.5% | 3.1% | 8,270 |
| | 2008 | 53.0% | −2.1% | 51.7% | 45.9% | 2.5% | 7,119 |
| | 2006 | 51.7% | −2.3% | 50.5% | 47.2% | 2.3% | 6,080 |
| | 2004 | 45.6% | −4.0% | 44.7% | 53.3% | 2.0% | 5,567 |
| | 2002 | 44.1% | −3.3% | 42.8% | 54.1% | 3.2% | 7,516 |
| | 2000 | 45.1% | −5.1% | 43.9% | 53.5% | 2.6% | 5,484 |
| | 1998 | 46.2% | −3.2% | 44.6% | 51.9% | 3.5% | 4,698 |
| | 1996 | 45.8% | −4.7% | 44.8% | 53.1% | 2.1% | 7,102 |
| | 1994 | 41.6% | −5.8% | 40.8% | 57.3% | 2.0% | 4,996 |
| | 1992 | 52.2% | −1.8% | 50.8% | 46.6% | 2.6% | 6,267 |
| | 1990 | 52.1% | −1.7% | 50.5% | 46.4% | 3.1% | 8,908 |
| | 1988 | 51.5% | −2.6% | 49.1% | 46.2% | 4.7% | 4,952 |
| | 1986 | 50.8% | −1.6% | 48.5% | 47.0% | 4.5% | 4,167 |
| | 1984 | 46.3% | −2.6% | 45.6% | 52.8% | 1.6% | 4,087 |
| | 1982 | 54.7% | −1.8% | 53.7% | 44.5% | 1.9% | 3,662 |
| | 1980 | 49.2% | −2.8% | 48.5% | 50.1% | 1.5% | 4,645 |
| | 1978 | 53.8% | −0.5% | 52.3% | 44.9% | 2.8% | 4,373 |
| | 1976 | 58.0% | 0.4% | 57.2% | 41.3% | 1.5% | 6,247 |
| | Average | 49.1% | −2.7% | 47.8% | 49.5% | 2.6% | |
| Female | 2010 | 49.5% | 3.2% | 48.1% | 49.1% | 2.8% | 9,195 |
| | 2008 | 57.0% | 1.9% | 55.6% | 42.0% | 2.5% | 9,327 |
| | 2006 | 56.0% | 2.0% | 55.1% | 43.3% | 1.5% | 7,091 |
| | 2004 | 52.9% | 3.3% | 52.1% | 46.3% | 1.6% | 7,030 |
| | 2002 | 50.2% | 2.7% | 49.0% | 48.7% | 2.3% | 8,782 |
| | 2000 | 54.5% | 4.3% | 53.4% | 44.6% | 2.0% | 6,024 |
| | 1998 | 52.6% | 3.2% | 51.1% | 46.0% | 2.9% | 4,973 |
| | 1996 | 54.7% | 4.2% | 53.7% | 44.5% | 1.8% | 8,056 |
| | 1994 | 52.7% | 5.3% | 51.9% | 46.5% | 1.5% | 5,206 |
| | 1992 | 55.5% | 1.6% | 54.2% | 43.5% | 2.2% | 6,938 |
| | 1990 | 55.3% | 1.5% | 53.8% | 43.5% | 2.7% | 9,467 |
| | 1988 | 56.5% | 2.4% | 53.7% | 41.4% | 4.9% | 5,488 |
| | 1986 | 54.0% | 1.5% | 51.3% | 43.8% | 4.9% | 4,540 |
| | 1984 | 51.5% | 2.6% | 51.1% | 48.1% | 0.9% | 4,429 |
| | 1982 | 58.3% | 1.8% | 57.5% | 41.1% | 1.4% | 3,725 |
| | 1980 | 55.1% | 3.0% | 54.4% | 44.4% | 1.1% | 4,775 |
| | 1978 | 55.0% | 0.6% | 54.1% | 44.3% | 1.5% | 3,855 |
| | 1976 | 57.1% | −0.5% | 56.5% | 42.4% | 1.1% | 6,198 |
| | Average | 54.4% | 2.5% | 53.2% | 44.6% | 2.2% | |

**Question Wording for Gender** (Coded: Male = 1; Female = 2):

**1972–1980:** "Interviewer recorded sex of respondent . . . Male (1); Female (2)"

**1982–2010:** "Are you . . . Male (2); Female (2)"

*Source:* National exit polls. See the section in Chapter 2 entitled "Creating a Cumulative National Data Set: Selecting Exit Polls" (pp. 28–29).

*Note:* When using these results to make inferences about the active electorate, the standard errors should be calculated using Table 2.2 (p. 36), which is explained in the adjacent section of Chapter 2, "Analyzing Exit Poll Questions: Estimating Sampling Error" (pp. 34–36). For a guide on how to understand the tables and figures of this chapter, see the section in Chapter 2 entitled "Presenting and Discussing the Exit Poll Data: Reading Chapter 5" (pp. 43–46). The rationale for using two-party percentages to show trends over time is given in Chapter 4, in the section entitled "Presidential Vote Choice" (pp. 124–131).

**Table 5.7** House Vote by Age, 1976–2010

| Category | Year | Two-Party House Vote | | Full House Vote | | | |
|---|---|---|---|---|---|---|---|
| | | Two-Party Democratic Vote | Difference from Mean Democratic Two-Party Vote | Democratic Vote | Republican Vote | Third-Party Vote | Number of Respondents |
| 18–29 | 2010 | 57.0% | 10.7% | 55.2% | 41.6% | 3.1% | 1,971 |
| | 2008 | 64.8% | 9.7% | 63.2% | 34.4% | 2.3% | 3,369 |
| | 2006 | 60.9% | 6.9% | 59.6% | 38.3% | 2.0% | 1,535 |
| | 2004 | 55.5% | 5.9% | 54.7% | 43.8% | 1.5% | 2,320 |
| | 2002 | 50.7% | 3.3% | 48.7% | 47.3% | 4.0% | 1,705 |
| | 2000 | 50.7% | 0.6% | 49.3% | 47.9% | 2.8% | 1,952 |
| | 1998 | 49.8% | 0.4% | 47.5% | 47.9% | 4.6% | 1,189 |
| | 1996 | 55.6% | 5.1% | 54.7% | 43.6% | 1.8% | 2,858 |
| | 1994 | 49.4% | 2.0% | 48.2% | 49.4% | 2.4% | 1,475 |
| | 1992 | 55.0% | 1.1% | 53.7% | 43.9% | 2.4% | 2,891 |
| | 1990 | 53.0% | −0.8% | 51.4% | 45.6% | 3.0% | 2,454 |
| | 1988 | 53.7% | −0.3% | 50.9% | 43.8% | 5.3% | 2,145 |
| | 1986 | 51.3% | −1.1% | 48.4% | 45.9% | 5.7% | 1,492 |
| | 1984 | 48.6% | −0.4% | 47.4% | 50.3% | 2.3% | 2,107 |
| | 1982 | 58.7% | 2.2% | 58.0% | 40.8% | 1.2% | 1,288 |
| | 1980 | 55.2% | 3.2% | 54.2% | 43.9% | 1.8% | 2,305 |
| | 1978 | 58.2% | 3.9% | 56.2% | 40.3% | 3.6% | 1,679 |
| | 1976 | 61.5% | 3.9% | 60.3% | 37.7% | 1.9% | 3,374 |
| | Average | 55.0% | 3.1% | 53.4% | 43.7% | 2.9% | |
| 30–44 | 2010 | 48.2% | 1.9% | 46.2% | 49.6% | 4.3% | 4,415 |
| | 2008 | 54.5% | −0.5% | 53.2% | 44.3% | 2.5% | 3,422 |
| | 2006 | 53.7% | −0.3% | 52.7% | 45.4% | 1.9% | 2,412 |
| | 2004 | 47.9% | −1.7% | 47.1% | 51.1% | 1.8% | 2,845 |
| | 2002 | 45.2% | −2.3% | 43.8% | 53.2% | 3.0% | 2,438 |
| | 2000 | 48.6% | −1.6% | 47.4% | 50.2% | 2.3% | 2,964 |
| | 1998 | 50.2% | 0.8% | 48.9% | 48.6% | 2.6% | 2,990 |
| | 1996 | 49.5% | −1.0% | 48.5% | 49.4% | 2.2% | 3,961 |
| | 1994 | 45.9% | −1.5% | 45.0% | 53.0% | 2.0% | 7,067 |
| | 1992 | 53.0% | −0.9% | 51.4% | 45.6% | 3.0% | 5,216 |
| | 1990 | 54.6% | 0.8% | 52.7% | 43.9% | 3.5% | 3,468 |
| | 1988 | 54.0% | 0.0% | 51.3% | 43.6% | 5.1% | 5,369 |
| | 1986 | 52.0% | −0.4% | 49.6% | 45.8% | 4.6% | 3,101 |
| | 1984 | 51.8% | 2.9% | 51.0% | 47.5% | 1.5% | 4,086 |
| | 1982 | 54.4% | −2.2% | 53.4% | 44.8% | 1.8% | 4,968 |
| | 1980 | 49.0% | −3.0% | 48.3% | 50.3% | 1.4% | 3,842 |
| | 1978 | 55.8% | 1.5% | 53.8% | 42.6% | 3.6% | 3,337 |
| | 1976 | 58.4% | 0.8% | 57.6% | 41.0% | 1.4% | 4,724 |
| | Average | 51.5% | −0.4% | 50.1% | 47.2% | 2.7% | |
| 45–59 | 2010 | 45.1% | −1.2% | 44.2% | 53.8% | 2.0% | 6,096 |
| | 2008 | 52.1% | −3.0% | 50.8% | 46.7% | 2.5% | 5,226 |

*(Continued)*

**Table 5.7**  House Vote by Age, 1976–2010 *(Continued)*

| | | Two-Party House Vote | | Full House Vote | | | |
|---|---|---|---|---|---|---|---|
| Category | Year | Two-Party Democratic Vote | Difference from Mean Democratic Two-Party Vote | Democratic Vote | Republican Vote | Third-Party Vote | Number of Respondents |
| 45–59 | 2006 | 53.6% | −0.4% | 52.6% | 45.6% | 1.8% | 4,658 |
| | 2004 | 50.2% | 0.6% | 49.3% | 48.9% | 1.8% | 3,952 |
| | 2002 | 46.8% | −0.6% | 45.7% | 51.9% | 2.4% | 5,803 |
| | 2000 | 50.4% | 0.3% | 49.4% | 48.6% | 2.0% | 3,557 |
| | 1998 | 52.3% | 2.9% | 50.2% | 45.9% | 4.0% | 3,154 |
| | 1996 | 50.0% | −0.5% | 48.9% | 48.9% | 2.2% | 4,255 |
| | 1994 | 46.7% | −0.7% | 45.9% | 52.3% | 1.8% | 3,001 |
| | 1992 | 52.0% | −2.0% | 50.8% | 46.9% | 2.3% | 3,343 |
| | 1990 | 52.3% | −1.5% | 50.7% | 46.2% | 3.1% | 4,954 |
| | 1988 | 53.5% | −0.5% | 51.0% | 44.3% | 4.7% | 2,474 |
| | 1986 | 53.9% | 1.5% | 51.5% | 43.9% | 4.6% | 2,219 |
| | 1984 | 47.9% | −1.0% | 47.6% | 51.8% | 0.6% | 1,963 |
| | 1982 | 56.3% | −0.2% | 55.3% | 42.9% | 1.8% | 1,931 |
| | 1980 | 52.7% | 0.7% | 52.3% | 46.9% | 0.8% | 2,086 |
| | 1978 | 54.2% | −0.1% | 53.3% | 45.0% | 1.8% | 2,108 |
| | 1976 | 55.5% | −2.2% | 54.9% | 44.1% | 1.0% | 3,031 |
| | Average | 51.4% | −0.4% | 50.2% | 47.5% | 2.3% | |
| 60+ | 2010 | 42.4% | −3.9% | 41.3% | 56.1% | 2.6% | 4,971 |
| | 2008 | 51.8% | −3.2% | 50.5% | 47.0% | 2.5% | 3,095 |
| | 2006 | 51.5% | −2.5% | 50.5% | 47.5% | 2.0% | 3,633 |
| | 2004 | 46.4% | −3.2% | 45.6% | 52.8% | 1.6% | 2,492 |
| | 2002 | 49.1% | 1.6% | 48.0% | 49.9% | 2.1% | 3,888 |
| | 2000 | 51.7% | 1.6% | 50.7% | 47.3% | 2.0% | 2,021 |
| | 1998 | 45.0% | −4.4% | 43.9% | 53.7% | 2.3% | 2,287 |
| | 1996 | 48.7% | −1.8% | 48.0% | 50.6% | 1.5% | 2,801 |
| | 1994 | 48.5% | 1.1% | 48.0% | 51.0% | 1.0% | 2,325 |
| | 1992 | 56.4% | 2.5% | 55.4% | 42.7% | 1.9% | 2,225 |
| | 1990 | 54.4% | 0.6% | 53.3% | 44.7% | 2.1% | 4,164 |
| | 1988 | 54.8% | 0.7% | 52.7% | 43.4% | 3.9% | 1,849 |
| | 1986 | 52.1% | −0.3% | 49.8% | 45.8% | 4.3% | 1,984 |
| | 1984 | 46.1% | −2.8% | 45.9% | 53.6% | 0.4% | 1,464 |
| | 1982 | 57.9% | 1.4% | 57.0% | 41.5% | 1.5% | 1,746 |
| | 1980 | 50.6% | −1.4% | 50.2% | 49.0% | 0.8% | 1,508 |
| | 1978 | 49.0% | −5.3% | 48.3% | 50.1% | 1.6% | 1,427 |
| | 1976 | 54.3% | −3.4% | 53.9% | 45.4% | 0.7% | 1,547 |
| | Average | 50.6% | −1.3% | 49.6% | 48.5% | 1.9% | |

**Question Wording for Age** (Coded: 18–29 = 1; 30–44 = 2; 45–59 = 3; 60+ = 4):

**1976 and 1980:** "To which age group do you belong? . . . 18–21 (1); 22–29 (1); 30–44 (2); 45–59 (3); 60 or over (4)"

**1978, 1982, and 1988:** "To which age group do you belong? . . . 18–29 (1); 30–44 (2); 45–59 (3); 60 or over (4)"

**1984–1986:** "To which age group do you belong? . . . 18–24 (1); 25–29 (1); 30–44 (2); 45–59 (3); 60 or over (4)"

## Table 5.7 *(Continued)*

**1990:** "To which age group do you belong? . . . 18–29 (1); 30–39 (2); 40–44 (2); 45–49 (3); 50–59 (3); 60 or over (4)"

**1992–1998:** "To which age group do you belong? . . . 18–24 (1); 25–29 (1); 30–39 (2); 40–44 (2); 45–49 (3); 50–59 (3); 60–64 (4); 65 or over (4)"

**2000–2010:** "To which age group do you belong? . . . 18–24 (1); 25–29 (1); 30–39 (2); 40–44 (2); 45–49 (3); 50–59 (3); 60–64 (4); 65–74 (4); 75 or over (4)"

*Source:* National exit polls. See the section in Chapter 2 entitled "Creating a Cumulative National Data Set: Selecting Exit Polls" (pp. 28–29).

*Note:* When using these results to make inferences about the active electorate, the standard errors should be calculated using Table 2.2 (p. 36), which is explained in the adjacent section of Chapter 2, "Analyzing Exit Poll Questions: Estimating Sampling Error" (pp. 34–36). For a guide on how to understand the tables and figures of this chapter, see the section in Chapter 2 entitled "Presenting and Discussing the Exit Poll Data: Reading Chapter 5" (pp. 43–46). The rationale for using two-party percentages to show trends over time is given in Chapter 4, in the section entitled "Presidential Vote Choice" (pp. 124–131).

## Table 5.8   House Vote by Sexual Orientation, 1996–2010

| Category | Year | Two-Party House Vote | | Full House Vote | | | |
| | | Two-Party Democratic Vote | Difference from Mean Democratic Two-Party Vote | Democratic Vote | Republican Vote | Third-Party Vote | Number of Respondents |
|---|---|---|---|---|---|---|---|
| Gay or | 2010 | 70.0% | 23.7% | 68.9% | 29.5% | 1.6% | 119 |
| Bisexual | 2008 | 81.1% | 26.1% | 79.8% | 18.6% | 1.6% | 139 |
| | 2006 | 75.6% | 21.6% | 74.7% | 24.2% | 1.1% | 186 |
| | 2004 | 75.9% | 26.3% | 75.1% | 23.9% | 1.0% | 210 |
| | 2002 | | | | | | |
| | 2000 | 67.5% | 17.4% | 63.9% | 30.7% | 5.4% | 223 |
| | 1998 | 66.8% | 17.5% | 65.2% | 32.3% | 2.5% | 195 |
| | 1996 | 72.0% | 21.5% | 69.5% | 26.9% | 3.6% | 181 |
| | Average | 72.7% | 22.0% | 71.0% | 26.6% | 2.4% | |
| Not Gay or | 2010 | 47.1% | 0.8% | 46.1% | 51.7% | 2.2% | 3,584 |
| Bisexual | 2008 | 54.6% | −0.5% | 53.0% | 44.2% | 2.8% | 3,632 |
| | 2006 | 52.9% | −1.1% | 51.9% | 46.3% | 1.8% | 5,624 |
| | 2004 | 48.2% | −1.4% | 47.3% | 50.9% | 1.8% | 5,741 |
| | 2002 | | | | | | |
| | 2000 | 48.2% | −1.9% | 47.1% | 50.5% | 2.4% | 5,140 |
| | 1998 | 48.2% | −1.2% | 46.8% | 50.3% | 2.9% | 4,299 |
| | 1996 | 50.1% | −0.4% | 49.3% | 49.1% | 1.6% | 3,293 |
| | Average | 49.9% | −0.8% | 48.8% | 49.0% | 2.2% | |

**Question Wording for Sexual Orientation** (Coded: Gay or Bisexual = 1; Not Gay or Bisexual = 2):

**1996–2010:** "Are you gay, lesbian, or bisexual? . . . Yes (1); No (2)"

*Source:* National exit polls. See the section in Chapter 2 entitled "Creating a Cumulative National Data Set: Selecting Exit Polls" (pp. 28–29).

*Note:* When using these results to make inferences about the active electorate, the standard errors should be calculated using Table 2.2 (p. 36), which is explained in the adjacent section of Chapter 2, "Analyzing Exit Poll Questions: Estimating Sampling Error" (pp. 34–36). For a guide on how to understand the tables and figures of this chapter, see the section in Chapter 2 entitled "Presenting and Discussing the Exit Poll Data: Reading Chapter 5" (pp. 43–46). The rationale for using two-party percentages to show trends over time is given in Chapter 4, in the section entitled "Presidential Vote Choice" (pp. 124–131).

**Table 5.9** House Vote by Region of Electoral Precinct, 1976–2010

| | | Two-Party House Vote | | Full House Vote | | | |
| | | Two-Party Democratic Vote | Difference from Mean Democratic Two-Party Vote | Democratic Vote | Republican Vote | Third-Party Vote | Number of Respondents |
|---|---|---|---|---|---|---|---|
| Category | Year | | | | | | |
| East | 2010 | 55.0% | 8.7% | 53.8% | 44.0% | 2.1% | 4,358 |
| | 2008 | 61.7% | 6.6% | 60.6% | 37.6% | 1.8% | 5,072 |
| | 2006 | 64.0% | 10.0% | 63.0% | 35.5% | 1.5% | 3,199 |
| | 2004 | 58.8% | 9.2% | 57.3% | 40.2% | 2.5% | 2,693 |
| | 2002 | 52.9% | 5.4% | 51.8% | 46.2% | 2.0% | 3,597 |
| | 2000 | 58.5% | 8.4% | 56.5% | 40.0% | 3.5% | 2,771 |
| | 1998 | 56.2% | 6.9% | 54.0% | 42.0% | 4.0% | 2,887 |
| | 1996 | 56.0% | 5.5% | 54.5% | 42.8% | 2.7% | 3,701 |
| | 1994 | 50.0% | 2.6% | 48.9% | 49.0% | 2.1% | 2,419 |
| | 1992 | 55.5% | 1.5% | 53.9% | 43.3% | 2.8% | 3,395 |
| | 1990 | 52.8% | −1.0% | 50.2% | 44.8% | 5.0% | 5,105 |
| | 1988 | 53.7% | −0.4% | 51.5% | 44.4% | 4.1% | 2,588 |
| | 1986 | | | | | | |
| | 1984 | 54.9% | 6.0% | 54.2% | 44.4% | 1.4% | 2,314 |
| | 1982 | 64.5% | 8.0% | 62.8% | 34.5% | 2.7% | 2,015 |
| | 1980 | 52.2% | 0.1% | 51.6% | 47.3% | 1.1% | 2,293 |
| | 1978 | 56.4% | 2.1% | 54.8% | 42.3% | 2.9% | 2,188 |
| | 1976 | 57.9% | 0.2% | 56.9% | 41.4% | 1.7% | 3,665 |
| | Average | 56.5% | 4.7% | 55.1% | 42.3% | 2.6% | |
| Midwest | 2010 | 45.4% | −0.9% | 43.8% | 52.6% | 3.6% | 5,556 |
| | 2008 | 53.9% | −1.1% | 52.9% | 45.2% | 1.9% | 4,516 |
| | 2006 | 52.8% | −1.2% | 52.1% | 46.6% | 1.3% | 3,534 |
| | 2004 | 49.4% | −0.2% | 48.9% | 50.0% | 1.1% | 3,413 |
| | 2002 | 47.3% | −0.2% | 46.1% | 51.5% | 2.4% | 3,909 |
| | 2000 | 49.7% | −0.5% | 49.0% | 49.7% | 1.3% | 3,154 |
| | 1998 | 46.9% | −2.4% | 46.0% | 52.0% | 2.0% | 3,013 |
| | 1996 | 50.4% | −0.1% | 49.5% | 48.7% | 1.8% | 4,198 |
| | 1994 | 45.5% | −1.9% | 45.0% | 54.0% | 1.0% | 2,617 |
| | 1992 | 52.0% | −1.9% | 50.9% | 46.9% | 2.2% | 3,605 |
| | 1990 | 54.0% | 0.2% | 53.0% | 45.1% | 1.8% | 4,026 |
| | 1988 | 55.4% | 1.3% | 53.4% | 43.0% | 3.6% | 2,927 |
| | 1986 | | | | | | |
| | 1984 | 47.5% | −1.4% | 46.9% | 51.9% | 1.2% | 2,504 |
| | 1982 | 49.3% | −7.2% | 48.9% | 50.3% | 0.8% | 2,153 |
| | 1980 | 50.4% | −1.6% | 49.9% | 49.0% | 1.1% | 2,672 |
| | 1978 | 51.1% | −3.3% | 50.0% | 47.9% | 2.1% | 2,553 |
| | 1976 | 55.1% | −2.6% | 54.5% | 44.5% | 1.0% | 2,823 |
| | Average | 50.4% | −1.5% | 49.5% | 48.8% | 1.8% | |
| South | 2010 | 37.6% | −8.7% | 36.5% | 60.6% | 2.9% | 4,558 |
| | 2008 | 49.0% | −6.1% | 47.6% | 49.6% | 2.8% | 4,299 |
| | 2006 | 46.4% | −7.6% | 45.4% | 52.5% | 2.1% | 4,090 |
| | 2004 | 43.6% | −6.0% | 43.0% | 55.6% | 1.5% | 4,162 |
| | 2002 | 42.4% | −5.0% | 41.2% | 55.9% | 2.8% | 5,476 |
| | 2000 | 44.0% | −6.1% | 43.2% | 54.9% | 1.9% | 3,291 |
| | 1998 | 45.4% | −4.0% | 44.0% | 53.0% | 3.0% | 2,562 |

**Table 5.9** *(Continued)*

| Category | Year | Two-Party House Vote | | Full House Vote | | | |
| | | Two-Party Democratic Vote | Difference from Mean Democratic Two-Party Vote | Democratic Vote | Republican Vote | Third-Party Vote | Number of Respondents |
|---|---|---|---|---|---|---|---|
| South | 1996 | 46.5% | −4.0% | 46.0% | 52.9% | 1.1% | 4,636 |
| | 1994 | 47.1% | −0.3% | 46.6% | 52.3% | 1.1% | 3,009 |
| | 1992 | 53.3% | −0.7% | 52.5% | 46.0% | 1.5% | 3,976 |
| | 1990 | 55.6% | 1.8% | 54.9% | 43.8% | 1.3% | 5,818 |
| | 1988 | 53.7% | −0.4% | 50.2% | 43.3% | 6.5% | 2,877 |
| | 1986 | | | | | | |
| | 1984 | 46.5% | −2.4% | 45.9% | 52.8% | 1.3% | 2,248 |
| | 1982 | 59.0% | 2.5% | 58.4% | 40.6% | 1.0% | 1,824 |
| | 1980 | 54.4% | 2.4% | 53.6% | 44.8% | 1.6% | 3,274 |
| | 1978 | 56.9% | 2.6% | 56.3% | 42.6% | 1.1% | 2,210 |
| | 1976 | 65.3% | 7.6% | 64.5% | 34.3% | 1.1% | 2,688 |
| | Average | 49.8% | −2.0% | 48.8% | 49.2% | 2.0% | |
| West | 2010 | 50.8% | 4.5% | 49.3% | 47.8% | 2.9% | 3,032 |
| | 2008 | 59.6% | 4.5% | 57.5% | 39.0% | 3.4% | 2,634 |
| | 2006 | 55.5% | 1.6% | 53.8% | 43.1% | 3.0% | 2,428 |
| | 2004 | 49.2% | −0.4% | 48.1% | 49.7% | 2.2% | 2,381 |
| | 2002 | 49.8% | 2.3% | 48.0% | 48.4% | 3.6% | 3,446 |
| | 2000 | 50.1% | 0.0% | 48.8% | 48.5% | 2.6% | 2,433 |
| | 1998 | 50.0% | 0.6% | 48.0% | 48.0% | 4.0% | 1,312 |
| | 1996 | 50.3% | −0.2% | 49.0% | 48.4% | 2.6% | 2,819 |
| | 1994 | 47.4% | 0.0% | 46.0% | 51.0% | 3.0% | 2,261 |
| | 1992 | 55.6% | 1.7% | 53.5% | 42.7% | 3.9% | 2,748 |
| | 1990 | 52.2% | −1.6% | 49.9% | 45.7% | 4.4% | 3,764 |
| | 1988 | 53.2% | −0.9% | 50.5% | 44.4% | 5.1% | 2,066 |
| | 1986 | | | | | | |
| | 1984 | 45.6% | −3.3% | 45.2% | 54.0% | 0.9% | 1,471 |
| | 1982 | 53.2% | −3.3% | 52.1% | 45.8% | 2.1% | 1,438 |
| | 1980 | 49.1% | −2.9% | 48.4% | 50.0% | 1.6% | 1,188 |
| | 1978 | 53.0% | −1.3% | 49.9% | 44.2% | 5.9% | 1,287 |
| | 1976 | 52.0% | −5.7% | 51.2% | 47.3% | 1.5% | 3,344 |
| | Average | 51.6% | −0.3% | 50.0% | 47.0% | 3.1% | |

**Classification for Region:**

**East:** Connecticut; Delaware; Maine; Maryland; Massachusetts; New Hampshire; New Jersey; New York; Pennsylvania; Rhode Island; Vermont; Washington, DC; West Virginia

**Midwest:** Illinois; Indiana; Iowa; Kansas; Michigan; Minnesota; Missouri; Nebraska; North Dakota; Ohio; South Dakota; Wisconsin

**South:** Alabama; Arkansas; Florida; Georgia; Kentucky; Louisiana; Mississippi; North Carolina; Oklahoma; South Carolina; Tennessee; Texas; Virginia

**West:** Alaska; Arizona; California; Colorado; Hawaii; Idaho; Montana; Nevada; New Mexico; Oregon; Utah; Washington; Wyoming

*Source:* National exit polls. See the section in Chapter 2 entitled "Creating a Cumulative National Data Set: Selecting Exit Polls" (pp. 28–29).

*Note:* When using these results to make inferences about the active electorate, the standard errors should be calculated using Table 2.2 (p. 36), which is explained in the adjacent section of Chapter 2, "Analyzing Exit Poll Questions: Estimating Sampling Error" (pp. 34–36). For a guide on how to understand the tables and figures of this chapter, see the section in Chapter 2 entitled "Presenting and Discussing the Exit Poll Data: Reading Chapter 5" (pp. 43–46). The rationale for using two-party percentages to show trends over time is given in Chapter 4, in the section entitled "Presidential Vote Choice" (pp. 124–131).

**Table 5.10** House Vote by Population Density of Electoral Precinct, 1984–2010

| Category | Year | Two-Party House Vote | | Full House Vote | | | |
|---|---|---|---|---|---|---|---|
| | | Two-Party Democratic Vote | Difference from Mean Democratic Two-Party Vote | Democratic Vote | Republican Vote | Third-Party Vote | Number of Respondents |
| City | 2010 | 57.5% | 11.4% | 56.0% | 41.4% | 2.6% | 4,954 |
| | 2008 | 64.6% | 9.6% | 62.8% | 34.4% | 2.8% | 4,935 |
| | 2006 | 62.1% | 8.1% | 60.6% | 37.0% | 2.4% | 3,910 |
| | 2004 | 55.1% | 5.6% | 54.4% | 44.2% | 1.4% | 3,976 |
| | 2002 | 58.8% | 11.4% | 57.4% | 40.2% | 2.3% | 5,243 |
| | 2000 | 63.3% | 13.1% | 62.1% | 36.1% | 1.8% | 3,591 |
| | 1998 | | | | | | |
| | 1996 | 56.1% | 5.6% | 55.2% | 43.2% | 1.6% | 4,957 |
| | 1994 | | | | | | |
| | 1992 | 63.0% | 9.1% | 61.6% | 36.2% | 2.2% | 3,821 |
| | 1990 | 58.8% | 4.9% | 57.1% | 40.1% | 2.8% | 4,709 |
| | 1988 | 61.4% | 7.3% | 58.4% | 36.7% | 5.0% | 2,986 |
| | 1986 | | | | | | |
| | 1984 | 60.4% | 11.5% | 59.3% | 38.8% | 1.8% | 2,519 |
| | Average | 60.1% | 8.9% | 58.6% | 38.9% | 2.4% | |
| Suburb | 2010 | 43.1% | −3.2% | 41.8% | 55.3% | 2.9% | 8,775 |
| | 2008 | 51.5% | −3.5% | 50.3% | 47.3% | 2.3% | 8,250 |
| | 2006 | 51.3% | −2.6% | 50.4% | 47.8% | 1.8% | 6,123 |
| | 2004 | 47.8% | −1.8% | 47.0% | 51.3% | 1.6% | 5,752 |
| | 2002 | 41.3% | −6.1% | 40.0% | 56.8% | 3.1% | 7,666 |
| | 2000 | 48.8% | −1.3% | 47.8% | 50.1% | 2.0% | 4,509 |
| | 1998 | | | | | | |
| | 1996 | 48.2% | −2.3% | 47.2% | 50.8% | 2.0% | 5,851 |
| | 1994 | | | | | | |
| | 1992 | 51.2% | −2.7% | 49.8% | 47.4% | 2.8% | 4,953 |
| | 1990 | 53.1% | −0.7% | 51.7% | 45.6% | 2.7% | 7,583 |
| | 1988 | 49.4% | −4.7% | 47.3% | 48.5% | 4.2% | 4,163 |
| | 1986 | | | | | | |
| | 1984 | 46.2% | −2.7% | 45.7% | 53.3% | 1.0% | 3,344 |
| | Average | 48.4% | −2.9% | 47.2% | 50.4% | 2.4% | |
| Rural | 2010 | 37.0% | −8.5% | 35.7% | 60.9% | 3.4% | 3,775 |
| | 2008 | 50.3% | −4.8% | 49.1% | 48.6% | 2.2% | 3,336 |
| | 2006 | 49.0% | −5.0% | 48.2% | 50.2% | 1.6% | 3,218 |
| | 2004 | 45.5% | −4.1% | 44.4% | 53.1% | 2.5% | 2,913 |
| | 2002 | 44.2% | −3.2% | 43.2% | 54.5% | 2.3% | 3,441 |
| | 2000 | 38.6% | −11.6% | 37.3% | 59.5% | 3.2% | 3,382 |
| | 1998 | | | | | | |
| | 1996 | 47.7% | −2.8% | 46.7% | 51.1% | 2.2% | 4,546 |
| | 1994 | | | | | | |
| | 1992 | 50.6% | −3.4% | 49.4% | 48.2% | 2.4% | 4,950 |
| | 1990 | 50.1% | −3.7% | 48.5% | 48.2% | 3.3% | 6,421 |

**Table 5.10**   *(Continued)*

| Category | Year | Two-Party House Vote | | Full House Vote | | | |
|---|---|---|---|---|---|---|---|
| | | Two-Party Democratic Vote | Difference from Mean Democratic Two-Party Vote | Democratic Vote | Republican Vote | Third-Party Vote | Number of Respondents |
| Rural | 1988 | 54.4% | 0.4% | 51.5% | 43.1% | 5.5% | 3,222 |
| | 1986 | | | | | | |
| | 1984 | 42.0% | −6.9% | 41.6% | 57.4% | 1.0% | 2,674 |
| | Average | 46.3% | −4.9% | 45.1% | 52.3% | 2.7% | |

**Classification for Population Density:**

**City:** Precinct residing within Census metropolitan statistical area (MSA) containing greater than 50,000 residents

**Suburb:** Precinct residing within Census MSA in close proximity to large urban area

**Rural:** Precinct residing within Census MSA with less than 50,000 residents not in close proximity to large urban area

*Source:* National exit polls. See the section in Chapter 2 entitled "Creating a Cumulative National Data Set: Selecting Exit Polls" (pp. 28–29).

*Note:* When using these results to make inferences about the active electorate, the standard errors should be calculated using Table 2.2 (p. 36), which is explained in the adjacent section of Chapter 2, "Analyzing Exit Poll Questions: Estimating Sampling Error" (pp. 34–36). For a guide on how to understand the tables and figures of this chapter, see the section in Chapter 2 entitled "Presenting and Discussing the Exit Poll Data: Reading Chapter 5" (pp. 43–46). The rationale for using two-party percentages to show trends over time is given in Chapter 4, in the section entitled "Presidential Vote Choice" (pp. 124–131).

**Table 5.11**   House Vote by Religious Affiliation, 1984–2010

| Category | Year | Two-Party House Vote | | Full House Vote | | | |
|---|---|---|---|---|---|---|---|
| | | Two-Party Democratic Vote | Difference from Mean Democratic Two-Party Vote | Democratic Vote | Republican Vote | Third-Party Vote | Number of Respondents |
| Protestant | 2010 | 39.6% | −6.7% | 38.3% | 58.5% | 3.2% | 2,025 |
| | 2008 | 45.8% | −9.3% | 44.6% | 52.8% | 2.6% | 1,940 |
| | 2006 | 44.9% | −9.0% | 44.1% | 54.1% | 1.8% | 3,408 |
| | 2004 | 42.5% | −7.1% | 41.9% | 56.7% | 1.4% | 4,942 |
| | 2002 | 38.3% | −9.1% | 37.6% | 60.5% | 1.9% | 4,239 |
| | 2000 | 42.4% | −7.8% | 41.6% | 56.6% | 1.8% | 4,515 |
| | 1998 | 41.6% | −7.8% | 40.4% | 56.9% | 2.7% | 2,469 |
| | 1996 | 43.2% | −7.3% | 42.4% | 55.8% | 1.7% | 3,936 |
| | 1994 | 41.6% | −5.8% | 41.1% | 57.6% | 1.3% | 2,729 |
| | 1992 | 47.1% | −6.8% | 46.2% | 51.9% | 2.0% | 3,863 |
| | 1990 | 48.3% | −5.5% | 47.4% | 50.7% | 1.9% | 4,960 |
| | 1988 | 49.1% | −5.0% | 46.7% | 48.5% | 4.8% | 5,645 |
| | 1986 | 47.6% | −4.8% | 45.5% | 50.0% | 4.5% | 4,565 |
| | 1984 | 41.0% | −7.9% | 40.6% | 58.5% | 0.9% | 4,777 |
| | Average | 43.8% | −7.1% | 42.7% | 54.9% | 2.3% | |

*(Continued)*

**Table 5.11** House Vote by Religious Affiliation, 1984–2010 *(Continued)*

| | | Two-Party House Vote | | Full House Vote | | | |
| | | Two-Party Democratic Vote | Difference from Mean Democratic Two-Party Vote | Democratic Vote | Republican Vote | Third-Party Vote | Number of Respondents |
|---|---|---|---|---|---|---|---|
| Catholic | 2010 | 44.4% | −1.9% | 43.4% | 54.5% | 2.1% | 998 |
| | 2008 | 56.6% | 1.5% | 55.1% | 42.3% | 2.7% | 1,030 |
| | 2006 | 55.6% | 1.6% | 54.8% | 43.8% | 1.3% | 1,610 |
| | 2004 | 49.3% | −0.3% | 48.8% | 50.2% | 1.0% | 2,341 |
| | 2002 | 54.5% | 7.1% | 53.4% | 44.5% | 2.1% | 1,941 |
| | 2000 | 51.1% | 0.9% | 50.2% | 48.1% | 1.7% | 2,065 |
| | 1998 | 53.1% | 3.7% | 51.1% | 45.2% | 3.8% | 1,396 |
| | 1996 | 53.8% | 3.3% | 52.8% | 45.4% | 1.9% | 2,055 |
| | 1994 | 47.1% | −0.3% | 46.2% | 51.9% | 1.9% | 1,448 |
| | 1992 | 56.7% | 2.8% | 55.1% | 42.0% | 2.8% | 1,948 |
| | 1990 | 55.6% | 1.8% | 53.9% | 43.1% | 3.0% | 2,055 |
| | 1988 | 55.2% | 1.2% | 52.7% | 42.7% | 4.6% | 2,800 |
| | 1986 | 54.9% | 2.4% | 52.4% | 43.0% | 4.6% | 2,565 |
| | 1984 | 56.1% | 7.2% | 55.3% | 43.3% | 1.5% | 2,264 |
| | Average | 53.1% | 2.2% | 51.8% | 45.7% | 2.5% | |
| Jewish | 2010 | 72.6% | 26.3% | 70.1% | 26.4% | 3.4% | 92 |
| | 2008 | 81.6% | 26.5% | 81.6% | 18.4% | 0.0% | 95 |
| | 2006 | 87.6% | 33.6% | 86.3% | 12.2% | 1.5% | 123 |
| | 2004 | 77.9% | 28.3% | 76.2% | 21.6% | 2.2% | 240 |
| | 2002 | 63.9% | 16.4% | 62.3% | 35.2% | 2.5% | 252 |
| | 2000 | 75.7% | 25.5% | 74.4% | 23.9% | 1.7% | 283 |
| | 1998 | 78.3% | 29.0% | 77.7% | 21.5% | 0.8% | 150 |
| | 1996 | 74.4% | 23.9% | 73.2% | 25.2% | 1.6% | 243 |
| | 1994 | 76.8% | 29.4% | 76.0% | 23.0% | 1.1% | 181 |
| | 1992 | 79.0% | 25.1% | 77.3% | 20.6% | 2.1% | 258 |
| | 1990 | 73.1% | 19.3% | 71.2% | 26.2% | 2.6% | 241 |
| | 1988 | 68.2% | 14.1% | 66.3% | 30.9% | 2.9% | 386 |
| | 1986 | 70.0% | 17.5% | 67.2% | 28.8% | 4.0% | 323 |
| | 1984 | 71.1% | 22.2% | 69.9% | 28.4% | 1.7% | 223 |
| | Average | 75.0% | 24.1% | 73.5% | 24.4% | 2.0% | |
| No Religion | 2010 | 69.2% | 22.9% | 68.1% | 30.3% | 1.6% | 408 |
| | 2008 | 74.4% | 19.4% | 72.1% | 24.8% | 3.1% | 479 |
| | 2006 | 77.0% | 23.0% | 74.4% | 22.3% | 3.3% | 652 |
| | 2004 | 67.7% | 18.1% | 65.1% | 31.1% | 3.8% | 960 |
| | 2002 | 67.7% | 20.3% | 64.3% | 30.6% | 5.1% | 614 |
| | 2000 | 65.5% | 15.3% | 61.8% | 32.6% | 5.5% | 764 |
| | 1998 | 66.7% | 17.3% | 64.6% | 32.3% | 3.1% | 344 |
| | 1996 | 61.5% | 11.0% | 60.0% | 37.6% | 2.3% | 528 |

**Table 5.11** *(Continued)*

| Category | Year | Two-Party House Vote | | Full House Vote | | | |
|---|---|---|---|---|---|---|---|
| | | Two-Party Democratic Vote | Difference from Mean Democratic Two-Party Vote | Democratic Vote | Republican Vote | Third-Party Vote | Number of Respondents |
| No | 1994 | 62.6% | 15.3% | 60.3% | 35.9% | 3.8% | 345 |
| Religion | 1992 | 69.5% | 15.6% | 66.4% | 29.1% | 4.5% | 492 |
| | 1990 | 59.2% | 5.4% | 54.4% | 37.5% | 8.1% | 660 |
| | 1988 | 65.2% | 11.1% | 61.4% | 32.8% | 5.8% | 550 |
| | 1986 | 58.7% | 6.3% | 56.1% | 39.4% | 4.4% | 374 |
| | 1984 | 66.2% | 17.3% | 64.9% | 33.1% | 2.0% | 424 |
| | Average | 66.5% | 15.6% | 63.9% | 32.1% | 4.0% | |
| Other | 2010 | 75.6% | 29.3% | 74.2% | 23.9% | 1.9% | 322 |
| Religion | 2008 | 78.7% | 23.6% | 75.8% | 20.5% | 3.7% | 271 |
| | 2006 | 74.2% | 20.2% | 70.8% | 24.7% | 4.6% | 384 |
| | 2004 | 71.7% | 22.1% | 68.6% | 27.1% | 4.3% | 602 |
| | 2002 | 67.7% | 20.3% | 64.3% | 30.6% | 5.1% | 522 |
| | 2000 | 69.2% | 19.0% | 65.6% | 29.3% | 5.1% | 563 |
| | 1998 | 63.6% | 14.2% | 58.1% | 33.2% | 8.7% | 297 |
| | 1996 | 71.9% | 21.4% | 69.4% | 27.2% | 3.4% | 451 |
| | 1994 | 65.0% | 17.6% | 62.1% | 33.5% | 4.4% | 212 |
| | 1992 | 66.1% | 12.2% | 64.6% | 33.1% | 2.3% | 492 |
| | 1990 | 64.9% | 11.0% | 60.3% | 32.7% | 7.0% | 503 |
| | 1988 | 71.6% | 17.6% | 66.5% | 26.3% | 7.1% | 596 |
| | 1986 | 68.4% | 15.9% | 63.1% | 29.2% | 7.7% | 494 |
| | 1984 | 64.2% | 15.3% | 62.4% | 34.8% | 2.7% | 439 |
| | Average | 69.5% | 18.5% | 66.1% | 29.0% | 4.9% | |

**Question Wording for Religious Affiliation** (Coded: Protestant = 1; Catholic = 2; Jewish = 3; No Religion = 4; Other Religion = 5):

**1984–1988:** "Your religion . . . Protestant (1); Catholic (2); Other Christian (1); Jewish (3); Something else (5); None (4)"

**1990:** "Your religious preference today? . . . Protestant (1); Catholic (2); Other Christian (1); Jewish (3); Something else (5); None (4)"

**1992–2000:** "Are you . . . Protestant (1); Catholic (2); Other Christian (1); Jewish (3); Something else (5); None (4)"

**2002:** "Are you . . . Protestant (1); Catholic (2); Other Christian (1); Jewish (3); Muslim (5); Something else (5); None (4)"

**2004–2010:** "Are you . . . Protestant (1); Catholic (2); Mormon/LDS (5); Other Christian (1); Jewish (3); Muslim (5); Something else (5); None (4)"

*Source:* National exit polls. See the section in Chapter 2 entitled "Creating a Cumulative National Data Set: Selecting Exit Polls" (pp. 28–29).

*Note:* When using these results to make inferences about the active electorate, the standard errors should be calculated using Table 2.2 (p. 36), which is explained in the adjacent section of Chapter 2, "Analyzing Exit Poll Questions: Estimating Sampling Error" (pp. 34–36). For a guide on how to understand the tables and figures of this chapter, see the section in Chapter 2 entitled "Presenting and Discussing the Exit Poll Data: Reading Chapter 5" (pp. 43–46). The rationale for using two-party percentages to show trends over time is given in Chapter 4, in the section entitled "Presidential Vote Choice" (pp. 124–131).

**Table 5.12**   House Vote by Religious Attendance, 2000–2010

| Category | Year | Two-Party House Vote Two-Party Democratic Vote | Difference from Mean Democratic Two-Party Vote | Full House Vote Democratic Vote | Republican Vote | Third-Party Vote | Number of Respondents |
|---|---|---|---|---|---|---|---|
| Once a Week or More | 2010 | 40.9% | −5.4% | 40.0% | 57.8% | 2.2% | 1,805 |
| | 2008 | 45.8% | −9.3% | 45.0% | 53.3% | 1.7% | 1,427 |
| | 2006 | 43.6% | −10.4% | 42.8% | 55.5% | 1.7% | 2,821 |
| | 2004 | 40.7% | −8.9% | 40.1% | 58.5% | 1.4% | 3,746 |
| | 2002 | 40.3% | −7.2% | 39.4% | 58.4% | 2.2% | 3,422 |
| | 2000 | 41.3% | −8.8% | 40.6% | 57.7% | 1.7% | 2,362 |
| | Average | 42.1% | −8.3% | 41.3% | 56.9% | 1.8% | |
| Less Than Once a Week | 2010 | 54.5% | 8.2% | 52.8% | 44.1% | 3.1% | 1,999 |
| | 2008 | 61.1% | 6.0% | 59.0% | 37.6% | 3.3% | 2,396 |
| | 2006 | 62.6% | 8.6% | 61.2% | 36.5% | 2.3% | 3,371 |
| | 2004 | 56.3% | 6.7% | 55.2% | 42.8% | 2.0% | 5,357 |
| | 2002 | 53.5% | 6.1% | 52.1% | 45.3% | 2.6% | 4,147 |
| | 2000 | 55.3% | 5.1% | 53.7% | 43.4% | 2.9% | 3,111 |
| | Average | 57.2% | 6.8% | 55.7% | 41.6% | 2.7% | |

**Question Wording for Religious Attendance** (Coded: Once a Week or More = 1; Less Than Once a Week = 2):

**2000–2008:** "How often do you attend religious services? . . . More than once a week (1); Once a week (1); A few times a month (2); A few times a year (2); Never (2)"

**2010:** "Do you attend religious services once a week or more? . . . Yes (1); No (2)"

*Source:* National exit polls. See the section in Chapter 2 entitled "Creating a Cumulative National Data Set: Selecting Exit Polls" (pp. 28–29).

*Note:* When using these results to make inferences about the active electorate, the standard errors should be calculated using Table 2.2 (p. 36), which is explained in the adjacent section of Chapter 2, "Analyzing Exit Poll Questions: Estimating Sampling Error" (pp. 34–36). For a guide on how to understand the tables and figures of this chapter, see the section in Chapter 2 entitled "Presenting and Discussing the Exit Poll Data: Reading Chapter 5" (pp. 43–46). The rationale for using two-party percentages to show trends over time is given in Chapter 4, in the section entitled "Presidential Vote Choice" (pp. 124–131).

**Table 5.13**  House Vote by Evangelical, 2004–2010

| Category | Year | Two-Party House Vote | | Full House Vote | | | |
|---|---|---|---|---|---|---|---|
| | | Two-Party Democratic Vote | Difference from Mean Democratic Two-Party Vote | Democratic Vote | Republican Vote | Third-Party Vote | Number of Respondents |
| Born Again | 2010 | 36.1% | −10.2% | 35.0% | 61.9% | 3.1% | 1,220 |
| | 2008 | 44.7% | −10.4% | 43.8% | 54.2% | 2.1% | 4,331 |
| | 2006 | 41.1% | −12.9% | 40.6% | 58.2% | 1.2% | 2,030 |
| | 2004 | 37.9% | −11.7% | 37.4% | 61.3% | 1.3% | 3,012 |
| | Average | 39.9% | −11.3% | 39.2% | 58.9% | 1.9% | |
| Not Born Again | 2010 | 54.3% | 8.0% | 53.0% | 44.5% | 2.4% | 2,499 |
| | 2008 | 61.3% | 6.3% | 59.6% | 37.5% | 2.9% | 7,584 |
| | 2006 | 60.4% | 6.4% | 58.9% | 38.7% | 2.4% | 4,035 |
| | 2004 | 55.7% | 6.2% | 54.7% | 43.4% | 1.9% | 5,928 |
| | Average | 57.9% | 6.7% | 56.5% | 41.0% | 2.4% | |

**Question Wording for Evangelical** (Coded: Born Again = 1; Not Born Again = 2):

**2004–2010:** "Would you describe yourself as a born again or evangelical Christian? . . . Yes (1); No (2)"

*Source:* National exit polls. See the section in Chapter 2 entitled "Creating a Cumulative National Data Set: Selecting Exit Polls" (pp. 28–29).

*Note:* When using these results to make inferences about the active electorate, the standard errors should be calculated using Table 2.2 (p. 36), which is explained in the adjacent section of Chapter 2, "Analyzing Exit Poll Questions: Estimating Sampling Error" (pp. 34–36). For a guide on how to understand the tables and figures of this chapter, see the section in Chapter 2 entitled "Presenting and Discussing the Exit Poll Data: Reading Chapter 5" (pp. 43–46). The rationale for using two-party percentages to show trends over time is given in Chapter 4, in the section entitled "Presidential Vote Choice" (pp. 124–131).

**Table 5.14**   House Vote by Education, 1986–2010

| Category | Year | Two-Party House Vote | | Full House Vote | | | Number of Voters |
|---|---|---|---|---|---|---|---|
| | | Two-Party Democratic Vote | Difference from Mean Democratic Two-Party Vote | Democratic Vote | Republican Vote | Third-Party Vote | |
| Did Not Complete High School | 2010 | 61.2% | 14.9% | 56.6% | 35.9% | 7.5% | 476 |
| | 2008 | 69.2% | 14.1% | 67.6% | 30.1% | 2.4% | 652 |
| | 2006 | 64.5% | 10.5% | 63.8% | 35.2% | 1.0% | 213 |
| | 2004 | 50.4% | 0.8% | 48.7% | 47.9% | 3.4% | 367 |
| | 2002 | 63.2% | 15.7% | 61.6% | 35.9% | 2.5% | 266 |
| | 2000 | 57.8% | 7.7% | 56.8% | 41.4% | 1.9% | 353 |
| | 1998 | 57.9% | 8.5% | 56.7% | 41.2% | 2.0% | 204 |
| | 1996 | 64.3% | 13.8% | 63.1% | 34.9% | 2.0% | 447 |
| | 1994 | 57.5% | 10.1% | 56.2% | 41.5% | 2.3% | 259 |
| | 1992 | 67.5% | 13.6% | 65.4% | 31.5% | 3.1% | 487 |
| | 1990 | 61.0% | 7.2% | 59.5% | 38.0% | 2.5% | 558 |
| | 1988 | 63.1% | 9.0% | 58.8% | 34.4% | 6.8% | 712 |
| | 1986 | 56.8% | 4.3% | 53.4% | 40.6% | 6.0% | 678 |
| | Average | 61.1% | 10.0% | 59.1% | 37.6% | 3.3% | |
| High School Graduate | 2010 | 46.8% | 0.5% | 45.7% | 52.0% | 2.3% | 2,954 |
| | 2008 | 56.5% | 1.4% | 55.2% | 42.6% | 2.2% | 3,212 |
| | 2006 | 55.5% | 1.5% | 54.7% | 43.8% | 1.5% | 1,242 |
| | 2004 | 49.7% | 0.1% | 49.2% | 49.7% | 1.1% | 1,908 |
| | 2002 | 52.3% | 4.9% | 51.2% | 46.7% | 2.1% | 1,573 |
| | 2000 | 50.3% | 0.1% | 49.4% | 48.9% | 1.7% | 1,710 |
| | 1998 | 51.4% | 2.0% | 49.5% | 46.8% | 3.7% | 1,015 |
| | 1996 | 54.9% | 4.4% | 53.3% | 43.9% | 2.8% | 1,752 |
| | 1994 | 46.6% | −0.8% | 46.0% | 52.7% | 1.3% | 1,075 |
| | 1992 | 58.0% | 4.0% | 56.5% | 41.0% | 2.4% | 1,817 |
| | 1990 | 57.9% | 4.1% | 56.1% | 40.8% | 3.1% | 2,511 |
| | 1988 | 56.7% | 2.6% | 54.1% | 41.4% | 4.5% | 2,741 |
| | 1986 | 54.9% | 2.5% | 51.9% | 42.6% | 5.5% | 2,575 |
| | Average | 53.2% | 2.1% | 51.8% | 45.6% | 2.6% | |
| Some College | 2010 | 44.5% | −1.8% | 42.8% | 53.5% | 3.7% | 4,853 |
| | 2008 | 54.3% | −0.7% | 53.2% | 44.8% | 2.0% | 5,061 |
| | 2006 | 51.6% | −2.4% | 50.5% | 47.4% | 2.1% | 1,875 |
| | 2004 | 47.7% | −1.9% | 46.9% | 51.4% | 1.7% | 2,968 |
| | 2002 | 46.5% | −0.9% | 45.4% | 52.1% | 2.5% | 2,419 |
| | 2000 | 47.7% | −2.5% | 46.5% | 51.1% | 2.4% | 2,653 |
| | 1998 | 46.7% | −2.7% | 44.7% | 51.1% | 4.1% | 1,279 |
| | 1996 | 50.3% | −0.2% | 49.2% | 48.6% | 2.1% | 2,064 |
| | 1994 | 41.0% | −6.4% | 40.2% | 57.9% | 1.9% | 1,381 |
| | 1992 | 52.6% | −1.3% | 51.3% | 46.1% | 2.6% | 2,076 |
| | 1990 | 53.2% | −0.6% | 51.4% | 45.2% | 3.4% | 2,597 |
| | 1988 | 52.9% | −1.2% | 50.2% | 44.7% | 5.1% | 3,017 |
| | 1986 | 50.3% | −2.2% | 48.1% | 47.6% | 4.3% | 2,399 |
| | Average | 49.2% | −1.9% | 47.7% | 49.4% | 2.9% | |

**Table 5.14** *(Continued)*

| Category | Year | Two-Party House Vote | | Full House Vote | | | |
| | | Two-Party Democratic Vote | Difference from Mean Democratic Two-Party Vote | Democratic Vote | Republican Vote | Third-Party Vote | Number of Voters |
|---|---|---|---|---|---|---|---|
| College | 2010 | 40.7% | −5.6% | 39.6% | 57.8% | 2.6% | 4,853 |
| Graduate | 2008 | 51.2% | −3.8% | 49.5% | 47.1% | 3.4% | 4,430 |
| | 2006 | 50.2% | −3.8% | 49.1% | 48.8% | 2.1% | 1,605 |
| | 2004 | 47.3% | −2.3% | 46.4% | 51.8% | 1.7% | 2,432 |
| | 2002 | 42.0% | −5.4% | 41.2% | 56.8% | 2.1% | 1,897 |
| | 2000 | 46.1% | −4.1% | 45.0% | 52.7% | 2.4% | 2,037 |
| | 1998 | 45.2% | −4.2% | 44.0% | 53.4% | 2.6% | 1,275 |
| | 1996 | 43.1% | −7.4% | 42.5% | 56.1% | 1.3% | 1,968 |
| | 1994 | 44.8% | −2.6% | 43.9% | 54.0% | 2.1% | 1,284 |
| | 1992 | 45.9% | −8.0% | 44.7% | 52.7% | 2.6% | 1,726 |
| | 1990 | 51.5% | −2.3% | 50.0% | 47.1% | 2.8% | 2,176 |
| | 1988 | 46.7% | −7.4% | 44.8% | 51.1% | 4.1% | 1,885 |
| | 1986 | 45.9% | −6.6% | 44.1% | 52.1% | 3.8% | 1,381 |
| | Average | 46.2% | −4.9% | 45.0% | 52.4% | 2.6% | |
| Postgraduate | 2010 | 53.7% | 7.4% | 52.6% | 45.3% | 2.1% | 3,560 |
| | 2008 | 56.9% | 1.8% | 55.7% | 42.3% | 2.0% | 2,958 |
| | 2006 | 58.7% | 4.8% | 58.0% | 40.8% | 1.1% | 1,141 |
| | 2004 | 53.5% | 3.9% | 52.3% | 45.5% | 2.1% | 1,552 |
| | 2002 | 46.9% | −0.5% | 45.4% | 51.4% | 3.3% | 1,473 |
| | 2000 | 54.4% | 4.2% | 53.1% | 44.5% | 2.4% | 1,512 |
| | 1998 | 53.8% | 4.4% | 51.8% | 44.5% | 3.7% | 880 |
| | 1996 | 50.9% | 0.4% | 50.3% | 48.5% | 1.2% | 1,321 |
| | 1994 | 56.8% | 9.4% | 55.7% | 42.4% | 1.9% | 869 |
| | 1992 | 54.7% | 0.8% | 53.6% | 44.3% | 2.0% | 1,185 |
| | 1990 | 53.8% | 0.0% | 52.4% | 45.0% | 2.6% | 1,585 |
| | 1988 | 53.5% | −0.5% | 51.1% | 44.3% | 4.6% | 1,581 |
| | 1986 | 56.0% | 3.6% | 54.0% | 42.4% | 3.6% | 1,213 |
| | Average | 54.1% | 3.0% | 52.8% | 44.7% | 2.5% | |

**Question Wording for Education** (Coded: Did Not Complete High School = 1; High School Graduate = 2; Some College = 3; College Graduate = 4; Postgraduate = 5):

**1986–1988:** "What was the last grade in school you completed? . . . Did not graduate from high school (1); High school graduate (2); Some college but not four years (3); College graduate (4); Postgraduate study (5)"

**1990–1998:** "What was the last grade of school you completed? . . . Did not complete high school (1); High school graduate (2); Some college, but no degree (3); College graduate (4); Postgraduate study (5)"

**2000–2010:** "What was the last grade of school you completed? . . . Did not complete high school (1); High school graduate (2); Some college or associate degree (3); College graduate (4); Postgraduate study (5)"

*Source:* National exit polls. See the section in Chapter 2 entitled "Creating a Cumulative National Data Set: Selecting Exit Polls" (pp. 28–29).

*Note:* When using these results to make inferences about the active electorate, the standard errors should be calculated using Table 2.2 (p. 36), which is explained in the adjacent section of Chapter 2, "Analyzing Exit Poll Questions: Estimating Sampling Error" (pp. 34–36). For a guide on how to understand the tables and figures of this chapter, see the section in Chapter 2 entitled "Presenting and Discussing the Exit Poll Data: Reading Chapter 5" (pp. 43–46). The rationale for using two-party percentages to show trends over time is given in Chapter 4, in the section entitled "Presidential Vote Choice" (pp. 124–131).

**Table 5.15**  House Vote by Employment Status, 1996–2008

| | | Two-Party House Vote | | Full House Vote | | | |
| Category | Year | Two-Party Democratic Vote | Difference from Mean Democratic Two-Party Vote | Democratic Vote | Republican Vote | Third-Party Vote | Number of Respondents |
|---|---|---|---|---|---|---|---|
| Employed | 2008 | 55.6% | 0.5% | 54.3% | 43.4% | 2.3% | 2,594 |
| Full Time | 2006 | | | | | | |
| | 2004 | 47.5% | −2.1% | 46.7% | 51.7% | 1.6% | 1,888 |
| | 2002 | 47.0% | −0.4% | 45.8% | 51.6% | 2.5% | 5,266 |
| | 2000 | 50.5% | 0.3% | 49.2% | 48.3% | 2.6% | 5,984 |
| | 1998 | 50.0% | 0.6% | 48.1% | 48.0% | 3.9% | 3,080 |
| | 1996 | 50.7% | 0.2% | 49.6% | 48.3% | 2.1% | 7,154 |
| | Average | 50.2% | −0.1% | 49.0% | 48.5% | 2.5% | |
| Not Employed | 2008 | 53.3% | −1.7% | 51.7% | 45.3% | 3.1% | 1,264 |
| Full Time | 2006 | | | | | | |
| | 2004 | 49.0% | −0.6% | 48.0% | 50.0% | 2.0% | 1,147 |
| | 2002 | 49.4% | 1.9% | 48.2% | 49.5% | 2.3% | 2,965 |
| | 2000 | 48.5% | −1.7% | 47.4% | 50.4% | 2.2% | 2,624 |
| | 1998 | 47.8% | −1.6% | 46.7% | 51.0% | 2.3% | 1,564 |
| | 1996 | 50.0% | −0.5% | 49.3% | 49.3% | 1.4% | 3,590 |
| | Average | 49.6% | −0.7% | 48.5% | 49.2% | 2.2% | |

**Question Wording for Employment Status** (Coded: Employed Full Time = 1; Not Employed Full Time = 2):

**1996 and 2000–2008:** "Do you work full time for pay? . . . Yes (1); No (2)"

**1998:** "Do you work for full time pay? . . . Yes (1); No (2)"

*Source:* National exit polls. See the section in Chapter 2 entitled "Creating a Cumulative National Data Set: Selecting Exit Polls" (pp. 28–29).

*Note:* When using these results to make inferences about the active electorate, the standard errors should be calculated using Table 2.2 (p. 36), which is explained in the adjacent section of Chapter 2, "Analyzing Exit Poll Questions: Estimating Sampling Error" (pp. 34–36). For a guide on how to understand the tables and figures of this chapter, see the section in Chapter 2 entitled "Presenting and Discussing the Exit Poll Data: Reading Chapter 5" (pp. 43–46). The rationale for using two-party percentages to show trends over time is given in Chapter 4, in the section entitled "Presidential Vote Choice" (pp. 124–131).

**Table 5.16**   House Vote by Marital Status, 1992–2008

| Category | Year | Two-Party House Vote | | Full House Vote | | | |
|---|---|---|---|---|---|---|---|
| | | Two-Party Democratic Vote | Difference from Mean Democratic Two-Party Vote | Democratic Vote | Republican Vote | Third-Party Vote | Number of Respondents |
| Married | 2008 | 49.1% | −6.0% | 47.8% | 49.5% | 2.7% | 2,411 |
| | 2006 | 48.4% | −5.5% | 47.6% | 50.6% | 1.8% | 4,156 |
| | 2004 | 43.3% | −6.3% | 42.6% | 55.8% | 1.6% | 7,551 |
| | 2002 | 42.9% | −4.5% | 42.1% | 56.1% | 1.8% | 5,324 |
| | 2000 | 44.9% | −5.3% | 43.9% | 53.9% | 2.1% | 5,350 |
| | 1998 | 43.8% | −5.6% | 42.3% | 54.4% | 3.3% | 3,336 |
| | 1996 | 45.7% | −4.8% | 44.9% | 53.3% | 1.8% | 6,870 |
| | 1994 | | | | | | |
| | 1992 | 50.3% | −3.7% | 49.1% | 48.6% | 2.3% | 4,687 |
| | Average | 46.0% | −5.2% | 45.0% | 52.8% | 2.2% | |
| | | | | | | | |
| Not Married | 2008 | 66.8% | 11.75% | 65.2% | 32.4% | 2.4% | 1,579 |
| | 2006 | 65.3% | 11.32% | 63.7% | 33.9% | 2.4% | 2,041 |
| | 2004 | 60.0% | 10.43% | 58.8% | 39.1% | 2.1% | 4,731 |
| | 2002 | 58.6% | 11.16% | 56.4% | 39.8% | 3.8% | 2,343 |
| | 2000 | 58.7% | 8.58% | 57.2% | 40.2% | 2.6% | 2,915 |
| | 1998 | 60.2% | 10.81% | 58.1% | 38.4% | 3.5% | 1,558 |
| | 1996 | 59.7% | 9.23% | 58.5% | 39.4% | 2.0% | 3,750 |
| | 1994 | | | | | | |
| | 1992 | 60.7% | 6.75% | 59.0% | 38.3% | 2.7% | 2,437 |
| | Average | 61.3% | 10.0% | 59.6% | 37.7% | 2.7% | |

**Question Wording for Marital Status** (Coded: Married = 1; Not Married = 2):

**1992:** "Are you . . . Married (1); Single, never married (2); Widowed (2); Divorced/Separated (2)"

**1996–2008:** "Are you currently married? . . . Yes (1); No (2)"

*Source:* National exit polls. See the section in Chapter 2 entitled "Creating a Cumulative National Data Set: Selecting Exit Polls" (pp. 28–29).

*Note:* When using these results to make inferences about the active electorate, the standard errors should be calculated using Table 2.2 (p. 36), which is explained in the adjacent section of Chapter 2, "Analyzing Exit Poll Questions: Estimating Sampling Error" (pp. 34–36). For a guide on how to understand the tables and figures of this chapter, see the section in Chapter 2 entitled "Presenting and Discussing the Exit Poll Data: Reading Chapter 5" (pp. 43–46). The rationale for using two-party percentages to show trends over time is given in Chapter 4, in the section entitled "Presidential Vote Choice" (pp. 124–131).

**Table 5.17**   House Vote by Child in Household, 1996–2010

| Category | Year | Two-Party House Vote | | Full House Vote | | | |
| | | Two-Party Democratic Vote | Difference from Mean Democratic Two-Party Vote | Democratic Vote | Republican Vote | Third-Party Vote | Number of Respondents |
|---|---|---|---|---|---|---|---|
| Child in | 2010 | 48.0% | 1.7% | 46.4% | 50.3% | 3.3% | 1,411 |
| Household | 2008 | 54.5% | −0.5% | 52.9% | 44.1% | 2.9% | 1,558 |
| | 2006 | 51.7% | −2.2% | 50.9% | 47.5% | 1.6% | 4,314 |
| | 2004 | 47.3% | −2.2% | 46.7% | 52.0% | 1.3% | 3,571 |
| | 2002 | 45.3% | −2.1% | 44.2% | 53.4% | 2.4% | 3,057 |
| | 2000 | 45.9% | −4.3% | 44.9% | 53.1% | 2.0% | 3,361 |
| | 1998 | 48.3% | −1.0% | 46.7% | 49.9% | 3.4% | 1,871 |
| | 1996 | 50.2% | −0.3% | 49.4% | 48.9% | 1.7% | 4,170 |
| | Average | 48.9% | −1.4% | 47.8% | 49.9% | 2.3% | |
| | | | | | | | |
| No Child in | 2010 | 48.2% | 1.9% | 47.2% | 50.8% | 2.0% | 2,554 |
| Household | 2008 | 55.6% | 0.6% | 54.3% | 43.3% | 2.4% | 2,437 |
| | 2006 | 55.4% | 1.4% | 54.3% | 43.7% | 1.9% | 8,032 |
| | 2004 | 50.1% | 0.5% | 49.1% | 49.0% | 2.0% | 5,708 |
| | 2002 | 49.1% | 1.7% | 47.9% | 49.7% | 2.4% | 4,611 |
| | 2000 | 52.3% | 2.1% | 50.9% | 46.5% | 2.5% | 4,940 |
| | 1998 | 49.4% | 0.0% | 47.7% | 48.9% | 3.4% | 3,029 |
| | 1996 | 50.6% | 0.1% | 49.6% | 48.4% | 2.0% | 6,633 |
| | Average | 51.3% | 1.0% | 50.1% | 47.5% | 2.3% | |

**Question Wording for Child in Household** (Coded: Child in Household = 1; No Child in Household = 2):

**1996:** "Do you have a child under 18 living at home? . . . Yes (1); No (2)"

**1998–2010:** "Do you have any children under 18 living in your household? . . . Yes (1); No (2)"

*Source:* National exit polls. See the section in Chapter 2 entitled "Creating a Cumulative National Data Set: Selecting Exit Polls" (pp. 28–29).

*Note:* When using these results to make inferences about the active electorate, the standard errors should be calculated using Table 2.2 (p. 36), which is explained in the adjacent section of Chapter 2, "Analyzing Exit Poll Questions: Estimating Sampling Error" (pp. 34–36). For a guide on how to understand the tables and figures of this chapter, see the section in Chapter 2 entitled "Presenting and Discussing the Exit Poll Data: Reading Chapter 5" (pp. 43–46). The rationale for using two-party percentages to show trends over time is given in Chapter 4, in the section entitled "Presidential Vote Choice" (pp. 124–131).

**Table 5.18** House Vote by Union Household, 1976–2010

| | | Two-Party House Vote | | Full House Vote | | | |
|---|---|---|---|---|---|---|---|
| | | Two-Party Democratic Vote | Difference from Mean Democratic Two-Party Vote | Democratic Vote | Republican Vote | Third-Party Vote | Number of Respondents |
| Category | Year | | | | | | |
| Union Household | 2010 | 62.4% | 16.1% | 61.1% | 36.9% | 2.1% | 703 |
| | 2008 | 65.4% | 10.3% | 64.4% | 34.1% | 1.5% | 899 |
| | 2006 | 64.9% | 11.0% | 63.7% | 34.4% | 1.9% | 1,502 |
| | 2004 | 62.2% | 12.6% | 61.4% | 37.3% | 1.3% | 2,164 |
| | 2002 | 63.0% | 15.5% | 61.5% | 36.2% | 2.2% | 1,830 |
| | 2000 | 61.2% | 11.0% | 59.9% | 38.0% | 2.1% | 2,350 |
| | 1998 | 63.7% | 14.4% | 60.9% | 34.6% | 4.5% | 1,153 |
| | 1996 | 63.0% | 12.5% | 61.3% | 36.1% | 2.6% | 1,772 |
| | 1994 | | | | | | |
| | 1992 | | | | | | |
| | 1990 | | | | | | |
| | 1988 | 63.2% | 9.2% | 59.8% | 34.8% | 5.4% | 2,676 |
| | 1986 | 62.5% | 10.1% | 59.6% | 35.7% | 4.7% | 2,371 |
| | 1984 | 61.8% | 12.9% | 61.0% | 37.7% | 1.3% | 2,280 |
| | 1982 | 67.8% | 11.3% | 66.8% | 31.7% | 1.5% | 1,902 |
| | 1980 | 62.9% | 10.9% | 62.2% | 36.6% | 1.2% | 2,793 |
| | 1978 | 65.0% | 10.7% | 63.5% | 34.2% | 2.4% | 2,534 |
| | 1976 | 66.8% | 9.2% | 66.0% | 32.8% | 1.2% | 3,902 |
| | Average | 63.7% | 11.8% | 62.2% | 35.4% | 2.4% | |
| Not a Union Household | 2010 | 44.5% | −1.8% | 43.3% | 53.9% | 2.8% | 3,113 |
| | 2008 | 52.0% | −3.1% | 50.4% | 46.6% | 3.0% | 2,937 |
| | 2006 | 50.3% | −3.6% | 49.5% | 48.8% | 1.8% | 4,971 |
| | 2004 | 45.0% | −4.6% | 44.2% | 54.0% | 1.8% | 7,077 |
| | 2002 | 42.9% | −4.6% | 41.8% | 55.7% | 2.5% | 5,796 |
| | 2000 | 45.4% | −4.8% | 44.2% | 53.2% | 2.6% | 6,256 |
| | 1998 | 45.0% | −4.4% | 43.6% | 53.3% | 3.0% | 3,710 |
| | 1996 | 45.7% | −4.8% | 44.9% | 53.2% | 1.9% | 5,436 |
| | 1994 | | | | | | |
| | 1992 | | | | | | |
| | 1990 | | | | | | |
| | 1988 | 50.4% | −3.7% | 48.1% | 47.4% | 4.5% | 7,226 |
| | 1986 | 48.1% | −4.4% | 45.8% | 49.5% | 4.7% | 5,954 |
| | 1984 | 43.5% | −5.4% | 43.0% | 55.8% | 1.2% | 5,865 |
| | 1982 | 51.5% | −5.0% | 50.7% | 47.7% | 1.6% | 4,985 |
| | 1980 | 46.3% | −5.7% | 45.8% | 53.1% | 1.2% | 5,764 |
| | 1978 | 49.5% | −4.9% | 48.5% | 49.5% | 2.1% | 5,014 |
| | 1976 | 53.1% | −4.6% | 52.3% | 46.3% | 1.4% | 7,219 |
| | Average | 47.5% | −4.3% | 46.4% | 51.2% | 2.4% | |

**Question Wording for Union Household** (Coded: Union Household = 1; Not a Union Household = 2):

**1976–1980:** "Are you or is anyone living in your household a union member? . . . Yes (1); No (2)"

**1982:** "Are you or is anyone living in your household a member of a labor union? . . . Yes (1); No (2)"

*(Continued)*

**Table 5.18** House Vote by Union Household, 1976–2010 *(Continued)*

**1984:** "Are you or is any person in your household a member of a labor union? . . . Yes, I do (1); Yes, other family member (1); No (2)"

**1986–1988:** "Are you or is any person living in your household a member of a labor union? . . . Yes, I do (1); Yes, other family member (1); No (2)"

**1996:** "Do you or someone in your household belong to a labor union? . . . Yes (1); No (2)"

**1998:** "Do you or does someone else in your household belong to a labor union? . . . Yes (1); No (2)"

**2000–2008:** "Do you or does someone in your household belong to a labor union? . . . Yes, I do (1); Yes, someone else does (1); Yes, I do and someone else does (1); No one does (2)"

**2010:** "Does someone in your household belong to a labor union? . . . Yes (1); No (2)"

*Source:* National exit polls. See the section in Chapter 2 entitled "Creating a Cumulative National Data Set: Selecting Exit Polls" (pp. 28–29).

*Note:* When using these results to make inferences about the active electorate, the standard errors should be calculated using Table 2.2 (p. 36), which is explained in the adjacent section of Chapter 2, "Analyzing Exit Poll Questions: Estimating Sampling Error" (pp. 34–36). For a guide on how to understand the tables and figures of this chapter, see the section in Chapter 2 entitled "Presenting and Discussing the Exit Poll Data: Reading Chapter 5" (pp. 43–46). The rationale for using two-party percentages to show trends over time is given in Chapter 4, in the section entitled "Presidential Vote Choice" (pp. 124–131).

**Table 5.19** House Vote by Party Identification, 1976–2010

| | | Two-Party House Vote | | Full House Vote | | | |
|---|---|---|---|---|---|---|---|
| | | | Difference from Mean | | | | |
| Category | Year | Two-Party Democratic Vote | Democratic Two-Party Vote | Democratic Vote | Republican Vote | Third-Party Vote | Number of Respondents |
| Democrat | 2010 | 92.4% | 46.1% | 91.5% | 7.5% | 1.0% | 6,215 |
| | 2008 | 93.2% | 38.1% | 92.2% | 6.8% | 1.0% | 7,575 |
| | 2006 | 93.4% | 39.4% | 92.6% | 6.5% | 0.9% | 4,989 |
| | 2004 | 91.4% | 41.8% | 90.3% | 8.5% | 1.2% | 4,777 |
| | 2002 | 89.9% | 42.4% | 88.6% | 10.0% | 1.4% | 5,859 |
| | 2000 | 88.5% | 38.4% | 87.4% | 11.3% | 1.3% | 4,345 |
| | 1998 | 88.8% | 39.5% | 87.1% | 10.9% | 1.9% | 3,537 |
| | 1996 | 86.1% | 35.6% | 85.4% | 13.8% | 0.7% | 6,147 |
| | 1994 | 88.7% | 41.3% | 88.0% | 11.2% | 0.7% | 3,553 |
| | 1992 | 88.8% | 34.9% | 87.3% | 11.0% | 1.7% | 5,322 |
| | 1990 | 80.0% | 26.2% | 77.7% | 19.4% | 2.8% | 6,396 |
| | 1988 | 83.2% | 29.1% | 80.0% | 16.1% | 3.9% | 4,090 |
| | 1986 | 80.7% | 28.3% | 77.4% | 18.5% | 4.1% | 3,579 |
| | 1984 | 83.9% | 35.0% | 83.1% | 15.9% | 1.1% | 3,405 |
| | 1982 | 89.9% | 33.3% | 89.1% | 10.0% | 0.9% | 3,279 |
| | 1980 | 83.4% | 31.3% | 82.5% | 16.5% | 1.1% | 4,560 |
| | 1978 | 85.4% | 31.0% | 83.7% | 14.4% | 2.0% | 3,363 |
| | 1976 | 87.0% | 29.4% | 86.2% | 12.8% | 0.9% | 5,300 |
| | Average | 87.5% | 35.6% | 86.1% | 12.3% | 1.6% | |
| Republican | 2010 | 4.6% | −41.7% | 4.6% | 94.3% | 1.1% | 6,065 |
| | 2008 | 9.2% | −45.8% | 9.1% | 89.2% | 1.7% | 4,490 |
| | 2006 | 7.7% | −46.2% | 7.6% | 91.3% | 1.0% | 4,157 |
| | 2004 | 6.6% | −43.0% | 6.6% | 92.9% | 0.5% | 4,265 |
| | 2002 | 6.1% | −41.3% | 6.1% | 92.9% | 1.0% | 5,847 |

**Table 5.19** *(Continued)*

| Category | Year | Two-Party House Vote | | Full House Vote | | | |
|---|---|---|---|---|---|---|---|
| | | Two-Party Democratic Vote | Difference from Mean Democratic Two-Party Vote | Democratic Vote | Republican Vote | Third-Party Vote | Number of Respondents |
| Republican | 2000 | 8.4% | −41.8% | 8.3% | 90.6% | 1.1% | 3,817 |
| | 1998 | 9.1% | −40.3% | 9.0% | 89.9% | 1.1% | 3,191 |
| | 1996 | 10.4% | −40.1% | 10.3% | 88.5% | 1.2% | 4,692 |
| | 1994 | 8.3% | −39.1% | 8.2% | 90.7% | 1.1% | 3,598 |
| | 1992 | 15.2% | −38.7% | 15.0% | 83.4% | 1.6% | 4,266 |
| | 1990 | 25.8% | −28.0% | 25.3% | 72.8% | 2.0% | 6,133 |
| | 1988 | 21.2% | −32.9% | 20.1% | 74.6% | 5.3% | 3,233 |
| | 1986 | 20.0% | −32.5% | 19.2% | 76.7% | 4.1% | 2,603 |
| | 1984 | 13.1% | −35.8% | 13.1% | 86.4% | 0.5% | 2,969 |
| | 1982 | 12.1% | −44.4% | 12.0% | 87.1% | 0.9% | 2,287 |
| | 1980 | 10.2% | −41.8% | 10.2% | 89.2% | 0.6% | 2,394 |
| | 1978 | 13.0% | −41.4% | 12.8% | 86.1% | 1.1% | 1,899 |
| | 1976 | 14.3% | −43.3% | 14.2% | 85.1% | 0.7% | 2,633 |
| | Average | 12.0% | −39.9% | 11.7% | 86.8% | 1.5% | |
| Independent | 2010 | 40.2% | −6.1% | 37.4% | 55.6% | 7.0% | 4,478 |
| | 2008 | 54.2% | −0.9% | 51.2% | 43.3% | 5.5% | 4,296 |
| | 2006 | 59.4% | 5.4% | 56.7% | 38.8% | 4.5% | 3,183 |
| | 2004 | 51.7% | 2.1% | 49.4% | 46.2% | 4.4% | 3,134 |
| | 2002 | 48.6% | 1.2% | 45.0% | 47.6% | 7.4% | 3,300 |
| | 2000 | 48.8% | −1.3% | 46.5% | 48.7% | 4.9% | 2,865 |
| | 1998 | 48.2% | −1.2% | 44.7% | 48.2% | 7.1% | 2,519 |
| | 1996 | 48.7% | −1.8% | 46.4% | 48.8% | 4.7% | 3,516 |
| | 1994 | 42.8% | −4.6% | 41.1% | 55.0% | 3.9% | 2,569 |
| | 1992 | 54.0% | 0.0% | 51.4% | 43.8% | 4.8% | 3,467 |
| | 1990 | 53.3% | −0.5% | 51.1% | 44.8% | 4.1% | 5,415 |
| | 1988 | 54.0% | 0.0% | 51.1% | 43.5% | 5.4% | 2,601 |
| | 1986 | 52.5% | 0.1% | 49.4% | 44.7% | 5.8% | 2,125 |
| | 1984 | 46.1% | −2.8% | 44.9% | 52.5% | 2.6% | 2,145 |
| | 1982 | 51.5% | −5.0% | 49.4% | 46.6% | 4.0% | 1,718 |
| | 1980 | 44.2% | −7.8% | 43.1% | 54.3% | 2.6% | 2,290 |
| | 1978 | 49.9% | −4.4% | 47.7% | 47.8% | 4.5% | 2,271 |
| | 1976 | 55.0% | −2.6% | 53.8% | 44.0% | 2.2% | 3,351 |
| | Average | 50.2% | −1.7% | 47.8% | 47.5% | 4.7% | |

**Question Wording for Party Identification** (Coded: Democrat = 1; Republican = 2; Independent = 3):

**1976–1988:** "Do you usually think of yourself as a . . . Democrat (1); Republican (2); Independent (3)"

**1990–2010:** "No matter how you voted today, do you usually think of yourself as a . . . Democrat (1); Republican (2); Independent (3); Something else (3)"

*Source:* National exit polls. See the section in Chapter 2 entitled "Creating a Cumulative National Data Set: Selecting Exit Polls" (pp. 28–29).

*Note:* When using these results to make inferences about the active electorate, the standard errors should be calculated using Table 2.2 (p. 36), which is explained in the adjacent section of Chapter 2, "Analyzing Exit Poll Questions: Estimating Sampling Error" (pp. 34–36). For a guide on how to understand the tables and figures of this chapter, see the section in Chapter 2 entitled "Presenting and Discussing the Exit Poll Data: Reading Chapter 5" (pp. 43–46). The rationale for using two-party percentages to show trends over time is given in Chapter 4, in the section entitled "Presidential Vote Choice" (pp. 124–131).

**Table 5.20** House Vote by Ideological Identification, 1976–2010

| Category | Year | Two-Party Democratic Vote | Difference from Mean Democratic Two-Party Vote | Democratic Vote | Republican Vote | Third-Party Vote | Number of Respondents |
|---|---|---|---|---|---|---|---|
| | | Two-Party House Vote | | Full House Vote | | | |
| Liberal | 2010 | 92.1% | 45.8% | 89.9% | 7.7% | 2.3% | 3,407 |
| | 2008 | 89.0% | 33.9% | 86.9% | 10.8% | 2.3% | 2,349 |
| | 2006 | 88.8% | 34.8% | 86.9% | 11.0% | 2.1% | 1,493 |
| | 2004 | 85.2% | 35.6% | 83.3% | 14.4% | 2.3% | 1,559 |
| | 2002 | 81.1% | 33.7% | 77.8% | 18.2% | 4.1% | 1,206 |
| | 2000 | 83.5% | 33.4% | 80.9% | 15.9% | 3.2% | 1,443 |
| | 1998 | 83.7% | 34.3% | 80.7% | 15.8% | 3.5% | 1,497 |
| | 1996 | 82.1% | 31.6% | 80.6% | 17.6% | 1.8% | 1,932 |
| | 1994 | 81.4% | 34.0% | 79.8% | 18.2% | 2.0% | 1,793 |
| | 1992 | 80.7% | 26.8% | 77.5% | 18.5% | 4.0% | 1,520 |
| | 1990 | 73.7% | 19.9% | 71.4% | 25.4% | 3.2% | 856 |
| | 1988 | 79.7% | 25.6% | 75.8% | 19.3% | 4.8% | 3,033 |
| | 1986 | 71.2% | 18.8% | 68.3% | 27.6% | 4.1% | 1,799 |
| | 1984 | 75.3% | 26.4% | 73.4% | 24.1% | 2.5% | 2,314 |
| | 1982 | 79.5% | 23.0% | 77.6% | 20.0% | 2.4% | 2,755 |
| | 1980 | 72.2% | 20.2% | 71.5% | 27.5% | 1.0% | 2,716 |
| | 1978 | 74.2% | 19.9% | 72.2% | 25.2% | 2.6% | 2,567 |
| | 1976 | 77.1% | 19.5% | 75.9% | 22.5% | 1.6% | 4,034 |
| | Average | 80.6% | 28.7% | 78.4% | 18.9% | 2.8% | |
| Moderate | 2010 | 56.6% | 10.3% | 55.1% | 42.2% | 2.7% | 6,667 |
| | 2008 | 62.4% | 7.4% | 60.7% | 36.7% | 2.6% | 7,099 |
| | 2006 | 61.2% | 7.2% | 60.1% | 38.1% | 1.8% | 5,840 |
| | 2004 | 56.6% | 7.0% | 55.6% | 42.6% | 1.8% | 5,485 |
| | 2002 | 54.3% | 6.9% | 53.0% | 44.7% | 2.3% | 7,140 |
| | 2000 | 53.9% | 3.8% | 52.8% | 45.2% | 2.0% | 5,374 |
| | 1998 | 55.3% | 5.9% | 53.5% | 43.2% | 3.2% | 4,521 |
| | 1996 | 57.2% | 6.7% | 56.1% | 41.9% | 2.0% | 6,679 |
| | 1994 | 56.5% | 9.1% | 55.4% | 42.6% | 2.0% | 2,145 |
| | 1992 | 57.3% | 3.4% | 56.2% | 41.9% | 1.9% | 3,464 |
| | 1990 | 57.8% | 4.0% | 56.2% | 41.0% | 2.8% | 4,353 |
| | 1988 | 57.2% | 3.1% | 54.8% | 41.0% | 4.2% | 4,686 |
| | 1986 | 57.7% | 5.3% | 55.0% | 40.3% | 4.7% | 3,845 |
| | 1984 | 54.3% | 5.4% | 53.8% | 45.2% | 1.0% | 3,711 |
| | 1982 | 60.4% | 3.9% | 59.7% | 39.1% | 1.2% | 3,864 |
| | 1980 | 56.5% | 4.5% | 55.8% | 42.9% | 1.3% | 4,545 |
| | 1978 | 59.3% | 5.0% | 58.2% | 39.9% | 1.9% | 3,502 |
| | 1976 | 60.9% | 3.3% | 60.3% | 38.7% | 1.0% | 5,163 |
| | Average | 57.5% | 5.7% | 56.2% | 41.5% | 2.2% | |

**Table 5.20**   *(Continued)*

| Category | Year | Two-Party House Vote | | Full House Vote | | | |
|---|---|---|---|---|---|---|---|
| | | Two-Party Democratic Vote | Difference from Mean Democratic Two-Party Vote | Democratic Vote | Republican Vote | Third-Party Vote | Number of Respondents |
| Conservative | 2010 | 13.4% | −32.9% | 13.0% | 83.9% | 3.0% | 6,390 |
| | 2008 | 23.3% | −31.8% | 22.9% | 75.1% | 2.0% | 4,450 |
| | 2006 | 20.3% | −33.7% | 20.0% | 78.4% | 1.6% | 3,755 |
| | 2004 | 17.7% | −31.9% | 17.5% | 81.4% | 1.1% | 3,821 |
| | 2002 | 18.9% | −28.6% | 18.5% | 79.4% | 2.1% | 4,928 |
| | 2000 | 19.1% | −31.1% | 18.7% | 79.6% | 1.7% | 3,181 |
| | 1998 | 17.6% | −31.8% | 17.1% | 80.3% | 2.6% | 2,813 |
| | 1996 | 20.9% | −29.6% | 20.6% | 77.8% | 1.6% | 4,473 |
| | 1994 | 18.9% | −28.5% | 18.6% | 79.8% | 1.6% | 1,850 |
| | 1992 | 27.9% | −26.0% | 27.4% | 70.6% | 2.0% | 1,982 |
| | 1990 | 38.8% | −15.0% | 37.6% | 59.2% | 3.2% | 3,200 |
| | 1988 | 34.0% | −20.1% | 32.2% | 62.3% | 5.5% | 3,246 |
| | 1986 | 35.2% | −17.2% | 33.4% | 61.6% | 4.9% | 2,866 |
| | 1984 | 28.3% | −20.6% | 28.0% | 71.1% | 0.8% | 2,838 |
| | 1982 | 35.4% | −21.1% | 34.8% | 63.4% | 1.8% | 2,150 |
| | 1980 | 33.1% | −18.9% | 32.6% | 65.9% | 1.5% | 2,814 |
| | 1978 | 36.6% | −17.8% | 35.7% | 61.9% | 2.4% | 2,409 |
| | 1976 | 39.8% | −17.8% | 39.2% | 59.3% | 1.6% | 3,274 |
| | Average | 26.6% | −25.2% | 26.0% | 71.7% | 2.3% | |

**Question Wording for Ideological Identification** (Coded: Liberal = 1; Moderate = 2; Conservative = 3):

**1976–2010:** "On most political matters, do you consider yourself . . . Liberal (1); Moderate (2); Conservative (3)"

*Source:* National exit polls. See the section in Chapter 2 entitled "Creating a Cumulative National Data Set: Selecting Exit Polls" (pp. 28–29).

*Note:* When using these results to make inferences about the active electorate, the standard errors should be calculated using Table 2.2 (p. 36), which is explained in the adjacent section of Chapter 2, "Analyzing Exit Poll Questions: Estimating Sampling Error" (pp. 34–36). For a guide on how to understand the tables and figures of this chapter, see the section in Chapter 2 entitled "Presenting and Discussing the Exit Poll Data: Reading Chapter 5" (pp. 43–46). The rationale for using two-party percentages to show trends over time is given in Chapter 4, in the section entitled "Presidential Vote Choice" (pp. 124–131).

**Table 5.21**  House Vote by Presidential Vote in Last Election, 1976–2010

| | | Two-Party House Vote | | Full House Vote | | | |
| | | Two-Party Democratic Vote | Difference from Mean Democratic Two-Party Vote | Democratic Vote | Republican Vote | Third-Party Vote | Number of Respondents |
|---|---|---|---|---|---|---|---|
| Democrat | 2010 | 85.8% | 39.4% | 83.6% | 13.8% | 2.6% | 4,149 |
| | 2008 | 91.2% | 36.2% | 88.1% | 8.5% | 3.4% | 1,701 |
| | 2006 | 93.3% | 39.4% | 92.3% | 6.6% | 1.1% | 2,800 |
| | 2004 | 88.1% | 38.5% | 86.3% | 11.6% | 2.1% | 1,161 |
| | 2002 | 88.0% | 40.6% | 85.8% | 11.7% | 2.5% | 2,944 |
| | 2000 | 81.6% | 31.5% | 79.8% | 18.0% | 2.3% | 2,569 |
| | 1998 | 82.4% | 33.0% | 80.5% | 17.3% | 2.2% | 2,314 |
| | 1996 | 83.2% | 32.7% | 82.1% | 16.6% | 1.2% | 6,574 |
| | 1994 | 84.3% | 36.9% | 83.1% | 15.5% | 1.4% | 4,177 |
| | 1992 | 89.5% | 35.6% | 87.5% | 10.3% | 2.2% | 3,963 |
| | 1990 | 81.6% | 27.8% | 78.9% | 17.8% | 3.3% | 2,930 |
| | 1988 | 85.4% | 31.3% | 82.7% | 14.1% | 3.1% | 3,123 |
| | 1986 | 83.4% | 31.0% | 80.3% | 16.0% | 3.7% | 2,719 |
| | 1984 | 85.4% | 36.5% | 84.6% | 14.5% | 0.9% | 2,725 |
| | 1982 | 89.1% | 32.5% | 87.9% | 10.8% | 1.3% | 2,433 |
| | 1980 | 75.7% | 23.6% | 74.9% | 24.1% | 0.9% | 4,601 |
| | 1978 | 77.7% | 23.3% | 76.5% | 21.9% | 1.6% | 3,946 |
| | 1976 | 86.8% | 29.1% | 85.6% | 13.1% | 1.3% | 3,517 |
| | Average | 85.1% | 33.3% | 83.4% | 14.6% | 2.1% | |
| Republican | 2010 | 7.6% | −39.2% | 7.4% | 90.8% | 1.7% | 3,909 |
| | 2008 | 19.4% | −35.7% | 19.1% | 79.5% | 1.4% | 1,485 |
| | 2006 | 15.5% | −38.4% | 15.3% | 83.2% | 1.5% | 2,820 |
| | 2004 | 13.1% | −36.4% | 13.0% | 86.0% | 0.9% | 1,167 |
| | 2002 | 14.4% | −33.1% | 14.1% | 84.0% | 1.9% | 3,836 |
| | 2000 | 10.3% | −39.8% | 10.1% | 88.0% | 1.9% | 1,783 |
| | 1998 | 9.4% | −40.0% | 9.2% | 88.6% | 2.2% | 1,736 |
| | 1996 | 12.9% | −37.6% | 12.8% | 86.0% | 1.2% | 4,687 |
| | 1994 | 11.4% | −36.0% | 11.3% | 87.8% | 1.0% | 3,822 |
| | 1992 | 31.9% | −22.0% | 31.2% | 66.5% | 2.3% | 7,102 |
| | 1990 | 38.4% | −15.4% | 37.5% | 60.1% | 2.3% | 5,676 |
| | 1988 | 34.9% | −19.2% | 33.1% | 61.7% | 5.2% | 5,388 |
| | 1986 | 34.5% | −17.9% | 32.9% | 62.4% | 4.7% | 4,790 |
| | 1984 | 22.8% | −26.1% | 22.6% | 76.4% | 1.0% | 4,045 |
| | 1982 | 31.2% | −25.3% | 30.8% | 67.8% | 1.4% | 3,707 |
| | 1980 | 20.7% | −31.3% | 20.6% | 78.7% | 0.7% | 2,889 |
| | 1978 | 24.2% | −30.2% | 23.4% | 73.3% | 3.3% | 2,864 |
| | 1976 | 36.8% | −20.8% | 36.4% | 62.5% | 1.1% | 4,958 |
| | Average | 21.6% | −30.2% | 21.2% | 76.9% | 2.0% | |
| Other Candidate | 2010 | 36.4% | −10.0% | 32.9% | 57.7% | 9.5% | 287 |
| | 2008 | 69.5% | 14.5% | 63.6% | 27.9% | 8.6% | 171 |
| | 2006 | 74.1% | 20.2% | 66.5% | 23.2% | 10.2% | 251 |
| | 2004 | 77.9% | 28.3% | 69.8% | 19.8% | 10.4% | 103 |
| | 2002 | 67.7% | 20.3% | 60.8% | 29.0% | 10.1% | 318 |
| | 2000 | 34.7% | −15.5% | 32.2% | 60.7% | 7.1% | 502 |
| | 1998 | 39.3% | −10.0% | 34.9% | 53.8% | 11.3% | 418 |

**Table 5.21** *(Continued)*

| Category | Year | Two-Party House Vote — Two-Party Democratic Vote | Difference from Mean Democratic Two-Party Vote | Full House Vote — Democratic Vote | Republican Vote | Third-Party Vote | Number of Respondents |
|---|---|---|---|---|---|---|---|
| Other Candidate | 1996 | 36.4% | −14.1% | 34.3% | 59.9% | 5.8% | 1,835 |
| | 1994 | 32.4% | −15.0% | 30.9% | 64.5% | 4.6% | 1,396 |
| | 1992 | 81.5% | 27.6% | 74.0% | 16.8% | 9.2% | 376 |
| | 1990 | 67.7% | 13.9% | 61.1% | 29.1% | 9.8% | 370 |
| | 1988 | 71.6% | 17.5% | 65.4% | 26.0% | 8.6% | 412 |
| | 1986 | 65.2% | 12.8% | 58.4% | 31.1% | 10.5% | 460 |
| | 1984 | 72.3% | 23.4% | 69.8% | 26.8% | 3.5% | 374 |
| | 1982 | 76.3% | 19.8% | 72.2% | 22.4% | 5.4% | 506 |
| | 1980 | 50.0% | −2.0% | 46.0% | 46.0% | 7.9% | 166 |
| | 1978 | 60.6% | 6.3% | 55.6% | 36.1% | 8.3% | 275 |
| | 1976 | 74.0% | 16.4% | 71.9% | 25.3% | 2.8% | 663 |
| | Average | 60.4% | 8.6% | 55.6% | 36.5% | 8.0% | |
| Did Not Vote | 2010 | 39.5% | −6.5% | 38.7% | 59.3% | 2.1% | 317 |
| | 2008 | 74.1% | 19.1% | 72.2% | 25.2% | 2.6% | 491 |
| | 2006 | 67.3% | 13.3% | 65.5% | 31.9% | 2.7% | 224 |
| | 2004 | 57.2% | 7.6% | 56.3% | 42.1% | 1.7% | 526 |
| | 2002 | 58.5% | 11.0% | 53.8% | 38.2% | 8.0% | 291 |
| | 2000 | 44.8% | −5.3% | 44.1% | 54.3% | 1.6% | 647 |
| | 1998 | 54.0% | 4.6% | 50.4% | 42.9% | 6.6% | 216 |
| | 1996 | 56.9% | 6.4% | 55.9% | 42.3% | 1.8% | 1,261 |
| | 1994 | 45.3% | −2.0% | 44.7% | 53.9% | 1.4% | 347 |
| | 1992 | 62.3% | 8.3% | 60.5% | 36.7% | 2.8% | 2,048 |
| | 1990 | 61.3% | 7.5% | 59.3% | 37.4% | 3.3% | 486 |
| | 1988 | 60.1% | 6.0% | 57.2% | 38.0% | 4.9% | 1,075 |
| | 1986 | 59.3% | 6.9% | 56.6% | 38.8% | 4.6% | 403 |
| | 1984 | 49.2% | 0.3% | 48.3% | 49.9% | 1.7% | 1,000 |
| | 1982 | 66.1% | 9.6% | 65.5% | 33.5% | 1.0% | 554 |
| | 1980 | 52.0% | 0.0% | 50.5% | 46.6% | 2.9% | 1,028 |
| | 1978 | 64.2% | 9.9% | 62.5% | 34.8% | 2.7% | 438 |
| | 1976 | 63.6% | 6.0% | 62.5% | 35.8% | 1.7% | 1,783 |
| | Average | 57.5% | 5.7% | 55.8% | 41.2% | 3.0% | |

Question Wording for Presidential Vote in Last Election (Coded: Democrat = 1; Republican = 2; Other Candidate = 3; Did Not Vote = 4):

**1976:** "In 1972, for whom did you vote? . . . Nixon (2); McGovern (1); Someone else (3); Did not vote (4)"

**1978:** "In 1976, for whom did you vote? . . . Carter (1); Ford (2); Someone else (3); Did not vote (4)"

**1980:** "In 1976, for whom did you vote? . . . Jimmy Carter (1); Gerald Ford (2); Someone else (3); Did not vote (4)"

**1982:** "How did you vote in the 1980 election for president? . . . Carter (1); Reagan (2); Anderson (3); Someone else (3); Did not vote for president in [Year] (4)"

**1984:** "Who did you vote for in the 1980 presidential election? . . . Carter (1); Reagan (2); Anderson (3); Didn't vote (4)"

**1986:** "Who did you vote for in the 1984 presidential election? . . . Reagan (2); Mondale (1); Someone else (3); Didn't vote for president (4)"

*(Continued)*

**Table 5.21** House Vote by Presidential Vote in Last Election, 1976–2010 *(Continued)*

**1988:** "Who did you vote for in the 1984 presidential election? . . . Reagan (2); Mondale (1); Someone else (3); Didn't vote (4)"

**1990:** "Who did you vote for in the 1988 presidential election? . . . George Bush (2); Michael Dukakis (1); Someone else (3); Didn't happen to vote in [Year] (4)"

**1992:** "Who did you vote for in the 1988 presidential election? . . . George Bush (Rep) (2); Michael Dukakis (Dem) (1); Someone else (3); Did not vote in [Year] (4)"

**1994:** "Who did you vote for in the 1992 presidential election? . . . George Bush (Rep) (2); Bill Clinton (Dem) (1); Ross Perot (Ind) (3); Someone else (3); Did not vote in [Year] (4)"

**1996:** "Who did you vote for in the 1992 presidential election? . . . George Bush (Rep) (2); Bill Clinton (Dem) (1); Ross Perot (Ind) (3); Someone else (3); Did not vote for president (4)"

**1998:** "Who did you vote for in the 1996 presidential election? . . . Bill Clinton (Dem) (1); Bob Dole (Rep) (2); Ross Perot (Ref) (3); Someone else (3); Did not vote for president in [Year] (4)"

**2000:** "In the 1996 election for president, did you vote for . . . Bill Clinton (Dem) (1); Bob Dole (Rep) (2); Ross Perot (Ref) (3); Someone else (3); Did not vote (4)"

**2002:** "In the 2000 election for president, did you vote for . . . Al Gore (Dem) (1); George W. Bush (Rep) (2); Ralph Nader (Gre) (3); Someone else (3); Did not vote (4)"

**2004:** "Did you vote in the 2000 presidential election? . . . Yes, for Al Gore (1); Yes, for George W. Bush (2); Yes, for another candidate (3); No, I did not vote (4)"

**2006–2008:** "In the 2004 election for president, did you vote for . . . George W. Bush (Rep) (2); John Kerry (Dem) (1); Someone else (3); Did not vote (4)"

**2010:** "In the 2008 election for president, did you vote for . . . Obama (D) (1); McCain (R) (2); Other (3); Didn't vote (4)"

*Source:* National exit polls. See the section in Chapter 2 entitled "Creating a Cumulative National Data Set: Selecting Exit Polls" (pp. 28–29).

*Note:* When using these results to make inferences about the active electorate, the standard errors should be calculated using Table 2.2 (p. 36), which is explained in the adjacent section of Chapter 2, "Analyzing Exit Poll Questions: Estimating Sampling Error" (pp. 34–36). For a guide on how to understand the tables and figures of this chapter, see the section in Chapter 2 entitled "Presenting and Discussing the Exit Poll Data: Reading Chapter 5" (pp. 43–46). The rationale for using two-party percentages to show trends over time is given in Chapter 4, in the section entitled "Presidential Vote Choice" (pp. 124–131).

**Table 5.22** House Vote by Presidential Approval, 1978–2010

| | | Two-Party House Vote | | Full House Vote | | | |
| | | Two-Party Democratic Vote | Difference from Mean Democratic Two-Party Vote | Democratic Vote | Republican Vote | Third-Party Vote | Number of Respondents |
| Category | Year | | | | | | |
|---|---|---|---|---|---|---|---|
| Approve | 2010 | 86.0% | 39.7% | 84.6% | 13.8% | 1.6% | 1,968 |
| | 2008 | 15.4% | −39.6% | 15.1% | 82.9% | 2.0% | 905 |
| | 2006 | 14.3% | −39.6% | 14.1% | 84.2% | 1.7% | 2,712 |
| | 2004 | 15.3% | −34.3% | 15.2% | 83.9% | 1.0% | 3,203 |
| | 2002 | 26.2% | −21.2% | 25.7% | 72.3% | 2.0% | 5,242 |
| | 2000 | 75.3% | 25.2% | 73.7% | 24.2% | 2.1% | 3,160 |
| | 1998 | 76.6% | 27.2% | 74.2% | 22.7% | 3.1% | 5,447 |
| | 1996 | | | | | | |
| | 1994 | 82.0% | 34.6% | 80.8% | 17.8% | 1.4% | 4,340 |
| | 1992 | | | | | | |

**Table 5.22** *(Continued)*

| Category | Year | Two-Party House Vote | | Full House Vote | | | |
| | | Two-Party Democratic Vote | Difference from Mean Democratic Two-Party Vote | Democratic Vote | Republican Vote | Third-Party Vote | Number of Respondents |
|---|---|---|---|---|---|---|---|
| Approve | 1990 | 40.6% | −13.2% | 39.7% | 58.2% | 2.1% | 10,763 |
| | 1988 | | | | | | |
| | 1986 | 36.2% | −16.3% | 34.4% | 60.8% | 4.8% | 4,983 |
| | 1984 | | | | | | |
| | 1982 | 25.5% | −31.0% | 25.1% | 73.2% | 1.7% | 3,587 |
| | 1980 | | | | | | |
| | 1978 | 72.9% | 18.5% | 71.6% | 26.7% | 1.7% | 3,650 |
| | Average | 47.2% | −4.2% | 46.2% | 51.7% | 2.1% | |
| | | | | | | | |
| Disapprove | 2010 | 11.9% | −34.4% | 11.4% | 84.4% | 4.2% | 2,316 |
| | 2008 | 68.8% | 13.8% | 66.8% | 30.3% | 2.9% | 3,020 |
| | 2006 | 84.0% | 30.0% | 82.1% | 15.6% | 2.2% | 3,943 |
| | 2004 | 89.1% | 39.5% | 86.9% | 10.7% | 2.4% | 3,178 |
| | 2002 | 88.2% | 40.8% | 85.6% | 11.4% | 2.9% | 2,896 |
| | 2000 | 14.3% | −35.8% | 13.9% | 83.2% | 2.9% | 2,291 |
| | 1998 | 14.3% | −35.1% | 13.9% | 83.2% | 2.9% | 4,110 |
| | 1996 | | | | | | |
| | 1994 | 16.8% | −30.5% | 16.5% | 81.7% | 1.8% | 5,137 |
| | 1992 | | | | | | |
| | 1990 | 73.8% | 19.9% | 70.6% | 25.1% | 4.2% | 6,725 |
| | 1988 | | | | | | |
| | 1986 | 79.4% | 27.0% | 75.6% | 19.6% | 4.7% | 3,106 |
| | 1984 | | | | | | |
| | 1982 | 90.0% | 33.5% | 88.7% | 9.9% | 1.5% | 3,204 |
| | 1980 | | | | | | |
| | 1978 | 38.1% | −16.2% | 37.1% | 60.2% | 2.7% | 3,517 |
| | Average | 55.7% | 4.4% | 54.1% | 42.9% | 3.0% | |

**Question Wording for Presidential Approval** (Coded: Approve = 1; Disapprove = 2):

**1978:** "On most political matters, do you approve or disapprove of the way [President] is handling his job as president? . . . Approve (1); Disapprove (2)"

**1982–2002:** "Do you approve or disapprove of the way [President] is handling his job as president? . . . Approve (1); Disapprove (2)"

**2004–2010:** "Do you approve or disapprove of the way [President] is handling his job as president? . . . Strongly approve (1); Somewhat approve (1); Somewhat disapprove (2); Strongly disapprove (2)"

*Source:* National exit polls. See the section in Chapter 2 entitled "Creating a Cumulative National Data Set: Selecting Exit Polls" (pp. 28–29).

*Note:* When using these results to make inferences about the active electorate, the standard errors should be calculated using Table 2.2 (p. 36), which is explained in the adjacent section of Chapter 2, "Analyzing Exit Poll Questions: Estimating Sampling Error" (pp. 34–36). For a guide on how to understand the tables and figures of this chapter, see the section in Chapter 2 entitled "Presenting and Discussing the Exit Poll Data: Reading Chapter 5" (pp. 43–46). The rationale for using two-party percentages to show trends over time is given in Chapter 4, in the section entitled "Presidential Vote Choice" (pp. 124–131).

**Table 5.23** House Vote by Congressional Approval, 1990–2010

| Category | Year | Two-Party House Vote | | Full House Vote | | | |
|---|---|---|---|---|---|---|---|
| | | Two-Party Democratic Vote | Difference from Mean Democratic Two-Party Vote | Democratic Vote | Republican Vote | Third-Party Vote | Number of Respondents |
| Approve | 2010 | 80.2% | 33.9% | 79.0% | 19.5% | 1.5% | 1,089 |
| | 2008 | 63.1% | 8.1% | 61.6% | 36.0% | 2.4% | 1,066 |
| | 2006 | 26.8% | −27.2% | 26.5% | 72.3% | 1.3% | 2,289 |
| | 2004 | | | | | | |
| | 2002 | 39.5% | −7.9% | 38.7% | 59.3% | 2.0% | 3,458 |
| | 2000 | | | | | | |
| | 1998 | 30.8% | −18.6% | 29.9% | 67.2% | 2.9% | 2,037 |
| | 1996 | | | | | | |
| | 1994 | 73.9% | 26.5% | 73.0% | 25.8% | 1.3% | 871 |
| | 1992 | | | | | | |
| | 1990 | 61.2% | 7.3% | 60.0% | 38.1% | 2.0% | 1,794 |
| | Average | 53.6% | 3.2% | 52.7% | 45.4% | 1.9% | |
| Disapprove | 2010 | 33.6% | −12.7% | 32.6% | 64.5% | 2.9% | 3,182 |
| | 2008 | 52.7% | −2.3% | 51.7% | 46.4% | 1.9% | 3,096 |
| | 2006 | 70.8% | 16.9% | 69.1% | 28.5% | 2.4% | 3,917 |
| | 2004 | | | | | | |
| | 2002 | 53.6% | 6.2% | 51.6% | 44.6% | 3.7% | 3,982 |
| | 2000 | | | | | | |
| | 1998 | 62.8% | 13.4% | 60.5% | 35.8% | 3.7% | 2,684 |
| | 1996 | | | | | | |
| | 1994 | 41.3% | −6.1% | 40.4% | 57.5% | 2.0% | 3,922 |
| | 1992 | | | | | | |
| | 1990 | 52.8% | −1.1% | 51.0% | 45.7% | 3.3% | 7,483 |
| | Average | 52.5% | 2.0% | 51.0% | 46.1% | 2.9% | |

**Question Wording for Congressional Approval** (Coded: Approve = 1; Disapprove = 2):

**1990–2002:** "Do you approve or disapprove of the way Congress is handling its job? . . . Approve (1); Disapprove (2)"

**2006–2010:** "Do you approve or disapprove of the way Congress is handling its job? . . . Strongly approve (1); Somewhat approve (1); Somewhat disapprove (2); Strongly disapprove (2)"

*Source:* National exit polls. See the section in Chapter 2 entitled "Creating a Cumulative National Data Set: Selecting Exit Polls" (pp. 28–29).

*Note:* When using these results to make inferences about the active electorate, the standard errors should be calculated using Table 2.2 (p. 36), which is explained in the adjacent section of Chapter 2, "Analyzing Exit Poll Questions: Estimating Sampling Error" (pp. 34–36). For a guide on how to understand the tables and figures of this chapter, see the section in Chapter 2 entitled "Presenting and Discussing the Exit Poll Data: Reading Chapter 5" (pp. 43–46). The rationale for using two-party percentages to show trends over time is given in Chapter 4, in the section entitled "Presidential Vote Choice" (pp. 124–131).

**Table 5.24**  House Vote by Perceived Direction of the Country, 1990–2010

| Category | Year | Two-Party House Vote | | Full House Vote | | | |
| | | Two-Party Democratic Vote | Difference from Mean Democratic Two-Party Vote | Democratic Vote | Republican Vote | Third-Party Vote | Number of Respondents |
|---|---|---|---|---|---|---|---|
| Right Direction | 2010 | 83.6% | 37.3% | 82.0% | 16.1% | 1.9% | 1,564 |
| | 2008 | 33.3% | −21.7% | 32.5% | 65.1% | 2.4% | 757 |
| | 2006 | 19.9% | −34.1% | 19.7% | 79.2% | 1.1% | 2,434 |
| | 2004 | 17.0% | −32.6% | 17.0% | 82.5% | 0.5% | 1,465 |
| | 2002 | 34.3% | −13.2% | 33.6% | 64.5% | 1.9% | 4,694 |
| | 2000 | 61.1% | 11.0% | 59.8% | 38.0% | 2.2% | 3,626 |
| | 1998 | 62.7% | 13.3% | 61.2% | 36.5% | 2.4% | 2,943 |
| | 1996 | 66.7% | 16.2% | 66.3% | 33.1% | 0.7% | 2,010 |
| | 1994 | 65.9% | 18.5% | 65.1% | 33.7% | 1.1% | 2,020 |
| | 1992 | | | | | | |
| | 1990 | 46.4% | −7.4% | 45.4% | 52.4% | 2.2% | 3,855 |
| | Average | 49.1% | −1.3% | 48.3% | 50.1% | 1.6% | |
| Wrong Track | 2010 | 22.4% | −23.9% | 21.8% | 75.6% | 2.6% | 2,645 |
| | 2008 | 62.8% | 7.8% | 61.1% | 36.2% | 2.7% | 3,010 |
| | 2006 | 79.9% | 25.9% | 78.2% | 19.7% | 2.1% | 3,525 |
| | 2004 | 83.6% | 34.0% | 81.0% | 15.9% | 3.1% | 1,625 |
| | 2002 | 68.0% | 20.6% | 65.7% | 30.8% | 3.5% | 3,267 |
| | 2000 | 24.5% | −25.6% | 23.8% | 73.3% | 2.8% | 1,757 |
| | 1998 | 28.2% | −21.1% | 27.3% | 69.4% | 3.3% | 1,721 |
| | 1996 | 30.5% | −20.0% | 29.3% | 66.7% | 4.0% | 1,535 |
| | 1994 | 33.1% | −14.3% | 32.4% | 65.4% | 2.2% | 2,922 |
| | 1992 | | | | | | |
| | 1990 | 60.3% | 6.5% | 58.1% | 38.3% | 3.5% | 5,415 |
| | Average | 49.3% | −1.0% | 47.9% | 49.1% | 3.0% | |

Question Wording for Perceived Direction of the Country (Coded: Right Direction = 1; Wrong Track = 2):

1990–2010: "Do you think things in this country today are . . . Generally going in the right direction (1); Seriously off on the wrong track (2)"

*Source:* National exit polls. See the section in Chapter 2 entitled "Creating a Cumulative National Data Set: Selecting Exit Polls" (pp. 28–29).

*Note:* When using these results to make inferences about the active electorate, the standard errors should be calculated using Table 2.2 (p. 36), which is explained in the adjacent section of Chapter 2, "Analyzing Exit Poll Questions: Estimating Sampling Error" (pp. 34–36). For a guide on how to understand the tables and figures of this chapter, see the section in Chapter 2 entitled "Presenting and Discussing the Exit Poll Data: Reading Chapter 5" (pp. 43–46). The rationale for using two-party percentages to show trends over time is given in Chapter 4, in the section entitled "Presidential Vote Choice" (pp. 124–131).

**Table 5.25** House Vote by Expected Life for Next Generation, 1992–2010

| | | Two-Party House Vote | | Full House Vote | | | |
|---|---|---|---|---|---|---|---|
| Category | Year | Two-Party Democratic Vote | Difference from Mean Democratic Two-Party Vote | Democratic Vote | Republican Vote | Third-Party Vote | Number of Respondents |
| Better Than Today | 2010 | 60.8% | 14.5% | 60.0% | 38.8% | 1.2% | 1,320 |
| | 2008 | | | | | | |
| | 2006 | 37.6% | −16.3% | 37.3% | 61.9% | 0.8% | 1,803 |
| | 2004 | | | | | | |
| | 2002 | | | | | | |
| | 2000 | 53.6% | 3.5% | 52.7% | 45.6% | 1.7% | 1,410 |
| | 1998 | | | | | | |
| | 1996 | 59.4% | 8.9% | 58.8% | 40.2% | 1.0% | 1,109 |
| | 1994 | | | | | | |
| | 1992 | 55.1% | 1.2% | 54.2% | 44.1% | 1.8% | 749 |
| | Average | 53.3% | 2.4% | 52.6% | 46.1% | 1.3% | |
| About the Same | 2010 | 53.5% | 7.2% | 51.9% | 45.1% | 3.1% | 1,050 |
| | 2008 | | | | | | |
| | 2006 | 52.7% | −1.2% | 51.7% | 46.4% | 1.9% | 1,720 |
| | 2004 | | | | | | |
| | 2002 | | | | | | |
| | 2000 | 51.4% | 1.3% | 50.3% | 47.6% | 2.2% | 824 |
| | 1998 | | | | | | |
| | 1996 | 51.8% | 1.3% | 51.1% | 47.5% | 1.5% | 1,312 |
| | 1994 | | | | | | |
| | 1992 | 44.5% | −9.5% | 43.2% | 54.0% | 2.8% | 779 |
| | Average | 50.8% | −0.2% | 49.6% | 48.1% | 2.3% | |
| Worse Than Today | 2010 | 33.9% | −12.4% | 32.8% | 63.9% | 3.4% | 1,524 |
| | 2008 | | | | | | |
| | 2006 | 67.2% | 13.3% | 65.6% | 32.0% | 2.4% | 2,541 |
| | 2004 | | | | | | |
| | 2002 | | | | | | |
| | 2000 | 40.3% | −9.8% | 39.1% | 57.9% | 3.0% | 611 |
| | 1998 | | | | | | |
| | 1996 | 39.5% | −11.0% | 38.7% | 59.3% | 2.0% | 1,205 |
| | 1994 | | | | | | |
| | 1992 | 59.1% | 5.2% | 57.1% | 39.5% | 3.4% | 900 |
| | Average | 48.0% | −3.0% | 46.7% | 50.5% | 2.8% | |

**Question Wording for Expected Life for Next Generation** (Coded: Better Than Today = 1; About the Same = 2; Worse Than Today = 3):

**1992–2010:** "Do you expect life for the next generation of Americans to be . . . Better than life today (1); Worse than life today (3); About the same (2)"

*Source:* National exit polls. See the section in Chapter 2 entitled "Creating a Cumulative National Data Set: Selecting Exit Polls" (pp. 28–29).

*Note:* When using these results to make inferences about the active electorate, the standard errors should be calculated using Table 2.2 (p. 36), which is explained in the adjacent section of Chapter 2, "Analyzing Exit Poll Questions: Estimating Sampling Error" (pp. 34–36). For a guide on how to understand the tables and figures of this chapter, see the section in Chapter 2 entitled "Presenting and Discussing the Exit Poll Data: Reading Chapter 5" (pp. 43–46). The rationale for using two-party percentages to show trends over time is given in Chapter 4, in the section entitled "Presidential Vote Choice" (pp. 124–131).

**Table 5.26**  House Vote by Position on Government Activism, 1992–2010

| | | Two-Party House Vote | | Full House Vote | | | |
| | | Two-Party Democratic Vote | Difference from Mean Democratic Two-Party Vote | Democratic Vote | Republican Vote | Third-Party Vote | Number of Respondents |
| Category | Year | | | | | | |
|---|---|---|---|---|---|---|---|
| Government Should Do More | 2010 | 78.7% | 32.4% | 77.1% | 20.9% | 2.1% | 1,773 |
| | 2008 | 76.5% | 21.5% | 75.6% | 23.2% | 1.2% | 2,474 |
| | 2006 | | | | | | |
| | 2004 | 67.1% | 17.5% | 65.9% | 32.3% | 1.8% | 1,492 |
| | 2002 | 66.8% | 19.3% | 65.2% | 32.4% | 2.4% | 3,400 |
| | 2000 | 73.4% | 23.2% | 71.5% | 26.0% | 2.5% | 2,719 |
| | 1998 | | | | | | |
| | 1996 | 71.8% | 21.3% | 70.1% | 27.5% | 2.3% | 1,676 |
| | 1994 | 70.2% | 22.9% | 69.3% | 29.4% | 1.4% | 1,988 |
| | 1992 | 68.4% | 14.5% | 66.5% | 30.7% | 2.8% | 1,397 |
| | Average | 71.6% | 21.6% | 70.2% | 27.8% | 2.0% | |
| Government Does Too Much | 2010 | 20.9% | −25.9% | 20.0% | 76.1% | 3.9% | 2,361 |
| | 2008 | 30.3% | −24.8% | 29.5% | 68.0% | 2.5% | 1,595 |
| | 2006 | | | | | | |
| | 2004 | 30.6% | −19.0% | 30.1% | 68.2% | 1.7% | 1,448 |
| | 2002 | 30.6% | −16.9% | 29.8% | 67.6% | 2.6% | 3,884 |
| | 2000 | 29.1% | −21.0% | 28.3% | 69.0% | 2.6% | 3,234 |
| | 1998 | | | | | | |
| | 1996 | 30.4% | −20.1% | 29.8% | 68.3% | 2.0% | 1,963 |
| | 1994 | 29.8% | −17.6% | 29.2% | 69.0% | 1.7% | 2,894 |
| | 1992 | 35.7% | −18.2% | 34.7% | 62.4% | 2.9% | 1,073 |
| | Average | 29.7% | −20.4% | 28.9% | 68.6% | 2.5% | |

Question Wording for Position on Government Activism (Coded: Government Should Do More = 1; Government Does Too Much = 2):

1992–1994: "Which comes closest to your view . . . Government should do more to solve national problems (1); Government is doing too many things better left to businesses and individuals (2)"

1996–2008: "Which comes closest to your view . . . Government should do more to solve problems (1); Government is doing too many things better left to businesses and individuals (2)"

2010: "Which is closer to your view . . . Government should do more to solve problems (1); Government is doing too many things better left to businesses and individuals (2)"

*Source:* National exit polls. See the section in Chapter 2 entitled "Creating a Cumulative National Data Set: Selecting Exit Polls" (pp. 28–29).

*Note:* When using these results to make inferences about the active electorate, the standard errors should be calculated using Table 2.2 (p. 36), which is explained in the adjacent section of Chapter 2, "Analyzing Exit Poll Questions: Estimating Sampling Error" (pp. 34–36). For a guide on how to understand the tables and figures of this chapter, see the section in Chapter 2 entitled "Presenting and Discussing the Exit Poll Data: Reading Chapter 5" (pp. 43–46). The rationale for using two-party percentages to show trends over time is given in Chapter 4, in the section entitled "Presidential Vote Choice" (pp. 124–131).

**Table 5.27** House Vote by First-Time Voter, 1996–2010

| Category | Year | Two-Party House Vote | | Full House Vote | | | |
|---|---|---|---|---|---|---|---|
| | | Two-Party Democratic Vote | Difference from Mean Democratic Two-Party Vote | Democratic Vote | Republican Vote | Third-Party Vote | Number of Respondents |
| First-Time Voter | 2010 | 51.5% | 5.2% | 45.6% | 42.9% | 11.6% | 138 |
| | 2008 | 64.6% | 9.5% | 63.1% | 34.6% | 2.4% | 961 |
| | 2006 | | | | | | |
| | 2004 | 53.3% | 3.7% | 53.0% | 46.4% | 0.6% | 715 |
| | 2002 | | | | | | |
| | 2000 | 51.1% | 0.9% | 50.1% | 47.9% | 2.0% | 781 |
| | 1998 | | | | | | |
| | 1996 | 59.0% | 8.5% | 57.4% | 39.8% | 2.8% | 696 |
| | Average | 55.9% | 5.6% | 53.8% | 42.3% | 3.9% | |
| Not First-Time Voter | 2010 | 45.8% | −0.5% | 44.5% | 52.6% | 2.9% | 4,391 |
| | 2008 | 53.3% | −1.8% | 51.9% | 45.5% | 2.6% | 6,908 |
| | 2006 | | | | | | |
| | 2004 | 49.2% | −0.4% | 48.3% | 49.9% | 1.8% | 5,469 |
| | 2002 | | | | | | |
| | 2000 | 49.6% | −0.5% | 48.4% | 49.1% | 2.5% | 7,857 |
| | 1998 | | | | | | |
| | 1996 | 50.1% | −0.4% | 49.2% | 48.9% | 1.9% | 6,481 |
| | Average | 49.6% | −0.7% | 48.5% | 49.2% | 2.3% | |

**Question Wording for First-Time Voter** (Coded: First-Time Voter = 1; Not First-Time Voter = 2):

**1996–2004 and 2010:** "Is this the first time you have ever voted? . . . Yes (1); No (2)"

**2008:** "Is this the first year you have ever voted? . . . Yes (1); No (2)"

*Source:* National exit polls. See the section in Chapter 2 entitled "Creating a Cumulative National Data Set: Selecting Exit Polls" (pp. 28–29).

*Note:* When using these results to make inferences about the active electorate, the standard errors should be calculated using Table 2.2 (p. 36), which is explained in the adjacent section of Chapter 2, "Analyzing Exit Poll Questions: Estimating Sampling Error" (pp. 34–36). For a guide on how to understand the tables and figures of this chapter, see the section in Chapter 2 entitled "Presenting and Discussing the Exit Poll Data: Reading Chapter 5" (pp. 43–46). The rationale for using two-party percentages to show trends over time is given in Chapter 4, in the section entitled "Presidential Vote Choice" (pp. 124–131).

**Table 5.28** House Vote by Household Income, 1994–2010

| | | Two-Party House Vote | | Full House Vote | | | |
|---|---|---|---|---|---|---|---|
| Category | Year | Two-Party Democratic Vote | Difference from Mean Democratic Two-Party Vote | Democratic Vote | Republican Vote | Third-Party Vote | Number of Respondents |
| Under | 2010 | 58.9% | 12.6% | 56.9% | 39.7% | 3.4% | 1,878 |
| $30,000 | 2008 | 68.3% | 13.2% | 66.9% | 31.1% | 2.1% | 2,876 |
| | 2006 | 65.2% | 11.3% | 63.5% | 33.8% | 2.6% | 2,211 |
| | 2004 | 61.7% | 12.1% | 60.2% | 37.3% | 2.4% | 2,574 |
| | 2002 | 59.6% | 12.2% | 57.9% | 39.2% | 3.0% | 2,842 |
| | 2000 | 57.7% | 7.5% | 56.2% | 41.2% | 2.6% | 2,297 |
| | 1998 | 56.2% | 6.8% | 54.0% | 42.2% | 3.8% | 2,086 |
| | 1996 | 58.4% | 7.9% | 57.0% | 40.6% | 2.4% | 4,658 |
| | 1994 | 54.7% | 7.3% | 53.4% | 44.2% | 2.3% | 2,868 |
| | Average | 60.1% | 10.1% | 58.5% | 38.8% | 2.7% | |
| $30,000– | 2010 | 52.2% | 5.9% | 50.8% | 46.4% | 2.8% | 2,200 |
| $49,999 | 2008 | 58.8% | 3.7% | 57.0% | 40.0% | 3.1% | 2,864 |
| | 2006 | 56.8% | 2.8% | 56.0% | 42.6% | 1.4% | 2,369 |
| | 2004 | 52.1% | 2.5% | 51.1% | 47.0% | 1.9% | 2,455 |
| | 2002 | 49.7% | 2.3% | 48.2% | 48.7% | 3.1% | 3,127 |
| | 2000 | 51.1% | 1.0% | 50.0% | 47.8% | 2.2% | 2,648 |
| | 1998 | 49.2% | −0.2% | 47.8% | 49.3% | 2.9% | 2,231 |
| | 1996 | 49.8% | −0.7% | 48.8% | 49.2% | 2.0% | 3,748 |
| | 1994 | 45.1% | −2.3% | 44.3% | 54.0% | 1.7% | 2,782 |
| | Average | 51.6% | 1.7% | 50.4% | 47.2% | 2.3% | |
| $50,000– | 2010 | 47.1% | 0.8% | 45.4% | 51.1% | 3.5% | 2,525 |
| $74,999 | 2008 | 52.8% | −2.3% | 51.4% | 46.0% | 2.7% | 3,186 |
| | 2006 | 50.8% | −3.2% | 49.8% | 48.2% | 2.0% | 2,572 |
| | 2004 | 44.7% | −4.9% | 44.0% | 54.4% | 1.6% | 2,670 |
| | 2002 | 45.6% | −1.9% | 44.6% | 53.3% | 2.1% | 3,416 |
| | 2000 | 47.8% | −2.3% | 46.9% | 51.2% | 2.0% | 2,660 |
| | 1998 | 44.6% | −4.8% | 43.6% | 54.2% | 2.2% | 2,235 |
| | 1996 | 47.1% | −3.4% | 46.4% | 52.2% | 1.4% | 2,876 |
| | 1994 | 45.4% | −2.0% | 44.7% | 53.8% | 1.6% | 2,051 |
| | Average | 47.3% | −2.7% | 46.3% | 51.6% | 2.1% | |
| $75,000– | 2010 | 43.1% | −3.2% | 42.3% | 55.8% | 1.9% | 1,873 |
| $99,999 | 2008 | 50.5% | −4.6% | 49.1% | 48.3% | 2.6% | 2,144 |
| | 2006 | 52.2% | −1.8% | 51.5% | 47.2% | 1.3% | 1,762 |
| | 2004 | 45.2% | −4.3% | 44.6% | 53.9% | 1.5% | 1,627 |
| | 2002 | 41.1% | −6.4% | 40.1% | 57.5% | 2.3% | 2,098 |
| | 2000 | 44.9% | −5.3% | 43.9% | 53.9% | 2.1% | 1,360 |
| | 1998 | 48.0% | −1.4% | 46.9% | 50.9% | 2.3% | 1,028 |
| | 1996 | 43.9% | −6.6% | 43.3% | 55.3% | 1.4% | 1,260 |
| | 1994 | 40.0% | −7.4% | 39.6% | 59.4% | 1.0% | 848 |
| | Average | 45.4% | −4.6% | 44.6% | 53.6% | 1.8% | |

*(Continued)*

**Table 5.28** House Vote by Household Income, 1994–2010 *(Continued)*

| Category | Year | Two-Party House Vote | | Full House Vote | | | |
|---|---|---|---|---|---|---|---|
| | | Two-Party Democratic Vote | Difference from Mean Democratic Two-Party Vote | Democratic Vote | Republican Vote | Third-Party Vote | Number of Respondents |
| $100,000 | 2010 | 40.9% | −5.4% | 40.1% | 58.0% | 1.9% | 3,310 |
| or More | 2008 | 49.1% | −6.0% | 48.2% | 50.0% | 1.9% | 3,892 |
| | 2006 | 47.6% | −6.3% | 46.9% | 51.6% | 1.5% | 2,577 |
| | 2004 | 42.0% | −7.6% | 41.5% | 57.4% | 1.1% | 2,126 |
| | 2002 | 35.6% | −11.8% | 34.8% | 62.9% | 2.2% | 2,762 |
| | 2000 | 44.1% | −6.1% | 43.2% | 54.8% | 2.0% | 1,566 |
| | 1998 | 45.3% | −4.1% | 44.1% | 53.3% | 2.6% | 1,057 |
| | 1996 | 36.8% | −13.7% | 36.3% | 62.4% | 1.2% | 1,206 |
| | 1994 | 36.3% | −11.1% | 35.9% | 63.1% | 1.0% | 727 |
| | Average | 42.0% | −8.0% | 41.2% | 57.1% | 1.7% | |

**Question Wording for Household** Income (Coded: Under $30,000 = 1; $30,000–$49,999 = 2; $50,000–$74,999 = 3; $75,000–$99,999 = 4; $100,000 or More = 5):

**1994–2002:** "[Previous Year] Total family income . . . Under $15,000 (1); $15,000–$29,999 (1); $30,000–$49,999 (2); $50,000–$74,999 (3); $75,000–$99,999 (4); $100,000 or more (5)"

**2004–2010:** "[Previous Year] Total family income . . . Under $15,000 (1); $15,000–$29,999 (1); $30,000–$49,999 (2); $50,000–$74,999 (3); $75,000–$99,999 (4); $100,000–$149,999 (5); $150,000–$199,999 (5); $200,000 or more (5)"

Source: National exit polls. See the section in Chapter 2 entitled "Creating a Cumulative National Data Set: Selecting Exit Polls" (pp. 28–29).

*Note:* When using these results to make inferences about the active electorate, the standard errors should be calculated using Table 2.2 (p. 36), which is explained in the adjacent section of Chapter 2, "Analyzing Exit Poll Questions: Estimating Sampling Error" (pp. 34–36). For a guide on how to understand the tables and figures of this chapter, see the section in Chapter 2 entitled "Presenting and Discussing the Exit Poll Data: Reading Chapter 5" (pp. 43–46). The rationale for using two-party percentages to show trends over time is given in Chapter 4, in the section entitled "Presidential Vote Choice" (pp. 124–131).

**Table 5.29**  House Vote by Two-Year Household Financial Situation, 1990–2010

| Category | Year | Two-Party House Vote | | Full House Vote | | | |
|---|---|---|---|---|---|---|---|
| | | Two-Party Democratic Vote | Difference from Mean Democratic Two-Party Vote | Democratic Vote | Republican Vote | Third-Party Vote | Number of Respondents |
| Better | 2010 | 61.7% | 15.4% | 60.1% | 37.2% | 2.7% | 696 |
| | 2008 | | | | | | |
| | 2006 | 28.1% | −25.9% | 27.6% | 70.8% | 1.6% | 1,924 |
| | 2004 | | | | | | |
| | 2002 | 33.7% | −13.8% | 33.0% | 64.9% | 2.1% | 2,241 |
| | 2000 | | | | | | |
| | 1998 | 59.4% | 10.0% | 57.9% | 39.6% | 2.5% | 3,927 |
| | 1996 | | | | | | |
| | 1994 | 59.7% | 12.3% | 59.0% | 39.8% | 1.2% | 1,305 |
| | 1992 | | | | | | |
| | 1990 | 47.1% | −6.7% | 46.1% | 51.9% | 2.0% | 2,815 |
| | Average | 48.3% | −1.5% | 47.3% | 50.7% | 2.0% | |
| About the Same | 2010 | 50.2% | 3.9% | 48.6% | 48.2% | 3.3% | 1,832 |
| | 2008 | | | | | | |
| | 2006 | 57.0% | 3.0% | 56.0% | 42.2% | 1.8% | 2,949 |
| | 2004 | | | | | | |
| | 2002 | 47.1% | −0.3% | 46.1% | 51.8% | 2.1% | 3,097 |
| | 2000 | | | | | | |
| | 1998 | 42.6% | −6.8% | 41.1% | 55.5% | 3.4% | 4,124 |
| | 1996 | | | | | | |
| | 1994 | 46.1% | −1.3% | 45.3% | 53.0% | 1.7% | 2,507 |
| | 1992 | | | | | | |
| | 1990 | 55.5% | 1.7% | 53.9% | 43.1% | 3.0% | 4,139 |
| | Average | 49.8% | 0.0% | 48.5% | 49.0% | 2.5% | |
| Worse | 2010 | 36.6% | −9.7% | 35.4% | 61.4% | 3.2% | 1,841 |
| | 2008 | | | | | | |
| | 2006 | 79.7% | 25.8% | 77.4% | 19.7% | 2.9% | 1,782 |
| | 2004 | | | | | | |
| | 2002 | 61.2% | 13.8% | 59.3% | 37.6% | 3.1% | 2,315 |
| | 2000 | | | | | | |
| | 1998 | 40.7% | −8.6% | 39.0% | 56.8% | 4.2% | 1,225 |
| | 1996 | | | | | | |
| | 1994 | 35.6% | −11.8% | 34.6% | 62.6% | 2.8% | 1,142 |
| | 1992 | | | | | | |
| | 1990 | 60.6% | 6.8% | 58.2% | 37.8% | 4.0% | 2,506 |
| | Average | 52.4% | 2.7% | 50.7% | 46.0% | 3.4% | |

**Question Wording for Two-Year Household Financial Situation** (Coded: Better = 1; About the Same = 2; Worse = 3):

**1990–2010:** "Compared to two years ago, is your family's financial situation . . . Better today (1); Worse today (3); About the same (2)"

*Source:* National exit polls. See the section in Chapter 2 entitled "Creating a Cumulative National Data Set: Selecting Exit Polls" (pp. 28–29).

*Note:* When using these results to make inferences about the active electorate, the standard errors should be calculated using Table 2.2 (p. 36), which is explained in the adjacent section of Chapter 2, "Analyzing Exit Poll Questions: Estimating Sampling Error" (pp. 34–36). For a guide on how to understand the tables and figures of this chapter, see the section in Chapter 2 entitled "Presenting and Discussing the Exit Poll Data: Reading Chapter 5" (pp. 43–46). The rationale for using two-party percentages to show trends over time is given in Chapter 4, in the section entitled "Presidential Vote Choice" (pp. 124–131).

**Table 5.30** House Vote by Judgments of Current National Economic Conditions, 1986–2010

| Category | Year | Two-Party House Vote | | Full House Vote | | | Number of Respondents |
|---|---|---|---|---|---|---|---|
| | | Two-Party Democratic Vote | Difference from Mean Democratic Two-Party Vote | Democratic Vote | Republican Vote | Third-Party Vote | |
| Performing Well | 2010 | 79.2% | 32.9% | 77.4% | 20.3% | 2.3% | 457 |
| | 2008 | 27.4% | −27.6% | 26.8% | 70.8% | 2.5% | 491 |
| | 2006 | 28.7% | −25.2% | 28.2% | 70.0% | 1.8% | 3,158 |
| | 2004 | 16.6% | −33.0% | 16.5% | 82.7% | 0.8% | 1,390 |
| | 2002 | 28.3% | −19.2% | 27.7% | 70.1% | 2.2% | 3,279 |
| | 2000 | 51.5% | 1.3% | 50.3% | 47.4% | 2.3% | 4,771 |
| | 1998 | 54.2% | 4.8% | 52.5% | 44.4% | 3.1% | 3,980 |
| | 1996 | 60.2% | 9.7% | 59.6% | 39.4% | 1.0% | 4,450 |
| | 1994 | 62.0% | 14.7% | 61.3% | 37.5% | 1.2% | 2,102 |
| | 1992 | 21.9% | −32.0% | 21.6% | 77.2% | 1.2% | 1,345 |
| | 1990 | 42.9% | −10.9% | 42.0% | 55.9% | 2.1% | 1,780 |
| | 1988 | | | | | | |
| | 1986 | 44.9% | −7.6% | 42.9% | 52.7% | 4.4% | 5,404 |
| | Average | 43.1% | −7.7% | 42.2% | 55.7% | 2.1% | |
| Performing Badly | 2010 | 42.6% | −3.7% | 41.2% | 55.6% | 3.1% | 3,908 |
| | 2008 | 56.5% | 1.5% | 55.0% | 42.4% | 2.6% | 7,401 |
| | 2006 | 78.8% | 24.9% | 77.0% | 20.7% | 2.3% | 3,477 |
| | 2004 | 79.1% | 29.5% | 76.9% | 20.4% | 2.7% | 1,771 |
| | 2002 | 61.8% | 14.3% | 60.2% | 37.2% | 2.6% | 5,012 |
| | 2000 | 35.8% | −14.3% | 34.8% | 62.2% | 3.0% | 752 |
| | 1998 | 27.0% | −22.4% | 26.3% | 71.4% | 2.3% | 823 |
| | 1996 | 37.7% | −12.8% | 36.5% | 60.3% | 3.2% | 3,217 |
| | 1994 | 36.6% | −10.7% | 35.8% | 61.9% | 2.2% | 2,872 |
| | 1992 | 62.1% | 8.1% | 60.3% | 36.9% | 2.8% | 6,004 |
| | 1990 | 57.4% | 3.6% | 55.6% | 41.2% | 3.2% | 7,607 |
| | 1988 | | | | | | |
| | 1986 | 67.1% | 14.6% | 63.9% | 31.3% | 4.8% | 2,821 |
| | Average | 53.5% | 2.7% | 52.0% | 45.1% | 2.9% | |

**Question Wording for Judgments of Current National Economic Conditions** (Coded: Performing Well = 1; Performing Badly = 2):

**1986:** "These days, is the condition of the nation's economy . . . Very good (1); Fairly good (1); Fairly bad (2); Very bad (2)"

**1990:** "These days, do you think the condition of the nation's economy is . . . Excellent (1); Good (1); Not so good (2); Poor (2)"

**1992–2010:** "Do you think the condition of the nation's economy is . . . Excellent (1); Good (1); Not so good (2); Poor (2)"

*Source:* National exit polls. See the section in Chapter 2 entitled "Creating a Cumulative National Data Set: Selecting Exit Polls" (pp. 28–29).

*Note:* When using these results to make inferences about the active electorate, the standard errors should be calculated using Table 2.2 (p. 36), which is explained in the adjacent section of Chapter 2, "Analyzing Exit Poll Questions: Estimating Sampling Error" (pp. 34–36). For a guide on how to understand the tables and figures of this chapter, see the section in Chapter 2 entitled "Presenting and Discussing the Exit Poll Data: Reading Chapter 5" (pp. 43–46). The rationale for using two-party percentages to show trends over time is given in Chapter 4, in the section entitled "Presidential Vote Choice" (pp. 124–131).

**Table 5.31**  House Vote by Judgments of Future National Economic Conditions, 1986–2008

| Category | Year | Two-Party Democratic Vote | Difference from Mean Democratic Two-Party Vote | Democratic Vote | Republican Vote | Third-Party Vote | Number of Respondents |
|---|---|---|---|---|---|---|---|
| | | | | Full House Vote | | | |
| Better | 2008 | 62.5% | 7.4% | 61.2% | 36.7% | 2.1% | 2,007 |
| | 2006 | | | | | | |
| | 2004 | | | | | | |
| | 2002 | | | | | | |
| | 2000 | 52.7% | 2.5% | 51.9% | 46.7% | 1.4% | 1,571 |
| | 1998 | 71.1% | 21.8% | 69.5% | 28.2% | 2.2% | 892 |
| | 1996 | | | | | | |
| | 1994 | | | | | | |
| | 1992 | | | | | | |
| | 1990 | 48.0% | −5.8% | 47.1% | 51.1% | 1.8% | 1,368 |
| | 1988 | | | | | | |
| | 1986 | 43.3% | −9.2% | 41.3% | 54.2% | 4.4% | 2,739 |
| | Average | 55.5% | 3.3% | 54.2% | 43.4% | 2.4% | |
| About the Same | 2008 | 54.1% | −0.9% | 52.9% | 44.8% | 2.3% | 999 |
| | 2006 | | | | | | |
| | 2004 | | | | | | |
| | 2002 | | | | | | |
| | 2000 | 48.6% | −1.5% | 47.4% | 50.1% | 2.5% | 3,144 |
| | 1998 | 48.3% | −1.0% | 47.3% | 50.5% | 2.3% | 2,827 |
| | 1996 | | | | | | |
| | 1994 | | | | | | |
| | 1992 | | | | | | |
| | 1990 | 50.8% | −3.0% | 49.8% | 48.2% | 2.0% | 3,019 |
| | 1988 | | | | | | |
| | 1986 | 52.2% | −0.2% | 49.8% | 45.5% | 4.7% | 3,966 |
| | Average | 50.8% | −1.3% | 49.4% | 47.8% | 2.7% | |
| Worse | 2008 | 45.9% | −9.1% | 44.4% | 52.3% | 3.2% | 879 |
| | 2006 | | | | | | |
| | 2004 | | | | | | |
| | 2002 | | | | | | |
| | 2000 | 43.5% | −6.7% | 41.4% | 53.9% | 4.7% | 683 |
| | 1998 | 34.7% | −14.7% | 32.9% | 61.9% | 5.2% | 1,052 |
| | 1996 | | | | | | |
| | 1994 | | | | | | |
| | 1992 | | | | | | |
| | 1990 | 59.0% | 5.1% | 56.7% | 39.5% | 3.8% | 5,370 |
| | 1988 | | | | | | |
| | 1986 | 67.2% | 14.8% | 63.8% | 31.1% | 5.1% | 1,622 |
| | Average | 50.0% | −2.1% | 47.9% | 47.8% | 4.4% | |

*(Continued)*

**Table 5.31** House Vote by Judgments of Future National Economic Conditions, 1986–2008 *(Continued)*

**Question Wording for Judgments of Future National Economic Conditions** (Coded: Better = 1; About the Same = 2; Worse = 3):

**1986:** "A year from now, will the U.S. economy be . . . Better than today (1); Worse than today (3); About the same as today (2)"

**1990–2008:** "During the next year, do you think the nation's economy will . . . Get better (1); Get worse (3); Stay about the same (2)"

*Source:* National exit polls. See the section in Chapter 2 entitled "Creating a Cumulative National Data Set: Selecting Exit Polls" (pp. 28–29).

*Note:* When using these results to make inferences about the active electorate, the standard errors should be calculated using Table 2.2 (p. 36), which is explained in the adjacent section of Chapter 2, "Analyzing Exit Poll Questions: Estimating Sampling Error" (pp. 34–36). For a guide on how to understand the tables and figures of this chapter, see the section in Chapter 2 entitled "Presenting and Discussing the Exit Poll Data: Reading Chapter 5" (pp. 43–46). The rationale for using two-party percentages to show trends over time is given in Chapter 4, in the section entitled "Presidential Vote Choice" (pp. 124–131).

**Table 5.32** Democratic Groups in House Elections Exit Polls, 1976–2010

| Group | Average Share of Exit Polls | Average Two-Party Democratic Vote | Democratic Share of Overall Vote 2010 | Last Year Voted For Other Party |
|---|---|---|---|---|
| *Base (67%+)* | | | | |
| Black | 10% | 88% | 90% | NA |
| Democrat | 39% | 88% | 92% | NA |
| Voted for Democratic candidate in last presidential election | 38% | 85% | 84% | NA |
| Disapprove of Republican president | 48% | 82% | NA | NA |
| Liberal | 19% | 81% | 90% | NA |
| Approve of Democratic president | 51% | 79% | 85% | NA |
| Jewish | 3% | 75% | 70% | NA |
| Gay or bisexual | 4% | 73% | 69% | NA |
| Think government should do more | 47% | 72% | 77% | NA |
| Hispanic/Latino | 4% | 70% | 60% | NA |
| Religion other than Protestant, Catholic, or Jewish | 6% | 70% | 74% | NA |
| Approve of Democratic Congress | 21% | 70% | 79% | NA |
| No religious affiliation | 8% | 67% | 68% | NA |
| | | | | |
| *Leaners (56%–66%)* | | | | |
| Union household | 26% | 64% | 61% | NA |
| Race other than white, black, Hispanic/Latino, or Asian | 2% | 63% | 53% | NA |
| Disapprove of Republican Congress | 58% | 62% | NA | NA |
| Did not complete high school | 6% | 61% | 57% | NA |
| Not married (last asked in 2008) | 34% | 61% | NA | NA |
| City precinct | 27% | 60% | 56% | NA |
| Voted for non-major-party candidate in last presidential election | 6% | 60% | 33% | 2010 |
| Household earns less than $30,000 annually | 24% | 60% | 57% | NA |
| Moderate | 48% | 58% | 55% | NA |
| Not born again | 64% | 58% | 53% | NA |
| Did not vote in last presidential election | 10% | 58% | 39% | 2010 |
| Easterner | 24% | 57% | 54% | 1996 |
| Asian | 2% | 57% | 58% | 1998 |
| Attend religious services less than once a week | 56% | 57% | 53% | NA |
| First-time voter | 9% | 56% | 46% | NA |
| Think future national economic conditions will be better (last asked in 2008) | 29% | 56% | NA | 1998 |

*Source:* National exit polls. See the section in Chapter 2 entitled "Creating a Cumulative National Data Set: Selecting Exit Polls" (pp. 28–29).

*Note:* NA = not applicable. When using these results to make inferences about the active electorate, the standard errors should be calculated using Table 2.2 (p. 36), which is explained in the adjacent section of Chapter 2, "Analyzing Exit Poll Questions: Estimating Sampling Error" (pp. 34–36). For a guide on how to understand the tables and figures of this chapter, see the section in Chapter 2 entitled "Presenting and Discussing the Exit Poll Data: Reading Chapter 5" (pp. 43–46). The rationale for using two-party percentages to show trends over time is given in Chapter 4, in the section entitled "Presidential Vote Choice" (pp. 124–131).

**Table 5.33**  Republican Groups in House Elections Exit Polls, 1976–2010

| Group | Average Share of Exit Polls | Average Two-Party Republican Vote | Republican Share of Overall Vote 2010 | Last Year Voted For Other Party |
|---|---|---|---|---|
| *Base (67%+)* | | | | |
| Republican | 34% | 88% | 95% | NA |
| Disapprove of Democratic president | 49% | 81% | 84% | |
| Voted for Republican candidate in last presidential election | 47% | 78% | 91% | NA |
| Approve of Republican president | 52% | 75% | NA | NA |
| Conservative | 34% | 73% | 84% | NA |
| Think government does too much | 53% | 70% | 76% | NA |
| Approve of Republican Congress | 42% | 68% | NA | NA |
| | | | | |
| *Leaners (56%–66%)* | | | | |
| Born again | 36% | 60% | 62% | NA |
| Attend religious services at least once a week | 45% | 58% | 58% | NA |
| Household earns $100,000 or more annually | 17% | 58% | 58% | NA |
| Think current national economic conditions are performing well | 44% | 57% | 20% | 2010 |
| Protestant | 55% | 56% | 59% | NA |

*Source:* National exit polls. See the section in Chapter 2 entitled "Creating a Cumulative National Data Set: Selecting Exit Polls" (pp. 28–29).

*Note:* NA = not applicable. When using these results to make inferences about the active electorate, the standard errors should be calculated using Table 2.2 (p. 36), which is explained in the adjacent section of Chapter 2, "Analyzing Exit Poll Questions: Estimating Sampling Error" (pp. 34–36). For a guide on how to understand the tables and figures of this chapter, see the section in Chapter 2 entitled "Presenting and Discussing the Exit Poll Data: Reading Chapter 5" (pp. 43–46). The rationale for using two-party percentages to show trends over time is given in Chapter 4, in the section entitled "Presidential Vote Choice" (pp. 124–131).

**Table 5.34**  Swing Groups in House Elections Exit Polls, 1976–2010

| Group | Average Share of Exit Polls | Average Two-Party Democratic Vote | Democratic Share of Overall Vote in 2010 | Last Year Switched Party Vote |
|---|---|---|---|---|
| 18–29 age group | 18% | 55% | 55% | 2000 |
| Female | 51% | 54% | 48% | 2010 |
| Postgraduate | 17% | 54% | 53% | 2004 |
| Think current national economic conditions are performing badly | 56% | 54% | 41% | 2010 |
| Catholic | 27% | 53% | 43% | 2010 |
| High school graduate | 23% | 53% | 46% | 2010 |
| Think life will be better for the next generation | 35% | 53% | 60% | 2010 |
| 30–44 age group | 31% | 52% | 46% | 2010 |
| Westerner | 20% | 52% | 49% | 2006 |
| Household earns $30,000–$49,999 annually | 23% | 52% | 51% | 2004 |
| Household finances have gotten worse in last 2 years | 27% | 52% | 35% | 2010 |
| 45–59 age group | 27% | 51% | 44% | 2010 |
| 60+ age group | 24% | 51% | 41% | 2010 |
| No child in household | 63% | 51% | 47% | 2010 |
| Think life will be about the same for the next generation | 31% | 51% | 52% | 1996 |
| Think future national economic conditions will be about the same (last asked in 2008) | 45% | 51% | NA | 2008 |
| Not gay or bisexual | 96% | 50% | 46% | 2010 |
| Midwesterner | 27% | 50% | 44% | 2010 |
| Southerner | 28% | 50% | 37% | 1994 |
| Employed full time (last asked in 2008) | 63% | 50% | NA | 2008 |
| Not employed full time (last asked in 2008) | 37% | 50% | NA | 2008 |
| Independent | 27% | 50% | 37% | 2010 |
| Not first-time voter | 91% | 50% | 45% | 2010 |
| Household finances have stayed the same in last 2 years | 45% | 50% | 49% | 2006 |
| Think future national economic conditions will be worse (last asked in 2008) | 27% | 50% | NA | 1998 |
| Male | 49% | 49% | 42% | 2010 |
| Some college | 30% | 49% | 43% | 2010 |
| Child in household | 37% | 49% | 46% | 2010 |
| Think country is moving in the right direction | 48% | 49% | 82% | 2010 |
| Think country is off on the wrong track | 52% | 49% | 22% | 2010 |

*(Continued)*

**Table 5.34** Swing Groups in House Elections Exit Polls, 1976–2010 *(Continued)*

| Group | Average Share of Exit Polls | Average Two-Party Democratic Vote | Democratic Share of Overall Vote in 2010 | Last Year Switched Party Vote |
|---|---|---|---|---|
| Suburban precinct | 43% | 48% | 42% | 2010 |
| Not a union household | 74% | 48% | 43% | 2010 |
| Think life will be worse for the next generation | 34% | 48% | 33% | 2010 |
| Household finances have gotten better in last 2 years | 28% | 48% | 60% | 2010 |
| Household earns $50,000–$74,999 annually | 23% | 47% | 45% | 2010 |
| White | 84% | 46% | 37% | 1992 |
| Rural precinct | 27% | 46% | 36% | 2010 |
| College graduate | 25% | 46% | 40% | 2010 |
| Married (last asked in 2008) | 66% | 46% | NA | 1996 |
| Disapprove of Democratic Congress | 79% | 45% | 33% | 1994 |
| Household earns $75,000–$99,999 annually | 13% | 45% | 42% | 2010 |

*Source:* National exit polls. See the section in Chapter 2 entitled "Creating a Cumulative National Data Set: Selecting Exit Polls" (pp. 28–29).

*Note:* NA = not applicable. When using these results to make inferences about the active electorate, the standard errors should be calculated using Table 2.2 (p. 36), which is explained in the adjacent section of Chapter 2, "Analyzing Exit Poll Questions: Estimating Sampling Error" (pp. 34–36). For a guide on how to understand the tables and figures of this chapter, see the section in Chapter 2 entitled "Presenting and Discussing the Exit Poll Data: Reading Chapter 5" (pp. 43–46). The rationale for using two-party percentages to show trends over time is given in Chapter 4, in the section entitled "Presidential Vote Choice" (pp. 124–131).

# Index

*Figures, tables, and notes are indicated by f, t, and n, respectively, following page numbers.*

education, 143–144
employment status, 144
evangelicals, 142
first-time voters, 156
four-year household financial situation, 160
future national economic conditions, judgment of, 161
gender, 133
government activism, position on, 155
household income, 158–159
House voter choice based on president, 211
ideological identification, 40, 42, 150
last presidential vote, 152
marital status, 145
overall presidential vote, 127
party identification, 149
perceived direction of the country, 154
population density, 139
presidential approval, 153
presidential vote in last election, 72
race, 132
regions, 137
religious affiliation, 47, 140
religious attendance, 141
sexual orientation, 136
timing of voter decision, 130
union households, 147
midterm election and, 73

P
Partisan predispositions
congressional voting preferences, 247–249
Democratic groups, 248, 295t
Republican groups, 248–249, 296t
swing groups, 249, 297–298t
presidential voting preferences, 162–166
Democratic groups, 164–165, 166t, 200t
Republican groups, 165, 201t
swing groups, 165–166, 202–203t
problems with, 5–7
Party identification, 68–69, 69f, 103t
congressional voting preferences, 230–231, 230f, 276–277t
presidential voting preferences, 147–149, 148f, 187t
Perceived direction of the country, 74–75, 75f, 107t
congressional voting preferences, 236–237, 237f, 285t
presidential voting preferences, 153–154, 153f, 192t
Perot, Ross, 125, 151

Physical characteristics, 51–56
age, 54–55, 54f, 93t
congressional voting preferences, 212–217
age, 215–216, 215f, 259–260t
gender, 213–215, 214f, 258t
race, 212–213, 212f, 255–256t
sexual orientation, 216, 217f, 261t
gender, 53–54, 53f, 92t
presidential voting preferences, 131–136
age, 134–135, 134f, 174t
gender, 132–133, 133f, 173t
race, 131–132, 132f, 172t
sexual orientation, 135–136, 135f, 175t
race, 51–52, 52f, 91t
sexual orientation, 55–56, 56f, 94t
Plumb, Elizabeth, 25n
Political orientations, 68–79
congressional voting preferences, 229–241
congressional approval, 73–74, 74f, 107t, 235–236, 236f, 284t
expected life for next generation, 237–239, 238f, 286t
first-time voters, 240–241, 240f, 288t
government activism, view of, 239–240, 240f, 287t
ideological identification, 43–46, 44f, 45t, 231–232, 232f, 278–279t
party identification, 230–231, 230f, 276–277t
perceived direction of the country, 236–237, 237f, 285t
presidential approval, 234–235, 234f, 282–283t
presidential vote in last election, 232–234, 233f, 280–281t
expected life for next generation, 75–77, 76f, 108t
first-time voters, 78–79, 78f, 109t
government activism, 77–78, 77f, 109t
ideological identification, 37–39, 37f, 69–70, 70f, 104t
last presidential vote, 70–72, 71f, 105t
party identification, 68–69, 69f, 103t
perceived direction of the country, 74–75, 75f, 107t
presidential voting preferences, 147–156
expected life for next generation, 154–155, 154f, 193t
first-time voters, 156, 157f, 195t
government activism, view of, 155, 156f, 194t
ideological identification, 39–43, 40f, 41t, 149–150, 149f, 188t